FROM CRITICAL TO SPECULATIVE IDEALISM

The Philosophy of Solomon Maimon

FROM CRITICAL
TO SPECULATIVE IDEALISM

The Philosophy of Solomon Maimon

by

SAMUEL ATLAS

Hebrew Union College-Jewish Institute of Religion
New York City

THE HAGUE

MARTINUS NIJHOFF

1964

PRINTED IN THE NETHERLANDS

TO CELIA

PREFACE

This volume is the first part of a larger work on the philosophy of Solomon Maimon and its systematic place in the history of thought. Here we deal with some of the fundamental themes of Maimon's philosophy, including his examination of Kant's philosophy, his relation to such immediate post-Kantians as Reinhold and Schulze, and the relation between him and Fichte. The second volume will concern itself with such aspects of Maimon's theoretical philosophy as the problem of the categories, the relation between idea and fiction, the concept of a universal soul, and practical philosophy, that is, ethics and the philosophy of law.

Chapters V, VII, and X of this volume contain, with substantial revisions in form and content, material that appeared originally in scholarly periodicals. Grateful acknowledgment is made to the *Hebrew Union College Annual* for permission to use the substance of my articles: "Solomon Maimon's Treatment of the Problems of Antinomies and Its Relation to Maimonides," *H.U.C.A.*, Vol. XXI; "Maimon and Maimonides," *H.U.C.A.*, Vol. XXII, part one; and to the *Journal of the History of Ideas*, for permission to use the substance of my essay "Solomon Maimon's Doctrine of Infinite Reason and Its Historical Relations," J.H.I., Vol. XIII, No. 2.

Thanks are due to the libraries of the Hebrew Union College-Jewish Institute of Religion in Cincinnati and New York, and of the Union Theological Seminary, New York City, for having made their resources available to me.

I acknowledge my gratitude to Jack Bemporad, M.A. and Dr. Julius Kravetz for their help in the phrasing and formulation of numerous passages and for their valuable suggestions. Mr. Jack Bemporad also assisted in the preparation of the index. Thanks are also due to Professor Fritz Bamberger, who read the manuscript and offered constructive comments.

Grateful appreciation is expressed also to Miss Marion Kuhn, L.L.B., for her assistance in editing the work, and to Mrs. Helen Lederer for typing the manuscript.

S.A.

TABLE OF CONTENTS

The Man:

...A monument of the striving of the human spirit... in defiance of all hindrances which are placed on its way.

(Lebensgeschichte I. p. 143)

His Thought:

The relation of philosophy to all other sciences is comparable to that of the godhead to the world. It is a relation of subordination, not of co-ordination. Just as the godhead permeates the world so philosophy pervades the sciences. Without godhead the world is incomplete, and without a world one could not attain cognition of godhead. Likewise, without philosophy science is incomplete, and without science philosophic knowledge cannot be attained.

(Logik, p. XIV)

His Achievement:

It is in the nature of genius to surpass and transcend itself: it is not concerned with the realization of an idea, but seizes it with enthusiasm, as if it were a divine inspiration. In the execution, however, one often feels the inadequacy of his powers.

Maimon on Leibniz (Streifereien, p.31)

CHAPTER I

INTRODUCTION

There are periods in the history of human thought which are characterized by an extraordinary concentration of creativity. Such periods are to be found in antiquity as well as in modern times. At the end of the eighteenth and the beginning of the nineteenth centuries, in the span of one generation between the appearance of Kant's *Critique of Pure Reason* in 1781 and the subsequent development of the systems of thought known as the philosophy of identity (Fichte, Schelling and Hegel), there evolved an array of systematic world conceptions which are distinguished by their scope and comprehensiveness. Kant was the first to attempt a revolution in human thought, his own Copernican revolution. Once this revolution got under way, however, it did not stop in the realm of critical thought, but swept on, begetting a variety of metaphysical conceptions far beyond Kant's original intention.

Among the philosophical systems of that period the philosophy of Solomon Maimon occupies an important place, for it forms a link, a necessary and logical transition, between critical thought and metaphysical speculation. Only a few specialists are acquainted with the place of Solomon Maimon in the history of European thought. He is generally known through his autobiography. However, the conception that his autobiography symbolizes can be fully comprehended only through a complete understanding of his philosophical writings.

The writing of the autobiography of a man of thought is, in a sense, one of the most difficult of the literary arts. To execute it with some degree of excellence the author must not only be discriminating, but he must also possess a good memory, literary skill, and – what is most important – the ability to find a point from which his whole life can be seen in perspective and to recognize the central idea that dominated it. In the case of Solomon Maimon the pursuit of truth and knowledge was a passion, and this drive is the central point from which the aspects of his life can be viewed in their proper relationships. Dedication to truth and the relentless search for logical consistency are manifest in all his philosophical writings. Never satisfied with a merely perfunctory grasp of a philosophical system, Maimon constantly sought to follow an idea to its ultimate conclusion, to pursue a concept to its final results, often trying to understand an author better than he might have understood himself.

Maimon's paramount concern was with fundamental philosophical problems, and to them was subordinated his interest in the history of philosophy. He entertained no scruples about interpreting previous writers in the light of his own philosophy. For instance, he interprets Aristotle in the light of critical philosophy (in *Die Kategorien des Aristoteles*).[1] He follows the same method in his exposition of Maimonides' *Guide for the Perplexed*.[2] He relates Leibniz to Spinoza, especially with reference to his own understanding of the pre-established harmony.[3] Thus Maimon's interpretations of philosophers who preceded him are of significance, not because of their historical accuracy, but because of the intrinsic systematic value which they possess for the understanding of his own philosophy.

The autobiography of Solomon Maimon is filled with tragedy;[4] his career presents a series of cruel paradoxes. In the history of human thought fate has played such havoc with few philosophers as it did with Solomon Maimon. His is the story of a beggar's struggle to attain the highest peak of the philosophical culture of his time, a time of out-

---

[1] See below, note 11.

[2] See below, note 14. He adopted the name Maimon out of reverence for Maimonides, as he himself testifies (*Lebensgeschichte*, II, 3). All his works in German appeared under that name. Some of his Hebrew essays were published under his original name, Solomon ben Joshua. Some of his works in manuscript (see below, note 5) bear the signature *Solomon ben Joshua* of Nieswicz.

[3] See below, p. 79 f.

[4] While the effect of Maimon's thought on the history of philosophy was limited to his own period, the story of his life had an impact on the cultural world of his time as well as on succeeding generations. His autobiography, which made him famous in wider circles, was edited several times. At the beginning of this century it was re-edited by Jakob Fromer, who provided it with a useful introduction and some valuable notes, and it appeared under the title "*Salomon Maimons Lebensgeschichte. Mit einer Einleitung und mit Anmerkungen neu herausgegeben* (Munich, 1911). The original work was translated into several languages. The English translation by J. Clark Murray, then Professor of Philosophy at McGill College, Montreal, entitled *Solomon Maimon: An Autobiography with Additions and Notes* (London, 1888), is not complete, the philosophical sections having been omitted. Nor, unfortunately, is it free of mistakes, especially in the translation of some philosophical passages. See, for instance, p. 23, where Maimon's analysis of the distinction between understanding and imagination is rendered inaccurately.

A contemporary of Maimon and one of his closest personal friends, Sabattia Joseph Wolff, published reminiscences of Maimon's life and work under the title *Maimoniana, oder Rhapsodien zur Charakteristik Salomon Maimons, aus seinem Privatleben gesammelt* (Berlin, 1813).

standing philosophical achievements. Having endowed him with great intellectual abilities, fate then placed him in circumstances that would have broken men of weaker fiber. Almost to the end of his days the struggle for existence consumed the greater part of his energy. Maimon's odyssey and heroic struggle against fate are a fascinating demonstration of the strength of the human will; it is one of the finest examples of the freedom and independence of the human spirit.

Quite apart from the individual and personal aspect, there is a general, larger aspect to the tragedy of Maimon's life: it epitomizes the struggle of the Jew to liberate his creative mind from the shackles of the ghetto. Consequently, Maimon's autobiography contains a wealth of historical material concerning the social, economic, and cultural conditions of Poland and of its Jewry in the second half of the eighteenth century. Indeed, Maimon took the social and cultural conditions of his time as a background against which to depict his personal life.

Maimon was born in 1752[5] in a village near Nieswiecz (Niesvies) and

[5] It is generally assumed that Maimon was born in 1754 or 1753. But the year 1752 seems more likely. Nowhere does Maimon mention his exact age, nor is there a reference to the exact date of his birth in his writings. Wolff, *Maimoniana*, p. 10, gives 1754 as the year of Maimon's birth. Abraham Geiger (*Jüdische Zeitschrift für Wissenschaft und Leben*, IV, Breslau 1866, p. 199), and Jakob Fromer (*Salomon Maimons Lebensgeschichte*, p. 482) tried to prove the approximate correctness of Wolff's dating. In his *Lebensgeschichte*, I, 262, Maimon mentions that he was about twenty-five years old on his arrival in Königsberg, and in an unpublished work of his in Hebrew (*Cheshek Shlomo*), now in the Bodleian Library, Maimon says that it was written "on his arrival" in Posen in the year 1778. The interval between the first stage of Maimon's odyssey, Königsberg, and his arrival in Posen was short.

However, we can establish 1752 as the year of Maimon's birth on the following basis. The expression "on his arrival" in Posen is not in the text; it is an addition by Fromer, as can be seen from the original passage quoted by Geiger (*op. cit.*, p. 192). As a matter of fact, Maimon arrived in Posen in the fall of 1777, and the Hebrew work was written in the first year of his two-year stay there. Maimon relates in his *Lebensgeschichte* that he arrived in Posen before the Jewish High Holidays. This must have been in the year 1777, since Rabbi Zvi Hirsh ben Abraham of Posen, Maimon's benefactor there, left the city for Fürth in the beginning of 1778 (cf. Geiger, *op. cit.*, p. 198). Maimon must have arrived in Königsberg in early summer of 1777 (and not, as Geiger writes, "in the late summer of 1777"), for he states that he spent the Fast of the Ninth of Ab (August) on the way from Stettin to Berlin, and the journey from Königsberg to Stettin took about five weeks. It seems, therefore, that Maimon was born in the year 1752, and on his arrival in Königsberg in the early summer of 1777 he was about twenty-five years old.

This conclusion is corroborated by the following autobiographical statement, which has escaped the attention of Maimon's biographers. In Maimon's *Geschichte seiner philosophischen Autorschaft in Dialogen. Aus seinen hinterlassenen Papieren*, which appeared in *Neues Museum der Philosophie und Literatur* (1804), Teil I, he writes (p. 136) that he was in his twenty-eigth year when he came to Germany. This refers to his second arrival in Berlin, after spending two years as a private teacher in Posen, since, on his first arrival from Königsberg, he was turned back. He left Posen for Berlin after the Jewish High Holidays, and this was in the year 1779. As he was then in his twenty-eight year, he could not have been born later than 1752; even 1751 cannot be excluded as a possible date of his birth.

Mir in the district of Nawaradok (Nowogrudek) in Lithuania, which
was then a part of Poland. As was customary he pursued Talmudic
studies, acquiring at a very early age a broad knowledge of the rabbinic
literature. He also read extensively in the Kabbalah and in the Chasidic
literature of the time as well as in philosophical works, especially
Maimonides' *Moreh Nebuchim*, and in such scientific books in Hebrew
as came his way. Though he revolted against the negative aspects of
ghetto-living, he retained throughout his life a great appreciation of
Judaism, of the truths contained in prophetic monotheism, as well as
in the ethico-religious teachings of the Talmud and the rabbinic writings.
He married at the extremely early age of eleven years and became a
father at fourteen. When he was twenty-five he left his wife and family
and went to Königsberg, Germany. From there he proceeded to Berlin
via Stettin, without, however, obtaining the permission necessary to
settle in Berlin. For about two months he carried the wanderer's staff
in the company of a professional beggar until he reached Posen, where
he remained for two years. At the age of twenty-seven he arrived in
Berlin, and, with the exception of a short stay in Holland, remained
in Germany until his death. While he was in Germany Maimon attended
a *gymnasium* in Hamburg for three years, acquiring there a fundamental
knowledge of languages, mathematics, and the sciences. He became
a friend of Moses Mendelssohn, Lazarus Ben David, and Markus
Herz, men prominent in the philosophy and culture of that period.
Through intensive reading he acquired a wide knowledge of philosophical
literature before he became acquainted with Kant's *Critique of Pure
Reason*.

From his Talmudic studies, which had taken up a large part of his
boyhood, he learned the technique of critical analysis, which served
him well in every field of learning; he could not read a text without
attempting to explore its implications and commenting on it. This was
the way in which he probed into the works of Wolff, Leibniz, Locke,
Hume, and Spinoza, and he applied this same method to the study
of Kant's *Critique of Pure Reason*. In trying to assimilate Kant's
ideas he compared them in his mind with the ideas of the philosophers
whom he had previously studied. The comments and the critical
notes he made while reading Kant's *Critique* developed into his first
work.

His friend Markus Herz, a famous physician in Berlin and a former
student and friend of Kant, sent the manuscript to the great philosopher,
and received a very favorable reply. Among other things Kant wrote:

"...but a glance at the manuscript soon enabled me to recognize its merits and to see not only that none of my opponents had understood me and the main problem so well, but that very few could claim so much penetration and subtlety of mind in profound inquiries of this sort as Herr Maimon..."[6]

Kant's praise encouraged Maimon to publish the manuscript, and the systematic maturity of this work placed him in the philosophical arena of the time. In this book he achieved a systematic viewpoint from which, except in a few minor points, he never swerved. This work of Maimons' appeared under the title *Versuch über die Transcendental-philosophie, mit einem Anhang über die symbolische Erkenntnis und Anmerkungen* (Berlin, 1790).[7]

In addition the following books came from Maimon's pen:

(1) *Philosophisches Wörterbuch, oder Beleuchtung der wichtigen Gegen-stände der Philosophie in alphabetischer Ordnung.* Erstes stück, Berlin, 1791.[8]

(2) *Salomon Maimons Lebensgeschichte; Von ihm selbst geschrieben und herausgegeben von K. P. Moritz.* In zwei Teilen. Berlin, 1792.[9]

(3) *Streifereien im Gebiete der Philosophie.* Berlin, 1793.[10]

(4) *Die Kathegorien des Aristoteles. Mit Anmerkungen erläutert und als Propädeutik zu einer neuen Theorie des Denkens.* Berlin, 1794. Bei Ernst Felisch. Second edition, 1798.[11]

---

[6] See *Briefe von und an Kant*, ed. Ernst Cassirer, I, 415 f.

[7] Henceforth referred to as *Tr*.

[8] See above, note 4.

[9] See above, note 4. Approximately the first half of the second part of this work is a presentation of the philosophy of Maimonides together with Maimon's explanations and critical remarks. The autobiography contains many philosophical aperçus and incisive remarks about various philosophical systems, religion in general and Jewish religious writings in particular. It also comprises a number of character sketches, noteworthy among which is that of Moses Mendelssohn.

[10] This work, henceforth referred to as *Str.*, consists of four essays: (1) "Über die Progressen der Philosophie" (pp. 3–58). This essay appeared previously as a separate publication. It was motivated by a question posed in 1792 by the Prussian Academy of Berlin for a prize essay, "What progress has metaphysics made since Leibniz and Wolff?" (2) "Über die Ästhetik" (pp. 61–176). (3) "Philosophischer Briefwechsel" (pp. 179–244). This contains the correspondence between Maimon and Reinhold, one of the most prominent philosophers of the time and famous as an expositor of Kantian philosophy. This correspondence is of importance for the understanding of the essential differences in Maimon's and Reinhold's conception of the Kantian *Critique* and of their approach to critical philosophy in general. (4) "Über die philosophischen und rhetorischen Figuren" (pp. 247–272).

[11] The *th* in "Kathegorien" is either a misprint or is due to Maimon's lack of knowledge of Greek. This work, henceforth referred to as *Kat. d. Arist.*, consists of two parts, the first of which is a translation into German from the Latin version, prepared by Buhle, together with Maimon's explanations and interpretations (pp. 1–90). The second part is a presentation of Maimon's theory of logic, central to which is the principle of determinability (pp. 93–257).

(5) *Versuch einer neuen Logik oder Theorie des Denkens. Nebst an-
gehängten Briefen des Philaletes an Änesidemus.* Berlin, 1794. Bei Ernst
Felisch. Second edition, 1798.[12]

(6) *Kritische Untersuchungen über den menschlichen Geist oder das
höhere Erkenntnis- und Willensvermögen.* Leipzig, 1797.[13]

Maimon also wrote commentaries on the works of other authors,
outstanding among which is his commentary in Hebrew on Maimonides'
Moreh Nebuchim (The Guide for the Perplexed) under the title *Giv'ath
Hamoreh*, Berlin, 1791.[14] His other commentaries are:

(1) *Bacons von Verulam neues Organon. Aus dem lateinischen übersetzt
von George Wilhelm Bartholdy. Mit Anmerkungen von S. Maimon.*
Berlin, 1793.

(2) *Anfangsgründe der Newtonischen Philosophie von Dr. Pemberton.
Aus dem Englischen mit Anmerkungen und einer Vorrede von S. Maimon.*
Berlin, 1793.

Among Maimon's works are a number of essays, some of them extensive, written for the various philosophical journals of the time.
Noteworthy among these are: (1) "Versuch einer neuen Darstellung des Moralprinzips und Deduktion seiner Realität" (*in Berlinische Monatsschrift*, Vol. 24, pp. 403–453); (2) "Über die ersten Gründe
des Naturrechts" (in *Philosophisches Journal*, Vol. I, Heft 2, pp.
141–174); (3) "Pragmatische Geschichte des Begriffs von Philosophie,
etc." (*ibid.*, Vol. 6, pp. 150–181); (4) "Über die ersten Gründe der Moral"

---

[12] Henceforth referred to as *Logik*. Of Maimon's major works, only this has been
republished in the present century. It was reissued in 1912 by the *Kantgesellschaft*
as a volume in the series *Neudrucke seltener philosophischer Werke*, the first volume
of which was *Änesidemus* by G. E. Schulze, a contemporary of Maimon. This edition
of Maimon's *Versuch einer neuen Logik* contains valuable notes and an extensive
bibliography by Bernhard Carl Engel.

[13] This work, which will be referred to as *Krit. Unt.*, has two parts, the first of which
deals with theoretical philosophy and the second with the problem of ethics. The first
section of the theoretical part (pp. 1–165) is presented in the form of a dialogue between
Kriton and Philaletes (Philaletes representing Maimon). This is followed by Prolegomena
(pp. 166–230) dealing with transcendental aesthetic, logic, and the antinomies. The
second part (pp. 231–270), dealing with ethics, is divided into "Prolegomena zu Kritik
einer praktischen Vernunft" and "Ethik nach Aristoteles."

[14] This commentary is limited to the first part of the *Guide*. It appeared anonimously
and has been republished several times. In the introduction to this work Maimon
presents a short history of philosophy containing the essence of the various systems of
thought leading up to Kant. It concludes with a concise summary of Maimon's own
position, which deviates from Kant in that he does not consider sensibility a separate
source of knowledge. The concepts of thought referring to objects of experience should
be regarded as actually related to the infinitesimals of sensation, and these infinitesimals are in themselves objects of thought. Maimon considers this doctrine to be in
accord with Leibniz' doctrine of monads. It is noteworthy that at that stage of his
development Maimon regarded the synthesis of Kant and Leibniz as the essence of his
philosophical position. This work of Maimon will be referred to as *Com. to Guide*.

(*ibid.*, Vol. 8, Heft 3, pp. 165–190); and (5) "Der grosse Man" (in *Neue Berlinische Monatsschrift*, Vol. 2, pp. 244–283).

Maimon's financial position remained precarious until Count Adolf von Kalkreuth, a nobleman with strong cultural and philosophical leanings, took an interest in him, both as an author and as a man, and offered him a home on his estate in Nieder-Siegersdorf, near Glogau, in Silesia, where he remained for about five years, until his death on November 22, 1800. There Maimon was able to use his hosts's large library, and it was there that he wrote a number of essays and his last major work, *Kritische Untersuchungen über den menschlichen Geist*, dedicated to his benefactor.

Maimon's philosophical career extended over a period of eleven years, from the appearance of his *Versuch über die Transcendentalphilosophie* in 1790 until 1800, the year of his death.

Shortly after his death he seems to have been entirely forgotten. His works lay unexamined in the archives of philosophy until the year 1846 when Johann Erdmann devoted a chapter in his history of philosophy to a treatment of Maimon's philosophical contribution. Most historians of philosophy up to Erdmann did not deem it necessary to appraise and evaluate Maimon's work.[15]

Maimon's appearance on the philosophical scene was like that of a meteor: sudden, of short duration and apparently leaving no trace. For almost fifty years after his death no proper appraisal of his contribution to philosophical thought was made, nor was there a thoroughgoing analysis of his importance and of his place in the history of philosophy.[16] Yet his influence on the development of philosophical thought was much deeper than it would seem at first.

Maimon has usually been lumped with the Kantian scholars of his time in a rather sweeping and indiscriminating manner, his name has

---

[15] Johann Eduard Erdmann, *Versuch einer wissenschaftlichen Darstellung der Geschichte der neueren Philosophie* (Leipzig, 1848). To Erdmann must go the credit for the resurgence of interest in Maimon. His example was followed by Eduard Zeller in his *Geschichte der deutschen Philosophie seit Leibniz* (1875) and by Kuno Fischer in his *Fichtes Leben, Werke und Lehre* [3](Heidelberg, 1900). From then on, all histories of philosophy have had sections devoted to Maimon. The most important of these are: (1) Ernst Cassirer, *Das Erkenntnisproblem*, III (Berlin, 1920); (2) Richard Kroner, *Von Kant bis Hegel* (1921); (3) Wilhelm Windelband, *Geschichte der neueren Philosophie* (2 vols.; Leipzig, 1922); (4) Nicolai Hartmann, *Die Philosophie des Deutschen Idealismus*, 2nd ed., (Berlin 1960).

[16] The most comprehensive analysis of Maimon's thought was presented by Friedrich Kuntze in his volume, *Die Philosophie Salomon Maimons* (Heidelberg, 1912). Other works devoted exclusively to the presentation of Maimon's thought as a whole, apart from essays and dissertations dealing with particular aspects, are: (1) M. Gueroult, *La Philosophie transcendentale de Salomon Maimon* (Paris, 1929); (2) Hugo Bergman, *Ha-philosofia shel Shlomo Maimon* (Hebrew) (Jerusalem, 1921).

been linked with those of Karl Leonhard Reinhold (1758–1823), Gottlob
Ernst Schulze (1761–1833), Friedrich Heinrich Jacobi (1743–1819), and
Jakob Siegmund Beck (1761–1842). And yet, on deeper analysis, he
stands out among these men.[17]

Very few of Maimon's contemporaries grasped the fundamental ideas
of critical philosophy and its perplexities as did Maimon. Kant himself
testified that Maimon had fathomed the meaning of the critical method
and has explored the problematic web involved in the "critique."
Moreover, Maimon seems to have anticipated some of the problems to
which Kant refers in his third "critique," *Kritik der Urteilskraft*. This
work appeared in 1790 and is concerned, among other things, with the
question of the unity of the various capacities of the human mind, a
problem with occupies a central place in Maimon's first work, which
appeared in the same year.

Comprehending the revolution implied in Kantian thought Maimon
pointed the way to its further development. He mastered the pivotal
ideas of the *Critique*, grasped the implications involved in critical philosophy, and discovered new systematic problems arising therefrom that
for the most part remained hidden from his contemporaries. Even
Reinhold, the most prominent exponent of Kantian philosophy reveals
in his correspondence with Maimon a total disregard for and misunderstanding of the problems that engaged him. Thus Maimon remained isolated and misunderstood throughout his life. His criticism
was regarded as hairsplitting: his keen analysis was looked upon as
frivolous, and his quest for certainty was taken as evidence of obsti-
nacy.

Maimon prophesied the fate of his career as an author in the following
words: "A writer who has a good *style* is read. One who has *expository
power* is studied. One who has neither the one nor the other, supposing
him, however, to be in possession of weighty and new truths, is used.
His *mind*, though not his *name*, is imperishable."[18] Shadworth H.
Hodgson, a noted English philosopher, who made an extensive study
of Maimon's work, as evidenced by his references to the latter, comment-
ed on this quotation: "Thy *name*, too, Maimon, if any words of mine

---

[17] Thus, for instance, Hans Vaihinger, who made much use of Maimon's conception
of fiction for his own doctrine in his *Philosophy of As-if*, writes of Maimon "as the most
penetrating mind among the immediate followers of Kant as Lambert was among the
immediate predecessors of Kant." See *Die Philosophie des Als-ob*, 4th ed., p. 43. A
comparison of Maimon and Lambert was also made by W. Dilthey, *Gesammelte
Schriften*, IV, 50.

[18] See *Philos. Wört.*, p. 155; *Philosophischer Briefwechsel*, in *Str.*, and Kuntze, *op. cit.*,
p. 511, n. 2.

could celebrate it. But he who now writes has a pen as little potent as thine own."[19] S. H. Hodgson considered Maimon the most important representative of Kantian thought, regarding him as the true successor and inheritor of the Kantian philosophy and of German Idealism generally.[20]

Maimon's prognostication as to the fate of his own philosophy came true. It would, he intimated, be that of the author who possesses neither a literary style nor systematic exposition. And from the point of view of style and systematic presentation Maimon's works are deficient. German was not his mother tongue, and he never acquired the facility with language required of a successful writer; neither did he have the patience to devote more effort to the planning of a systematic presentation of his ideas or to subject his writings to careful examination. On the other hand, "there are passages in Maimon's writings in which the thought bursts forth with truly resplendent power, forcing the language, even playing with it, in modes of expression that are astounding."[21]

In his autobiography Maimon refers to a childhood inclination toward painting and writes: "Yet I judge myself at present that, if I had been kept at it, I would have become a great, though never an exact painter, i.e., I would have been able to sketch with ease the main features of a picture, but would not have had the patience to work it out in detail." This characteristic of his applies equally well to his career as a philosophical writer, for he never had the patience to give his work a more complete, finished, and rounded-out form. The reader gets the impression that it is all written in great haste, with little concern for form, as though the author were afraid he would not have time to finish and wanted, as it were, to take the world by storm.

Maimon's first book, *Versuch über die Transcendentalphilosophie*, illustrates very well the manner and method of his writing. It consists of four parts: the first part (pp. 1–166) is a criticism of Kant's theoretical philosophy, the Aesthetic and the Analytic of the *Critique*; the second part (pp. 167–262), under the title "Kurze Uebersicht des ganzen Werkes," is a kind of commentary to the first, including also Kant's theory of the antinomies and his ontology; the third (pp. 263–332), under the title "Symbolische Erkenntnis und philosophische Sprache," and the fourth parts (pp. 333–444), "Anmerkungen und Erläuterungen, etc.," are again a kind of commentary to the preceding parts. The

---

[19] Shadworth H. Hodgson, *Philosophy of Reflection* (London, 1878), p. 17.
[20] *Ibid.*
[21] See Kuno Fischer, *Geschichte der neuen Philosophie*, Vol. VI, *Fichtes Leben, Werke und Lehre*, 3rd ed., p. 70.

headings of the chapters as well as the juxtaposition of various concepts
and themes are characteristic of his unsystematic exposition.

Of the technique by which this first book was composed, Maimon
writes in his *Autobiography*: "The method by which I studied this work
(i.e., Kant's *Critique of Pure Reason*) was quite peculiar. On the first
perusal I obtained a vague idea of each section. This I endeavored
afterwards to sharpen by my own reflection and thus to penetrate into
the author's meaning. This is properly the process which is called
thinking onself into a system. But as I had already mastered in this way
the systems of Spinoza, Hume, and Leibniz, I was naturally led to think
of a *coalition-system*. This, in fact, I found, and gradually I put it into
writing in the form of explanatory observations on the *Critique of Pure
Reason*, as this system unfolded itself to my mind. Such was the origin
of my transcendental philosophy. In it each of the above-mentioned
systems is so developed that the point of convergence of all of them is
evolved. Consequently, this book must be difficult to understand for
the man who, owing to the inflexible character of his thinking, has made
himself at home in just one of these systems without regard to any other."

The book deals with a variety of problems, the connections among
which are at first difficult to discern. It presents at random a galaxy of
diverse ideas without any apparent interrelation. It is written in the
form of aphorisms, and the ideas are not presented in a continuous flow
of thought. Because of these characteristics Maimon's work is one of
the most difficult in the history of philosophical literature. No wonder,
then, that his contemporaries refused to review the book, admitting
their inability to fathom the author's meaning.

In Maimon's second work, *Philosophisches Wörterbuch*, the systematic
order of problems has been replaced by the alphabetical order. It is
characteristic of him that he conceived the idea of writing a philosophical
dictionary. It is as though he himself admitted the difficulties he had
in finding an adequate systematic form for his thoughts. He resorts
to alphabetical order, forgetting that a dictionary, too, is subject to
laws of order, namely, completeness and a certain proportion in the
treatment of the subjects. That his dictionary should begin with an
article on *Aberglauben* and end with an essay on *Zweifel* may suggest
the thought that it summarizes in a way, Maimon's own development
from "superstition" to "skepticism." It will, however, be pointed out
in the course of this study that skepticism was not Maimon's ultimate
position, but only one aspect of his thought, an alternative to speculative
idealism. Maimon's criticism of Kant's solution of Hume's difficulties

concerning the reality of our fundamental concepts does not generate skepticism but a spirit of idealism. The skeptical method is for Maimon not an end but a means leading to the assumption of an infinite mind.

Even in such works, as *Versuch einer neuen Logik*, and *Kritische Untersuchungen über den menschlichen Verstand*, in which he attempts to construct a system of thought, the ideas are buried beneath the debris of unsystematic form.

Maimon's contemporary critics, therefore, could always blame his style and ascribe their inability to follow him to the form of his writing. When Rheinhold, in his correspondence with Maimon, is hard pressed by the latter with an objection or a question, he often takes refuge in reminding Maimon of his linguistic deficiencies. "There is no excuse for us to argue any longer, we don't understand each other." Maimon's reply was: "If you don't understand me, as you admit, how can you possibly say that I do not understand you?" It was Reinhold who advised Maimon to wait with the formulation of his system of thought until he had mastered the language and had acquired a better style. It must be pointed out, however, that Maimon himself was aware of the faults in his style. Apologetically he writes to Reinhold that in spite of his infelicity of expression he has made his points sufficiently clear and is ready to offer further elucidation of his point of view.

In another connection Maimon confesses that his writings are intended not for the public at large but for independent thinkers. But the independent thinkers of Maimon's time and of the following generation were too busy with the elaboration and formulation of their own systems of thought. Among the ranking philosophers of Maimon's day only Fichte pays generous tribute to him. Fichte recognizes the debt he owes to Maimon's skepticism, mentioning him together with Aenesidemus-Schulze and stating that from their writings he has gained the conviction that philosophy has not yet attained the rank of a science. He calls Maimon "one of the greatest thinkers of our time," and in another connection he refers to him as "the extraordinary Maimon."[22] However, he never fully acknowledges the relationship of his own thought to Maimon's concept of the thing in itself, his doctrine of time and space, and his idea of an infinite reason.

Fate was no kinder to Maimon the philosopher than it was to Maimon the man. In his lifetime he was misunderstood and misinterpreted.

[22] Cf. Fichte's *Werke*, ed. Medicus, I, p. 227; Fichte's *Leben und literarischer Briefwechsel* (2nd edition, 1826) II, p. 205; Fichte, *The Science of Rights*, transl. A. E. Kroeger (1889), p. 22.

Even Kant who was the first to appreciate Maimon's work, later seems to have entirely forgotten his own favorable appraisal. In a letter to Reinhold (dated 28 March 1794) he refers unfavorably to Maimon's attempt "to improve on critical philosophy." Kant seems to have approved of Reinhold's exposition and interpretation of his thought, and Reinhold's "principle of consciousness" was apparently considered by Kant to be a further development of his own system. This indicates that he followed neither the relevant contemporary literature nor the controversy between Reinhold and Maimon in its detailed implications. In fact, Kant admitted in this connection that it was difficult for him at his age to follow the thought of other thinkers. As will be shown in this study, Reinhold's analysis of consciousness leads to the assumption of a thing in itself as a metaphysical entity and to consequences incompatible with a consistent system of critical philosophy. However, Maimon's criticism of Reinhold and of some aspects of Kantian thought is more consistent with Kantianism than Reinhold's defense of it.

But if Maimon was misunderstood in his own time, he was nevertheless noted as one of its most remarkable men. His fame, however, seems to have been due more to his extraordinary life than to his work. His autobiography attracted the attention of the greatest men of his time. Goethe and Schiller became interested in the author's personality; in their correspondence they speak of him with admiration. Goethe was so fascinated by Maimon's heroic struggle that he invited him to Weimar. Schiller sent Goethe an essay by Maimon, in which the latter undertook an analysis of the various aspects of Goethe's creative genius – his poetical creations and his contributions to natural science – attempting to establish a unifying principle for them. Maimon's life was regarded as an illustration of the struggle of the human will, of the freedom and sovereignty of the mind, and of the capacity of the human spirit to overcome all obstacles to the attainment of intellectual pre-eminence.

Indeed, Maimon's life considered from the standpoint of the sum total of energy spent in the service of truth resembles the life of the great thinkers of all time. Maimon writes of himself: "In the search for truth I left my people, my country, and my family. It should not, therefore, be assumed that I shall forsake the truth for any lesser motives."

It would seem that Maimon's prognostication that his philosophy would have the same fate as that of Spinoza and Hume, i.e., only his contemporaries would not recognize his achievement, was not fulfilled. Indeed, precisely the opposite occurred. While in his own day he was highly esteemed and admired by many, even though misunderstood, after his death he sank into almost complete oblivion. This was partly due to the fact that, apart from his style of writing, his was the era of the growth and development of the metaphysical systems of Fichte, Schelling, and Hegel. The interest of the German philosophical world was entirely engaged by the eminence and splendor of their speculations; their grandeur had, as it were, overshadowed the critico-skeptical analyses and the speculative investigations of Maimon. These metaphysical systems, however, represent a deviation from the foundations laid by Kant and a departure from the methods of critical philosophy. It was natural, therefore, that in such a climate of ideas there should be no interest in Maimon, whose investigations were centered in Kant and whose analyses were directed to the problematic that had grown out of critical philosophy.

In the forefront of the history of philosophical thought are those personalities who have distinguished themselves by their capacity for synthesis, while the thinkers who have concentrated on philosophical analysis are often ignored or not fully appreciated. Admitting that genius expresses itself in synthesis rather than in analysis, it should not be overlooked that analysis is the necessary precondition for synthesis, and very often the former leads to the latter. Thus, Hume's analysis of the principle of causality contributed to the synthesis of empiricism and idealism that is the very essence of Kantianism.

Maimon's genius rests in analysis rather than in synthesis. This analysis of the concept of the thing in itself, the questions of *quid facti* and *quid juris*, the Kantian assumption of scientific experience (that is, the reality of synthetic propositions) as the basis on which the structure of critical philosophy rests, and the criticism of the Kantian deduction of the categories, are judicious and incisive. However, his synthesis of Kant's criticism, Hume's skepticism and Leibniz's metaphysics are less convincing. The fate of Maimon's philosophy is thus bound up with the fate of critical philosophy in general. When Kantianism as a whole is regarded as a passing phase in the history of human thought, then Maimon's contribution will be ignored. If, however, the tenets of critical philosophy are considered to be of paramount validity, if Kantianism contains within itself elements of a perennial nature – not this particular concept or that special doctrine, but the principles and method of critical philosophy as a whole – then Maimon's contribution is not to be disregarded. The speculative elements of a metaphysical nature in Maimon's thinking are, to my mind, of no more than historical interest. It is the critical component of his thought: his conception of the thing in itself, his treatment of the problem *quid facti*, his principle of determinability, and especially his conception of fiction and its role and scope in science and philosophy, are fruitful and provocative. Some consider Maimon's doctrine of fiction to be his most important contribution. We will, however, try to show that fiction was conceived by Maimon as a creative idea laid down by the mind for attaining order and completeness, and not as referring to something that is unreal, as fiction is usually taken to mean. For Maimon fiction sometimes connotes an idea in the Kantian sense, that is, a regulative idea. But, since the Kantian distinction between a regulative idea and a constitutive principle is not rigorously maintained by Maimon, for a regulative idea has also a constitutive function, a fiction can sometimes attain the status of a constitutive principle.

Kant's critical philosophy left its imprint on succeeding thought; indeed, it has dominated the development of philosophy down to the present day. Two streams of thought originating from Kant have contended with each other for supremacy: the critical and the metaphysical. For about fifty years, beginning with the last decade of the eighteenth century, the speculative-absolutist trend, culminating in the metaphysical systems of the philosophy of identity, was dominant. In the second half of the nineteenth century the critical trend gained ascendancy with the rise of Neo-Kantianism. At that time, when the rapid and successful development of science was challenging the claim of metaphysics that it is capable of comprehending the essence of reality independently of scientific investigation, the call went out for a return to Kant, i.e., to the critical trend in Kant's thought. In Neo-Kantianism this trend was revived. Both strains issuing from Kant's thought, the metaphysical as well as the critical, were stressed by Maimon, the critical aspect predominating.

With Maimon there begins a line of thought in the interpretation of the Kantian concept of a thing in itself which tries to understand it in a manner compatible with the *Critique* as a whole. From the last decade of the eighteenth century until our own time there have been two main schools of thought vying with each other in the understanding of Kantian philosophy. One school begins with Johann Schulz, a Königsberg pastor, and other contemporaries of Kant. In the nineteenth century, Kuno Fischer, Friedrich Paulsen, Benno Erdmann and Alois Riehl, to mention but a few, belong to the same group. According to them, Kant is to be understood, in consonance with the literal meaning of some of his statements, to have assumed the reality of things in themselves existing independent of the subject. These transcendent entities (*noumena*) affect the mind.

Not the effect of the appearances (*phenomena*), but the effect of the things in themselves is maintained. Kant speaks of the effect of the things in themselves on the subject. This is to be understood as referring not to the appearances (*phenomena*), but to the transcendent things existing in themselves; that is, the *noumena* affect our conception of the objects. To be sure, we can know only the phenomena, but the noumena actively affect our knowledge of the phenomena.

An opposing school of thought originates with Maimon, and continues with Fichte and the Neo-Kantian school of Marburg (Hermann Cohen, Paul Natorp and others). This school attempts to remove the contradiction implied in the assumption of things in themselves existing independently and affecting our mind in its cognition of the appearances. Such an assumption is contrary to the very essence of the Critique, which maintains that knowledge is restricted to the realm of appearances and that the categories of understanding are applicable only to objects of experience.

Maimon's philosophy is, properly speaking, dominated by a few fundamental thoughts systematically connected with one another. It is preoccupied at first with one central problem, which then evolves into a whole series of questions systematically and consistently developed. This is the problem of the relation of pure thought to real objects, i.e., the possibility of "real thought" (*reales Denken*) as distinguished from formal thought.

The importance of Maimon's thought does not consist merely in being an object of historical curiosity; it represents more than an episode in the history of thought. His philosophy presents a new conception that had an effect on the development of philosophical thought. It contains systematic implications for the development of critical philosophy, as well as for that of the metaphysical systems of the post-Kantian period. Broadly speaking, Maimon's contribution to metaphysics, which is of historical interest, is his synthesis of Kantianism with Leibniz-Spinoza, and in this respect he is the precursor of Fichte, whose philosophical conception is a synthesis of Spinoza and Kant. Fichte's concept of the ego takes the place of the Kantian subject, and his pantheistic indentification of the world with the absolute ego, God, is a Spinozian idea. The world as a projection of the ego is the object of consciousness. God, however, according to Fichte, is more than an object of consciousness; He is living action, the living fountain of consciousness itself. God is not the known object but knowing itself. Inasmuch as the world is, in Fichte's view, a manifestation of the existence of God, the world is pantheistic. Schelling's natural philosophy stresses the object in opposition to Fichte's emphasis on the ego as the primary element producing the non-ego. And Hegel represents a great synthesis of Fichte's egoism and Schelling's objectivism. The whole metaphysical movement starting with Fichte and culminating in Schelling's and Hegel's systems, known as the philosophy of identity, of tremendous significance for the development of European philosophy, was inaugurated by Maimon with his concept of the human reason as a part of the divine reason and his concept of synthetic propositions as dissolvable into analytic ones in the infinite intellect. Maimon's contribution to metaphysical thought made Fichte's conception possible; Fichte's thesis produced its antithesis in Schelling's, and the tension between Fichte and Schelling – between thesis and antithesis – produced the comprehensive synthesis of Hegel.

Maimon's metaphysical conception is thus the connecting link between Kant and Fichte, who was the first of the three stars in the metaphysical firmament at the end of the eighteenth and the beginning of the nineteenth century. But this is only of historical interest. The development from Kant's criticism all the way to speculative idealism is made continuous through Maimon, and the whole process leading from critical to speculative idealism is without gap or interruption. There is another aspect to Maimon, of even greater importance, namely, his contribution to a proper understanding of Kant and of critical philosophy in general.

Maimon's analysis of the concept of thing-in-itself, demonstrating the superfluity of this concept in a critical system of thought and offering a psychological explanation of its origin in the human mind, is a lasting contribution to critical idealism. This analysis makes it possible to interpret Kant in the spirit of true critical idealism.

Certain inconsistencies and contradictions in Kant's *Critique* had been pointed out by Maimon's contemporaries, Friedrich H. Jacobi and Aenesidemus-Schulze (G.E. Schulze). Maimon, however, was not satisfied with a merely negative criticism of Kant; he drew certain positive conclusions which he believed followed necessarily from his criticism. On the foundation of Kant's critical principles Maimon developed a philosophical conception which was distinguished by its consistency. The destructive criticism of Kant by some of Maimon's contemporaries led them away from critical philosophy to either romanticism or dogmatic skepticism and to the adoption of a philosophical viewpoint diametrically opposed to that of Kant, but Maimon's constructive criticism of the latter leads to a consistent system of critical philosophy.

Maimon's philosophy is thus a high peak in the history of philosophy from which to survey and evaluate Kant's transcendental feat as well as the metaphysical systems of the post-Kantian period. It is a vantage point for a double orientation: first, the critical elements in Maimon's thought help us better to understand the transcendental idealism of Kant, and second, the metaphysical elements of Maimon's thought constitute the transitional link connecting Kant with Fichte, the first of the speculative metaphysicians following Kant.

The ambiguities in Kant are due in part to the fact that he was struggling to present something totally new with tools of expression that were charged with old meanings. Concepts such as "subject" and "*a priori*" came down to Kant from dogmatic rationalism where they had a meaning entirely different from that which Kant intended to convey. It is through Maimon's criticism of Kant that we are frequently able to acquire a better insight into the Kantian world of thought as well as into the spirit of critical philosophy as a whole. From a study of Maimon we may perceive what Kant, going beyond his predecessors, succeeded in establishing, what he left unsolved, and what still remains to be clarified. Even when Maimon's suggestions and conclusions are not acceptable to a critical idealist they nevertheless are helpful in acquiring a better understanding and appraisal of Kantianism as a whole. It is of interest to note that the two lines of thought springing from the problems contained in Kantianism – one leading to speculative metaphysical idealism, the other leading to critical idealism – were pointed out in their initial stages by Maimon. The way leading to Fichte's metaphysics as well as to a critical interpretation of Kant, as manifested in the critical idealism of the Neo-Kantian movement, was initially intimated by Maimon. And this is the best proof of Maimon's deep insight into the whole fabric of Kantianism.

Herein lies Maimon's importance. His philosophical conception is not an isolated phenomenon in a particular philosophical period; it is a signpost on the highroad of the great movements of thought in one of the most tensely charged philosophical periods in the history of man. Maimon characterized his conception as "a system based on a coalition" (*Koalizion-system*), implying that ideas of Leibniz, Spinoza, Hume, and Kant were incorporated in his synthesis. In another connection, however, Maimon described his philosophy not as a system but as a "system-free" conception (*Nicht-system*). He may have meant to imply

by this designation that his conception is not formally developed
enough to be considered a system, or he may have had in mind his own
definition of his philosophical conception as being, on the one hand,
empirical skepticism and, on the other, rational dogmatism. Since these
do not form a synthesis but represent, rather, two possible alternatives,
they constitute, not a unified philosophical system, but a "system-free"
conception. However, what Maimon intended to imply by the term
Nicht-system is irrelevant. A proper appraisal and evaluation of a
philosophical conception can best be attained by grasping the world of
the thinker in its totality and by understanding the main ideas in which
the whole is centered. Maimon's empirical skepticism is grounded on
the conviction that the question *quid facti* had not been satisfactorily
solved by Kant, that on the basis of experience we are unable to prove
that reality conforms to *a priori* forms of thought. In other words, Kant
had not succeeded in refuting Hume. On the other hand, relative certainty based on empirical experience is quite sufficient for the purpose
of scientific experience. If, however, we are not satisfied with relative
certainty derived from empirical experience and are searching for absolute certainty, then we have to assume an infinite mind in relation to
which all reality is dissolvable into analytic propositions. In this last
doctrine Maimon's rational dogmatism is rooted. Between these two
alternatives Maimon's thought constantly oscillates as between two
poles. These two aspects of his philosophy are consistently thought out,
and Maimon is conscious of this. "It is my deepest conviction," he writes,
"that my system of thought is as fully developed as any other."[23] But
these two main aspects of his thought do not form a synthesis, a unity;
they are two opposite poles rather than the two foci of an ellipse.
Maimon considered his philosophical conception as a critical skepticism
that is essentially a synthesis of Hume and Leibniz as seen with the
binocular vision of Kantian criticism. Just as the Kantian conception
is a synthesis of English empiricism and continental rationalism, so
Maimon's conception is a combination of Hume's skepticism and
Leibniz' rationalism. The question *quid facti*, which he raises against
Kant, constitutes the crux of his skepticism; and Maimon's epistemological monadism[24] forms the center of his rationalism. However,
with reference to Maimon's conception the term "coalition" is to be
preferred to "synthesis" because the two main elements of his thought
do not constitute a unity but are, rather, two possible alternatives.

[23] *Tr.*, p. 443.
[24] That is the infinitesimals of sensation. See below, Chap. VI.

When, in the second half of the last century, the call "Back to Kant" was heard, it was little realized how much Maimon had anticipated the ideas and conceptions that motivated it. Some of the main thoughts developed in the various trends of Neo-Kantianism of the second half of the last century had already been expressed by Maimon, though perhaps not in the same form. In consequence of certain aspects of his thought, and especially because of his concept of the thing-in-itself, Maimon may truly be called the first Neo-Kantian. Almost seventy-five years of philosophical development separate the early beginnings of the Neo-Kantian movement from Maimon, yet it is amazing to see how much they have in common. The call "Back to Kant" does not mean a return to the whole body of Kantian teachings, for there are in Kant many elements that are conditioned by the position of science in his time and are no longer tenable. The return to Kant that is called for is merely a return to the transcendental method and to the main principles of critical philosophy. Through Maimon's incisive criticism of Kant we learn to winnow the chaff from the grain, to separate the transitory from the enduring. Certain of Kant's doctrines, which are historically conditioned and dependent on Newtonian physical concepts, must be divorced from the transcendental method, which is the form of critical idealism and is independent of any particular stage in the development of scientific thought. This is not to say that Maimon reached the heights of critical thought – far from it. But his analysis and criticism help us to gain a better insight into the Kantian problematic and to acquire a facility in distinguishing the abiding elements of critical philosophy from the historical Kant, which constitutes the very essence of Neo-Kantianism.

The importance of Maimon's thought for a renaissance of critical idealism is, we believe, much greater than appears at first thought. Elements of critical idealism are as old as the history of human thought. In modern times it was Kant who formulated its doctrines. However, because of certain ambiguities in Kant himself and difficulties arising from Kant's formulation, critical idealism has suffered setbacks through the development of idealistic speculative metaphysics, on the one hand, and through empirisicm and positivism as a reaction to this metaphysics, on the other. A revival of the spirit of critical idealism is thus possible only through a return to Kant, that is to say, a return to the Kantian method. And Maimon's criticism of certain Kantian doctrines can lead to a distinction between the actual doctrines of Kant and the critical method.

CHAPTER II

THE THING-IN-ITSELF

The problem of the concept of the thing-in-itself (*Ding an sich*) in Kant's thought, its meaning and significance, became the pivotal point of philosophical thinking in the period immediately following the appearance of Kant's *Critique*. All the discussions and arguments in the various philosophical schools revolved around this concept, and Maimon's philosophy was no exception. Maimon attacked the problem of the thing-in-itself in a variety of contexts and from several different angles. Not satisfied with proving the untenability of the concept in a critical system of thought, as Jacobi and Schulze had already done, he attempted to define its positive meaning in critical philosophy. If the thing-in-itself is understood to mean, as it usually is, an object independent of a thinking subject, then it is just as contradictory as the concept of a squared circle. It is tantamount to stating that we can imagine something that is in principle unimaginable, or that we can be conscious of something that in principle transcends all consciousness. As it is impossible to know something that is in principle unknowable, and as it is inconceivable for the subject to have an idea of an object that cannot be brought within the sphere of comprehension of the subject, the thing-in-itself is an illogical concept. Our task, therefore, is to explain the origin of this self-contradictory concept in our mind by positively establishing its meaning and rightful place in the realm of consciousness.

Maimon's philosophy is thus based, first, on the disproof of metaphysical entities, such as things-in-themselves, understood as substances bearing appearances, and, second, on the reflective analysis of the phenomena of consciousness as such, establishing the necessity for a complete correlation between consciousness and its object.

The contradictory nature of the concept of the thing-in-itself in the Kantian system of thought was first pointed out by Friedrich Heinrich Jacobi in his essay *"Über den Transcendentalen Idealismus,"* which was appended to his treatise *David Hume über den Glauben, oder Idealismus und Realismus* (1787). Jacobi epitomized the inconsistency of this concept thus: "For several years I have felt the need to start anew the study of Kant's *Critique of Pure Reason* because of the confusion in my mind resulting from the fact that, on the one hand, I could not enter into the system without the assumption of the concept of the thing-in-itself and, on the other hand, I could not remain in it with this concept."

The criticism Jacobi leveled against the concept of the thing-in-itself was shared by Aenesidemus-Schulze. He, too, pointed out the contradictory nature of this concept in the Kantian system. The *Critique of Pure Reason* is based on the principle that all human knowledge begins with the effect of objectively existing things upon our senses, i.e., that there are things-in-themselves which affect our consciousness. This assumption, however, is not proved, nor is it consistent with the results of the *Critique*. According to Kant's transcendental deduction of the pure concepts of understanding, the categories of causality and reality are applicable only to empirical intuitions, i.e., to objects perceived in time. Outside the realm of experience the categories have no meaning whatsoever. In Schulze's view Kant is supposed to have assumed that the thing-in-itself furnishes the material of the intuitions by affecting our sensibility. But the thing-in-itself is not an object of intuition or of sensuous perception; it is fundamentally incompatible with and independent of all perceptions. Consequently, neither the concept of causality nor that of reality, which are categories of thought applicable only to objects of experience, can possibly be applied to things-in-themselves. In the assumption of things-in-themselves as the causes of appearances, the principles of causality and of sufficient reason are applied by Kant to an objective world in itself (*noumena*) and not only to the realm of appearances (*phenomena*), a procedure inconsistent with the Transcendental Deduction of the categories.[1]

Maimon's objection to Schulze's skepticism points out the dogmatic suppositions implied in his criticism of critical philosophy. A sharp distinction must be made between the two modes of skepticism. While Schulze's can be designated as dogmatic skepticism, Maimon's is critical skepticism. Maimon analyzes their different attitudes toward the problem of the thing-in-itself. He makes the point that Aenesidemus-Schulze's intention is to prove that skepticism consists, first, in the doctrine that philosophy has not definitely established, on the basis of

---

[1] Cf. Gottlob Ernst Schulze, *Aenesidemus, Neudrucke seltener philosophischer Werke*, edited by the *Kantgesellschaft*, Vol. I, with notes by Arthur Liebert (Berlin, 1911). p. 199. This work was originally published anonymously in 1792, which edition bears the full title: *Aenesidemus oder über die Fundamente der von dem Herrn Professor Reinhold in Jena gelieferten Elementar-Philosophie nebst einer Verteidigung des Skepticismus gegen die Anmassungen der Vernunftkritik.*

secure and generally valid principles, the existence or the non-existence of things-in-themselves and their qualities, and, second, that philosophy has factually determined the limitations of the cognitive capacity of man.[2]

Aenesidemus' skepticism is opposed to critical philosphy only with reference to the second part of the statement, namely, that concerning the limits of the cognitive capacity. But with respect to the first part, i.e., that philosophy has not definitely established the existence or non-existence of things-in-themselves and their qualities, critical philosophy is in full agreement with Aenesidemus' skepticism. Critical philosophy differs from Aenesidemus on the limitations of the cognitive capacity, for it maintains not only that philosophy has not, up till now, succeeded in establishing the existence or non-existence of things-in-themselves, but it claims much more, namely, that it has definitely established a principle which implies the impossibility of any assertion concerning things-in-themselves, including the existence or non-existence of such entities. It demands the withholding of any statement concerning things-in-themselves.

While Aenesidemus' philosophical position may be said to be a statement of a historical fact, that philosophy has not succeeded as yet in establishing anything definite about metaphysical entities, critical philosophy claims to have discovered a definite principle from which it conclusively follows that the human mind is incapable of asserting anything concerning things-in-themselves. The recognition of the essence of the cognitive process as synthesis, which is subject to certain conditions, leads inexorably to the law of restriction, that is, that cognition is confined to the realm of experience, and any attempt to transscend it leads to the domain of fancy and not to scientific knowledge.

Maimon maintains that the skepticism of Aenesidemus involves a dogmatism. Aenesidemus does not go so far as critical philosophy "in declaring insoluble in principle the questions concerning the existence or non-existence of things-in-themselves, their real and objective qualities, and speculations concerning matters transcending the limits of our cognitive capacity."[3] Aenesidemus-Schulze merely

---

[2] Cf. Logik, pp. 298 f.

[3] Cf. *Logik*, p. 300: "Er [Schulze] erklärt keineswegs [as critical philosophy does] die Fragen, welche die menschliche Vernunft über das Dasein und Nichtsein der Dinge an sich, über ihre reellen und objektiven Eigenschaften und über die Gränzen der Erkenntniskräfte aufwirft für schlechterdings unbeantwortlich..." It seems to me that we have here either a misprint or an unfortunate formulation. "Über die Gränzen der Erkenntniskräfte" cannot mean that the question concerning the limits of human reason is insoluble. Rather the reverse is true, for critical philosophy delimits the range

states the fact that speculative metaphysics has not as yet succeded in solving metaphysical questions. But the possibility of metaphysics as a science is in principle not excluded, since he does not fix the limits of our cognitive capacity. Critical philosophy, however, has deduced the impossibility of the science of metaphysics from principles determining the limitations of our cognitive capacity.

Kant's concept of the thing-in-itself was generally understood by his contemporaries as well as by many of his interpreters in the following generations in a realistic sense, as the substratum underlying appearances. Though things as they appear to us (*phenomena*) and as they are in themselves (*noumena*) are essentially different, the former are affected by the latter, *noumena* are the source of appearances (*phenomena*). The question naturally arises: since *noumena* cannot be objects of cognition, for we have no means at our disposal for the cognition of metaphysical entities abstracted from the manner in which they appear to us, how can we posit their reality as substrata of appearances? Furthermore, since they are so radically different from *phenomena*, how can we maintain that they affect *phenomena*? The relation of cause and effect can exist only among things of the same order. This is a problem that Kant has not solved successfully; it constitutes an incongruity in the whole structure of his philosophy.

Maimon therefore conceives of things-in-themselves as nothing other than the complete cognition of appearances. Metaphysics is not a science of objects that are beyond the realm of appearances but merely a science of the limits of the process of cognition or of the last elements of the series of appearances. These limits are ideas in the critical sense, i.e., they constitute the final goal toward which the cognition of appearances strives. What is outside the realm of experience cannot be an object of cognition; *noumena* cannot, therefore, constitute a subject matter for the science of metaphysics, nor can we presuppose them as substrata for the *phenomena*. Since they are so different from each other, the supposition that the former affect the latter is baseless, for a causal nexus cannot be presupposed among objects of totally different and absolutely heterogeneous natures. We have, therefore, to conceive of things-in-themselves as the complete series of appearances, or as

of our cognitive capacity, with the result that the validity of our forms and concepts of understanding is confined to the realm of experience, and problems concerning matters beyond the realm of experience are in principle insoluble. I have, therefore, rendered this passage in Maimon as referring to "speculations concerning matters transcending the limits of our cognitive capacity," but not to the "limits" themselves, as being insoluble.

the absolute solution of all problems regarding the objects of experience. It is an ideal which the mind sets itself for the complete cognition of the whole series of appearances. The thing-in-itself is thus, for Maimon, a limiting concept. "These final elements of the series as ideas are truly no objects of cognition. They are, however, so closely connected with the objects of experience that without them the complete cognition of experiential objects is impossible. We constantly approach the cognition of the last limiting elements of the series corresponding to the degree of the progress of our cognition of appearances."[4]

Maimon argues against the conception of his contemporaries, who understood the Kantian concept of things-in-themselves as the substrata of appearances, that is, entities existing outside the mind. It was generally held that while appearances have objective reality only in relation to the mind with its forms of sensibility and understanding, transcendent entities exist in themselves and affect our sensibility, which is itself only a receptive mode of cognition. Receptivity implies that something is given from without and that "something" is real in itself; its existence is independent of and apart from its relation to our mind with its constitutive forms and essential modes of cognition.

To this Maimon counters that, since things-in-themselves are essentially different from the objects as appearances, there is no method by which we can possibly attain knowledge of things abstracted from the mode of our sensibility and understanding. We know of an object only through the medium of the forms of sensibility and understanding, not as it is in itself.

The difference between sensibility and understanding is to be understood, according to Maimon, as a qualitative and gradual distinction of consciousness. They differ from each other not essentially but in degree. That is to say, while sensibility is an incomplete, indistinct mode of cognition, understanding in terms of concepts is a complete mode of cognition. This doctrine of Leibniz', which Maimon reintroduced, was a determining factor in post-Kantian thought.

The receptive nature of sensibility is therefore to be modified. Through the capacity of sensibility the mind does not passively receive something "given" from without; the receptive act of the given transcendent reality is determined by apperception and forms of thought. Receptivity as a passive mode of consciousness is a mere abstraction.

---

[4] Cf. Bacon's *Von Verulam neues Organon. Aus dem Lateinischen übersetzt von G. W. Bartholdy. Mit Anmerkungen von S. Maimon* (Berlin, 1793), p. 217. This work, which has a short history of philosophical systems and mathematical inventions at the end, will henceforth be referred to as *Bacon*.

Realizing that the mind is always active, moulding and shaping the capacity of sensibility, we must understand the receptive mode of consciousness in an immanent sense, i.e., as arising from within conciousness.

Maimon writes: "The term 'given' which Kant so often employs to signigy the material of sensibility means for him, as well as for me, not something given in us, i.e., to our mind, the cause of which is beyond us. Such a relation could only be deduced, not directly and immediately perceived. To be sure, the conclusion from a given effect to a definite cause is always hazardous, since the effect may be the result of various causes. Hence the relation of perceptions to their causes is always doubtful, whether the latter are immanent within or transcendent beyond the mind. Consequently, the concept 'given' should be understood as referring merely to a presentation (*Vorstellung*) existing in our mind, the cause of which is unknown to us."[5]

Thus, we do not perceive through the senses something "given" from without. Sensibility is not receptive in the sense that it is aware of some transcendent object existing outside consciousness; it is receptive in the sense that our mind does not know the cause of the consciousness of something, not having reduced it to concepts of understanding.

The concept of the thing-in-itself is thus neither cognizable nor incognizable; it is, rather, unthinkable. It is an imaginary and irrational entity, like the concept of $\sqrt{-a}$ in mathematics. The thing-in-itself "is an impossible concept, an absolute *Nihil*."[6] That something is given in our consciousness means more than that there is present in our mind something of which neither the cause nor the mode of its generation (*essentia realis*) is known to us. We have an incomplete cognition of it, or our consciousness of it is not complete. Since we do not possess the means for the possible cognition of a thing-in-itself, the conditions for its presentation being absent, the concept of a thing-in-itself is just as much an object of general logic as the concept of $\sqrt{-a}$ is an object of mathematics. To be sure, algebra employs the concept of $\sqrt{-a}$ not as a determined object, but rather in order to exhibit the impossibility of an object corresponding to such a concept. It was generally understood

---

[5] *Tr.*, p. 203. This interpretation of Kant, though in accord with a consistent system of critical idealism, is not borne out by some passages in Kant, which would indicate rather a casual relation between phenomena and things-in-themselves. The ambiguities in Kant have caused conflicting interpretations of the *Critique*. Maimon here offered an interpretation of Kant which was later expounded in Neo-Kantianism.

[6] *Krit. Unt.*, pp. 158, 191.

in mathematics that an equation resulting in an imaginary number of $\sqrt{-a}$ indicates that the formulation of the problem is incorrect. This is the meaning of Maimon's statement that the concept of $\sqrt{-a}$ shows the impossibility of an object corresponding to it. In like manner, transcendental logic employs the concept of the thing-in-itself in order to demonstrate the impossibility of such a concept having objective reality, since the transcendental conditions necessary for the determination of reality, such as the forms of time and space, are absent with reference to the concept of a thing-in-itself.[7]

The conception of the idea of the thing-in-itself as a fiction, or an illusion, or a *nihil* like the square root of minus 2 ($\sqrt{-2}$), is negative, since each of these definitions implies the impossibility of such a concept having objective reality. This is, however, only one aspect of Maimon's doctrine of the thing-in-itself. There is another aspect to it in Maimon's conception of the thing-in-itself as a limiting concept. According to Maimon the "given" is the consciousness of something, the cause of which and the mode of whose generation in our mind is unknown to us. "This incomplete consciousness can, however, be thought of as gradually decreasing in the manner of a descending series approaching nullity. Hence the merely 'given,' that is, what is present in our mind and unamenable to formulation by concepts of thought (or to rationalization and categorization), is a mere idea of a limit of this series toward which it is constantly possible to approach, as to an irrational root in mathematics, but which can never be reached."[8]

Maimon thus considers the idea of the thing-in-itself as implying the complete cognition of appearances. "Metaphysics is not the science of something transcendent existing beyond the mind behind appearances, but only of the limits (ideas) of appearances, or of the ultimate members (*Glieder*) of their series."[9]

Now the concept of the "limits" or the "ideas" of appearances can be understood in two different ways. It may mean the infinitesimals of sensation in which the objects of experience, as appearances, are grounded. It may also be understood as the ultimate goal of attaining the complete solution of all problems concerning an object, i.e., the attainment of absolute unity, which is the ideal goal of all science. In other words, the "limits" of appearances are either the original elements in which the object of appearance is grounded, or the ultimate goal of

[7] *Tr.*, pp. 419 f.
[8] See *Tr.*, pp. 219 f.
[9] See *Philos. Wört.*, pp. 176 f.

absolute cognition of an object, toward which the human mind strives through scientific processes.

From the modification that Maimon added to his definition of the concept of the thing-in-itself – the limits of appearances – neither of the two possibilities is excluded. Maimon writes: "Though these limits in themselves cannot be objects of cognition, they are so closely connected with the objects cognized, that no complete cognition of objects as appearances is possible without conceiving their limits. With the gradual growth of our knowledge of objects reaching out toward completion, we continuously approach the cognition of the limits thereof."[10]

The close connection between the cognition of objects and their limits and the emphasis on the impossibility of comprehending objects without conceiving their limits would suggest that the limits refer to the infinitesimals in which the objects of experience are grounded. We are reminded of Maimon's doctrine of the infinitesimals of sensation as the *noumena*, i.e., the metaphysical entities, in which appearances have their ultimate root.[11] On the other hand, the concluding remark, that with the gradual increase of our knowledge of objects we continuously approach the cognition of the limits thereof, points in the direction of absolute unity as the goal of all knowledge of an object. The thing-in-itself is thus identified with the complete solution of all problems concerning an object. This is the ideal goal toward which the process of thought is continuously approaching. In this case the limits or "ideas" constitute the *terminus ad quem*, while in the conception of the limits as the infinitesimals of sensation there is involved the idea of the thing-in-itself as a *terminus a quo*. The former is a critical concept, for by the limits of the object is understood the ideal focus that we asymptotically approximate; the latter is a metaphysical idea, for the limits imply the infinitesimals of sensation from which appearances are derived.

In connection with Maimon's criticism of the metaphysical concept of the thing-in-itself as an object existing beyond the subject and inaccessible to consciousness, he gives the following definition of his idea of the thing-in-itself. "By the idea of the thing-in-itself," he writes, "I understand nothing other than the concept of an indefinite synthesis in general [*überhaupt*], while the idea of the thing is the product of a definite synthesis."[12]

---

[10] *Ibid.*
[11] *Tr.*, pp. 27 ff.
[12] See *Str.*, p. 206: "Unter Ding an sich kann ich nichts anderes verstehen als den

In order to understand the difference between a definite and an indefinite synthesis, we must realize that a synthesis is an act of unification of a manifold consisting of definite elements. The perceptions are brought into a unity of consciousness, the comprehension of which constitutes the conception of a definite object. In the proposition A is B, the elements thought at first to be different are brought into a unity. This is a definite synthesis.[13] The unification of elements that are not known and not clearly comprehended is an indefinite synthesis. The process of scientific development consists in the extension of the area of comprehension of reality, i.e., of definite syntheses. However, no object is fully and completely comprehended. There is always a residuum of problems with reference to the object, which is not mastered by our thought, i.e., not synthesized. These problems constitute the unknown X. We think of this unknown, the X, as one object; this is an indefinite synthesis. In other words, the idea of an object as a unity, when the object is unknown and not mastered by our thought, is an indefinite act of unification. This is what Maimon means by the definition of the thing-in-itself as referring to the problems, the X, of an object. The idea of this X as one object, which is an indefinite synthesis, implies, however, the expectation and the hope of a possible solution of the problems and their unification. An indefinite synthesis implies the idea of the possible attainment of a definite synthesis. It is thus the formulation of a task.

The thing-in-itself is, therefore, not the idea of a transcendent object existing beyond the subject and entirely outside the sphere of consciousness. We cannot possibly have an idea of such an object, which is in principle inaccessible to comprehension. The thing-in-itself is also not the concept of an indefinite object, but rather the concept of an indefinite synthesis. A transcendent object existing beyond consciousness is a concept of an undetermined object. This is the metaphysical concept of the thing-in-itself. An indefinite synthesis is an undetermined concept of an object, not a concept of an undetermined object. This is an idealistic, critical concept of the thing-in-itself. The distinction between a definite and an indefinite synthesis is a distinction of various areas of consciousness. The indefinite synthesis is just as immanent to consciousness as the definite synthesis. The comprehension of an object by an act of synthesis is a definite synthesis. But the cognition of any object is never complete and final; there are always

Begriff einer unbestimmten Synthesis überhaupt; unter dem vorgestellten Dinge aber die schon vor sich gegangene bestimmte Synthesis."
[13] See *Str.*, p. 207.

problems in relation to any cognized object which are not solved and ordered by the mind. The idea of the solution of all problems in relation to an object as constituting the totality of the object is to be considered as the indefinite synthesis.

Perceptions as such do not immanently contain any reference to a real object existing beyond the subject and its states. Only when the perceptions are unified into an object by an act of synthesis are they related to an object. Synthesis is thus no less a process of objectification than it is a process of unification. Now thing-in-itself means, according to Maimon, that which constitutes the concept of a real object in general, i.e., the indefinite synthesis, as separated from all its particular features resulting in a definite synthesis by which our consciousness may conceive it. The concept of the thing-in-itself is thus an immanent concept of thought, for it is the result of an indefinite synthesis. And, like the definite synthesis, an indefinite synthesis is a process of objectification.

The thing-in-itself as an indefinite synthesis thus imposes on the mind the endless task of defining it and making of it a definite synthesis. Since, however, we can only asymptotically approach a final solution of all the problems, the synthesis of an indefinite object will never be fully transformed into a synthesis of a definite object; there will always remain something undefined in the object. Even though the area of definition may expand endlessly, the area of the undefined, not rationalized, will never be completely eliminated.

Maimon is therefore critical of Reinhold's conception of the thing-in-itself as the mere material of the perception abstracted from its form. He maintained that the mere material of the sensuous perceptions does not belong to any object altogether but is entirely subjective. Perceptions as such do not contain any reference to something existing beyond the subject. Hence it is incongruous to speak of the material of perceptions abstracted from its form as the thing-in-itself. Only the perceptions unified by an act of synthesis into a unity of consciousness are related to an object. The perceptions are then conceived as presentations and ideas, not of a mere subjective state and not of a logical object of thought, but of a real object. A thing-in-itself, therefore, cannot refer to the material of the perception, as Reinhold asserted, but to the concept of a real object in general, i.e., an indefinite synthesis abstracted from the definite determinations of the object which constitute the definite synthesis.[14]

Thus, the criticism of the dogmatic metaphysical concept of a thing-

14 *Ibid.*, and note.

in-itself applies also to the doctrine of those critical philosophers who, like Reinhold, though not admitting a relation between our ideas and things-in-themselves as though they were recognizable objects, nevertheless maintain that there is a relation between our ideas and things-in-themselves, not as recognizable objects, but as objects thought of in a definite manner.

There is a correspondence between Maimon's conception of consciousness in general (*überhaupt*) and that of the thing-in-itself as an indefinite synthesis in general. Under consciousness in general Maimon understands the indefinite flow of consciousness, which is at the bottom of every particular act of consciousness; the relation of the latter to the former is that of determinations to the determinable. Just as space is the determinable and the particular mathematical figures are its determinations, so the general flow of consciousness is the determinable and the particular definite acts of consciousness its determinations. The same applies to the relation between existence in general, which is a determinable, and the individual things thought of as existing, which are its determinations.[15] Likewise, the thing-in-itself, as the indefinite synthesis, is the determinable, and the particular definite acts of synthesis are its determinations. In other words, the indefinite synthesis is the material of the definite synthesis, which is its form. However, the thing-in-itself, as the material of the synthesis, means for Maimon something entirely different from Reinhold's conception of it as the material of the forms of consciousness. For the latter the material is given from outside; for the former the material, as an indefinite synthesis, is given from within consciousness as a task for a determination by a definite synthesis.

We can bring the idea of the thing-in-itself as an infinite task which can be approached endlessly into relation with Maimon's analysis of the various methods of construction in mathematics. There are, according to Maimon, two methods of constructing a mathematical object, one of which may be designated as an objective construction and the other as a schematic construction. With the first method, the construction of the object is accomplished in accordance with the conditions conceived *a priori* by our understanding. With the second method, the object is obtained, not through *a priori* understanding, but only by means of an empirical presentation.

As an illustration of these two modes of construction let us consider the two methods employed in the construction of a circle. The algebraic

[15] *Ibid.*, p. 209.

equation of a circle defines the circle by determining a certain number of points. This is an *a priori* determination of a circle by our understanding. But the points are merely the *loci geometrici* of the formula of a circle, not the circle itself as a continuous magnitude presented by a single line. In order to obtain the circle as one and a single object, the points must be connected by lines drawn between them. Hence the construction of the circle as determined by the algebraic equation does not fully correspond to its object, since the equation determines merely the geometrical points, not the object itself. Only by drawing the lines connecting the points do we attain the object of a circle in its totality. However, the concept of motion is an empirical concept, not an *a priori* concept.

In the case of the description of a circle as an object resulting from the movement of a line around one of its ends, as in ordinary geometry, the construction fully corresponds to the concept of the object, but it is not *a priori*, since the concept of motion is empirical.[16] An ideal determination of a circle as a single whole would be an *a priori* definition of all of its points, eliminating the need for the employement of empirical concepts, such as motion.

Here reason demands an increase *ad infinitum* in the determination of the points of the circle, thereby continuously approaching the *a priori* construction of the object as a whole fully corresponding to its concept. A determination of all the points of a circle by means of pure understanding is an objective *a priori* construction of a real object. However, this ideal mode of construction cannot be fully attained; we can only strive to approach it through an endless process.

Thus in the determination of a circle by the algebraic equation, the construction is *a priori*, but it does not produce the object in its totality. According to the description of a circle as a line, each point of which is at an equal distance from a given point (the centre), its construction is performed by the motion of a line on one of its end points. This construction fully corresponds to the object, but it is not *a priori*, since it requires motion and the concept of motion is *a posteriori*. Both methods are thus schematic constructions, not objective *a priori* constructions. In order to attain an objective *a priori* construction of a circle, it is necessary to determine all its points algebraically, and this is impossible. We can only strive to determine as many points of the object as possible, thus endlessly approaching but never attaining the *a priori* construction

16 *Bacon,* pp. 233 ff.

of the object in its totality.[17] We can, I think, use Maimon's definition of the two modes of construction as an illustration of his idea of the thing-in-itself as an endless task.

All constructions of mathematical objects that require the movement of a line for the completion of the object are schematic constructions. An objective *a priori* construction by the understanding that fully corresponds to the object is an ideal that can be approached but never fully attained. In view of the concept of the thing-in-itself as an endless task, we can interpret the ideal mode of *a priori* construction fully corresponding to the object as the idea of the thing-in-itself. By achieving an *a priori* construction of the object in complete agreement with its concept, the identity of thought and being will be attained, and this is an endless task. In any schematic construction of an object accomplished by means of the motion of a line, which is an empirical procedure, there is no identity of thought and being. We have to recognize and clearly distinguish between the *a priori* and the *a posteriori* elements in the objective construction and then search for a further reduction of the latter, thus approaching the ideal objective construction in which the *a priori* elements will be constantly increased and the *a posteriori* elements decreased. The complete objective *a priori* construction, which is an endless task of the identity of thought and being, is the thing-in-itself.

Reason demands the deduction *a priori* of an object fully corresponding to its concept. The schematic construction contains a formal incompleteness, as the object is presented exclusively by means of an empirical concept, that is, the motion of a line. But the objective construction by *a priori* concepts of understanding suffers from a material incompleteness, as is the case with an algebraic equation of a circle. For only certain points of the circle are determined *a priori*, the object as a whole having to be constructed by drawing a line connecting the points. The attainment of an ideal objective *a priori* construction of a concept, in which formal completeness is not at the expense of material incompleteness, but in which the formal fully corresponds to the material content of the object, is an endless task which we approach asymptotically. This harmonious unity of the formal with the material can, I submit, be defined as the idea of the thing-in-itself.

The denial of the reality of things-in-themselves as conceived by dogmatic philosophy must now be supplemented by an explanation of the mode of the generation of the idea of the thing-in-itself in our

[17] *Ibid.*, p. 226.

consciousness. The criticism of this metaphysical concept will be complete only if we succeed in identifying its psychological origin.[18]

The origin of this concept lies in an illusion, the psychological basis of which is easy to identify. The habit by which we generally relate our perceptions and ideas to an object and thus perform a synthesis by which the object is determined, leads to the illusion that when we do not have a definite object to which to relate our ideas, there exists an indefinite object which we imagine as real. By revealing the psychological basis of the concept of the thing-in-itself Maimon exposed (to use a Kantian phrase) the supposedly legitimate child of logic as an illegitimate offspring of psychology.

The place of a thing is its relation in space to other objects. The thing-in-itself, however, is thought of not in relation to other objects in space and consequently has no place at all; at the same time it is impossible to think of a thing-in-itself in universal, empty space, since space is only the relation of objects to one another. Absolute empty space cannot be imagined; it is an illusion. The same considerations apply to motion. Motion necessarily involves change of place, and just as space cannot be imagined by itself without relation to the objects in it, so motion cannot be imagined as absolute, but only in relation to other objects in space. Nevertheless, we do think of motion in empty space.[19]

These concepts are illusions, the basis of which can be psychologically explained. Imagination draws false conclusions from that which can be thought of in relation to no particular definite object to that which can be thought of in relation to no object at all. Thus, for instance, absolute space is to be critically defined as nothing more than the relation of an object A in space, not only to an object B (with which it stands in a definite relationship), but to any other object that can be imagined in space. Since any other object can be thought of instead of B, we make the leap from thinking of A in relation to any object other than B to thinking of A in relation to no object at all, that is, empty space.

The same argument applies to the concept of absolute motion. One cannot think of absolute motion as completely unrelated to objects. Absolute motion is to be understood as nothing other than the change of an object A in space not only in relation to a particular object B, but in relation to any other object that can be imagined instead of B. But our imagination makes the leap from the presentation of any object

---

[18] *Str.*, pp. 270 f.
[19] *Ibid.*

imaginable to the presentation of the motion of A in relation to no object at all. And just as these illusions of absolute space and absolute motion have their roots in a leap of the imagination from the concept of no definite object to that of no object at all, so the concept of the thing-in-itself is an illusion deriving from a leap of the imagination from a definite to an indefinite synthesis, which is assumed as referring to a real object.

These illusions Maimon calls fictions. Just as other sciences have successfully employed fictions, so in philosophy, too, fictions have a legitimate place. The only qualifying condition for their use is that we must not take the fiction for a real object, but must be aware of its nature and function.[20]

In Leibniz' philosophy of nature monads are not real objects but the same as differential magnitudes in mathematics, namely, limits of relations. The idea of a moral sense is for Kant not a real object but merely an idea problematically assumed for the sake of the construction of a moral science. The followers of Leibniz and Kant frequently confused the merely subjective with the objective, the relative with the absolute. In like manner they substituted a definite mode of imagination for an indefinite act of perception.

In the construction of his system Leibniz used what Maimon referred to as the method of fiction, which will presently be explained. Science as well as philosophy used this method, and many theories, scientific as well as philosophic, can be properly understood when seen in its light. The *methodus indivisibilium* is a case in point. This method treats a magnitude as though it were composed of indivisible parts, a line as though made up of points, a surface as though consisting of lines, and a body as though formed of surfaces, and in this way the relation between the magnitudes is determined. The relation obtaining between the objects comprising the indivisible parts are considered equivalent to the relation obtaining between the indivisible parts in which the objects are grounded. On first thought it would seem that this method involves a contradiction, since a magnitude can be thought of as infinitely divisible. In fact, it is to be understood as a fiction. "It does not mean that a line consists of points and a surface of lines, but that the relation of all lines that can be drawn on one surface to all lines that can be drawn on another surface determines the relation of the surfaces to each other, as though the surface consists of lines."[21]

Leibniz' system of monads is to be understood in a similar way.

[20] *Ibid.*
[21] *Ibid.*, p. 29.

His intention is not to teach that infinitely divisible bodies consist of monads; in the system of monads he has applied this same *methodus indivisibilium* as a mere fiction. This does not mean that a body is composed of monads, but only that in order to understand correctly the relation of bodies to one another and their mutual influence and to determine this relation precisely, we have to think of the bodies as consisting of infinitely small parts and out of the relation of these parts to determine the relation of the bodies, thus considering the bodies as if they consisted of monads. This process of the dissolution of bodies into infinitely small parts is impossible for us to accomplish, but it serves as a goal, an idea that we can approach continually in our search after the nature of bodies and their mutual relation. In this way the monads are to be understood, not as if they were things in themselves but as fictions or ideas. Thus Leibniz' system is interpreted by Maimon in the spirit of critical idealism.

The method of interpolations is likewise a process of thought based on a fiction, i.e., the calculation of the intermediary values on the basis of the observed ones. Leibniz employs this method in his theory of confused and indistinct ideas. It does not mean that we actually have ideas during our sleep, but only that according to the law of continuity we must interpolate the presence of ideas in our mind even when we are not conscious of them; that is to say, on the basis of the concept of the soul as always active, we have to assume that if it were possible for us to observe ourselves while asleep, we would discover ideas in our mind. The theory of the soul as an active substance is thus the basis for this interpolation, which is nothing but a fiction. The same is true of the theory of innate ideas. These ideas are not to be treated as things-in-themselves but only as useful fictions helping us to understand the process of cognition. Since it is impossible to learn necessary truths by experience, we cannot explain knowledge otherwise than by assuming innate ideas. The step from here to declaring the Kantian categories to be fictions is very obvious, for the innate ideas of Leibniz have the same function as the categories, namely, to explain the necessary truths that cannot possibly be derived from sensuous experience. This step has been taken by Hans Vaihinger. Nowhere in Maimon's writings, however, do we find that he considers the categories as fictions. Moreover, there is a great difference between the meaning of the term "fiction" as Maimon understands it and the implication of the term in the "philosophy of as-if" by Vaihinger.[22]

[22] Hans Vaihinger, *Die Philosophie des Als-Ob*, 1st ed., 1911.

Maimon has at times explained the term "fiction" as an idea in opposition to a real thing. He seems to have conceived of fiction as a scientific method in a manner totally different from that of Vaihinger. The latter, in his "philosophy of as-if," bases his system of fictions on a biological concept of knowledge, an epistemology that conceives of truth as a weapon in the struggle of man for survival, in which there is implied the denial of truth as a value in itself. It teaches the identification of truth and usefulness. Knowledge of truth has no value other than that it is a means for action in man's struggle for existence. Thus a proposition is truthful if it leads to action that is purposeful, and a proposition is false if it leads to action that is harmful. The criterion of truth is thus utility or usefulness. The characteristic marks of fiction as a scientific method are, according to Vaihinger, first of all the logical contradiction implicit in it and, secondly, the utility and usefulness implied in it. In the latter rests its justification. Fiction is thus distinct from error as well as from hypothesis. Error is not only false but also useless; hypothesis is not only useful, but it claims to be true, corresponding to reality. At the same time, there is a certain community of ideas between the three concepts: Falseness is common to fiction and error, and usefulness is common to fiction and hypothesis. Thus fiction occupies a place between error and hypothesis.

For Maimon, however, the systematic place of fiction in our thought is a totally different one. Falseness is not its characteristic mark, since it is related to a realm of our thought to which the terms "false" and "true" are not applicable. Trueness and falseness are terms related to the realm of understanding. Fiction is the result of an act of the imagination and is applied only where understanding cannot be employed. Thus, to think of an infinite series as concluded is an act of the imagination, for it is impossible to think of an infinitude as concluded by our understanding. The validity of an imaginary act such as fiction lies in its contribution to the completion of our conception of the world. And when we speak of useful fictions, "useful," according to Maimon, is to be understood, not in a biological, but in a purely theoretical sense, i.e., contributing to the completeness of our conception of the world. Consequently fiction has nothing in common with error or with hypothesis, for error and hypothesis belong to the realm of the understanding, whereas fiction is an act of the imagination; they are thus incommensurable magnitudes. In Maimon's view fiction has also the distinguishing mark of a regulative idea in the Kantian sense.

The thing-in-itself, considered as an idea of ultimate unification of the object, is an endless idea. Hence the concept of a thing-in-itself as a fiction has two aspects. It is unreal, an illusion, when it is understood as a transcendent entity. It has the aspect of an endless idea to the extent it is understood to be a limiting concept implying the task of striving for the ultimate unity of the object. The vision of a complete unity is a fiction having the function of a regulative idea.

CHAPTER III

THE COPERNICAN REVOLUTION IN PHILOSOPHY: SUBJECT AND OBJECT*

In taking up Kant's comparison of the critical method in philosophy with that of Copernicus, Maimon defines the essence of the Kantian revolution in metaphysics in connection with his own distinct position regarding the problem of the thing-in-itself.[1] Maimon's position, as it emerges from his conception of the essence of the Copernican revolution, can be summarized by the following principle: Being cannot be explained by another mode of being, but by the laws of thought as creative functions of consciousness.

The essence of critical idealism does not consist in the derivation of the object from the subject, with its forms of thought as constant patterns of being, but in the doctrine that objects, i.e., phenomena of experience, are results of creative functions of thought. As *phenomena* cannot be explained by *noumena*, so objects cannot be derived from the self as a *noumenon*. The principle that one form of being, i.e., *phenomena*, cannot be explained by another form of being, i.e., *noumena*, implies that *phenomena* should be considered neither as grounded in *noumena* nor as having their ground in the subject, the self, as a form of being, i.e., as a *noumenon*.

Kant introduced the Copernican method in philosophy on the following grounds. It had until then been generally assumed that our cognition must conform to the objects of reality. Consequently, all attempts at attaining knowledge of reality through necessary synthetic propositions had to fail. Objects of reality can be known only through experience, which is *a posteriori*, and experience can grant us only comparative certainty, not general validity. Kant, therefore, proposed to reverse the relationship between subject and object, on the assumption that objects are not prior to the subject, but conform to the subject with its forms of intuition and concepts of thought. In metaphysics we should try to apply a method along the lines of Copernicus' primary hypothesis. "Failing of satisfactory progress in explaining the move-

---

* This section with minor variations is the author's contribution to the Harry A. Wolfson Jubilee Volume, The American Academy for Jewish Research, New York City,
[1] Cf. *Krit. Unt.*, pp. 5–14.

ments of heavenly bodies on the supposition that they all revolved around the spectator, he tried wehther he might not have better success if he made the spectator to revolve and the stars to remain at rest."[2]

This similarity of the critical method in metaphysics to the hypothesis of Copernicus can be understood in various ways. It may mean that while, according to the first dogmatic supposition, objects in themselves are endowed with a definite constitution which determines our perception of objects, the new hypothesis proposes that our faculty of intuition and understanding is endowed with a definite constitution which determines the objects. This would imply a causal connection between things-in-themselves. According to the first supposition, objects as things-in-themselves constitute the cause, and the things conceived are its effect. However, by reversing the relationship between subject and object and by considering the cause of the connection between them as being in the subject instead of the object, there is implied the conception of the subject as a thing-in-itself, and thus the principle of causality is applied to a *noumenon*. This would contradict the critical conception of the categories as being confined to the world of experience. Thus, neither things-in-themselves nor the subject, as a thing-in-itself, can be considered the cause of phenomena of experience. Though Maimon did not explicitly formulate the problem in this way, it seems to be implied in his analysis of the analogy between the Copernican revolution and the method of critical philosophy. And we shall show from different texts that this was Maimon's intent and purpose in his conception of the Copernican revolution.

Now, what is the difference between the Ptolemaic and the Copernican world systems? What does it mean that, according to the former, the sun revolvers around the earth, and that, according to the latter, the earth rotates on its axis and around the sun? Since the change of position of the two bodies proceeds in such a manner as to preserve the same relationship between them, what difference is there between the two systems?

It is clear that the difference between them concerns not the relative movements of the two bodies in relation to each other, but their absolute motion. Absolute motion, however, can have different meanings. First, it may refer to the movement of a body, i.e., the change of its position, in absolute empty space. But movement of this kind is only thinkable, not perceivable. Imagine a single body A existing in an absolute void. The thought of this object changing its place is possible, but it cannot

[2] See *Critique of Pure Reason*, Smith translation, p. 22.

be cognized, for the various places this body occupies at different times are not recognizable in themselves.

Second, absolute motion may mean the movement of a body in space filled with bodies. Its movement is recognizable in relation to other bodies. The movement of the body is absolute in the sense that it changes its place not only with reference to this or that object, but with reference to all objects in the space. Thus, for instance, the movement of a boat on a river may be considered absolute, because it changes its place in relation to all objects on its banks, while the movement of objects on the banks is considered relative because they change their place only in relation to the boat but not in relation to one another. But "absolute" motion in this sense also is not a proper term for the distinction between the two astronomical systems. With regard to the daily movement (disregarding the yearly movement) the earth changes its position not only with respect to the sun but also in relation to all other heavenly bodies. The sun, however, changes its position only in relation to the earth, and not with reference to the other heavenly bodies. This fact is also recognized in the Ptolemaic system, and yet this system does not attribute absolute motion to the earth. Thus the difference between the two systems cannot be grounded in the conception of absolute motion as the movement of a body in relation to all objects.

Thirdly, absolute motion can mean the movement of a body as determined by a general law *a priori*. Thus, when a stone falls from the top of a tower, the change in the position of the tower is relative with regard to the stone, while the motion of the stone is absolute. This is so not because it moves with reference to all other objects but because it is determined by the general law of gravitation. But this meaning of absolute motion, too, cannot explain the difference in the change of place of the two bodies. The law of gravitation applies equally to the stone and to the tower. Each of them moves with an equally accelerated velocity, though in different directions. Through the law of gravitation absolute movement cannot be recognized and differentiated from relative motion, just as the motion of a body in empty space cannot be recognized.

Absolute motion can, however, have a fourth meaning, namely, movement as determined by a general law *a priori*, so that in its universal application the motion of each object is recognized and distinguished from the motion of the correlative object. Even though the phenomenon as a whole of the two moving bodies in their relation to each other is one, and the motion of each is equal to that of the other, yet when the change of place of each of them is considered separately, it is differently determined. This is the case with the law of general attraction. Let us assume two bodies, A and B, of different masses at a certain distance from each other. According to the general law of attraction, the change of place of A will be determined by the mass of B, and conversely, the change of place of B by the mass of A. Since, however, the masses of the two bodies are different, the change of place of each of them will be differently determined. The absolute motion of A is determined by the mass of B according to the law of attraction, and vice versa.

In this way absolute motion can be distinguished from relative in that the former is originally determined by the law of attraction and the latter is a derivation thereof. Thus, the motion of A, as determined by the mass of B according to the law of attraction, is absolute. The motion of B in relation to A, though equal to that of A in relation to B, is relative, since it is derived from the former and is secondary to it. The same applies to the motion of B. Inasmuch as it is determined by the mass of A according to the law of attraction, it is primary and absolute, and the motion of A in relation to B is relative and secondary, since it is a derivation from the former.

Now, the difference between the two astronomical systems lies in absolute motion. The relative motion of the sun and the earth in relation to each other is the same in both systems. They differ in that the Ptolemaic system considers the motion of the sun as the absolute, primary motion on the basis of mere appearance without demonstrating it sufficiently, while the Copernican system determines absolute, primary motion on the basis of the general law of attraction discovered by Newton.

Let us now analogically try the same analysis with the relationship between subject and object according to dogmatic and critical systems of philosophy. The employment of pure concepts *a priori* is a fact of our consciousness, like the phenomenon of the movement of the heavenly bodies, for we assume the reality of necessary synthetic propositions. Just as the various astronomical systems agree as to the fact of the consciousness of motion, so dogmatic and critical philosophy agree as to the fact of our consciousness of pure, *a priori* concepts. They are definite modes of relationship between the subject and object of cognition. The problem, however, is in which of them, the subject or the object, are these concepts grounded? Since *a priori* concepts are operative in the actual cognition of objects as phenomena, in which both the subject and the object are intertwined, we may attribute them just as well to one as to the other.

If we assume that objects are the cause and the ground of necessary *a priori* concepts, then these concepts are in the objects in a primary, original sense, while they are in the subject by derivation, that is, the presentations in our mind are dependent upon and derived from objects. This is the view of dogmatic metaphysics. It considers pure concepts *a priori* as applied to objects to be determinations of the objects as they are in themselves. But the mere fact of the relationship between subject and object is no reason for holding one or the other as the ground of these concepts. Since objects as they are in themselves cannot be known, such an assumption is only thinkable, not recognizable. In order that the ground for *a priori* concepts be cognized and not merely thought, it is necessary to consider the general applicability of these concepts, corresponding to the second meaning of absolute motion. The concepts are necessarily binding not only in relation to this or that object, but in relation to all objects. Just as the movement of the boat is recognized as absolute because it moves in relation to all objects on the river's banks, while objects on the banks change their place only in relation to the boat, so concepts *a priori* are valid and binding for the cognition of all objects. We assume, therefore, that *a priori* concepts have their root in the subject, because of their general applicability.

But the fact of general applicability is insufficient ground from which to derive the origin of *a priori* concepts, just as the boat's motion cannot be considered absolute because the boat changes its place in relation to all objects on the river's banks. Furthermore, while dogmatic rationalism, like critical philosophy, will admit the general validity of pure concepts *a priori* with reference to all objects of experience, it nevertheless considers objects to be the cause and ground of these concepts. Thus the consideration of the general applicability of pure concepts *a priori* with regard to all objects of experience does not give us the right to determine the subject or the object as the original ground of these concepts.

Let us now consider the third possibility of determining the relationship between subject and object, corresponding to the third conception of absolute motion. In this instance, absolute motion is determined by a general law through which it is recognizable, such as the law determining the fall of the stone from the tower. The priority of the subject as the ground of the *a priori* concepts is likewise derived from a general law. Kant believed he had found such a law in the transcendental deduction of the categories, which consists in the demonstration that pure concepts *a priori* are indispensable with reference to all objects of experience, for no experience, that is, no cognition of objects, is at all possible save through them. The principle of the possibility of experience corresponds to the law of gravitation governing the fall of bodies. Just as the latter determines the fall of the stone as the primary, absolute motion, and the change of the place of the tower in relation to the stone as secondary and derivative, so the former determines the subject as the ground of *a priori* concepts.

But it is equally impossible in this manner to determine the subject as the source and ground of *a priori* concepts. We have seen that the same law that determines the fall of the stone from the tower also determines the change of place of the tower in relation to the stone. Hence the general principle of possibility of experience cannot determine the ground of *a priori* concepts to be the subject. So long as we consider subject and object as separate entities, that is, things-in-themselves, the question of the origin and source of *a priori* concepts is insoluble; they can be attributed alike to subject or to objects. Since cognition in the form of synthetic propositions is the result of a synthesis of something "given" from outside through the forms of sensibility and pure concepts of thought, the subject is not the sole agent of this synthesis. Assuming the reality of things-in-themselves, which are not objects of cognition, by what right do we attribute the absolute source of the necessary concepts to the subject rather than to the unknown factor, things-in-themselves? Just as the law of gravitation applies both to the stone and the tower, so in metaphysics it is impossible to determine the absolute priority of the subject in this subject-object relationship, so long as we assume the reality of things-in-themselves.

The analogy of the Copernican revolution in philosophy can be meaningfully applied only by discarding the assumption of the transcendent reality of things-in-themselves. Critical philosophy does not search for a ground of our cognitions in a thing-in-itself, either in the objects or in the subject. It strives only to discover the principles of cognition, i.e., the concepts *a priori* as they determine the objects of experience.

Maimon's position (with regard to the thing-in-itself) is fundamentally different from those who interpreted critical idealism as implying the assumption of the reality of a thing-in-itself. Accordingly, he applies the fourth view of absolute motion as an analogy of the Copernican revolution in metaphysics. As we have seen, the fourth meaning of absolute motion is derived from a general law by which the object of motion is determined. And in metaphysics, too, phenomena should not be understood as appearances of some transcendent objects (*noumena*), but as determined by the laws governing the systematic unity of our immanent knowledge. Thus the concept of the thing-in-itself is entirely discarded, for it involves a contradiction to maintain, on the one hand, that every cognitive act must necessarily conform to and be a function of the categories of thought, and, on the other hand, to entertain the idea of a thing existing in itself, which is by definition incapable of being apprehended.

When our thought in its search for the final cause and source of all appearances goes beyond the limits of experience, it reaches out towards the unconditioned, i.e., the thing-in-itself. By assuming the existence of the unconditioned as the necessary condition of all contingent reality the series of conditions is concluded. But the thing-in-itself as the unconditioned condition of appearances is unthinkable without a contradiction. "If everything cognizable must be conditioned by something incognizable, it follows that the unconditioned is the necessary counterpart of everything conditioned. But the antecedent is by no means proved...."[3] To be sure, we consider objects of experience as appearances, implying the assumption of something that appears. But it is not warranted to attempt to conclude the series of causes and to reach out towards the unconditioned, i.e., the thing-in-itself, as the cause of the conditioned.

Hence Maimon writes: "Not only is absolute motion of an object in empty space not cognizable by us, but I do not even see the need for adding the idea of absolute motion to every relative motion cognized by us." Similarly, it is unnecessary to add to the appearance of an object the concept of a thing-in-itself as its cause. Absolute motion of an object in empty space is an idea resulting from a mere abstraction. But motion of an object determined by the mass of another object according to the general law of attraction is cognized by us. In like manner, the concept of a thing-in-itself is the result of an abstraction of the forms in which objects of experience appear. It is a concept that cannot be cognized, but only thought. Since all knowledge is determinable by the forms and concepts of thought, the idea of an object transcending the forms of thought is just as illegitimate as that of motion in empty space.

Maimon's idea of the thing-in-itself is compatible with the Kantian conception of ideas as distinguished from concepts. The ideas of absolute subject, absolute cause, and the totality of the world are for Kant not

[3] See *Krit. Unt.*, pp. 13 f.

concepts of cognition (*Erkenntnisbegriffe*), but concepts of thought (*Denkbegriffe*), that is to say, ideas of reason that can only be thought, not cognized. Since cognition by the necessary forms of thought is confined to the realm of experience, the way from the conditioned to the unconditioned leads from objects of cognition to ideas of reason. Thus the thing-in-itself as the unconditioned is an idea of reason that can only be thought, not cognized. As such it can be supposed neither to affect the objects of cognition nor to stand in any relationship with them and thus be a factor determining our cognition.

Since any attempt to conclude the series of cotingencies by reaching out beyond the sphere of the immanent into the transcendent is unwarranted, we are entitled to speak neither of the object in itself nor of the subject in itself as the absolute cause of the subject-object relationship. In accounting for this relationship, it is imperative to remain within the sphere of immanent consciousness.

This conception of the Copernican revolution in metaphysics implies the elimination of the possible misunderstanding that critical philosophy assumes a causal, noumenal connection between subject and object. Instead of placing the cause of the subject-object relationship in objects themselves, as dogmatic rationalism does, critical philosophy supposedly conceives of the subject-in-itself as the cause of this relationship. Both conceptions are equally wrong in Maimon's view, since they assume the existence of a thing-in-itself, whether it be the object or the subject, as the unconditioned cause of experience which is conditioned. As we have seen, the problem of the relation of sun and earth cannot be solved by considering them isolated phenomena, for then we are not in a position to prove the Copernican theory as against the Ptolemaic, since absolute motion of an object by itself cannot be established. Absolute motion, according to the fourth explanation, means the deduction of the motion of a body from a general law governing the fall of all bodies. Similarly in metaphysics the hypothesis is proposed that *a priori* forms of thought determine objects, that is to say, the priority of the subject over the object. But the subject is not to be understood as a transcendent entity, as a thing-in-itself. We have to remain within the bounds and limits of experience and deduce the priority of the forms of thought from the general law, which states that without those forms of intuition and categories of thought no experience is at all possible or thinkable.

In the fourth conception of absolute motion no specific motion is recognized as absolute in itself beyond and outside relative motion

given by experience. Only that motion is determined as absolute which
is derived from the general law of attraction. The relation between the
subject and the object in metaphysics is to be determined in the same
manner. Neither the object in itself nor the subject in itself is to be
considered as the source and root of the phenomena of being. The law
conceived by thought should replace the subject as an entity in itself.
The laws conceived are functions of thought, and a function is grounded
in an act and not in a mode of being. Thus by the priority of the subject
we mean the priority of creative activity, not a mode of being. This is
what we meant by stating at the outset that being cannot be explained
by another mode of being.

The idea of a thing-in-itself fulfils a certain function in our thought;
it sets a goal toward which to strive, but it is not to be posited as something existing in itself and by itself beyond the realm of experience. In
our struggle with the problem as it presents itself in the "given" the
goal is its final and complete solution. Thus the thing-in-itself is identical
with the ideal of absolute unity and order.

The revolution in metaphysics brought about by Kant is thus analogous to the Copernican revolution. Just as the latter proved the
assumed absolute motion to be relative and vice versa, so critical
philosophy reversed the accepted relationship between subject and
object. That which dogmatic metaphysics assumed to be the absolute
source of the elements *a priori* in our thought, i.e., the object, critical
philosophy declares to be derivative, and what the former assumed
to be derivative, i.e., the creative subject, the latter puts forth as the
primary factor in the subject-object relationship.

In this analysis of Maimon's conception of the Copernican revolution
in metaphysics there is implied an answer to the following objection,
which may be raised against Kant's comparison of his method with that
of Copernicus. While Copernicus did away with the geocentric and
anthropocentric view of the Ptolemaic system, Kant proposed an anthropocentric view by declaring the subject to be the source of all
knowledge and perception of objects. To Maimon, however, the
significance of the revolution brought about by critical philosophy does
not lie in the reversal of the relationship between subject and object,
but rather in the proper identification of the primary and the derivative
factors in the process of cognition. Copernicus realized that the supposedly absolute motion of the sun is based on mere appearance, while
the supposedly relative motion of the earth is absolute, in accordance
with our definition of absolute, as the primary motion determined by

the general law of attraction. In the same manner, critical philosophy dethroned the object as the supposedly primary source of concepts *a priori*. In both cases the primary factor is determined by the general law from which it is derived.

We are not to search for the ground of our cognition in a mode of being but in cognition itself. Cognition is to be explained by its own principles rather than by a mode of being outside consciousness or by the mind as an *ens per se* and a mode of being. The objects of cognition are not to be derived from that which lies outside the process of cognition but from the principles of cognition themselves as they are manifested in the objects of experience, which are the objects of cognition.

We do not gain anything by the assumption that the unknown things in themselves constitute the ground of our cognition of objects and that our knowledge of objects is due to the effects of the things on our mind. The conception of cognition as an act of copying, that is, that its essence consists in the description of things as they are in themselves, does not account for the necessary synthetic propositions. Since things-in-themselves are entirely unknown to us, we cannot possibly know the mode of their effect on our cognition. And as we cannot know the manner of this effect, its supposition does not explain the reality of the necessary synthetic propositions.

Just as cognition cannot be derived from things-in-themselves, so it cannot be derived from the subject as a thing-in-itself. A thing-in-itself cannot be the ground of cognition of phenomena of experience. Hence the derivation of the general principles of cognition from the mind does not imply that the mind is a mode of being, a thing-in-itself. This is the very essence of critical philosophy in contradistinction to dogmatic philosophy. The characteristic feature of the latter is that it searches for the ground and the origin of cognition in a mode of being, while the former strives to explain cognition through principles of cognition. That is to say, critical philosophy tries to explain cognition as a creative process and not as the effect of a mode of being, be it a subject or a thing-in-itself. This creative process manifests itself in the objects of experience as cognized by us.

Maimon held that Locke and Leibniz sought for the real ground of cognition. While the former derived cognition from sense perceptions, the latter derived it from innate ideas. Both, however, derived cognition from a mode of being: either sensations affected by the things or ideas innate in the mind. "But the *Critique of Pure Reason* determines neither the objects nor the subject as the origin and ground of our cognition; it seeks merely to establish what is contained within cognition itself."[4] In other words, instead of revealing the origin and ground of our cognition in a mode of being, either in the objects or in the subject, critical philosophy strives to discover the laws and principles contained within the process of cognition. Even if we suppose the ground of cognition to reside in things-in-themselves or in the subject itself, the manner in which cognition arises still remains unknown, since a thing-in-itself cannot be known; it is therefore a useless assumption. Hence we have to restrict our philosophic investigation to an analysis of the process of cognition as such and explain cognition by the principles contained within it and not look for its ground outside itself.

According to our understanding of the purport of the *Critique*, the Copernican revolution in philosophy intended by Kant cannot mean placing the subject in the centre instead of the object. It can mean only what Maimon intended by his fourth conception of this revolution. The third view of the Copernican revolution is compatible with a subjective interpretation of Kantianism, that is, the view that the subject is endowed with certain *a priori* forms of sensibility and understanding, which the mind imposes upon reality, just as a seal with a certain pattern or device is stamped upon some material. But this is not Maimon's understanding of the essence of the *Critique of Pure Reason*.

In another context Maimon clearly defined his conception of the essence of the *Critique* with reference to the Kantian concept of the mind as the origin of synthetic propositions. Schulze raised the objection against Kant that, by applying the principle of sufficient reason, he determined the mind (*Gemüth*) as the cause and ground of the necessary synthetic propositions, thus employing a concept of understanding (causality) with reference to a thing-in-itself, the mind. Maimon held that this criticism lacked any foundation. The *Critique* does not determine the mind as the cause of the necessary synthetic propositions. "Just as Newton does not mean by the power of attraction something apart from the bodies mutually attracting each other as the cause of this attraction, but merely the effect of this power as determined by law, so Kant understands by the forms of cognition merely the general modes of their operation or the rules thereof, but is by no means concerned with their cause."[5] Kant, then, according to Maimon, does not determine the mind, the subject, as the cause of the necessary synthetic

---

[4] Cf. *Logik*, pp. 353 ff.
[5] *Logik.*, pp. 347 f.

propositions, and does not apply the principle of causality with reference to a thing-in-itself.

The relevance of this conception of Kant's aim and purpose to the meaning of the Copernican revolution in philosophy is clear. It cannot mean that the object has been replaced by the subject, that is, that instead of the object determining the subject, the subject, as a thing-in-itself, determines the object. Since Kant does not determine the subject as the cause and ground of the necessary cognitions, but solely the laws governing the relation between subject and object or the effects of the forms of cognition on the objects of cognition, the essence of the *Critique* does not consist in placing in the centre of the revolution one thing (subject) instead of another (object). Its essence consists in replacing a thing with a relation, or rather with the law of a relation, that is, the rules governing the creative role of the forms of cognition in our knowledge of objects of experience.

The distinction between the third and fourth views of the meaning of the Copernican revolution in philosophy consists in that the former implies subjective idealism and the latter is compatible with objective idealism. But the identification of the third view with the Kantian position, as some have suggested, cannot be supported, at least not according to Maimon's conception of the essence of the *Critique*. We have demonstrated that he understood its essence to imply objective idealism. By "subject" (*Gemüth*, in Kantian language) is not meant the individual subject, as an entity *per se*, a thing-in-itself, but the process of thought as it evolves in the struggle with the problems of reality and as it manifests itself in the objects of cognition. Maimon's objection to the third view of the Copernican revolution is directed against a subjective interpretation of Kantianism, but not against Kant himself as Maimon understood him. To look for the ground of cognition in a mode of being is the method of pre-Kantian dogmatic philosophy. Aenesidemus-Schulze, who understood the essence of the *Critique* as establishing the subject as the ground of the necessary forms of cognition, is quoted by Maimon: "A derivation of the necessary and universal notions in our cognition from the mind [*Gemüth*] does not explain any better the existence of the necessary ideas than their derivation from the objects beyond us and from their effect upon us."[6] Schulze's thought was rooted in dogmatic, pre-Kantian philosophy, since he considered the subject and the objects as isolated entities confronting each other. Maimon held, therefore, that there was nothing to be gained by deriving the necessary

[6] *Logik.*, p. 353.

concepts from the subject instead of from the objects and their effect upon our mind. By pointing out the essential difference between dogmatic and critical philosophy, namely, that the *Critique* does not intend to derive the necessary forms and concepts from the subject as an entity in itself, but rather to establish the necessary principles of cognition as manifested in the objects of cognition, Maimon's objection was directed against the interpretation of Kant in the sense of subjective idealism.

Some scholars have interpreted the third view of the relation between subject and object as referring to Kant and the fourth conception as being Maimon's own view.[7] To my mind, Maimon here interpreted the critical philosophy of Kant as he understood it, in contradistinction to those philosophers of his time who interpreted Kantianism as necessarily implying the transcendent reality of things-in-themselves. There is no compelling reason to assume that Kant himself proposed the transcendent reality of things-in-themselves. Such an assumption would involve us in contradictions, for it is inconsistent with the essence of critical idealism. In recent times, Hermann Cohen and Paul Natorp and the scholars belonging to this school of thought (the Marburg School) understood the Kantian thing-in-itself to be a limiting concept, an idea, not a transcendent reality existing in itself, a *noumenon* behind the *phenomenon*. And Maimon was the first to conceive the Kantian thing-in-itself not as a transcendent reality but as immanent to consciousness, i.e., those elements of consciousness with regard to an object that are not categorized and rationalized are designated as the thing-in-itself.

There is no indication in Maimon of the assumption that the third view of the relation between subject and object, implying the reality of things-in-themselves, refers to Kant. We have demonstrated that in defending Kant against his critics Maimon maintained that the essence of the *Critique* consists in the establishment of *a priori* concepts as the indispensable conditions of the cognition of objects of experience, not in the discovery of some entity in itself as the source of these concepts. Consequently the Kantian concept of "appearance" with reference to objects of experience does not imply the appearing of some reality in itself. Maimon writes: "The designation of the cognized object as appearance presupposes some thing that appears. But I cannot see the justification for such a supposition."[8]

    [7] Cf. M. Gueroult, *La Philosophie transcendentale de Salomon Maimon* (Paris, 1929), pp. 18–21, and Hugo Bergman, *Ha-philosophia shel Shlomo Maimon*, Hebrew, (Jerusalem, 1932), p. 20.
    [8] Cf. *Krit. Unt.*, p. 14.

The third view concerning the relation between subject and object does not, therefore, refer to Kant as Maimon understood him, but to those expositors of Kant, such as Jacobi, Schulze, and Reinhold, who considered the supposition of the reality of things-in-themselves as an indispensable component of critical philosophy. Those expositions of Maimon that consider the third view of the relation between subject and object as referring to Kant are grounded in the conception of Kantianism as presupposing the reality of things-in-themselves. Thus their preconceptions of the essence of Kantianism determined their identification of the third view with that of Kant.

The same applies to Friedrich Kuntze,[9] the author of the most exhaustive work on Maimon, whose conception of Kant determined his exposition of Maimon's view of the Copernican revolution in philosophy. Kuntze recognized the difference between the third and fourth conception of the relation between subject and object as this: the former assumes the reality of things-in-themselves, while the latter derives the relation between subject and object from the laws of cognition determining the objects, eliminating the assumption of things-in-themselves. But he does not interpret Maimon to have attributed the third view to Kant; Kuntze regards the fourth view as Maimon's interpretation of Kant's conception of the Copernican revolution. With reference to Maimon he writes as follows: "He intends by that analysis of the analogy [between the Copernican revolution in astronomy and in philosophy] to understand the Kantian enterprise better than Kant understood himself."[10] Being a critical realist Kuntze assumed the metaphysical reality of things-in-themselves and interpreted Kant accordingly. Our conception of phenomena is the function of both things-in-themselves and the concepts of understanding. This is the essence of the transcendental deduction, according to Kuntze.[11] He therefore considers Maimon's discarding of the thing-in-itself as an unwarranted iterpretation of Kant.

The following reason has been advanced for believing that the third view of the relation between subject and object is that of Kant. Kant had to assume the reality of things-in-themselves in order to account for the application of the categories of thought. Without the assumption of things-in-themselves as determining factors in the employment of the concepts *a priori* it would be impossible to account for the experi-

---

[9] Friedrich Kuntze, *Die Philosophie Salomon Maimons* (Heidelberg, 1912).
[10] *Ibid.*, p. 37, f.
[11] Cf. Friedrich Kuntze, "Salomon Maimons theoretische Philosophie und ihr Ort in einem System des Kritizismus," *Logos*, III, 298 f.

ence of the world. The question, "Why do we apply in one case a definite *a priori* concept and in another case a different concept?" cannot be resolved except by the assumption of things-in-themselves, which determine in each particular case the application of a definite category.[12]

But if this was Kant's view, what is left of the Copernican revolution? If objects as they are in themselves determine the application of concepts *a priori*, then concepts revolve around objects. Such a realistic conception is analogous to the Ptolemaic and not to the Copernican world-system.

Furthermore, if objects determine the application of the necessary *a priori* concepts, and these concepts are real in things-in-themselves, what is gained by positing the categories as necessary principles of thought? What is gained by this duplication, that is, by considering the categories as principles of thought and attributing them to things-in-themselves? This double-world theory is in agreement with the Aristotelian doctrine of the categories, but not with critical philosophy. Maimon would have been the last person to have held such a view of Kantianism.

It has also been proposed that the thing-in-itself has, according to Kant, a necessary relationship to the material given through sensibility, which, in conjunction with the concepts *a priori*, determines the objects of experience. Hence the third view of the relation between subject and object must refer to Kant. The empirical object is the result of a double relationship: it is the effect, first, of the relation between material given through sensibility and concepts of understanding, and second, of the relation between the material of appearance and the thing-in-itself.[13] According to this interpretation, the function of the thing-in-itself is not to determine the application of the categories but to supply a source of the material given through sensibility.

Such an interpretation of Kant is also unjustified. For if the thing-in-itself provides the material of sensuous perceptions, it is a determining factor in the cognition of objects of experience, and our knowledge of these objects is no longer the result of the cognitive functions of our understanding, since the "given" material is grounded in some metaphysical entity. The "given" should rather be defined as the awareness of a problem and the imposition of a task for unification, and not as a manifestation or an "appearance" of a thing-in-itself. Just as the *Critique*

---

[12] Cf. Bergman, *op. cit.*, pp. 20 f.

[13] Cf. Gueroult, *op. cit.*, p. 19: "L'object empirique est comme le résultat d'un double rapport: rapport de la matière à l'esprit, rapport de la matière à la chose en soi..."

is, according to Maimon, not concerned with the search for a source of our cognitions in the subject, it is also not seeking for a ground of the "given" material in things-in-themselves. Both attempts are unwarranted, for they presuppose the principle of causality, which is a concept of understanding restricted to the realm of experience. It cannot therefore be applied to a metaphysical entity transcending the limits of experience. Hence it cannot be proposed that the cause of the "given" material lies in the thing-in-itself beyond the appearances.

The assumption of a metaphysical reality as the source of the "given" material lacks any basis. Since it is by its very definition beyond the scope of possible experience, it cannot possibly have any function in our cognition of the phenomena. It is therefore meaningless to assume a relationship between things-in-themselves and the material given to our sensibility. An ontological interpretation of Kantianism is self-contradictory.[14] Maimon could not have meant to imply that Kant held the cognition of objects of experience to be the result of a double relationship.[15]

[14] The following passage in Maimon's first work (*Versuch über die Transcendentalphilosophie*, Berlin, 1790, pp. 419 f.) should dispel the possibility of attributing to Maimon the view that Kant propounded the "given" as the determining factor in the application of the forms of understanding. Maimon writes: "The given in the presentation (*Vorstellung*) cannot mean, according to Kant, that something beyond the capacity of presentation is the cause of the presentation." Such a conception on the part of Kant would not agree with the doctrine that "the thing in itself (*noumenon*) cannot be cognized as the cause of the presentation, since the schema of time is lacking here. The capacity of presentation itself can just as well be the cause of the presentation as the object beyond it. The given can thus be nothing else but that element in our consciousness, the cause and the mode of whose generation (*Essentia realis*) are unknown to us, i.e. of which we have an incomplete consciousness. This incompleteness can, however, be thought of as subject to constant diminution, so that by an endless series of grades it can be reduced to naught (*Nichts*). Hence the given (i.e. what is present in our mind without being deduced from forms of thought and without consciousness thereof) is only an idea of the limit of this series – a limit which, like an irrational root in mathematics, can be approached but never attained."

[15] Cf. Gueroult, *op cit.*, who puts forth the parallelism between the double relationship determining the motions of objects and the double relationship obtaining in the cognition of objects: "... de même que le mouvement de la pierre résultait d'une double détermination, l'attraction de la pierre sur les autres choses et l'attraction des autres choses sur la pierre." This parallelism seems to me to be rather forced and artificial. There is only one law of attraction determining the relation between objects; each object attracts and is attracted by other bodies. Thus, the motion of an object is the result of a mutual, not a double relationship, since both aspects of the attraction are determined by the same law. According to Gueroult, however, objects of experience are actually the result of two different relationships: the relationship of a metaphysical reality to an object "given" through the forms of sensibility and the relationship between sensibility and concepts of understanding.

CHAPTER IV

THE COPERNICAN REVOLUTION:
SUBJECT AND CONSCIOUSNESS

Maimon's criticism of Reinhold's principle of consciousness is tied in with his criticism of the concept of a thing-in-itself. By considering representation (*Vorstellung*) as related to an object and a subject, Reinhold presupposes the reality of both, object-in-itself and subject-in-itself. A relation between A and B as between two objects presupposes their reality as separate entities. Only in a dogmatic system of thought, according to which the reality of things-in-themselves is assumed, is it proper to speak of representation as related to an object.

The distinction must be made, according to Maimon, between presentation (*Darstellung*) and representation (*Vorstellung*) of an object. The latter implies that the concept of the object is related to the object as it is in itself, just as a copy is related to the original. The German word *Vorstellung* consists of two words, *vor* and *Stellung*, meaning that the concept of the object represents the thing, places it before us. But presentation (*Darstellung*) implies the immanent process of thought presenting an object; its relation to an object outside consciousness is not implied. The assumption of the reality of an object outside consciousness corresponding to the concept is the result of our imaginative faculty. Reinhold's analysis of consciousness of an object as an act of representation, i.e., as necessarily implying a relation to an object outside consciousness, is grounded in a lack of understanding of the difference between representation and presentation. Or, as Maimon maintains, the perception of an object does not actually represent a thing outside consciousness. When we conceive it as representing an object, it is due to an illusion of the imaginative faculty.[1]

The assumption that a thing-in-itself is the source and ground of our conception of the object is illegitimate. "It is analogous to the case of the Indian who, on being told that the world rests upon a pair of elephants and the elephants upon an immense tortoise, asked naïvely: And the tortoise, on what does it rest?"[2]

---

[1] See *Logik*, p. 319.

[2] See *ibid.*, p. 321. This analogy is also used by Fichte (see *über den Begriff der Wissenschaftslehre* ,1794, p. 51). Kuntze (*Die Philosophie Salomon Maimons*, p. 352, n. 1) is inclined to think that Fichte borrowed the analogy from Maimon. But this is not

In Maimon's criticism of Reinhold and in his distinction between presentation and representation there is implied the principle that no concept of a phenomenon can be derived from a mode of being. And this applies to the subject as well as to the object; neither should be considered as the ground and source of our concepts. Maimon's conception of the soul is determined by the same reasoning.

Maimon conceived of substance not as the constantly existent *substratum* underlying the various changes as accidents but in an exclusively idealistic manner as that concept of the synthesis which can be thought of by itself.[3] In the same way the concept of the soul as a substance was evolved by Maimon as the transcendental condition of objective thought, and not as a transcendent, metaphysical entity. The understanding of substance as an independent concept and not as a transcendent reality and the conception of the soul as a transcendental condition of cognition of objects are consistent with Maimon's rejection of the thing-in-itself as a transcendent entity underlying appearances.

The proposition that the soul is a substance means no more than that the soul must be thought of as one and the same in the various manifestations of its activity. The presentations and ideas of the mind concerning reality can attain objective validity only on the assumption of the unity of consciousness in its various manifestations. This assumption is an indispensable condition, without which no coherent and comprehensible concept of the object of reality can be formulated out of the continuous flow of consciousness. In order to bring about a synthesis of various notions and presentations that constitute the essence of cognition of an object, the unity of the mind must be presupposed.

When the mind has an idea *A* and following upon it an idea *B*, this is merely a sequence of ideas in time. To constitute a unity, the ideas must be connected with each other in the form of a synthetic proposition, such as *A* is *B* (an assertoric proposition), or *A* can be *B* (a problematic proposition). This is possible to attain only by assuming the unity of the subject. The same subject must perceive the various ideas prior to the formulation of the synthetic proposition. For if the various ideas were conceived by various minds, there could not arise the

conclusive. Fichte may have known it from another source, for it is of a much older date than Maimon. John Locke employs this analogy with reference to the concept of substance (cf. *An Essay concerning Human Understanding*, chap. XXIII).

[3] See below, chap. VIII, Principle of Determinability.

synthetic proposition connecting the ideas into a unity. Thus the conception of the soul, that is, the thinking capacity, as a substance does not mean to imply the continuous duration of the soul as an entity, a thing-in-itself, but solely the assumed unity of consciousness as an *a priori* condition of all "real thought" (*reales Denken*), i.e., thinking of objects. This can also be designated as a transcendental condition, for it makes possible the transition of thought from the bounds of consciousness towards the forming of an object of reality.

The soul is a substance only for the cognition of phenomena; that is to say, we have to think of the soul as a substance for the purpose of attaining unity of cognition; we cannot recognize the soul as a substance through its own features. But the unity of consciousness is a necessary condition of phenomena as unified objects. The concept of the soul as a substance means only the unity of consciousness. The activity of the soul in producing ideas has to be unified, and the ideas produced have to be brought into a causal relation; for this purpose the soul has to be thought of as a substance. The concept of substance is thus grounded in its function, which is the connection of the ideas. "When the soul ceases its activity, as, for instance, in sleep, there is no need for the connection of the ideas. ... If, however, we continue to think of the soul as a unity and a substance even when it is not active, that is due to the method of interpolation, that is to say, it is merely a fiction."[4] This idea of Maimon is contrary to Leibniz' conception of the soul as a substance continuously active, unless, as in another connection, Leibniz is understood by Maimon to have based his conception of the soul on an interpolation which is a fiction.

The conception of the soul as a logical subject and not as a metaphysical entity entails the elimination of the possible consideration of the soul as the cause of its ideas and mental presentations. A logical subject is posited as a necessary transcendental condition of the possible cognition of the phenomena of reality. We can say of a thing that it is the cause of another thing when the former is thought to exist by itself and its existence is the necessary condition of the latter. But the term "soul" implies merely the unity of consciousness and not the existence of an entity in itself. There is no sufficient reason for positing the existence of the soul as a transcendent entity apart from its function in the process of cognition. We should not, therefore, attribute to the soul a separate existence divorced from its function, that is, apart from the forms of thought that are manifest in the cognized objects.

---

[4] See *Magazin zur Erfahrungsseelenkunde*, 10 Bd., 3 Stück, pp. 139 f.

Kant has demonstrated that the absolute subject is a mere idea, like the other metaphysical ideas (God and the world in its totality); they are ideas of reason, not concepts of thought. This critical attitude towards metaphysics is the basis for Maimon's conception of the soul as the assumed unity of consciousness. As a logical subject of the forms of thought the soul has no existence of its own apart from the existing forms. "It is therefore just as incongruous to state that the soul is the cause of the forms of thought as it is absurd to state of a thing that it is the cause of its own self."[5]

By conceiving of the soul as the transcendental condition of the unity of consciousness Maimon's position is that of transcendental idealism, which is equally opposed to subjective idealism and to dogmatic realism. The characteristic feature of these latter philosophical positions is that both presuppose the existence of a metaphysical entity, a transcendent reality, out of which cognition is derived. While dogmatic realism presupposes the existence of objects in themselves, subjective idealism conceives of the mind as an entity in itself, in which the presentations and the ideas have their root and source. Both, however, are dogmatic, since they presuppose a metaphysical reality for the explanation and the derivation of our presentations and ideas of objects. Transcendental or critical idealism maintains that it is just as wrong to assume that the subject is an existing entity as it is to presuppose the reality of things-in-themselves. Both assumptions transcend the limits of experience and are in the realm of the imagination. Every concept concerning an object of experience involves the junction of subject and object, form and matter, thought and being; it is a meeting of two ingredients the separation of which is the result of an abstraction. The conception of the subject and the object as discrete entities is not grounded in experience. This is what Maimon means by stating that the soul is the logical subject of the unity of consciousness; the logical subject is an *a priori* necessary condition for the cognition of objects of reality. And a necessary transcendental condition should not be hypostatized into a transcendent, metaphysical reality.

Bound up with Maimon's repudiation of the concept of substance is his critical conception of force in natural science as a relational, functional idea. The concept of force or power as employed in natural science must be understood as nothing but the regularity with which a natural phenomenon takes place. Power is not to be hypostatized into an object, a substance that is the cause of another object. Thus

[5] See *Bacon*, p. 83.

the law of attraction or of repulsion should not be attributed to a power existing in an object, which is the cause of the phenonemon of attraction; it means merely the regular form in which the natural phenomenon of the relation between the two objects takes place.[6]

In the dogmatic understanding of natural forces as inhering in substances, constituting the cause of certain phenomena, it is assumed that every natural phenomenon has its cause in the existence of a corresponding substance. Instead of seeking for the functional relation obtaining between objects, it looks for the substance that is supposedly the cause of the relation between the objects. What has been said with reference to substance and soul applies with equal validity to the concept of force. Force in natural science should not be attributed to a substance, a metaphysical entity, but the concept of force should be understood as a relational concept signifying the regularity of the relation obtaining between the objects.

The transformation of the concept of substance into a concept of function in the course of the history of modern scientific development has been traced by Ernst Cassirer.[7] This transformation is a confirmation of critical idealism, which repudiates the concept of substance as a transcendent entity.

Not without reason does Kant place the category of substance among the categories of relation. For the concept of substance is a relational concept. In Maimon this trend of thought is fully developed. The predominance of relation over transcendent reality is manifest in his definition of the concept of substance, the concept of soul, and the concept of force.

Analogously, William James, a leading representative of pragmatism, criticized the classic conception of consciousness as it was understood by Descartes and the whole seventeenth century, namely as an entity contrasted to matter, the characteristic feature of which is extension. In an essay, "Does Consciousness Exist?" published in 1904, James writes: "To deny plumply that consciousness exists seems so absurd on the face of it – for undeniably thoughts do exist.... Let me then immediately explain that I mean only to deny that the word stands for an entity, but insist most emphatically that it stands for a function." The distinction between an entity and a function is the same as that between substance and a logical subject, or between a thing-in-

---

[6] See *ibid.*, pp. 84 ff.

[7] Cf. *Substanzbegriff und Funktionsbegriff*, English translation entitled *Substance and Function* by W. C. Swabey and M. C. Swabey.

itself and a transcendental condition. The former (substance or thing-in-itself) is thought to exist by itself without considering its function; the latter (logical subject, transcendental condition) cannot be thought of otherwise than in relation to the objects conceived, that is, its function.

We have here a striking example of the compatibility of some central ideas of pragmatism with those of critical idealism. Critical philosophy tries to show that the concept of substance has to be replaced by the concept of function. Pragmatism, which is grounded in totally different suppositions, has also replaced the concept of entity as applied to consciousness by that of function.

A. N. Whitehead writes with reference to James' conception of consciousness: "James denied that consciousness is an entity, but admits that it is a function. The discrimination between an entity and a function is therefore vital to the understanding of the challenge which James is advancing against the older modes of thought.... But he does not unambiguously explain what he means by the notion of an entity, which he refuses to apply to consciousness."[8] James seems to understand by entity an object similar to the objects in the natural world, that is, objects perceived by common sense on a natural level. He thinks in naturalistic terms when he writes: "There is, I mean, no aboriginal stuff or quality of being, contrasted with that of which material objects are made, out of which our thoughts of them are made; but there is a function in experience which thoughts perform, and for the performance of which this quality of being is invoked. That function is *knowing*. 'Consciousness' is supposed necessary to explain the fact that things not only are, but get reported, are known."[9]

Thus, things do exist as we perceive them, and the function of consciousness is to report, to know things as they are in themselves. Moreover, it seems that consciousness as a function is understood by James to be a function of things, not of the creative activity of the mind, for he writes: "Consciousness is supposed necessary to explain the fact that things not only are, but get reported, are known." Since he understands by "entity" a material stuff, consciousness as a function implies the fact that things "get reported." This is diametrically opposed to the concept of consciousness as a function as understood by critical philosophy in general and by Maimon in particular.

In summing up, we would say that Maimon's conception of the Copernican revolution in philosophy consists in the following. The relation

---

[8] See *Science and the Modern World*, A Mentor Book, p. 143.
[9] Quoted by Whitehead, *op. cit. ibid.*

of the idea, or the representation, to the object is not to be understood as a causal thing-relationship, a notion generally ascribed to Kant. Maimon rejects such a conception. The Copernican revolution in philosophy, which maintains that the object is regulated by, and revolves around, the idea and not vice versa, is meant only as an ideal dependence of the former on the latter, and not a dependence of one thing on another thing. It does not mean that cognition produces its object as one thing produces another thing. It means, rather, that the knowledge of an object, that is, the objective necessity of the laws and the relations that determine the object as an object of knowledge, presuppose certain general principles. These general principles, which make the object an object of knowledge, comprise the concepts of understanding, but they are not to be conceived as constituting the subjective capacity of the human mind. If these general principles were inherent in the human mind, thus constituting the psychological make-up of the subjective cognitive faculty, our understanding, which determines the object, would be a real thing, among other things, and the relation between our understanding and the object would be a causal relation between definite entities, i.e., real things.

This is not the intention of the Copernican revolution, as Maimon tries to show. The general principles presupposed in the enterprise of cognition are not psychological capacities of our subjective mind, but are universal general principles. The term "understanding" comprises the sum-total of the general principles without which cognition of objects is impossible. These principles are not beyond the realm of cognized objects but within them. In order to establish the relation between the idea and the object, it is not necessary to transcend the realm of cognized objects as they are presented in a systematic order, for the general principles determining the systematic order of the objects are contained within the systematic order itself. The principles are the necessary conditions of the knowledge of things. We cognize an object when we establish the synthetic unity of the manifold of sensibility. The cognized object is thus dependent logically upon the assumption of these general principles. But a cognitive act of synthesis always transcends that which is given through the senses.

The Copernican revolution does not reverse the relationship between subject and object, as between separate things, nor does it seek a causal relationship between two distinct entities; rather, it looks for the ideal dependence of the cognized object upon its logical conditions. This is what we mean when we say that one mode of being should not be explained by, or derived from, another mode of being. The subject, or the idea, should not be explained by, and derived from, the object, nor should the object be derived from the subject. Both methods are equally dogmatic. But the knowledge of things is dependent upon the assumption of general principles, without which things could not be cognized. Hence things are dependent upon those principles which constitute the general objective mind, or general consciousness. This is what is meant when it is stated that things revolve around the understanding.

CHAPTER V

INFINITE MIND

In the time immediately following the appearance of Kant's *Critique of Pure Reason* the old metaphysical systems were being undermined by the "all-crushing" (*"der alleszermalmende"*) Kant and the new metaphysics of Fichte and the Philosophy of Identity had not yet come into their own. In this transitional period the attention of the philosophical world in Germany was centered in the interpretation of Kantian philosophy, and especially in the understanding of the concept of the thing-in-itself. With reference to the latter Jacobi and Maimon went further than their contemporaries. Reinhold and Beck, whose contributions consisted in interpreting and explaining Kant,[1] made the Kantian philosophy accessible to wider circles. Reinhold's interpretation of Kant betrays the difficulties and apparent contradictions of critical philosophy. Jacobi and Maimon, however, grasp the full implications of the new philosophy and with respect to the problem of the thing-in-itself draw the conclusions that necessarily follow from the principles of critical philospohy. Jacobi questions the possibility of the very concept of the thing-in-itself in a system of thought that declares the object of cognition to be confined to the realm of phenomena. His analysis, however, led him away from critical philosophy to romanticism and to the adoption of a philosophical viewpoint in opposition to Kant. Maimon, on the other hand, declares that the concept of the thing-in-itself belongs to the realm of ideas in the Kantian sense, which can be approached endlessly but never fully attained. Maimon thus gives meaning and significance to the concept of the thing-in-itself in the authentic spirit of the Kantian philosophy.

Maimon thus anticipated the position of Neo-Kantianism, which appeared on the philosophical scene in the second half of the nineteenth century, two generations after his death, the outstanding exponents of which were Otto Liebmann, Hermann Cohen, and Paul Natorp. Maimon was the first to present a deduction of the concept of the

---

[1] See Karl L. Reinhold, *Briefe über die Kantische Philosophie* (1790), and Siegmund Beck, *Einzig möglicher Standpunkt aus welchem die kritische Philosophie beurteilt werden muss* (1796).

thing-in-itself in a purely transcendental and critical sense. As we have said, for him the thing-in-itself is that element in our consciousness which cannot yet be rationalized. It is present in our consciousness; it is not a reality outside of it.[2] It is regrettable that this aspect of Maimon's philosophy, i.e., his critico-analytical method, was not taken up by the philosophical systems of the post-Kantian period, which instead turned toward dogmatic metaphysics.[3]

There is, however, another aspect to the philosophy of Maimon, which had its effect upon the development of the philosophy of Fichte and the philosophy of identity as evolved by Schelling and Hegel – all of whom may be said to constitute the trend toward pantheism – and this is Maimon's doctrine of an infinite reason. The idea of an infinite reason, presented by Maimon as an outgrowth of epistemological considerations, took on the form of pantheism in the constructions of the speculative metaphysicians.

Maimon was one of the few constructive critics of Kant who had a decisive influence on the development of post-Kantian thought. His criticism of Kant is that of a follower, not that of an opponent, for he considered the Kantian philosophy on the whole as irrefutable as Euclidean geometry was supposed to be. It is directed only against certain of Kant's doctrines on the basis of critical idealism. To be sure, with regard to the concept of the thing-in-itself, Maimon is an uncompromising critic, for he tries to demonstrate the untenability of the assumption of a thing-in-itself as an *ens reale*, as the bearer of the appearances. And with respect to the question of *quid juris* – the explication of the relation of concepts of thought *a priori* to objects of reality, that is, objects given through the forms of intuitions (*Anschauung*), Maimon is also critical of the Kantian deduction. He therefore introduces the metaphysical idea of an infinite reason, in relation to which all objects are simply the product of its thought. Hence the synthetic propositions of limited, human thought, in relation to an infinite mind, are dissolvable into analytic propositions.

Maimon's viewpoint, then, is both a criticism of Kant and an attempt to present a new synthesis on the basis of critical idealism. Kant's theoretical philosophy is concerned mainly with the solution of the

---

[2] *Tr.*, p. 419; *Kat. d. Arist.*, p. 143; *Krit. Unt.*, pp. 155–158.

[3] Cf. Wilhelm Dilthey, *Gesammelte Schriften*, IV, 50, where he writes of Fichte that he prepared the way for the development of the concept of the objective spirit and of the form of pantheism that was evolved through metaphysical dialectics, and then adds: "If the methods of critical analysis, as developed by Lambert, Kant and Maimon, had been further pursued... the course of the development of philosophy would have been entirely different."

problem posed by Hume's skepticism. Kant referred to Hume as having denied the possibility of deducing causality from experience, and as having declared causality to be merely a psychological phenomenon. He then tried to give this illegitimate child of psychology a logical and legitimate birthright by pointing out that without *a priori* forms of thought no experience would be possible at all. The legitimacy of these forms of thought lies in their function, namely, to make experience possible.

Thus Maimon is to be identified with Kant in maintaining the reality of *a priori* forms of thought, as opposed to Hume; but in opposition to Kant he asserts the impossibility of deducing the legitimacy of the forms of thought from their functional value. We cannot prove that the objects of experience are actually moulded by the *a priori* forms.

Maimon tries to prove that Kant failed to solve satisfactorily the problem of the application of the categories of understanding, which are *a priori*, to objects given through intuition (*Anschauung*). This is the essence of the question *quid juris*. He therefore sets himself he task of solving this problem with the help of a metaphysical concept that apparently presents a deviation from the path of critical thought.

One aspect of Maimon's thought is defined by him as "empirical skepticism." But what is the nature of this skepticism? He does not deny the reality of *a priori* forms of thought; he doubts only the possibility of establishing the legitimacy of *a priori* forms of thought from their function in making experience possible, as Kant proposes. Maimon does not believe that it can be proved that the phenomena of experience are necessarily subject to *a priori* forms of thought and ordered by them. "Critical philosophy and skeptical philosophy," writes Maimon, "stand in the same relationship to each other as the first man and the serpent: 'He [the man] will bruise you upon the head' (which means that the critical philosopher will always disturb the skeptic with the demand for necessary and universally valid principles which are required for scientific knowledge), but 'you, the serpent, will bite the heel of the man' (that is to say, the skeptic will always annoy the critical philosopher with the assertion that his necessary and universally valid principles have no reality, *quid facti*)."[4]

Experience can give us neither necessity nor universality, only comparative certainty, but for the purpose of experience comparative (or relative) certainty is sufficient. However, if we are not satisfied with relative certainty, but seek absolute certainty, necessity and uni-

----

[4] See "Über die Progressen der Philosophie," in *Str.*, p. 58.

versal validity of the principles, then we have to look for them in the realm of metaphysics rather than in the realm of experience. That is to say, we have to assume that the comparative certainty of experience has its foundation in an infinite mind, for which all synthetic propositions are analytic.[5] Maimon thus introduces a metaphysical idea for the purpose of granting experience a true reality. And he introduces this idea in order to solve the problem of *quid juris*.

With respect to the question of *quid facti*, therefore, Maimon is a skeptic, for he does not believe that the logical forms of thought *a priori* can be deduced from the facts of scientific experience. In other words, Hume's skepticism cannot be refuted on the basis of experience. But with reference to the problem of *quid juris*, Maimon introduces a metaphysical idea in order to justify the application of forms of thought *a priori* to objects of experience. In doing so, he is a transcendental rationalist.

In the center of the Kantian critique stands the question *quid juris* and its solution, i.e., the problem of the deduction of the categories and the application of the forms of thought *a priori* to objects of reality. In the process of cognition we employ certain concepts and principles, which science, the most precise and developed form of cognition, takes for granted without questioning their validity and without examining their meaning and origin. The question arises, therefore: What is the justification of this assumption? By what right do we claim that the concepts of causality and substance, for instance, have reality in the objective world, so that the phenomena of reality are actually subject to them? What is the basis for the assumption of the objective validity of these concepts and principles? Where does one find the guarantee for their rightful application to the phenomena and the real objects of experience?

The problem could be solved satisfactorily if we were in a position to compare objective reality with the content of our cognition, i.e., with the forms of thought and its principles. However, it is impossible to undertake such a comparison, since we cannot compare the world as it is in itself with the contents of our thought; we can only compare one set of ideas about the world with another set of ideas about it. The world as it is is inaccessible to us because every act of cognition is subject to forms of thought that are constitutive of the thinking process as such. Since we cannot recognize reality except through general and constitutive forms of thought, we are entitled to speak only in terms

[5] Cf. *Tr.*, pp. 171, 443.

of our ideas about reality, and not of reality as it is in itself, independent
of a cognitive subject and of the forms of thought to which the process
of cognition is subject.

Consequently, a special method is required for satisfactorily
approaching the question *quid juris* in order to find a justification for
the application of forms of thought to phenomena of reality and their
objectification. Kant's great achievement lies in his introduction of
a new mode of thought in philosophy, the transcendental method, which
he compared with the new method introduced by Copernicus into the
natural sciences. Just as the Copernican revolution reversed the
accepted relation of the astronomical bodies to one another, so Kant's
revolution in philosophy reversed the generally assumed relation between thought and reality, between our concepts of objects and the
objects themselves.

The essence of the Kantian deduction of the categories is the recognition that they must be deduced from the very nature of the cognitive process as such. Should we succeed in establishing that the
cognition of any object must inevitably proceed according to a certain
pattern and is subject to certain general and necessary forms, i.e.,
categories of thought, we could then justifiably conclude that the objects
of cognition must necessarily correspond to these forms of thought. The
"objective validity" and the actual signification of the categories of
thought will then be established or "deduced." Thus, in order to solve
the problem of deduction, we must first gain clarity and certainty about
the essence of cognition as such. We must know of what the essence
of cognition consists before we try to deduce from it its constitutive
forms as necessarily belonging to it.

Furthermore, we must recognize that when we speak of the essential
elements of cognition, we mean by cognition not the individual cognitive act, which is a psychological process of the subjective consciousness, but cognition in the systematic order in the most exact form of
scientific thought, i.e., natural science. The latter presents an objective
manifestation of human thought, of human, scientific consciousness.
In the systematic order of the laws and principles formulated by science,
cognition is inherent as an objective reality; and as such it does not
begin and end in time like the individual psychological act of cognition.
Whereas the psychological, individual act of cognition is a process
occurring in time, having a beginning and an end, cognition as an
objective reality in the scientific and systematic order is a timeless
structure. Only the latter can be described meaningfully by the logical

terms of right and wrong, true and false. The former, as a temporal process having a beginning and an end, can be described correctly only by psychological, not logical, terms.

Cognition in a systematic order is expressed in the form of propositions having a subject and a predicate. Thus, the analysis of the essence of cognition has to start with the analysis of the propositions that logic has ordered in definite groups and classes. Kant defines the process of cognition as an act of synthesis, and the essence of cognition as a unity established through the synthetic act. The subject and the predicate are the concepts unified and synthesized in the proposition. This process of unification is not merely the result of a subjective association, but the presentation of a connection between the concepts in the object as such. From this analysis of the concept of cognition as synthesis it necessarily follows that the process of cognition is based on the assumption that a material manifold must first be given and known to us in order to make the synthesis possible.

Since the very process of cognition consists of an act of synthesis, the elements of the synthesis must previously have been given to us. In order to have cognition as a synthesis in the form of systematically formulated propositions, another kind of knowledge is prerequisite, i.e., knowledge of objects derived through the forms of sensibility. Mere knowledge through sensibility is, of course, not real knowledge, nor can it be described by the logical terms true or false, since it is not knowledge expressed in the form of propositions. On the other hand, knowledge that can be said to be true is impossible without correlative knowledge through intuition. "Just as intuitions without concepts are blind, so concepts without intuitions are empty."

The forms in which this intuitive knowledge appears are time and space, which are *a priori*. In these two forms the multitude of all real objects appears to man. Thus the material world, which is the object of our intuition and our science, is an objective world only for the human species, since the possible existence of worlds of different phenomena for other intelligences cannot in principle be ruled out.

The problem of the thing-in-itself thus arises of necessity. Since our cognition is dependent on a material "given" presented to us in the forms of our intuition, which is not logically deducible, it is quite possible to imagine a material "given" in other forms. In other words, what is logically deducible must be thought of as binding for all thinking subjects. On the other hand, what is factually given and not logically deducible does not necessarily belong to the essence of thought; hence the possibility must be admitted that there may be thinking subjects for whom these particular forms of intuition are not necessary. Herein lies a great limitation of the Kantian deduction, that some "given" material must be assumed which cannot be further deduced, i.e., the forms of intuition, of sensibility.

The process of thinking is the application of a general concept produced by the mind to an object of experience. This process presupposes two elements: (1) the matter, i.e., something given to the mind through intuition, and (2) the form, i.e., the general rules and concepts without which the given would not be an object of thought. The concept may arise either simultaneously with the intuition of the object or prior to it. Thus, for instance, in the concept of a straight line, the material of which is the intuition of a line in space and the logical form (straightness, unity of direction), is the concept that arises simultaneously with the intuition, for the drawing of the line is from the start subject to the concept or rule determining it. The reality of the synthesis of the subject "line" with its predicate "straight" rests on the possibility of construction by intuition, since the intuition as well as the concept are both *a priori*. This is generally the case with mathematical objects. The possibility of joining matter and form is here given by the fact that they are of the same *a priori* nature. In the case of an intuition *a posteriori*, however, when matter is given from without and not produced by the mind *a priori*, the question *quid juris* arises, i.e., by what right do we apply a form of thought to given matter and thus grant objective reality to a formal, symbolical concept?[6]

There are cases in which the concept precedes the intuition. Thus, for example, the mind conceives of the concept of a circle as a figure subject to the rule according to which all lines drawn from the center to the periphery are equal. We have here a *definitio nominalis* but no *definitio realis*, i.e., we know the rule governing this mathematical figure, but we do not know whether it can be realized. This concept remains problematical as long as its reality is not demonstrated through a construction *a priori*. In fact, Euclid devised a method of constructing a circle by rotating a line about one of its ends. In this manner the objective reality of this concept is shown.[7]

With regard to the concept of causality, however, which is the form of the hypothetical judgment in relation to a definite object of ex-

---

[6] Cf. *Tr.*, pp. 48 f.
[7] *Ibid.*, p. 50.

perience, the question of *quid juris* is urgent. The essence of this concept is that when A is assertorically given, B must follow categorically. The question is, how can the objective reality of this concept be proved, and by what right do we apply a logical concept to reality? Since the concept refers to *a posteriori*, given objects of experience, and not to *a priori* intuitions, how can we justify the application of the *a priori* concept of causality to the *a posteriori*, given objects of experience? Kant answered this problem in the following way: We apply these concepts, not directly to the material of intuition, but rather to its *a priori* form, time, and it is through the medium of form that these concepts are applied to the intuition. When we say that *A* is the cause of *B*, meaning that when *A* is given, *B* is necessarily also given, we do not mean the material contents of *A* and *B*, which are *a posteriori*, but merely their formal aspects, i.e., the preceding of *A* and the following of *B* in time are related. *A* is determined as *A*, not because of its material content, but because of its *a priori* form preceding in time; similarly, *B* is determined because of its form following in time. The relation of the preceding to the following corresponds to the relation of the antecedent to the consequent in a hypothetical judgment. The justification for the application of *a priori* concepts to objects of experience, which are heterogeneous, is to be found in the form of time.

Maimon, however, raises the following objection to this deduction: What compels our understanding to subsume the regular succession of *B* upon *A* under the form of a hypothetical judgment? The fact that phenomena occur in time and that time is *a priori* does not command necessity for their being equivalent to the logical relation of antecedent and consequent. So far the answer to the question *quid juris* has merely shown that the succession of phenomena through the medium of time is not of a different order from the logical *a priori* form, and they *may* therefore correspond to one another, but it has not shown the necessity of this correspondence. The Kantian cannot convince us of this necessity. He can only refer to the fact of experience; he cannot know the reason for the harmony existing between the logical form of causality and the succession of phenomena.[8] For instance, that a straight line is the shortest distance between two points is recognized as an apodictic statement referring to the union of two predicates (straightness and being the shortest), which the mind prescribes as necessary for the construction of a certain line. We cannot explain the reason why these

[8] *Ibid.*, p. 51.

two predicates must be together in the subject; it is sufficient for us to understand the possibility of this union.[9]

The same reasoning applies in our case. In answering the question *quid juris* Kant does not intend to reduce synthetic propositions to analytical ones but merely to prove their logical possiblity.[10] Since we are convinced by experience of the fact of the reality of the synthetic propositions,we need to prove only their logical possibility.The synthetic propositions may be explained through the medium of time as *a priori* but not as pure. The distinction between *a priori* and pure knowledge is this: *A priori* concepts are those general concepts which constitute the conditions for the knowledge of particular objects, and consequently they must precede such knowledge. An *a priori* intuition is an intuition that constitutes the form or condition of all particular intuitions, such as time and space. A concept is *a priori* when it is the necessary condition of the thinking of all objects in general, such as the concepts of identity and contradiction. (In the propositions A is identical with A, A is opposed to non-A, we must understand by A not a definite but any definable object.)

That is pure which is a product of the mind alone, not of the senses. Everything that is pure is also *a priori*, but that which is *a priori* is not necessarily pure. All mathematical concepts are *a priori* but not pure. The possibility of a circle is not recognized on the basis of the perception of an object of experience. Consequently, a circle is an *a priori* concept, not a pure one, since it is dependent on the intuition of space, which is not produced by the mind. "All relational concepts, such as identity, substance, causality, and the like, are both *a priori* and pure, for they are not given representations but thought relations between given representations."[11]

What is true of concepts is true also of propositions. *A priori* propositions are those which necessarily follow from concepts by the law of contradiction, quite independent of whether the concepts are pure or not; pure propositions are those which follow from pure concepts. All mathematical propositions are *a priori* but not pure, since they are dependent on intuitions of space and time, whereas the proposition, every event must have a cause, is *a priori* and pure, since it follows necessarily from a pure *a priori* concept, i.e., causality, for causes without effects as well as effects without causes are unthinkable. According to

---

[9] *Ibid.*, p. 54.
[10] By logical possibility is meant the deduction of reality from *a priori* principles, and not merely freedom from contradiction. Cf. below, Chap. VIII.
[11] *Tr.*, pp. 56 f.

Maimon, the notions of time and space are *a priori*, since they are prior to all particular, sensuous perceptions, but they are not pure, since they themselves flow from perceptions of the variety of things.[12]

In order to answer satisfactorily the question *quid juris*, we must be able to demonstrate the logical possibility of the object, that is, we must be able to explain the relation of the a *priori* concept to the *a posteriori* object and to allow the object to be generated from the concept. We are fully in possession of an object when we are capable of deducing it *a priori*.

Accordingly, we must, first of all, achieve clarity concerning the meanings of the term "possibility." "Possibility" may mean first the explanation of a concept by presenting a certain given object in intuition (i.e. sensibility) corresponding to it, that is, material possibility. But the genesis of this concept is still not explained. Through intuition the concept is established as a matter of fact, but its logical possibility is still problematical. Through intuition (*Anschauung*) the concept is made possible *materialiter* but not *formaliter*. The square root of 2 is possible *formaliter*, for it is the product of the multiplication of a number with itself, but it is impossible *materialiter*, since we cannot find the object. This is the second kind of possibility. Here the rule by which the object is attained is given but not the object itself. The square root of -a ($\sqrt{-a}$) is impossible both *formaliter* and *materialiter* because the concept involves a formal contradiction: according to the very rule of multiplication, no multiplication of a number with itself can produce a negative number.[13]

The possibility of mathematical propositions is of the first kind. Their significance can be demonstrated through intuition, but their genesis cannot be made logically possible. That a straight line is the shortest distance between two points can be made evident by the actual construction of a straight line. But its genesis cannot be made logically possible; we are unable to explain the necessity of the connection between straightness and shortness. We have to draw an individual line in order to perceive the connection between the two predicates, straightness and shortness. But we are not in possession of a general *a priori* rule from which this relation can be deduced. Wherever the possibility of a phenomenon is explained only by reference to individual facts, the *questio quid juris* remains. For how can we account for the fact that our reason posits with apodictic certainty the existence in the

---

[12] *Ibid.*, p. 57; cf. below, Chap. IX.
[13] *Tr.*, pp. 58 f.

object of a certain necessary connection between predicates? Our reason can maintain with certainty the existence of predicates only with respect to such objects as are produced *a priori* by itself but not with respect to objects that impose themselves on the mind from without. Since time and space are mere intuitions and not *a priori* or pure concepts, by their mediation only the connection of the predicates can be presented to our intuition, *not* their necessity and certainty. Thus the question remains: How are synthetic propositions in mathematics possible?

With regard to the concept of causality Kant maintains that through the medium of time *a priori*, which is its schema, the causal relation gains *a priori* certainty. Maimon's objection to this deduction is that although space and time are *a priori*, they are not pure, for they are only intuitions, not *a priori* concepts. Consequently, through the medium of time the causal relation can be presented to our intuition, but its logical possibility cannot be explained nor its genesis deduced. Its certainty and necessity with respect to objects of reality cannot be obtained through the intuitive presentation of a logical form. And the question *quid juris* is still unanswered.

A proposition is absolutely true only when its material, i.e., the object of thought, is completely given in the very form of thought. That is to say, a proposition is absolutely true only when the matter and form of the proposition are identical. This is the case only with the propositions of logic, the law of identity and the law of contradiction: *A* is identical with *A*, or *A* is opposed to non-*A*. These propositions refer to the thinking of objects in general, quite independent of the actual object of thought, i.e., its material, since its material is any thinkable object. The laws of logic are concerned with the thinkability of objects in general; they are formal, not material, since they refer to the process of thinking as such, quite independent of the material of thought, i.e., of the objects. Therefore, the question *quid juris* does not arise in connection with logic, since the material to which the propositions refer is fully given in the very form of thought, i.e., in the propositions themselves. We have here the absolute identity of thought and reality.

With regard to propositions concerning objects of experience, which are not fully contained in the form of thought, but are given from without, or mathematical objects which require a construction through intuition for their presentation, the question *quid juris* has not been solved. Even though the fact of the reality of these propositions may be certain, their logical possibility is not explained. That is to say, we are not able to deduce their necessity logically. In other words, the ideal knowledge consists in reducing reality to necessity; it must show that factual reality must be as it is and cannot be otherwise. To perceive fully means to dispense with the accidental and to transform factuality into necessity. So long as this is not done, reality is passively perceived in its factuality, and as such it is merely accidental.

If it were possible to dissolve synthetic propositions into analytic ones, the question *quid juris* would be satisfactorily solved. For in that case propositions concerning experience would be identical with logical, formal propositions, and the former like the latter would contain an identity of form and matter. In fact, the concept of an *intellectus infinitus* implies for Maimon the idea of an *a priori* anticipation of the logical possibility of reality, i.e., a reality dissolvable into analytical propositions.

In order to explain the possibility of the relation of the synthetic propositions to reality it is necessary, writes Maimon, to assume that the synthetic connection between the subject and the predicate flows from the very essence of the subject itself. So, for instance, the synthetic proposition that a straight line is the shortest distance between two points would follow necessarily and become an analytic proposition if we were able to recognize the very essence of the straight line and define it accordingly. For the ideal knowledge is the recognition of the predicate as being contained in the subject and flowing from it analytically. This assumption actually implies the denial of the reality of synthetic propositions. "I cannot think otherwise," writes Maimon, "than that Kant assumed the reality of synthetic propositions only with reference to our limited understanding, and with this I readily agree."[14] It is actually Maimon's intention, in introducing the idea of an infinite reason, to point out the problematic nature of synthetic propositions. Synthetic *a priori* propositions are the result of the limitation of our understanding; to the infinite mind, however, they are all dissolvable into analytic propositions, and in this rests their legitimacy.

The whole development of the metaphysical systems of the post-Kantian period is centered in the problem of deduction. All these systems attempt to overcome the dualism of sensibility and understanding and to make the logical deduction complete, thus embracing the whole object. This process of thought reaches its culmination in Hegel. By eliminating the Kantian requirement of a material "given" presented through the forms of intuition, and by attempting to deduce

[14] *Ibid.*, p. 62.

the objects of cognition in their entirety from logical forms, Hegel tries to solve the problem of deduction by proposing a metaphysical identification of being and thought.

Without the link formed by Maimon we cannot grasp fully the entire unfoldment from Kantian critical thought with its dualism of forms of intuition, on the one hand, and spontaneous forms of understanding, on the other, up to the philosophy of the identity of thought and reality, in which the attempt is made to deduce the object in its entirety from the forms of thought. As we have said, for the purpose of solving the problem of *quid juris*, Maimon introduces the metaphysical idea of an infinite reason, in relation to which each and every synthetic proposition is dissoluble into an analytic one. When we read Maimon in the light of the further development of the philosophy of identity, we grasp the full import of his role in inaugurating the attempt to solve the problem of "deduction" on a metaphysical basis and in overcoming the Kantian dualism.

The question *quid juris* constitutes for Maimon, as for Kant, the very core of the philosophic problem. He tries to show how the question *quid juris* engaged the attention of all philosophers, though in a form different from that of critical philosophy. The question of the union of soul and body, as well as the problem of the creation of the world, including matter, by an Intelligence are, upon deeper analysis, seen to be the same as the question *quid juris*.[15]

All reality consists of ourselves and of external objects to the extent that we are conscious of them. External existence has two elements: first, the forms, i.e., the general concepts with which our mind operates in the process of thought and which are *a priori* in us; second, matter, i.e., presentations, given *a posteriori*, of the particular objects which, in combination with the forms, constitute the known, particular objects. The forms pertain to the soul, matter to the body. The question of the union of soul and body can thus be reduced to the following: How is it conceivable that forms of thought *a priori* can unite with objects given *a posteriori*? With respect to the problem of creation, the question can be reduced to this: How can the generation of matter, which is something sensuously perceived, not thought, be explained by the assumption of an Intelligence that is *only* thought, since matter and thought are so heterogeneous?

In the realm of epistemology the question *quid juris* resolves itself to this: If our understanding were capable of producing objects out of

---

[15] *Ibid.*, pp. 62 ff.

itself according to laws dictated by itself without requiring something given from the outside, the question *quid juris* would never arise. Since, however, our mind is not capable of creating objects out of nothing, but must have given to it objects that are subject to laws and regulations not dictated by it, the question *quid juris* arises. How can our mind extend its power to given objects that are outside the realm of its sovereignty?

According to the Kantian system, sensibility and understanding are two totally different sources of cognition, and the question *quid juris* cannot be satisfactorily solved. However, in the system of Wolff and Leibniz, sense-knowledge is not really distinguished from intellectual knowledge by its genesis; they both flow from one and the same source. They differ only with respect to their clearness, distinctness, and completeness. Whereas intellectual knowledge is clear and distinct, the qualities with which sense-knowledge deals are spatially extended and confused. The question *quid juris*, concerning the relation of *a priori* thought to sensory reality, can thus be easily solved. The application of *a priori* forms of thought to reality is justified by the consideration of the fact that sense-knowledge is not essentially, but only relatively, different from intellectual knowledge.

Thus, for instance, with regard to the concept of causality, i.e., the necessity for a sequence B to follow upon a given A, it is impossible in the Kantian system to explain by what right we unite a concept of understanding (necessity) with occurrences given to our intuition, such as a sequence of events in time. Kant tries to solve this difficulty by pointing out that time and space are *a priori* forms of intuition, and therefore we can justifiably apply the concept of necessity, which is *a priori*, to a definite sequence of occurrences in time, inasmuch as this, too, is *a priori*. But since intuition, though *a priori*, is nevertheless essentially different from forms of understanding, the application of the latter to the former cannot be fully and satisfactorily justified. For Leibniz, on the other hand, time and space are forms of thought concerning the relation of things to one another. Though confused and unclear, they are, nevertheless, of the same nature as the forms of understanding; they differ only in the degree of distinctness. Therefore, they can justifiably be subordinated to the forms of understanding and can be molded by them.

In this connection Maimon introduces the idea of an infinite mind. "Let us assume," he writes, "at least as an idea, an infinite reason in relation to which the forms of thought are simultaneously objects of understanding, or which produces out of itself all possible relations and associations of objects (i.e., their ideas). Our human reason will be of the same kind as the infinite reason, though in a limited degree. This sublime idea, when completely developed, will, I believe, solve the difficulty of the relation of the *a priori* forms to sensuous objects."[16] By this happy combination of Leibniz' ideas that sense-knowledge and intellectual knowledge are of the same nature and that time and space are relations of thought instead of forms of intuition, with the idea of an infinite reason, Maimon tries to solve the problem of *quid juris*.

It appears that the idea of an infinite reason was suggested to Maimon by Maimonides. In Maimon's philosophy, which he himself designates as a *coalition-system*,[17] ideas of Maimonides alongside with those of Hume, Spinoza, Leibniz, and Kant enter as constituent elements into the shaping of his thought.

In his *Guide for the Perplexed* (Book I, chapter 1), Maimonides interprets the Hebrew term *tzelem* ("image," "form") in the Biblical passage, "In the image of God created He him" (Genesis 1 : 27), as referring to the intellectual capacity of man, which is man's ability to conceive the universal forms of reality. This interpretation of the Biblical passage is valid only on the assumption that the human intellect (finite) and the divine intellect (infinite) are of the same nature and differ only in degree. Maimon realizes this and, accordingly, interprets Maimonides in this manner: There are two distinct modes of thought: one is a process from *a priori* to *a posteriori*; the other is a process from *a posteriori* to *a priori*. This distinction is valid only with regard to finite reason, such as human intellect, for which the existing objects are given through experience and are not the result of its own thought. But with regard to infinite reason, the distinction between these two processes of thought has no meaning; since objects cannot be given to it externally, they must be the product of its own thought. Consequently, the thinking of the infinite reason can only be *a priori*.

Now, it is clear that an intellect can conceive itself or the universals that constitute the essence of reality, but it cannot comprehend existents, particular existing things, as the latter are not logically deducible. Infinite reason can thus conceive of a limited intellect by imagining itself in a finite manner. It conceives of a finite reason by the process of limiting its own absolute and infinite reason. Likewise, a finite reason can imagine infinite reason by the process of negating its own limitations.

---

[16] *Ibid.*, pp. 64 ff.
[17] *Lebensgeschichte*, II, p. 253.

"Finite reason and infinite reason are thus of the same kind; they differ only in degree. This is the real meaning, according to Maimonides, of the Biblical passage: 'In the image of God created He him [man]'."[18]

The very fact that Maimon introduces the concept of infinite reason in his commentary on that chapter in the *Guide* which deals with the relation of human and divine reason seems to indicate that the original impulse behind the development of this concept in his thought came to him from Maimonides. Although, in this instance, he read into Maimonides more than the passage actually warrants, he did so because of his recognition of the general similarity between his own and Maimonides' thought.

In order to understand Maimon's point of view and the basis of his whole philosophy, we have to go back to Leibniz, as Kuntze correctly points out, and to his fundamental distinction between *vérités de raison* (truths of reason) and *vérités de fait* (truths of fact).[19]

The idea that an object is ideally defined by propositions that attribute predicates to subjects is common to all rationalistic systems of the seventeenth century. We attain complete knowledge of an object only when it is deducible from the primary elements, which cannot and need not be further derived. This is the ideal of knowledge for which we have to strive.

According to Leibniz, every true judgment is ultimately reducible to a proposition that attributes a predicate to a subject. In any such true proposition the predicate is actually contained within the subject. Even in those cases where it is impossible to reduce an object of cognition completely to its logical elements, the predicates are still contained in the subject, though implicitly, not explicitly. "Subject" is thus to be understood as the basic concept, the underlying reality that is, on the one hand, the bearer of accidents and, on the other, the basis from which the consequents follow. Thus every true judgment of subject and predicate is ultimately analytic, except for existential propositions, which are in our limited knowledge synthetic. The kind of knowledge in which the predicate constitutes a part of the notion of the subject is possible for man only with regard to truths of reason which are necessary propositions. Existential propositions are synthetic and contingent; therefore, they express only truths of fact. Necessary truths are deducible from elementary or primary principles, as, for instance, in logic, the laws of which are confined to the thinking of objects in

---

[18] *Com. on the Guide, qiv'at Hammoreh* (Hebrew), p. 9b, also 12a.
[19] Friedrich Kuntze, *Die Philosophie Salomon Maimons*, pp. 276, 307, and 341.

general, or in mathematics, where we deal with real and specific objects that are, however, constructed by our mind out of the spontaneity of our thought. But with regard to contingent, factual truths, this kind of knowledge is impossible for us. Here an absolute, logical deduction of the object is beyond our capacity; we can strive to approach it, but we can never fully attain it.

The dissolution of a complex object, such as a contingent, into its simple elements and ideas is impossible of attainment by us. Empirical objects are refractory to an exclusively logical analysis. By the very nature of contingent objects and of our limited mind, these objects resist an absolute reduction to simple elements and to analytic ideas. Nevertheless, such simple elements must exist, even though we are unable at any given time to discover all of them.

The assumption of the reality of these elements is part of all rationalistic thought, including that of Maimon. This is particularly apparent in his idea of an infinite reason, in reference to which the contingent is dissoluble into logical relations. Truths of fact are thus for the infinite mind truths of reason. Such ideal truth can be approached by means of our reason even though we are unable to attain it. In order that the contingent should also have a certain validity and be amenable to logical analysis, it must be of the same nature and structure as the logically necessary. The contingent is factually not susceptible to a reduction to logical elements; yet the eventual reduction to logical elements must in principle be possible, and this constitutes an eternal problem for our thinking. Truths of fact are not of a totally different nature from truths of reason; both are equally rooted in reason. The purpose that lies behind Maimon's idea of an infinite reason is the establishment of this connecting link between truths of fact and truths of reason.

Leibniz' distinction between truths of reason and truths of fact is not, to my mind, to be understood as setting up two totally different, parallel spheres having nothing in common, as some commentators have interpreted it, but rather as a statement of the limitation of our understanding, i.e., that there is a factual reality not yet rationalized. This factual reality is not, however, devoid of reason; it, too, is rooted in reason and is capable of being rationalized, even though at present we have to confine ourselves to statements of a factual nature.

Nor does it seem to me that Leibniz' dichotomy between perceptual knowledge, which is confused, and rational knowledge, which is clear and distinct, should be interpreted as meaning two different, independent, and parallel spheres of knowledge. By calling perceptual knowledge confused, Leibniz intends to imply that knowledge cannot be attained by the senses; the senses can only provoke our minds and set in motion the processes of thought which culminate in the understanding of the object. In other words, perceptual knowledge is not knowledge at all, but constitutes the material for knowledge which can be attained only through understanding and thought.

Thus the distinction between necessary and contingent truths is to be understood as referring to human limitations. The human mind is incapable of comprehending fully contingent, empirical objects, and of dissolving them into purely logical, mathematical relations and thus transforming the truths of fact into the truths of reason. For God, however, there are *only* truths of reason. Maimon understands Leibniz' concept of a pre-established harmony in the sense that the world of ideas and the world of matter are both rooted in God. Consequently, truths of fact and truths of reason are not two separate realms. Maimon writes: "The pre-established harmony of body and soul is not merely an accidental and external harmony resulting from an arbitrary act; it should rather be understood as an essential and immanent harmony inherent in the objects, dependent on a will that has its ground in the very nature of the objects."[20]

Maimon insists that we must understand the concept of a pre-established harmony with reference to the spirit of Leibniz' system as a whole, and not merely on the basis of certain isolated statements of Leibniz'. And then he adds: "I understand Leibniz in the sense that the infinite reason of God refers to all possible objects or worlds which are, of course, real in relation to God. The real world of man is nothing else but the totality of all possible objects as comprehended in a restricted manner by our limited mind. Of the totality of all possible objects only so much is comprehended as real by our mind as matter and sensibility, which impose restrictions on our understanding, permit. In this sense we say that matter resists the infinite reason of God, so that in relation to the human, limited mind not all possible objects are real."[21]

---

[20] Cf. *Str.*, p. 26: "... nicht eine zufällige äussere, sondern eine wesentliche innere Harmonie, die nicht bloss von einer Willkür sondern von einem Willen, der in der Natur der Objekte selbst seinen Grund hat, abhängt."

[21] *Ibid.*, p. 36: "Nach der Art wie ich mir Leibnizens System denke, ...bezieht sich der unendliche Verstand Gottes auf alle mögliche *Dinge*... die in Ansehung seiner zugleich wirklich sind. Die in Ansehung unserer wirklichen Welt ist nichts anderes als der *Inbegriff aller möglichen Dinge von uns auf eine eingeschränkte Art vorgestellt.* Von diesem Inbegriff

In support of the validity of Maimon's understanding of Leibniz' concept of a pre-established harmony, I submit the following considerations. Leibniz compares the difference between necessary and contingent truths with the distinction that exists between rational numbers and surds.[22] The characteristic mark of surds is that we cannot fully attain their numerical value; we can only approach them endlessly, that is, the resolution of the surd proceeds to infinity. This is so, however, only with respect to limited human reason. For an infinite reason, like that of God, there is no essential difference between rational numbers and surds, between finite and infinite sequences. The conclusion to be drawn from this is that since for God there is no difference between rational numbers and surds, the distinction between the necessary and the contingent does not hold true for Him either.

This interpretation of Leibniz is borne out by another passage, in which Leibniz says: "The difference between necessary and contingent truths is indeed the same as that between commensurable and incommensurable numbers. For the reduction of commensurable numbers to a common measure is analogous to the demonstration of necessary truths, or to their reduction to such as are identical. But just as in the case of surd ratios the reduction involves an infinite process and yet approaches a common measure, so that a definite but unending series is obtained, so also contingent truths require an infinite analysis which God alone can accomplish."[23] Here also the idea is apparent that the difference between the necessary and the contingent does not apply to God but only to man, because of his human limitations.

Bertrand Russell, however, interprets Leibniz differently. He attempts to prove that the difference between the necessary and the contingent is metaphysically true, and not merely the result of our human limitations.[24] According to Russell, Leibniz taught a real dualism, maintaining that the division between the necessary and the contingent is metaphysically true and refers to God as well as to man, the bridge connecting them being the pre-established harmony. Thus the pre-established harmony is a mechanical link connecting the two totally different realities. Against Russell's view we hold with Maimon that the pre-established harmony should be understood rather as

alles möglichen wird nur so viel *als wirklich* von uns vorgestellt, wie viel die *Materie* (unsere eigene Einschränkung) zulässt..."

[22] G. W. von Leibniz, *Philosophische Schriften* (Gerhard edition), VII, 309.

[23] *Ibid.*, p. 200. The translation is by Bertrand Russell. Cf. Bertrand Russell, *The Philosophy of Leibniz* (Cambridge, 1900), p. 61.

[24] Russell, *op. cit.*, p. 62. However, cf. A. O. Lovejoy, *The Great Chain of Being. A Study of the History of an Idea* (Cambridge, Mass., 1936), p. 354, n. 68.

having its roots in the concept of the identical nature of the contingent and the necessary. Thus the pre-established harmony follows from the metaphysical monism implied in Leibniz. Since the opposition of the necessary and the contingent does not apply to God, the idea of the pre-established harmony derives from the concept of the contingent as being of the *same* nature as the necessary.

Maimon's concept of the infinite reason is to be understood, therefore, as an interpretation of Leibniz, that is to say, the distinction between the necessary and the contingent refers only to our human limitations; metaphysically they are both of the same essence. And this monistic interpretation of Leibniz as offered by Maimon was subsequently corroborated by the publication of previously unknown writings of Leibniz.[25]

Kant also speaks of an *intellectus archetypus*, an infinite or intuitive reason that creates objects through mere thought. But Kant's idea of an infinite reason has an entirely different function from that of Maimon. It is not to be understood as a reality in itself, in which our human reason is rooted, as is the case with Maimon's concept, but rather as a limiting concept whose function is to emphasize the essential limitations of the human mind. Our process of cognition is bound up with forms of intuition, i.e., sensibility. We cannot cognize an object unless it is given to us through intuition. The infinite reason is totally different; it is not bound up with intuition; it creates objects only through thought. Maimon, on the other hand, strives to eliminate the ultimate distinction of intuition and thought within the sphere of the limited human mind. For if intuition and thought are essentially and radically different, how can pure forms of thought be made applicable to objects of intuition? To resolve this Maimon introduces the idea of an infinite reason of which our human mind is a part. Since, in relation to the infinite reason, there are not two different realms, that of intuition and that of thought, but all is thought, the objects given to us through intuition do not constitute a separate realm in themselves. Only insofar as the objects have not yet been fully mastered by reason are they given to us and perceived through forms of intuition. Pure concepts of thought can be applied to objects of intuition because of the assumption that intuition is in its essence confused thought. The difference between intuition and thought is a difference in degree, not in essence. Whereas Kant conceives the idea of an infinite reason in order to accentuate the

---

[25] Cf. L. Couturat, *Opuscules et fragments inédits de Leibniz* (Paris, 1903). See especially p. 18.

ultimate dualism inherent in the process of human thought and to emphasize the limitations of the human mind, Maimon attempts through the same idea to overcome this dualism.[26]

It appears to me that for Maimon the function of the idea of an infinite reason is to enable us not to stop at contingent reality as something final and irreducible, but to continue endlessly with the process of rationalization. The idea of an infinite reason imposes upon the human mind the task of searching endlessly after the rational elements of reality. If the necessary and the contingent were two heterogeneous, parallel spheres of truth referring to metaphysical realities, our task would only be to discover the contingent and there to rest in our knowledge that we have reached the limits of possible understanding. Since, however, contingent, empirical reality is also rooted in reason, even though we may be unable at a certain stage in our scientific experience to master it by logical means, it constitutes a problem for further investigation and an endless task for our thought. Maimon writes: "Reason demands that the 'given' in the object should not be considered as something final and irreducible, but merely as the result of the limitation of our faculty of thought. In relation to a higher, infinite reason, the 'given' would disappear and be reduced to logical relations. Reason thus demands an infinite progress by which the rationalization of the object is constantly being increased and the 'given' decreased to an infinitely small degree."[27] The question here is not how far we can go in this direction. We must view the object in relation to the most perfect reason, which implies an infinite idea towards which we must always strive.

Maimon's idea of the relation of contingent and necessary truths

[26] Friedrich Paulsen is thus incorrect in interpreting the Kantian concept of an infinite reason in the following manner: "The reality, as it is in itself, is thought by us as having its roots in an *intellectus archetypus*, in an absolute and intuitive reason, which conceives as a system of existing ideas" (cf. Friedrich Paulsen, "Kants Idealismus," in *Kritizismus, eine Sammlung von Beiträgen aus der Welt des Neu-Kantianismus*, ed. Friedrich Myrho [Berlin, 1926], p. 3). This interpretation of Paulsen is bound up with his dogmatic conception of the Kantian things-in-themselves as realities *per se* to which our thinking is inexorably and necessarily driven. Paulsen writes: "We determine by necessary thinking the realm of 'things-in-themselves,' i.e., the intelligible world... we determine them as a system of ideas which have their root and unity in an absolute spirit" (*ibid.*). Such a conception of Kant's position would involve us in contradictions and difficulties and is incompatible with the very spirit of critical philosophy, which confines the realm of cognition to the sphere of phenomena. Things-in-themselves must therefore be understood in a critical sense as limiting concepts, and correspondingly, the idea of an infinite reason cannot be arrived at through the medium of things-in-themselves as real entities. According to Kant, the infinite reason is rather an idea conceived for the purpose of stressing the limitations of the human mind arising from its inherent dualism of sensibility and understanding.

[27] *Philos. Wört.*, p. 169.

seems also to have been suggested to him by his reading of Maimonides. Maimonides defines the knowledge of God, as it differs from human knowledge, in the following manner: God cannot acquire knowledge which he did not possess previously, neither can God's knowledge include any plurality, nor is His knowledge subject to any change. Therefore, God's knowledge must *a priori*, as it were, extend over all things, including particulars, otherwise His knowledge would change with the coming and passing of things. Maimonides refers to the opinion of the philosophers, who maintained that the object of knowledge cannot be a nonexisting thing and therefore God's knowledge of an object cannot precede the existence of the thing, nor can God's knowledge comprise that which is infinite. Further, it is impossible for God to know any transient thing, for that would imply a change in His knowledge. He can, therefore, know only what is constant and unchangeable. But even this kind of knowledge presents a problem, for His knowledge would then include a plurality according to the number of objects known[28]

Maimonides maintains that all these assertions are based on a common error, namely, the belief that God's knowledge is like ours. The truth is that God's knowledge is essentially different from our own. He has no attribute which is not identical with His essence. His knowledge and His essence are one. Therefore, His essence knows everything by His knowing Himself. His knowledge includes the infinite and extends over all particular objects. The term "knowledge" with reference to our knowledge and to that of God is a homonym; only the words are the same, but the things designated by them are different. Thus what seems contradictory with reference to our knowledge, i.e., the harmonization of the idea of *a priori* truth, which is independent of experience, with *a posteriori* knowledge of particular, individual objects, which is experiential, is not irreconcilable with respect to the divine, infinite knowledge. And since our intellect is incapable of comprehending the true idea of God's knowledge, we may not ask how the *a priori* character of God's knowledge is to be reconciled with His knowledge of particular, individual objects. In his insistence that God's knowledge extends also to particulars *qua* particulars, Maimonides departs radically from the teaching of Aristotle, since it is the latter's doctrine that God's knowledge encompasses only the universal forms of reality. In this fundamental divergence of Maimonides from Aristotelianism we may find the ultimate source of Maimon's doctrine that the contingent and the necessary are, in relation to the infinite mind, identical.

[28] *Guide*, III, 20.

Since Leibniz identifies the empirically particular with truth of fact and the analytically universal with truth of reason, we may translate Maimonides' thought into Leibnizian language thus: For the human mind there is a difference between truths of reason and truths of fact, between the universal and the particular, between the essential and the existential; for God, however, no such difference exists. What is for us truth of fact is for God truth of reason. Through endless analysis by the infinite mind all existing objects are dissolvable into logical and mathematical relations. And the distinction between truths of fact and truths of reason, between the particular and the universal, between the existent and the essential, between the accidental and the necessary, obtains only with regard to our limited, human mind, and not with regard to the infinite mind. Maimon thus read Leibniz with the eyes of a student of Maimonides and interpreted Leibniz accordingly.

The Aristotelean principle that God is the *intellectus, ens intelligens* and *ens intelligibile* (See Metaphysic, XII, Chap. 7 and 9), which plays such an important part in Maimonides' thought, expresses the idea that for the infinite reason there is an identity of thought and reality. Man, before comprehending a thing, has the potentiality of comprehending it. When he actually comprehends an object by abstracting the form from the substance, he performs an act by which he acquires the idea of the thing. In this case the intellect is not distinct from the thing comprehended. Whenever the intellect is in action, the intellect and the thing comprehended are not two different things, but one and the same thing. The principle of the identity of intellect, intelligence, and the intelligible applies to the limited mind of man as well as to the infinite mind of God. The difference between God's intellect and that of man consists merely in the fact that God's intellect is always in action, for there is in Him at no time a mere potentiality, while man's intellect is potential before becoming actual and requires a cause for the transition from potentiality to actuality.[29]

Since, for Maimonides, knowledge of reality consists in knowing the forms, knowledge in general has a finite, limited character, as it is exhausted in the knowledge of the forms of reality which can be attained by the human mind. In Maimon's view, as in Leibniz', the ideal knowledge of an object is its dissolution into logical and mathematical relations, which is an endless process. For the infinite mind nothing is given, all is thought; for the finite mind the task is the reduction of the "given" as much as possible to its logical, analytical elements. Conse-

[29] *Ibid.*, I, 68.

quently, for Maimon the distinction between the limited, human mind and the *intellectus infinitus* consists in that to the former something is given from without, while to the latter nothing is given, all being pure thought. But inasmuch as the object is rationalized, there is an identity of thought and being. For the infinite intellect, the identity of thought and being is complete; for the limited mind, this ideal identity is an endless task which we can approach but can never completely attain, since there is always in the object something not yet fully mastered by our mind. In spite of these differences, Maimonides' concept of the identity of *intellectus, intelligens*, and *intelligibile*, in conjunction with his concept of God's knowledge as extending over particulars as such, suggested to Maimon the adventurous idea of employing the concept of an infinite reason for the solution of the problem of *quid juris*.

ii

Now that we have shown the necessity of the concept of infinite mind for the solution of the problem *quid juris* and have illustrated its systematic relationship to the philosophy of Leibniz and Maimonides, it is important for us to consider the consequences of this concept for the understanding of Maimon's philosophy as a whole.

The assumption of the idea of an infinite mind is necessary, according to Maimon, for the explanation of scientific knowledge, which consists of synthetic propositions claiming certainty and general validity. *A priori* synthetic judgments cannot possibly be derived from mere experience. The certainty claimed for the synthetic propositions of scientific knowledge points to an idea that lies beyond the realm of empirical and sensuous experience.

We have to consider Maimon's position in the light of the idealistc trend of philosophical thought in various phases of the history of human thought. The concept of *a priori*, in whatever form it appears in the history of philosophy – whether that of a metaphysical idea, such as the idea of *anamnesis* of Plato, or that of a psychological concept, such as the doctrine of *ideae innatae* of Descartes – is always proposed as a necessary assumption for the explanation of scientific knowledge. All the idealistic philosophers – Plato, Descartes, and Kant – recognized that the content of scientific knowledge comprises much more than mere empirical experience accounts for. The claim of certainty and of general validity that scientific knowledge raises goes beyond empirical experience; in its very essence it is something totally different from the mere sensuous experience. The concept of *a priori*, in whatever form it may appear, cannot *be derived from* experience but is proposed *for the explanation* of experience. Since the idea of *a priori* is totally different from concepts grounded in sensuous experience, the former cannot possibly be derived from the latter. The reality of *a priori* concepts can be proposed only on the basis of its necessity for the explanation of scientific knowledge. The justification of the idea of *a priori* resides in the function it fulfills in the explanation of scientific experience. Thus its deduction is attained by the recognition of its indispensability for explaining the reality of scientific experience which claims certainty and general validity for its propositions.

In the same manner Maimon deduces the idea of an infinite reason; he proposes the assumption of such an idea for the sole purpose of explaining the possibility of synthetic propositions claiming certainty and general validity. The reality of synthetic propositions, of which our scientific knowledge consists, can be accounted for only on the assumption of an infinite mind, in relation to which our synthetic propositions are analytic.

Although Maimon does not designate his assumption of the idea of an infinite mind as a deduction, we may, in view of the spirit of his philosophy as a whole, consider his assumption as being grounded in a deduction, since he introduces it for the sole purpose of explaining and accounting for the reality of scientific knowledge. Deduction in the Kantian transcendental sense means the method by which a concept is derived from a given fact. It consists of a demonstration of the necessity and the indispensability of a concept for the explanation of the reality of a phenomenon.

Maimon is critical of the Kantian deduction of the categories because the reality of synthetic *a priori* propositions is subject to doubt; one may deny their reality, maintaining that the synthetic propositions are the result of an illusion grounded in habit. He formulates this skeptical attitude in the question *quid facti*. At the same time, this skepticism with reference to the reality of synthetic propositions in experience, i.e., natural sciences, did not prevent him from recognizing the reality of synthetic propositions in our thought. The presence of synthetic propositions in mathematics, which is the product of thought, testifies to their reality.

The reality of synthetic propositions can be explained only on the assumption that our mind shares in an infinite mind in which synthetic propositions are dissolvable into analytic propositions. The thinking process of man demands supplementation by the idea of an infinite mind. In other words, our regarding of synthetic propositions as real implies the supplementary idea of an infinite mind. Human thought in its very essence surpasses itself, that is, thought is self-transcending. This is apparently the implication in Maimon's conception of the idea of an infinite mind; it follows from the analysis of human thought as self-transcending. The idea of an infinite mind is necessary for the explanation of the creative nature of human thought, for synthetic propositions are not confined to the realm of thought; since the predicate is not derived from the subject but adds to it something new, these propositions are creative. And since the idea of an infinite mind is necessary for the explanation of synthetic propositions, the method by which it is derived can be designated as deduction.

In introducing the idea of an infinite mind, Maimon writes: "Let us assume, at least as an idea..."[29a] The words "at least as an idea," a subsidiary phrase enclosed in brackets, may mean that the assumption of the idea of an infinite mind, which is required for a philosophical account of scientific experience, is a mere idea, not a metaphysical reality; the hypostatization of the idea into a metaphysical reality is not warranted. We cannot deduce the transcendent reality of an idea from its assumption as an explanatory hypothesis. In postulating a hypothesis for the explanation of a phenomenon we must be mindful of the principle that only the minimum required should be posited. As the idea of an infinite mind is introduced for the purpose of explaining scientific experience, with the aim of giving certainty to the synthetic propositions, this function may perhaps be served by the mere idea of such a mind. That is to say, the idea is a goal that we have to strive to approach. We have thus in view the synthetic propositions in relation to this goal. So long as we have not succeeded in dissolving the synthetic propositions into analytic ones, we assume that the former are grounded in the latter. It is a hypothesis that gives, not the certainty of reality, but the certainty of a goal. Thus, the reality of an idea should not be converted into an idea of reality, and a hypothesis should not be transformed into a hypostasis.

This critical interpretation of the idea of an infinite mind is, however, not borne out by Maimon's system as a whole. It seems clear from the various contexts in which this idea occurs in Maimon's writings that

[29a] See above, p. 75.

he consciously posits it as a metaphysical reality and not as a mere idea in the sense of a limiting concept and an endless goal. The apparently critical and non-metaphysical understanding of this idea in the text before us should therefore not be taken as an expression of Maimon's definite and settled view of the matter, but rather as a passing remark introduced for the sole purpose of making the idea acceptable even to a follower of critical philosophy.

And herein lies the difference between the idea of an infinite mind, according to Kant, and Maimon's conception of the idea as a metaphysical reality. The idea of an infinite mind, *intellectus archetypus*, in Kant is merely a limiting and methodological concept, introduced for the purpose of delimiting and defining the finite human mind by contrasting it with the infinite, intuitive mind.

The function of the idea of an infinite mind is for Maimon not confined to the explanation of the possibility of synthetic propositions; its scope is much wider. Through this idea the concept of causality with reference to objects of experience is detached from the form of time with which the phenomena are associated; the causal connection acquires thus the rank of a pure logical relation. "Just as the actual coexistence of the various features of an object has its ground in the ideal coexistence, i.e., logical connection of these features in an infinite capacity of cognition, so the regular succession of various phenomena one upon another must also have its ground in the infinite capacity of cognition which thinks of this regular succession of the phenomena in terms of a logical antecedent and a logical consequent."[30]

In other words, our perception of a regular sequence of phenomena occurring in time, which is the basis for our conception of a causal connection between the objects, must be thought of as being conceived by the infinite mind as a logical, not a temporal sequence. An infinite mind thinks only in terms of logical relations. The assumption of such a mind constitutes the logical foundation of our conception of causality, which is derived from the observation of a sequence of phenomena occurring in time. The concept of a causal connection between phenomeena in time, which is based on experience, does not command certainty because the causal nexus between them is subject to doubt. By assuming an infinite mind, of which the human mind is a part, the causal connection of phenomena in time must be thought of as grounded in a logical connection of premise and consequence. What is for the limited, human mind a regular, temporal sequence of phenomena must be thought of,

[30] *Magazin zur Erfahrungsseelenkunde*, Vol. X, *2tes Stück*, p. 55.

by an infinite mind, as grounded in a necessary logical relation. The relation between A and B, which we conceive in the form of cause and effect is, with regard to an infinite capacity of cognition, a logical relation of antecedent and consequent. The concept of causality can be philosophically justified only on the basis of such an assumption. "We can thus problematically assume an intellectual being whose relation to all objects of nature is akin to the relation of our thinking capacity to the objects of mathematics."[31] That is, just as we think of the relation between mathematical objects in terms of logical relations between ground and consequence, so must we think of the relation between natural objects, with respect to an infinite capacity of cognition as a relation of logical premise and consequence, and not as a relation of cause and effect bound up with the form of time, as is the case with reference to the limited human cognition.

The relation of the idea of an infinite mind to Leibniz' system of thought (of which Maimon is aware) is clearly revealed in the following statement. "The infinite mind conceives all objects in the clearest possible manner. We can, according to this system of thought, have no idea of any other substance except that of our own ego and our own capacity of representation, for the corporeal substances are in this system not real but fictitious. All possible objects as substances are therefore nothing else but all possible representations [*Vorstellungen*] by the thinking capacity. These representations are in their essence no more than the effect, the sum total of the activity of the infinite capacity of presentation restricted in an infinite variety of ways. The infinite capacity of cognition presents itself as restricted in all possible forms and diverse modes. The representations [*Vorstellungen*] of an infinite mind are at the same time presentations [*Darstellungen*] of real objects; that is, by the mere act of representation the ideas acquire objective reality as existing substances outside of the mind. Every object of nature, i.e., every act of the thinking capacity is, according to Leibniz, a mirror of the universe. ...It represents in a restricted mode the whole universe, since it represents the infinite mind in a restricted manner. The artist of the universe operates thus all in all."[32]

With the assumption of the idea of an infinite mind the phenomena of the world can be thought of as determinable. The principle of determinability has been defined by Maimon as an ideal mode of

[31] *Ibid.*, p. 61.
[32] *Ibid.*, p. 62.

determination.[33] The subject is neither that which endures forever, nor the substratum of the predicates, but that which can be thought of by itself, and the predicate is that which cannot be thought of by itself, but only in connection with the subject. The determination of subject and predicate is similar to the determination of objects as thought of by the infinite mind. What the infinite mind thinks as possible is the subject; that which follows from it necessarily is the predicate. The subject is thus thinkable by itself; the predicate, as the necessary consequence of the subject, is not thinkable by itself but only in connection with the subject.

This ideal mode of determination, however, is applicable only to objects of mathematics, not to given objects of experience. To the infinite mind, which thinks of all objects in terms of logical and mathematical relations, all objects are thoroughly determined by this mode. But not so to the finite mind. "For a finite reason subject is not what is merely thinkable by itself, but what is merely given by itself, and predicate is that which is thinkable only in relation to the former as an object."[34] It would seem that the definition of the subject, which is given by itself, refers to the subject of objects of experience. For with regard to mathematical objects, the subject is not given but is thought by itself. On the other hand, even in mathematics, the subject, such as a line, which is produced by the mind, is "given" to our intuition. The subject is not merely thought but also "given." Hence, even with regard to mathematical objects, the subject can be defined as that which is given by itself as a result of the productive act of our thinking capacity.

In the Kantian idea of an "intuitive mind" there is implied the vision of a union of the ideal with the real, the abstract with the concrete, the transcendent with the immanent, the supratemporal with the temporal, the timeless with the historical. These realms, which for the human mind are apparently inharmonizable and incompatible entities, are conceived in relation to an "intuitive reason" as one harmonious whole. In the theoretical realm this means a union of understanding and sensibility, of discursive thinking and intuition. While for the human mind the categories of thought and the forms of intuition (time and space) constitute two different realms, one dependent upon the other (the former without the latter is empty, the latter without the former is blind), for the intuitive reason, which creates the object through intuitive creative thought, no such dualism exists. In the ethical,

---

[33] Cf. below, Chap. VIII, "Principle of Determinability."
[34] See *Tr.*, p. 87, n.

practical realm the "intuitive reason" involves the union of the final goal of the totality, i.e., humanity, as a unified whole, with the ethical will of the free individual personalities constituting the totality.

It must be emphasized, however, that for Kant the concept of an "intuitive reason" was merely a methodological fiction. He conceived it for the sole purpose of stressing the inherent limitations of the human mind, and the immanent tensions of the human personality. In his striving for mastery of the problems in the theoretical realm, man should recognize his modest role and the limited possibilities that exist. He can never attain an "intuitive reason" by which the object of knowledge is intuitively comprehended and created through intuition. A union of intuition and understanding, in which the intellect is intuitive and the intuition is intellectual (*intellectuelle Anschauung*), is an exclusive distinction of the infinite, divine mind. The finite human mind is characterized by the dualism of intuition and understanding. Thus the idea of an "intuitive reason" serves merely the purpose of emphasizing that which is closed and unattainable for the human mind in the theoretical realm. In the practical realm it serves the purpose of recognizing the dualism that obtains between being and the "ought to be," between the real and the ideal.

Kant never attempts to raise the "intuitive reason" to the status of an attainable goal of human knowledge. The finite human mind, with the inherent dualism of the capacities of sensibility and of understanding, remains always in a state of tension in relation to the infinite "intuitive reason." The same reasoning applies to the practical, ethical realm and to ethics as a science dealing with the rules of conduct. Here the idea of "intuitive reason" takes the form of the idea of love; it means the ideal state in which there is an absolute unity of the communal good with the will of the many individuals endowed with the capacity for freedom. In the idea of a state of love there is no dualism between the ideal good and the will of the free individuals; there is absolute unity between being and the "ought to be," between the real and the ideal, just as there is absolute' unity of intuition and understanding in the "intuitive reason" in relation to objects of cognition. This ideal state of man, however, is merely an imaginary focus conceived as an endless goal. In the concrete historical situation man must always remain in a state of tension in relation to the ideal.

This is also what Kant means when he defines the ideal state as a thing-in-itself. Just as the thing-in-itself in the theoretical realm is impossible of attainment by means of the categories of thought, which are confined to the realm of phenomena, so the ideal state, as a thing-in-itself, a *noumenon*, is beyond the reach of human attainment. It is an endless idea towards which to strive.

The idea of an infinite mind, which fulfills for Maimon the function of the various Kantian ideas, can be characterized as a metaphysical monism. He does not present this idea as a result of intellectual intuition; it is neither an entity to be approached by a mystical act in the manner of those who pretend to have the capacity of perceiving the ultimate reality *uno actu*, nor is it a transcendent, selfsufficient reality. Moreover, Maimon does not posit the idea of an infinite mind as a metaphysical, all-embracing reality in the manner of Spinoza's pantheism, nor is it to be understood as a transcendent source of all values and purposes conceived by man as guiding principles for our ethical conduct. It is rather closely connected with the thinking process of man and with the human will striving for the objectivization of ideas and actions. It is conceived solely for the purpose of giving reality to our synthetic propositions concerning objects of experience as well as to actions that are grounded in the striving for the realization of a general objective will. Furthermore, the idea of the ultimate truth, i.e., a mind comprehending all objects of reality in terms of analytic propositions, gives direction and purpose to our struggle to attain the highest truth, which, according to Maimon, consists in analytic knowledge. And the idea of an infinite will, i.e., a will in which the highest good is realized, serves as a goal toward which to strive, namely, the realization of the general and objective will. It is thus bound up with the totality of human experience, the theoretical as well as the ethical.

It may seem that the two aspects of this idea, namely, the aspect of an infinite mind and that of an infinite will, imply a dualism. However, by considering the function and the role of this idea and the method by which Maimon derived it, the methodological and systematic unity of Maimon's philosophical conception is not impaired.

In Maimon's systematic monism the assumption is implied that reality is itself a system that can in principle be known and may in the future be fully comprehended in terms of analytic propositions. This is particularly true of the first stage of Maimon's philosophy, in which the idea of an infinite mind and the doctrine of the infinitesimals of sensation,[35] two conceptions closely connected with each other, play a central role. The comprehension of this system in terms of human knowledge is the goal of the scientific process. The conception of a goal,

---

[35] See below, Chap. VI.

the attainment of which can be reached gradually in the course of the development of scientific and philosophic thought, suggests stages leading up to it. It also implies the reality of progress. All human experience, consisting of the different stages in the development and growth of scientific and philosophic knowledge, leads up to this one systematic reality. Each stage of this endless process is real because it approaches the ideal of systematic unity. The concept of a hierarchy consisting of levels of truth and reality leading up to the highest truth and the highest reality is grounded in the conception of the reality of the world as being in its essence a single non-contradictory system. The various stages in the growth of human thought can be considered rungs of the ladder leading to the ultimate goal of absolute systematic unity. On the assumption of the reality of progress, that is to say, that the history of scientific and philosophic thought is continuously approaching the highest goal, the various stages of this process can be arranged according to the rungs of the ladder of perfection.

The conception of a hierarchy of various levels of truth and value leading up to the most real being and to the highest good is based on the assumption that reality is or can be arranged into a single systematic unity. While the dogmatic metaphysician holds that the concept of such a hierarchy actually follows from the essence of reality as being itself so organized, the critical idealist, who considers human thought and consciousness the root and basis of all reality, may arrange the various levels of human consciousness, i.e., the various stages of the development of scientific thought, in such a hierarchy, believing that human thought is continuously growing and ascending towards the most real being and the highest truth. However, both the dogmatic metaphysician and the critical idealist envisage the ideal good as the attainment of absolute systematic unity; they both hold that the attainment of this goal is within the possible reach of man. Hence there follows the conception of the different levels and stages of truth as rungs of a ladder leading to the ultimate goal.

Maimon actually employs the ladder as a figure of speech to illustrate the interconnection of the various concepts into a systematic unity. It may likewise be used as an appropriate figure of speech for the presentation of his conception of the different levels of consciousness leading up to the highest truth and absolute unity, which consists in the complete mastery of the objects of reality by our thought and the ultimate dissolution of our cognition from synthetic propositions into analytic propositions. That is to say, the attainment of the highest truth consists in the realization of the absolute identity of thought and being. As a figure of speech the ladder can also be used to illustrate Maimon's conception of the relation between the finite and the infinite mind, that is, for the process of ascending from the finite human mind to the idea of an infinite mind by the method of abstraction and for the process of descending from the infinite mind to the finite mind by the method of limitation.

Maimon says that the human mind is capable of employing various methods of thought, namely, the method of abstraction, which proceeds from the particular to the general, and the method of limitation or concretization, which proceeds from the general to the particular. Thus, for instance, with regard to the concept of a rectangular triangle, which is an object determined by a definite relation between its sides, the particular property of the relation of the sides of a triangle to one another may be abstracted from the concept. By way of such an abstraction a more general concept will be obtained, namely, a triangle in general. By a further process of abstraction the property of three sides, by which space is enclosed in a triangle, may be ignored, thus obtaining a more general concept of a geometrical figure. On the other hand, the mind can proceed in the opposite direction, from the general to the particular. It can first conceive the idea of a geometrical figure in general and then proceed to limit this general concept by the addition of special properties to it, such as being enclosed by three sides, thus obtaining the concept of a triangle. By a further limitation of this concept the mind may add to it a definite property, namely, a special relation existing between its sides, thus obtaining a rectangular triangle. As the human mind is limited in its very essence, it is impossible for the process of abstraction or of limitation to proceed endlessly. Each of these modes of thought will reach a limit, after which no further abstraction or limitation will be possible. Only the infinite mind can be thought of as having no limits; it can proceed endlessly in both directions. But for the human mind the ladder has its limitations. On the one hand, it is limited by the material, sensuous perceptions; on the other hand, it is limited by the most abstract forms of thought, which the human mind is not capable of transcending.

Similarly, the finite mind attains the idea of an infinite mind by abstracting the limitations of its own mind; and the infinite mind conceives of the finite mind by thinking of itself in a restricted manner, that is to say, by thinking of its own self as restricted in various modes, it can conceive of the finite mind.[36]

[36] *Com. to the Guide*, Chap. 1.

A frequent phenomenon in the history of philosophy is the discovery in human consciousness of an appeal to an ultimate transcendent reality in which one finds rest and assurance for the validity of human thought. The way from human consciousness to an infinite, transcendent consciousness, which is supposed to be the guarantor of the reality of our limited, finite thought, is characteristic of many philosophical systems. In the centre of these systems of thought is the idea that a philosophical account of the essence of the world must start neither with the world, nor with God, nor with the absolute, but with man.

Thus Augustine maintains that the reality of the highest truth is presupposed in the very distinction between the true and the false as such; this presupposition is the indispensable condition of the possibility of our judgments and propositions. Every act of jugdment is grounded in the assumption of the highest ultimate truth. Descartes likewise proposes that our conception of a scale of the degrees of perfection, which we apply in our value judgments, is grounded in the supposition of a most perfect being. This idea makes possible the conception of a gradation of perfection, ascending as well as descending. The belief in the transcendent reality of ideas and values, without which the cognition of the temporal experiential world could not be accounted for, is posited also in the Platonic idea of recollection (*anamnesis*) as the basis of all our cognitions. Plato explains the process of the intellectual cognition of the phenomena of the world only by appealing to the transcendent, super-mundane reality of ideas. And in modern times, Kant recognizes in our consciousness of the unconditional categorical imperative the manifestation of an absolute consciousness, a thing-in-itself, that is, a thing-in-itself in the sense of an idea, an endless goal.

When we consider the problems that Maimon tries to solve by introducing the idea of an infinite mind, and when we observe the role and function of this idea in his system, we must conclude that the originality of his conception is not impaired by the recognition of its place in the history of human thought. In spite of this metaphysical concept, Maimon still remains in the realm of transcendental critical idealism, to which he gave a new stimulus and impetus. The process of continuous perfection in all areas of human endeavor, intellectual, ethical, and esthetic, is for him the only basis of reality. The identity of thought and being is the aim of all our strivings; and the ideal of the completeness of its attainment as the final goal is the product of the imagination. Thus the idea of the infinite mind is a function of the imagination.

The historical references to the occurrence of the idea of an infinite, transcendent reality in various metaphysical systems are intended merely to show that the appeal to the transcendent is a motif appearing and reappearing in various forms in the course of human thought. It must be recognized, however, that the idea of an infinite mind in the critical, transcendental system of Maimon is fundamentally different from the concept of a transcendental reality in the various metaphysical systems.

God and man, the infinite and the finite, are two ideas, each of which could lead to the other by the application of a different method. We may start from the idea of God as the infinite mind and come down to man as the finite mind by applying a method of limitation. We can imagine that the infinite mind thinks of the finite mind by a limiting process; that is, by thinking of itself as restricted and as imposing limitations upon itself, the infinite conceives of the finite. Aristotle defined God as "thought thinking thought." In order to understand the possibility of God, the infinite, thinking of the finite, Maimon invents the method of self-restriction.

On the other hand, we may start from the concept of man as the finite mind and reach out in our imagination to God as the infinite mind by the application of a method of elimination. That is to say, by a process of thought that eliminates and abstracts the restrictions inherent in the finite mind we may reach out to the infinite.[37]

However, the way from the finite to the infinite by the method of elimination and the way from the infinite to the finite by the method of restriction are possible only on the assumption that they differ from each other in degree but not in essence. For if the infinite were the "wholly other," differing from the finite in its very essence, the method of restriction could not lead from the infinite to the finite, nor could the method of elimination lead from the finite to the infinite.

This possibility of reaching out to the infinite offers a positive basis for metaphysics. Since the human mind is aware of the continuous growth and development of its thought, as manifested in the continuous growth of science and mathematics, and since it is in possession of the idea of infinite development, it can conceive of the idea of an infinite mind by a process of eliminating its own restrictions. Thus metaphysics, the subject matter of which is the absolute and the infinite, is a possible science. The idea of God, which is only regulative for Kant, becomes for Maimon a constitutive idea derived by a sort of transcendental deduction. The idea of an infinite mind approximates the status of an

[37] *Ibid.*

idea deduced by the transcendental method. Though Maimon does not explicitly designate the method of elimination as a "transcendental method," it is, I think, legitimate to interpret it in this way.

The human mind in its creativeness produces various cultural phenomena. Science, law, and state are its manifestations. The idea of endless progress is assumed and demanded, for without it the actual attempt at creative initiative would not take place. Hence it is a necessary and indispensable idea. In other words, the idea of endless growth and development makes the progress of thought possible. Thus the way from the finite to the infinite is a constitutive idea for cultural phenomena. The characteristic feature of the transcendental method is the deduction of a concept from the objective phenomena of culture (e.g., mathematics and science) by demonstrating the necessity and the indispensability of the concept for these phenomena. Deduction is not an analysis of the subjective mind of man detached from the phenomena in which the creative function of mind manifests itself. This is true also of the idea of an infinite mind in Maimon's system of thought. The idea is deduced from the phenomena of culture produced by the human mind.

Kant's formulation of the transcendental question with reference to mathematics and science differs fundamentally from that of metaphysics. In relation to the former, assuming the factuality of mathematics and science, the question is, how are synthetic *a priori* propositions in mathematics and science possible? The reality of these sciences is assumed. The task of philosophy is to show their possibility, that is to say, to demonstrate that they are rooted in *a priori* principles. The aim is to deduce the reality from the logical possibility. Possibility in the transcendental logical sense amounts to a deduction of reality from *a priori* principles. With regard to metaphysics, however, the question is raised: Is metaphysics as a science possible? This query puts in question the very reality of metaphysics. And the Kantian answer to it is negative, for the *a priori* principles, such as causality and substance, are not entities in themselves but functions of the mind in the scientific cognition of the phenomena of experience. Their application and validity as ordering principles are, therefore, confined to the realm of experience.

Maimon, however, shows that the possibility of synthetic propositions in mathematics and science cannot be deduced without the assumption of the idea of an infinite mind, in relation to which each and every one of the synthetic propositions is reducible to analytic propositions. The idea of an infinite mind is thus necessary for the deduction of the synthetic propositions in mathematics and science. In other words, the deduction of the transcendental possibility of mathematics and science is dependent on the metaphysical assumption of the idea of an infinite mind. The ground is thus laid for the deduction of the possibility of metaphysics. By proving the interdependence of the solution of the transcendental questions concerning mathematics and physical science and that of metaphysics, the latter is no longer isolated and separated from the former. The possibility of metaphysics in the form of the assumption of an infinite mind is guaranteed by proving the possibility of mathematics and science on the basis of the same assumption. By the deduction of the latter the former is deduced *ipso facto*.

Maimon thus defines the idea of an infinite reason in terms relating to human thought, while Kant defines it merely negatively, as distinct from the limited, human reason. Moreover, for Maimon this idea has a positive function in explaining the possibility of synthetic knowledge. It is because of this function that the reality of an infinite reason is asserted, at least as an idea having a positive function in our cognition of the phenomena of the world, for in this idea the possibility of synthetic knowledge is grounded. Maimon's idea of an infinite mind may therefore be defined as a limiting concept in the sense of a *terminus ad quem*, in contradistinction to the conception of it as *terminus a quo*. This is especially evident in, and closely connected with, Maimon's conception of the thing-in-itself as an infinite task.

The dualism of Kant appears not only in his separation of the forms of intuition from the categories of thought, i.e., the "Aesthetic" from the "Analytic"; in the "Analytic" itself there is the dichotomy of the noumenal (things-in-themselves) and the phenomenal worlds. This dualism cannot be bridged by interpreting the *phenomena* as appearances of the *noumena*, i.e., the former as manifestations of the latter, as some realists and metaphysicians expound the Kantian position. If this interpretation were valid, the transition from the "Analytic" to the "Dialectic," which constitutes the very heart of the *Critique of Pure Reason*, would be entirely incomprehensible. For if the *phenomena* are appearances of the *noumena*, the application of the categories would not be confined to the realm of *phenomena*, but would be valid also in relation to the *noumena* as the essences that manifest themselves in the *phenomena*. And if this were so, metaphysical entities could become objects of cognition, and this is incompatible with the fundamental Kantian position.

While dualism is the characteristic feature of the Kantian "Aesthetic"

and "Analytic," the characteristic feature of the "Dialectic" is its pluralism. The various transcendental ideas stand side by side without
any attempt by Kant to reduce them to a unity. The dualism between
the "Aesthetic" and the "Analytic," i.e., between forms of sensibility
and concepts of understanding, must be overcome. Therefore, sensibility
must not be considered a separate function of our consciousness, i.e.,
a capacity fundamentally different from that of understanding;
rather, it must be looked upon as the lowest form of understanding. For
this reason Maimon regards time and space, not as forms of intuition,
but as forms of the heterogeneity of objects. These forms are also
forms of thought; they give us only an obscure idea of the variety and
heterogeneous character of the objects. A clear idea of the true essence
of the objects can be attained only through the concepts of thought,
namely, the categories.

The dualism of *phenomena* and *noumena* must also be overcome.
Maimon therefore considers the thing-in-itself not as the "given" object
having a transcendent reality beyond our consciousness, but rather as
that element of our consciousness of an object that is not yet synthesized and categorized by the forms of thought. The "given" signifies
the irrational aspects of our consciousness in relation to an object
which are clamoring for rationalization and of which our consciousness
is aware. The "given" thus presents a problem and a task for further
investigation and inquiry, aiming at the complete rationalization of
the object. By the conception of the affinity of the human, finite mind
with the infinite, intuitive mind, the idea of the latter implies an ideal
goal towards which to strive. Through the solution of all problems
concerning an object, i.e., its complete rationalization and categorization, and by the transformation of our synthetic knowledge into
analytic knowledge, identity of thought and being will be attained and
the "given" will be eliminated. This is an endless task, the solution of
which we can hope to attain only at the end of the historical process,
i.e., at the end of man's struggle with the problems of reality. In this
sense we define the idea of an infinite, intuitive mind as a *terminus ad quem*, since it is the ideal goal toward which the human mind
strives.

With Maimon the idea of an infinite reason acquires a functional
value for the concept of the thing-in-itself as an endless goal. In
assuming an infinite mind in relation to which all reality is dissolvable
in thought, i.e., into analytical propositions, the possibility is put forth
that the human mind endlessly approaches this ideal mode of know-

ledge. The "given" should not be thought of as necessary and constitutive of the finite, human thought. In principle, the "given" is
subject to dissolution into pure, creative thought. The "given" thus
imposes a task upon the human mind. Implicit in the idea of an infinite
reason is the idea that with respect to it all real objects are the result
of creative thought and all synthetic propositions of the human,
limited mind are dissolvable into analytic propositions. This idea implies
the possibility, in principle, that the human mind can also dissolve the
"given" in pure thought and strive for the conversion of synthetic
propositions into analytic ones, even though this process may require
an infinite time for its achievement.

Likewise, in the interest of greater unity, the various ideas of the
Kantian "Dialectic" that imply a pluralism are to be replaced by one
dominant and overriding idea. Maimon holds that the idea of an infinite
mind alone is sufficient to fulfill the function of the various Kantian
ideas.[38]

Maimon defines the human mind as a *schema* of the infinite mind.[39]
Being a schema implies that the human mind possesses the idea of an
infinite mind – without it the striving to approach it would be impossible – but it does not mean that the human mind is part and parcel
of the infinite mind, of which it is an instrument, nor does it imply
that the creations of the finite reason are manifestations of the infinite
reason. We can define Maimon's conception of the human mind thus:
The finite reason is seen in the light of, or brought into relation with,
the infinite reason, but not in the sense that the infinite mind is considered as operating through the finite mind.

The concept of the human mind as an instrument and vehicle of
the infinite mind, i.e., that the absolute, objective spirit realizes itself
through the medium of the human, finite mind, is evolved by the
speculative metaphysics of Fichte, Schelling, and Hegel. The conception
of the human mind as a *schema* is a whole world away from the metaphysical conception of the human mind as a medium of the absolute
spirit. Whereas, in the conception of the human mind as a medium and
instrument of the absolute, the infinite is seen in the finite, in the
conception of the human mind as a *schema*, the finite is seen in relation
to the infinite.

The distinction between Kant's and Maimon's ideas of an infinite

---

[38] See *Tr.*, p. 366.
[39] *Ibid.*, p. 365.

reason is thus bound up with the difference between their views of the thing-in-itself as well as with their various conceptions of time and space. For Kant, as he was generally understood, there is an essential dualism in our thought: time and space as forms of intuition, on the one hand, and categories of understanding, on the other. The latter is dependent upon the former. Therefore, a divine reason, in relation to which no such dualism exists, is totally and essentially different from the human mind, which is dependent upon two heterogeneous sources. Maimon conceives of time and space as forms of thought and not as forms of intuition. Consequently, no such fundamental dualism in relation to human thought exists. The human mind can thus be thought of as a *schema* of the infinite mind. With regard to the concept of the thing-in-itself, Kant's view seems to imply a certain dogmatism, namely, that there are objects (*noumena*) underlying the appearances (*phenomena*). Maimon has dispensed entirely with the metaphysical reality of the things-in-themselves. The "given" is for him not a metaphysical reality, but merely the irrational elements of our consciousness. And the idea of an infinite reason is, as it were, the guarantee of the possibility of the complete solution of the "given" into pure thought. This is what is implied in the conception of the human mind as a *schema* of the infinite mind.

According to his own statement, Maimon differs from Kant in the following. First, Kant postulates various metaphysical ideas, while Maimon considers one idea to be sufficient, namely, the idea of infinite reason. Second, whereas Kant holds that ideas are not objects of cognition, Maimon maintains that the idea of an infinite reason, though not an object of cognition in the same way as are objects given through the forms of intuition, is an object of understanding arrived at through the analysis of our own cognitive process. This process posits the reality of synthetic propositions, which demands the assumption of an infinite reason. Even though this idea cannot be directly and immediately recognized as a real object, it can become an object of cognition through its *schema*, i.e., through the definite objects of thought cognized by us.

Thus Maimon asserts the reality and the metaphysical existence of the ideal object, the infinite reason. "An idea is a method by which the transition is made from the concept of an object to the object itself. Though the idea does not designate an object of intuition, it nevertheless determines a real object, the *schema* of which is an object of sensibility. So, for instance, our human reason is the *schema* of the idea of an infinite reason. The *schema* symbolizes the idea, and the idea indicates the thing as such or its existence, without which this idea and its *schema* would be impossible."[40]

This reasoning would seem to be a lapse into ontological thinking. That "the idea indicates the thing as such or its existence, without which this idea and its *schema* would be impossible," is an argument firmly rooted in the ontological mode of thought, which makes an unwarranted transition from mere thought to the reality of the object.[41] It would seem that Maimon here affirms the metaphysical reality of the infinite intellect. Moreover, the very idea of our human reason as the *schema* of the infinite reason contains an essential departure from Kant's concept of *schema*. While Kant's doctrine of schematism should be understood as a critical method by which the application of the concepts of understanding to objects of intuition is legitimized and justified, Maimon employs the method of schematism in a metaphysical sense.

In the chapter of the *Critique of Pure Reason* entitled "The Schematism of the Pure Concepts of Understanding," Kant deals with the problem of how pure concepts of understanding, which are totally different from empirical intuitions, are applicable to appearances, i.e., to objects given through the forms of intuition. He is looking for some third thing, which is homogeneous with the categories of thought, on the one hand, and, on the other hand, with appearances. Only such an intermediate representation, which is in one respect akin to concepts of understanding and in another related to the forms of sensibility, can justify the application of the former to the latter. Kant locates it in the concept of time, which is homogeneous with the category of understanding as well as with appearances.

---

[40] *Ibid.*

[41] This seems to be ontological thinking in the same way that it is implied in some trends of modern phenomenology, especially as developed into ontological phenomenology by Max Scheler and Nicolai Hartmann. They all make the transition from the intentional character of our thought, i.e., that it is directed towards an object, to the ontological reality of the object.

Maimon seems to have been aware of this problem. In his *Krit. Unt.*, p. 161, Maimon tries to show that we have a concept of the absolute totality of the conditions implying the idea of an unconditional reality. This concept must have its ground in the function of our cognitive capacity. And since our sensibility and understanding are confined to the empirical realm and cannot be the basis for the unconditioned, this concept must have its ground in the capacity of reason (*Vernunft*). Having in mind the objection that may be raised, that it is not legitimate to make a transition from a mere form of reason to an object, Maimon writes: "Nevertheless, the concept cannot be completely empty; even though it is not of a constitutive nature and cannot determine an object, it has a regulative use, in that it directs our understanding to search constantly for the totality of the conditions and to proceed from condition to condition, and so on, *ad infinitum*."

Kant thus formulates his doctrine of *schematism* for the solution of the same problem designated by Maimon as the question *quid juris*, i.e., how can pure concepts of thought be applied to objects of intuition, since they are essentially different from each other. Kant tries to show that time is a representation homogeneous with the category of understanding and with the form of sensibility; as such it can serve as a bridge between the concepts of understanding and the forms of intuition, and the application of the former to the latter is thus justified. Maimon, however, who is critical of the Kantian solution of the problem, introduces the idea of an infinite reason for its solution, thereby giving to the concept of *schema* a metaphysical turn, considering the human mind an image of the infinite mind.

Kant defines the essence of *schema* thus: "The *schema* is in itself always a product of the imagination. Since, however, the synthesis of imagination aims at no special intuition, but only at unity in the determination of sensibility, the *schema* has to be distinguished from the image. If five points be set alongside each other, thus..... I have an image of the number five. But if, on the other hand, I think only a number in general, whether it be five or a hundred, this thought is rather the representation of a method whereby a multiplicity, for instance, a thousand, may be represented in an image in conformity with a certain concept, than the image itself. For with such a number as a thousand the image can hardly be surveyed and compared with the concept. This representation of a universal procedure of imagination in providing an image for a concept I entitle the schema of this concept."[42]

The Kantian definition of *schema* comprises two elements: one positive, the other negative. The positive part of the definition stresses the pure synthetic character of the *schema*, the negative part warns against confusion of the *schema* with the image; the two are not identical. The function of the synthesis of the *schema* is to bring the multiplicity of sensibility into a unity. Kant does not explicitly state what kind of unity he refers to. That time and space as such constitute definite forms of unity, had already been established by the transcendental "Aesthetic." Here, however, we are dealing with another kind of unity, which has not been dealt with by Kant before, that is, the unity of thought and intuition or the unity of the categories of understanding with the forms of sensibility.

Through an analysis of Kant's thought we may arrive at the following conclusions which are of immediate interest for our purpose: first, that

[42] *Critique of Pure Reason*, Smith translation, p. 182.

Kant defines the *schema* as the product of the capacity of the imagination; second, the *schema* should not be identified with image; and third, the *schema* is "the representation of a method whereby a multiplicity, for instance, a thousand, may be represented in an image." The product of the capacity of the imagination is not an image, but the function of a method. Wherever method is spoken of, however, a functional relation of thought to reality is implied. The function of the *schema* is thus the same as that of the categories of thought, for they, too, are methods for the establishment of the reality of objects, and like the categories the *schema* is also confined to the realm of experience.

Kant's very definition of the function of the *schema* implies a limitation, namely, a limitation restricting its application to the realm of experience. Kant writes: "The categories, therefore, without *schemata*, are merely functions of the understanding for concepts, and represent no object. This objective meaning they acquire from sensibility, which realizes the understanding in the very process of restricting it."[43] The words "restricting it" are of great importance for us, since they reflect the limited function of the concept of *schema*. The function of the categories is confined and restricted through the *schemata* to the objects of sensibility; their application beyond the realm of sensibility is not warranted.

Maimon, however, identifies the *schema* with the image; he thus extends the realm of its application beyond the bounds of empirical experience and employs the concept of *schema* for the establishment of a metaphysical reality, an infinite reason.

A straight roads leads from Maimon's concept of *schema* as an image to speculative metaphysics, the philosophy of identity. While with Kant it is the function of schematism to establish the unity of thought and sensibility, for the philosophers of identity the duality of thought and sensibility is entirely eliminated and the unity of thought and being is presupposed. For them the dualism of thought and sensibility poses no problem. They hold that the purpose of schematism is to show the rise in human consciousness of the individual objects deviating from the general concepts that are identical with being.

Maimon constitutes the transition between Kant and the philosophy of identity. While Maimon relates the finite, human reason to the infinite reason, the philosophy of identity detects the infinite in the finite. Maimon looks upon this ideal concept as a solution of the problem *quid juris*, for only thus can certainty be given to synthetic propositions.

[43] *Ibid.*, p. 187.

In the philosophy of identity of the post-Kantian period the subject and object are identified, and the problem of the application of pure concepts of thought to objects given through the forms of sensibility loses its acuteness.

It is of interest to note how this development is bound up with the development of the different conceptions of *schema* and its function. Kant originates the concept of schematism for the purpose of bridging the two heterogeneous sources of our knowledge, intuition and understanding, and in order to overcome the dualism and heterogeneity of receptive sensibility and spontaneous concepts. The schematism of Schelling, on the other hand, is based on the assumption of the complete identity of intuition and understanding. For Schelling it is the function of schematism to explain how the separate objects of reality arise from the general concept, which is identical with its object. The question, How do our concepts harmonize with the objects and penetrate reality? is no problem at all for Schelling and for the philosophy of identity in general, since the object and its concept and, vice versa, the concept and its object, are, outside human consciousness, one and the same; their separation from each other arises only with the rise of human consciousness. Consequently, the question of the application of forms of thought to objects of intuition is meaningless. This question arises only on the assumption of the fundamental difference between sensibility and understanding, between the forms of intuition and concepts of understanding.

In positing the problem Maimon follows Kant, for whom the incongruity of sensibility and thought is presupposed. But he deviates from Kant in the solution of the problem, and this consists in the conception of sensibility as a lower form of thought and in his conception of the human mind as the *schema* of an infinite mind. The Kantian conviction of the heterogeneity of sensibility and understanding has to be discarded. Maimon therefore conceives of time and space not as forms of intuition distinct from forms of thought. For him space is the category of heterogeneity and diversibility, and time is the category of succession; thus he considers the forms of time and space as forms of thought. But in the philosophy of identity, which conceives the idea of the absolute unity of thought and being, there is no place even for positing the problem.

In Maimon's thought the same tension can be detected that is evident in Maimonides. On the one hand, Maimonides positively defines the essence of God's knowledge as the intellect, the intelligence, and the intelligible; on the other hand, he emphasizes that it is impossible for man to comprehend fully the essence of God's knowledge. Furthermore, it seems that Maimonides' rationalism conceives of the human mind as part of the divine mind. But in connection with certain metaphysical problems, such as freedom of the will, divine knowledge of the infinity of particulars and of things of the future, that is knowledge of non-being, Maimonides stresses the essential difference between the divine mind and the human reason, i.e., that divine knowledge is something totally different from human knowledge.

This reasoning constitutes a tension rather than a contradiction in Maimonides' thought. It is a kind of *analogia mentis*, implying the idea that the elements of the analogy are neither identical nor radically dissimilar; or, positively expressed, they are in some respects similar and in others entirely different.[44] With regard to the understanding of the process of human cognition in the comprehension of the logical and mathematical laws and the essential forms of being, the human mind is capable of abstracting the pure forms of reality and the pure forms of thought from the sense data and from the sensuous objects in which these forms are realized. Such an ideational act of cognition by the human mind is accomplished by abstracting the pure forms of reality from the sensuous perceptions. This process of ideation, which is not accomplished through the instrumentality of the senses, is similar to the cognitive act of divine thought; it can be designated as a part of divine thought. However, with respect to the comprehension of the essence of the divine mind as bearing on the solution of the ultimate metaphysical questions – the problem of the reconciliation of freedom of the will with God's omniscience, the problem of the ultimate purpose of the universe, and similar metaphysical questions – we have to recognize that the human mind is incapable of fully comprehending the essence of the divine mind. We must acknowledge not merely the gradual but the essential difference between divine knowledge and human knowledge. This cognition must lead to the understanding of the term "knowledge," in its application to human and to divine thought, as a homonymous term, that is, a term employed to designate two essentially and wholly different objects.

This same tension occurs in Maimon, though the problems with which he grapples are entirely different from those dealt with by Maimonides. Maimon maintains that the synthetic propositions concerning objects of experience are the result of the inherent limitations

[44] Cf. below, Chap. X, p. 192 f.

of the human mind, which is incapable of an infinite process of reducing experiential propositions to purely logical and analytic propositions. But for an infinite mind our synthetic knowledge is in reality reducible to analytic knowledge.

We can grant reality to our synthetic porpositions with reference to objects of experience only on the assumption that these propositions are reducible to analytic propositions by a mind capable of an infinite process of reduction. In relation to an infinite mind in a metaphysical sense, the essential attribute of which is analytic knowledge, it is incongruous to speak of the reduction of synthetic knowledge to analytic knowledge, since the knowledge of an infinite mind is intuitive and spontaneous and therefore all analytic. However, the idea of an infinite mind implies, for the human mind, the possibility of an endless process of reduction of synthetic knowledge to analytic knowledge. The idea of the metaphysical reality of analytic knowledge holds out to man an endless task of a possible reduction of the synthetic propositions to analytic propositions.

But what is the guarantee for the reality of such an assumption? Its only guarantee seems to reside in the recognition that without it skepticism must necessarily follow. To guard us against skepticism the assumption of an infinite mind is indispensable.

The question may be raised, the infinite mind is perhaps of such a nature that its analytic, spontaneous knowledge is of a totally different kind, and thus has no relation whatever to our synthetic knowledge? In order to maintain that our synthetic knowledge is real because it is dissolvable into analytic knowledge by an infinite mind, something more is required, namely, that the same propositions that are derived from observation, experience, and analogy by the human mind are reducible to analytic propositions by the infinite mind. This is possible only on the assumption that our finite human thought, operating in terms of synthetic propositions, is of the same nature as the infinite mind. That is to say, the finite and the infinite mind stand in a relationship of "more or less" to each other; they differ from each other only in degree, not in essence. For if they were essentially different from each other, the idea of an infinite mind could not guarantee the certitude of our experiential knowledge, which consists of synthetic propositions. Such an idea of an infinite mind would be purposeless and meaningless, for it would be transcendent and far removed from any relation to the problem of the possibility of the certitude of our synthetic knowledge, which is our main concern. In order that the infinite mind may fulfill the function for which it was conceived, it must be brought down from its transcendence and metaphysical seclusion; it must be thought of as possessing the same kind of thought as our finite mind. The infinite mind must be regarded as differing from the finite mind, not in its essence and quality, but only in degree.

However, according to Maimon, the human mind is the *schema* of the infinite mind, and a *schema* is a special kind of image. The finite mind is not the vehicle and instrument of the infinite mind; the former is not a manifestation of the latter. Maimon thus retreats from his original position, which demands a close relationship between the finite and the infinite mind, as if in fear that this daring conception may bring the finite too close to the infinite.

CHAPTER VI

INFINITESIMALS OF SENSATION

In order to obtain a clear concept of the content of an act of perception, it is necessary to look for the ultimate elements of which that perception consists. In other words, a process of analysis is required, by which the perception is dissolved into its constituent elements. As a preliminary condition of such an analysis the perception must be abstracted from all quantity and all quality, extensive and intensive alike. The analysis of the perception of a patch of red color, for instance, will lead to the abstraction of all extension, and the object will then be thought of as consisting of an infinite number of points, the combination of which results in the particular perception. These points constitute the differential elements of extension. Any given perception must thus be thought of, according to Maimon, as consisting of elements that constitute its differentials. In order that we may be conscious of a perception, it must have a certain degree of extension as well as a certain degree of quality, for we are incapable of perceiving the infinitesimals, i.e., the infinitely small points of which it consists. We are conscious only of the compound, i.e., of an object that has a certain degree of extension and quality.[1]

We must assume, further, that different perceptions are composed of different elements, that is to say, their infinitesimals are different, otherwise there would be no difference among objects, and all things would appear as one and the same. In the difference of the infinitesimals lies the foundation of the variety of perceptions.

Even though we are not conscious of the individual elements, they are nevertheless present in any definite given perception. Just as in accelerated motion the preceding motion does not disappear but is joined to the following, so the single elements of perception join the ones that follow until they reach the degree necessary for an awareness. The comparison of similar single elements of perception and their integration is a necessary condition of the unity of the manifold that makes up conscious perception. This process of unification is not the result of a conscious act, in which the single elements of sensation are

[1] *Tr.*, pp. 27 f.

compared; it takes place subconsciously. It is not like the process of understanding, which, being a synthesis of the manifold of objects, is a conscious process of unification of various objects. We have to assume the presence of elementary sensations in any given perception on the basis of the general law of nature that no force, no effect, is destroyed except by an opposing force.[2]

Understanding, as we have just said, is a conscious process, and by it the various sensuous objects of our consciousness are related to one another through pure concepts of thought. Sensibility thus furnishes the differential elements of consciousness; the imagination produces out of these elements a definite object of intuition (*Anschauung*) and perception; and the understanding establishes the relation of the objects of intuition, i.e., the sensuous objects resulting from the integration of the various differential elements of sensation.

"The differential elements of the objects are the *noumena*; the objects that spring from them are the *phenomena*. The differential element of an object in itself with regard to intuition is equal to 0; $dx = 0$; $dy = 0$. The relation between them, however, is not equal to 0, but can definitely be determined through perceptual intuitions that spring from them."[3]

Definite perceptions of objects are, as it were, the integrals of the infinitesimal elements of perception. The *noumena* are the things-in-themselves of the *phenomena*. According to Maimon, however, they are not transcendent but immanent to our consciousness, though we are not conscious of them, for we are aware only of the integrals, not of the infinitesimals. While the Kantian *noumena* may appear to be the substrata of the *phenomena*, Maimon's *noumena* constitute the differential elements of conscious perception. "The *noumena* are ideas of reason conceived by the mind as principles by which to explain the generation of objects."[4]

In the perception of red as different from green, for instance, the pure concept of difference is not to be understood as related to the sensuous qualities of perception, for if it is so understood, there arises the question of *quid juris*, that is, how can a pure concept be applied to sensuous objects that are given; rather, the pure concept of difference must be considered as related to forms *a priori*. For this reason Maimon maintains that it refers to the relation of the differential elements, which are ideas of reason *a priori*.

[2] *Ibid.*, p. 31.
[3] *Ibid.*, p. 32.
[4] *Ibid.*

Thinking is a process by which the unity of a manifold is produced. Consequently, understanding cannot think of an object otherwise than by the rule governing the generation of the object. For only in this way is a manifold thought of as a unity. The essence of thought thus consists in thinking of an object, not as already existing, but as resulting from a process of generation, i.e., as becoming. The particular rule of the generation of an object makes it a definite object, and the relation of various objects to one another flows from the relation of their rules of generation, or of their differentials, which are the elements out of which objects as integrated entities are generated.

Our mind behaves passively in perception. This is merely a receptive process. Our consciousness of objects, on the other hand, is the result of an active process, in which an act of the imagination synthesizes a number of various sensuous perceptions and perceives the manifold as a unity. When I say I am conscious of something, this something is not to be taken as existing by itself outside of consciousness. It implies a contradiction to speak at one and the same time of consciousness and of an object existing outside myself and its states. "Consciousness" here refers to a definite kind of consciousness, the process of consciousness itself, in which a reference to an existing object is implied.[5] The primitive imagination assumes the existence of the things it imagines. Actually, however, the process of imagination is not a representation (*Vorstellung*) of something existing outside the mind, but rather the presentation (*Darstellung*) of something as existing, which in fact did not exist before.

The infinitesimals of perception are to be considered ideas conceived by the mind as necessary constituents of a definite intuition. Consciousness of the primary, constituent elements of a synthesis as well as the complete synthesis are both ideas; they are limiting concepts. Consciousness of a complete and perfect synthesis embraces infinity, which is not attainable by a limited capacity of cognition. Only a mind that can conceive an object in its completeness, without leaving any unsolved problem regarding the object, can attain perfect synthesis. Nor can the infinitesimals become objects of cognition for a limited mind without an endless process of abstraction that cannot be fully accomplished. However, we have to posit the reality of the infinitesimals, since without them the law of continuous generation of a definite synthesis is impossible to establish. Thus the process of cognition always begins and ends in the middle. The same reasoning holds true with

[5] *Ibid.*, pp. 29 f.

reference to our system of numbers, in which the unit is always arbitrary, since we can always imagine a unit smaller or larger than any given one. The absolute unit is merely an idea, which can never be given in intuition, since the forms of units are time and space, which can be divided endlessly. In the same way, the infinitesimals as well as the complete synthesis are ideas, for they cannot be attained by our consciousness, though we can approach them endlessly.[6]

A complete and perfect synthesis embracing the totality of the relations of objects as well as a full comprehension of their infinitesimal elements are beyond the scope of human capacity, which is capable of conceiving only integrals. The infinite intellect, however, comprehends the totality of objects through the thought of the totality of the relations prevailing among their differentials. While the process of human, limited thought moves from integrals to differentials, the thinking process of the infinite reason proceeds in the opposite direction. In establishing a law governing the relations among phenomena, the human mind conceives a principle that relates to their differentials. The assumption that the relations among phenomena are grounded in similar relations among differentials is the basis of the law. For the infinite reason, however, the reality of phenomena flows from the comprehension of the totality of the relations of the differentials.

Maimon elaborated his theory of fictions and of the role they play in human thought, scientific as well as metaphysical, at a later stage in his development. In his *Versuch über die Transcendentalphilosophie,* which deals with the doctrine of differentials, Maimon does not treat of fiction as a method of human thought. However, the concept of fiction is implicit in his distinction between different kinds of infinitesimals. We have to differentiate, he writes, between two kinds of infinitesimals, one symbolical and the other real. The former is not presentable in intuition, the latter is. The former signifies a process by which a quantity is being constantly approached without ever being reached; the latter implies that the same relation obtains between objects independent of their quantity. Here the infinitesimal does not negate quantity as such; it means merely that the relation is independent of a definite quantity. For example, the proposition that the angle formed by two parallel lines is infinitely small means only that the farther from their beginning two lines meet, the smaller will be the angle. This can be carried to the point where the lines will not meet at all and thus will not form an angle. The infinitely small angle is merely a limiting

[6] *Ibid.,* p. 349.

concept, which an angle can approach; it is a symbolical infinitesimal.

With regard to a real infinitesimal, however, the differential equation of a quantity does not indicate that this quantity ceases at any time to be what it is; it implies an undetermined yet determinable situation. Thus, when we say $dx : dy = a : b$, we do not mean: x abstracted from all quantity is related to y abstracted from all quantity as a is to b, for zero related to zero does not constitute a real relation. We mean, rather, that whatever value we may give x, i.e., we may make it as small or as large as possible, it will follow from the equation of these magnitudes that $x : y = a : b$. Here we determine x as the smallest possible magnitude, from which it will follow that $dx : dy = a : b$. Differential calculus deals not with magnitudes but with relations between magnitudes. The differential quotient $dx : dy$ implies that the relation between dy and dx is constant, quite independent of the quantitative value of the variables, and this is a real infinitesimal. The symbolical infinitesimal has no reality, but is intended by mathematicians merely to serve the purpose of making their propositions as general as possible. The real infinitesimal, however, can be thought of as a real object, even though it cannot be represented in our intuition.[7] Since the symbolical infinitesimal bears the characteristics by which Maimon defines a fiction – it is the product of the imagination for the completion of a series – it is to be regarded as such.

Metaphysical infinitesimals, i.e., the infinitely small elements of which a perception is composed, are real. For quality as such can be considered as abstracted from all quantity. A patch of color is a synthesized manifold, i.e., quality given in a certain quantity. An infinitesimal point of the patch will be quality abstracted from all quantity, and sensation as a whole is to be regarded as consisting of such primary elements. It is on the basis of this analysis that Maimon tries to solve the question *quid juris*. The pure concepts of understanding are not to be directly related to the intuitions, to the sensations, but to their infinitesimal elements, which are ideas of the generation of these intuitions. Through the medium of these ideas the pure concepts of understanding are related to the intuitions. Just as in mathematics we determine the relations between magnitudes on the basis of the ratio of the differentials, so our understanding refers the relation between objects given through intuition to the relation obtaining between the differentials of these objects. Thus the proposition, fire melts wax, is not directly related to fire and wax as objects of intuition but to their

---

[7] *Ibid.*, p. 351.

constituents, their differential elements, which are thought by our understanding as standing in relation of cause and effect. "I hold," writes Maimon, "that our understanding has the capacity, not only to conceive general relations between definite objects of intuition but also to determine objects by determining the relation between their elements. Understanding is therefore justified in establishing different relations *a priori*."[8]

Since all relations between integrals can be reduced to relations between differentials, causality, which is a relation between two *phenomena*, A and B, can be reduced to a relation between *noumena*, that is, between the differential A and the differential B. These *noumena* are not things-in-themselves, substrata of *phenomena*, but ideas of reason.

Maimon is well aware of the objection that might be raised against the introduction of the mathematical concept of infinity into philosophy. "I maintain, however," he writes, "that in truth these concepts actually belong to philosophy. Philosophy is their natural domain, and from there they were transferred to mathematics. And the great Leibniz was led to the discovery of differential calculus through his system of monads (Monadology)."[9] Since the differentials of intuition are themselves *a priori*, the concepts of thought *a priori* can be related to them. Herein lies the answer to the question *quid juris*. We do not apply *a priori* forms of thought to *a posteriori* objects, but to *a priori* elements of intuition, that is, infinitesimals.

The question *quid juris* has two aspects for Maimon: first, the question is, How can *a priori* concepts be related to *a posteriori* objects? and second, How are synthetic propositions dissolvable into analytic ones? Maimon's solution is intended to apply to both aspects of the problem. The function of the differentials of intuition is to explain both how *a priori* forms of thought can be applied to *a posteriori* objects and how synthetic propositions are dissolvable with reference to an infinite reason into analytic ones.

We have already pointed out that Maimon gives great scope to the question *quid juris* by including metaphysical problems that have engaged philosophers of the past, such as the creation of the material world by a God who is absolute spirit and the harmony of soul and body, two essentially heterogeneous entities. Here, too, Maimon tries to solve at the same time the epistemological question of the relation

---

[8] *Ibid.*, p. 355.
[9] *Ibid.*, p. 27.

of *a posteriori* objects to *a priori* concepts and the problem of how synthetic propositions can be reduced to analytic ones in the infinite mind.

Maimon strives to eliminate the implication of a relation between empirically given objects and pure ideas. He searches, therefore, for a doctrine setting forth our conception of objects as grounded in relations of ideas. The philosophy of immanence demands that our concepts concerning reality be dissolved into relations of ideas instead of relations between objects and ideas or between things-in-themselves and phenomena. With this aim in view Maimon proposed the theory of differentials, that is, infinitesimals of sensation.

It has been suggested that the concept of differentials of sensibility serves for Maimon the same purpose as does the concept of the thing-in-itself for Kant.[10] This comparison is based on the assumption that things-in-themselves are transcendent realities affecting phenomena. The variety of empirical objects is explained by the effect of things-in-themselves on our consciousness, according to the realistic conception of *noumena*. Things-in-themselves as substrata of phenomena are determining factors in our conception of phenomena; the infinitesimals of sensation likewise determine our sensations and conscious perception of an object. But the thing-in-itself can be defined either as the problem in the object that is not categorized and rationally comprehended, i.e., an X, thus imposing a task for further investigation, or as an ideal goal of the complete solution of an object into relations of thought. The thing-in-itself neither determines nor constitutes an integral part of our cognition of an object. According to this view of the Kantian concept, it cannot be maintained that the infinitesimals of sensation serve the same purpose as the thing-in-itself. The infinitesimals constitute the basic elements of our conscious perception of an object. They thus fulfill a totally different function in the epistemological account of the process of cognition, as they are a determining factor and an integral part of our perception. The thing-in-itself, on the other hand, is a problem, an X, or an idea, that is, the ideal of the final and complete solution of all problems relating to an object.

Maimon calls the differentials *noumena*, as opposed to empirical objects, which are *phenomena*. "These *noumena* are ideas of reason, principles that serve the purpose of explaining the generation of objects."[11] The *noumena* are ideas of reason, not the substrata of phe-

[10] Fr. Kuntze, *op. cit.*, p. 331.
[11] *Tr.*, p. 32.

nomena affecting them. Ideas of reason are immanent to our consciousness, not transcendent. "In mathematics as well as in philosophy infinitesimals are mere ideas; they are not objects but represent the mode of generation of objects, that is, they are mere limiting concepts, which we can always approach but never attain. They arise through a process of reduction *ad infinitum* of the consciousness of an intuition."[12]

The very essence of critical idealism consists in the conception of ideas, pure concepts of thought, as the basis of cognized reality. Therefore *noumena* (differentials), as ideas of reason, can be understood as immanent ideas of thought for the explanation of our perception of objects, but not as real elements of sensation. If we accept the infinitesimals as metaphysical elements of sensation, we have left the ground of idealism and retreated into sensualism, and it does not make any difference whether we declare the given sensation or its differential elements to be the basis of our conception of reality. Moreover, the infinitesimals cannot be "given" to the senses; they can only be thought. By declaring differentials to be the basis of reality, the "given" is entirely overcome and dissolved into pure thought. "Reason requires," says Maimon, "that the 'given' in the object should not be considered as something unchangeable and constant in the very nature of the object, but merely a result of the limitation of our faculty of thought. The 'given' disappears in relation to a higher, infinite intellect. Reason thus demands progress *ad infinitum*, by which the rationalization of an object is increased and the 'given' diminished to an infinitely small quantity... And we must constantly and increasingly try to approach the idea of an infinite reason."[13]

In formulating his theory of the infinitesimals of sensation, Maimon must have been influenced by Kant's analysis.[14] Kant says: "From empirical consciousness to pure consciousness a gradual transition is possible... There is also possible a synthesis in the process of generating the magnitude of a sensation from its beginning in pure intuition = 0, up to any required magnitude." "Between reality and negation there is a continuity of possible realities and of possible smaller perceptions. Every color, for instance red, has a degree, which, however small it may be, is never the smallest..."[15]

On the basis of this analysis Maimon conceives the idea of a reality devoid of all quantity, an infinitesimal entity that is identical with

---

[12] *Ibid.*, p. 28, note.
[13] *Philos. Wört.*, p. 169.
[14] *Critique of Pure Reason*, Smith transl., pp. 201 ff.
[15] *Ibid.*, pp. 203 f.

thought. The "given" must have extension; the infinitesimal can only be thought, therefore its concept and reality are one and the same.

It seems, however, that Maimon's doctrine of the infinitesimals of sensation is grounded in a different conception. He does not maintain a consistently idealistic view of the infinitesimals, but permits the possibility of a realistic interpretation. One is left with the impression that the infinitesimals are for him transcendent entities, constituting the elements of perception. That is to say, any given sensation, any given quality of perception, can be abstracted from its quantity and reduced to its constituent elements, i.e., differentials. The latter are the primary elements of which any given perception is composed. Accordingly, differentials are *noumena*, that is, transcendent things-in-themselves, constituting the elements from which phenomena are derived. Differentials are *noumena* in the realistic, metaphysical interpretation of the concept of the thing-in-itself. We are conscious of phenomena, i.e., the compounds, not of their primary, constituent elements. *Noumena* are nevertheless present in the act of perception, even though we are not conscious of them, for they constitute the basic metaphysical elements of reality.

Such a conception has its systematic place in sensualism and metaphysical dogmatism, for, as we have pointed out, it does not make an iota of difference whether we declare the given sensations or the infinitesimal points of sensation to be the basis and root of our conception of reality. In both cases we have assumed a transcendent reality given to our consciousness from without, that is, a metaphysical reality determining our cognition of phenomena.

Such a doctrine is untenable, as are all other forms of sensualism and dogmatism. For to have something "given" and not to be conscious of it is self-contradictory. We arrive at the concept of the infinitesimals through a process of continuous abstraction. The law of continuity itself, however, is not given to our senses, but is rather the result of an act of creation by the mind. The assumption of the reality of infinitesimals of sensation is therefore an idea, a hypothesis in the original meaning of the term (from *tithemi*, placing), that is, a principle purposefully put forth as a basis for the derivation of a law of generation of a phenomenon of experience. Such an assumption should not be turned into a thing-in-itself, a hypostasis (*stasis*, standing), implying a metaphysical entity underlying the phenomenon of experience.

As an illustration of the reality of the differentials of sensation and of their presence in any given definite sensation, Maimon adduces the fact of accelerated motion, in which the previous motion is contained, even though we are not conscious of it, on the basis of the natural law that a force is destroyed only by an opposing force.

The objection may be raised, however, that this law itself is not derived from sensuous perception; it is rather the result of a thinking process, which is creative. This law of continuity is a hypothesis, a deductive principle for the derivation of a law of nature, rather than the result of an induction from the observation of phenomena of nature. Thus, in order to arrive at the reality of infinitesimals, we have to employ ideas of reason, deductive principles.

The doctrine of differentials should therefore be understood to mean that the infinitesimals are ideas of reason having their root in the creativity of the human mind; they are immanent ideas invented by the mind for the purpose of deducing reality, with the help of the law of continuity, from principles posited by the mind. Maimon, however, does not hold to this position consistently. He seems to maintain that the infinitely small magnitudes, the infinitesimals, are metaphysical entities out of which phenomena are composed.

In order to solve the problem of the antinomy of the absolute, or the infinitely small motion, Maimon has to assume the reality of the infinitely small. "We must assume," he writes, "the real infinity as the element of the finite. It is not a mathematical or potential infinity, which implies merely the possibility of endless divisibility."[16]

The assumption of the infinitely small magnitude as a real entity is the basis of Maimon's doctrine of the infinitesimals of sensation. To be sure, in modern mathematics the concept of the infinitesimals as real entities has been entirely discarded. But this does not invalidate the metaphysical investigations that operate with the idea of the infinitesimals as real entities. The reasons for the legitimacy of this concept in philosophy are twofold, historical and philosophical. On the historical side is the fact that the inventors of calculus seem to have actually thought of infinitesimals as real entities. And even though mathematicians regard this concept as superfluous, for mathematics can do without it, philosophy is entitled to assume the reality of the infinitely small if it serves the purpose of greater systematic unity in the construction of a philosophical conception of the world.

As to the historical basis for the idea of the reality of infinitely small magnitudes Maimon saw a connection between Leibniz' doctrine of the monads and his invention of calculus. The former was the fore-

16 *Tr.*, p. 236.

runner of the latter, that is to say, the conception of the monads as metaphysical entities led to the conception of infinitesimals and the invention of calculus. Hermann Cohen likewise saw the relation between the metaphysical conception of the monads and the mathematical concept of infinitesimals, but he comes to different conclusions.

Cohen sees in the idea of the infinitesimal the vehicle through which the groundlessness of sensualism and empiricism, which emphasize sense-perceptions as the foundation of the cognition of reality, can be conclusively demonstrated. He does not think of infinitely small magnitudes as metaphysical entities. The idea of such an entity, which the mind posits as a basis upon which to construct a scientific conception of the world, discloses the nature of scientific thought. Its fundamental concepts are not derived from sense data, but originate in the human mind. Such ideas and concepts reveal the creative character of cognition as the basis of scientific thought. Hence critical idealism is scientific idealism in contradistinction to subjective idealism. While the latter is grounded on a psychological analysis of the individual's subjective reaction to impressions and empirical data received from without, the former is oriented towards systematic thought as laid down in the scientific account of the phenomena of reality in the form of a system of laws. Scientific idealism, therefore, is actually realism, since a true and coherent account of reality is to be found in science and not in our common-sense conception of the world, which is grounded in our subjective impressions and sense-data.

Thus there is an unbridgeable gap between Maimon's conception of infinitesimals as real metaphysical magnitudes and Cohen's conception of the idea of the infinitely small as an ideal concept posited by the mind as a foundation upon which to build a system of laws determining natural phenomena. While for Maimon infinitesimals are metaphysical entities, Cohen sees them as grounded in the creative process of pure thoutht. Though there is this fundamental difference between them, it is nevertheless indicative of a common aspect of their philosophies. Both men see the origin of the finite in the infinite. Cognition of reality can be explained only through the idea of infinetely small magnitudes, and the infinite is the basis of the finite. With Maimon the priority of the infinite is twofold. Scientific thought, which is presented in the form of a system of synthetic propositions, can claim validity only on the assumption that synthetic propositions are dissoluble into analytic propositions by the infinite mind. Then the basis of the law of causality, for instance, connecting objects of experience resides in the assumption that the

infinitesimals of sensation are connected by this law. All laws governing
empirical objects are valid only on the metaphysical assumption that
these laws are grounded in objects of thought, i.e., infinitesimals.
Consequently, finite empirical objects can be ordered by laws of thought
only on the supposition that the finite is grounded in the infinite. The
logical priority of the infinite is a necessary presupposition, without
which there is no escape from skepticism. In Cohen's view the idea of
an infinite progress takes the place of Maimon's idea of an infinite mind.
Being is identified with categorized and rationalized thought. Thought
in the form of a system of laws, as presented in natural science, is
identical with being. But as problems are never fully solved, being is
never complete. In every stage of scientific development reality as
cognized and ordered in a system of laws is the only reality. The validity
of synthetic propositions resides in their function of ordering reality.
There is no need to resort to a metaphysical idea of an infinite mind in
order to grant reality to synthetic propositions; the reality of these
propositions is vouched for by their function.

Like Maimon, Cohen interprets the philosophy of Leibniz as the
forerunner of Kant. He shows that the doctrine of monads must be
understood in the light of and in agreement with critical idealism.
Monads are, according to Cohen, grounded in the idea that matter is
rooted in something that is not material. Extension is the characteristic
feature of matter. But extended material is inadequate ground on which
to explain the generation of being. Leibniz, therefore, posits something
not extended as the basis of reality. Extension should not be considered
the first substance (contrary to Descartes); it cannot be the *prius* for
the explanation of reality. *Immo extensione prius* (i.e. something prior
to extension) must be posited as the substance. That is to say, something
not extensive must be the underlying ground of all being.

Non-extension, however, is a negative concept; it implies merely
the absence of extension. A mere negation cannot serve as the ground
for the generation of reality. Hence the non-extensive must have
something positive, owing to which it can serve as the ground of being.
This positive moment, which is a substitute for extension, resides in
the concept of force. And the concept of force is to be understood as intensity. Consequently, the non-extensive element must have the feature
of intensity in order to be the ground of reality. Through the conception
of the intensive Leibniz discovered the new number, the infinitesimal.
This infinitely small number stands in opposition to the finite extended
number. It is defined as substance, and as such it is beyond extension

and therefore grounded in pure, unalloyed thought. Since the infinitely small is not extended, it is incomprehensible by the sensuous imagination or by intuition (*Anschauung*). The concept of the infinitesimal and that of intensity, in which reality is grounded and by which the concept of matter is determined, are grounded in pure thought.

Along with the determination of matter, the concept of thought and the criterion of truth attain a different and more exact definition. While for Descartes the criterion of truth lies in the evidence and the distinctness of ideas, for Leibniz these are insufficient. Since the infinitesimal, which is the basis of reality, is not subject to perception or intuition, evidence and distinctness cannot determine the truth of an idea.

If monads were pure ideas posited as necessary conditions of matter and of objects of experience, there could be no objection to such a doctrine on the part of critical idealism. However, Kant's objection to the *Monadology* of Leibniz is justified, according to Cohen, because monads are not conceived exclusively as pure ideas, creations of the human mind, but rather as ontological entities. The turn towards dogmatic ontology implied in the *Monadology* is the reason for Kant's rejection of the doctrine of monads. While the mathematical foundation of monads, the infinitesimal magnitudes, is conceived by Leibniz as a pure idea, in his account of the world he thinks of them as metaphysical entities. The infinitely small magnitudes, the simple monads, thus take on the features of metaphycisal substance and ontological reality. The objects of nature and the phenomena of consciousness are derived from and explained by them. In his picture of the world, as presented in the *Monadology*, Leibniz' metaphysical interest overshadows his philosophical-critical interest in the examination of the capacity, scope, and limitations of human cognition. It is this dogmatism that constitutes the basis of Kant's objection to Leibniz.[17]

Now Cohen writes: "With our freer historical view we can extricate the deep and wide trend of the scientific discoverer from the world-view of his system." That is to say, a free attitude toward the history of

---

[17] Cf. H. Cohen, *Kants Theorie der Erfahrung*, 3rd ed. (Berlin, 1918), pp. 51 ff. Cf. also *ibid.* p. 584 f., where Leibniz is quoted: "In rebus corporeis esse aliquid praeter extensionem, imo extensione prius..." Cohen then quotes Kant's reaction to this statement of Leibniz: "Leibniz, to whom human reason owes so much, teaches that the body possesses an essential force which is prior to extension"; and Cohen comments: "In *imo extensione prius*, there is expressed the generating function of the intensive". That is to say, the intensive has priority over the extensive. See also the valuable essay of Prof. Hugo Bergmann, ,,S. Maimon and H. Cohen" (Hebrew), in Jubilee Volume for J. N. Epstein, p. 284 f., Jerusalem, 1950.

ideas does not record ideas as matters of fact but seeks the inner motives and implications of ideas with reference to their function in the construction of a world-view. We can thus permit the deep trend implied in the concept of the infinitesimal to appear in its full eminence and not allow it to be obscured by the metaphysical conception of Leibniz' world-view. "We can conceive of the monad as being grounded in the creative capacity of the mind, generating the concepts that are constitutive for matter and objects of reality. Such a concept of the monad, which is bound up with a definition of thought, is accordingly not a thing, but one of the *aeternae veritates*, in which, according to Leibniz, all truth and certitude of cognition, i.e., reality of things, are grounded. In this scientifically firm and singularly fruitful sense, it can be said that the ideas of reason constitute the formulation and the guarantee of the reality of things. Thus matter finds its lasting ground in thought and not in extension."[18]

Cohen thus conceives the monads as pure, creative ideas, and not as metaphysical, ontological entities; and the concept of the infinitesimal magnitude he regards as the basis of the conception of monads as the ground of reality. Both these ideas are anticipated by Maimon, even though they do not attain that clarity of thought and precision of expression characteristic of Cohen.[19]

The difference between Maimon's and Cohen's conception of the infinitesimal can be summarized thus: For Cohen the emphasis is on the infinitesimal as a pure concept of thought, intensive and non-extensive, constituting the basis of reality. Monads should be stripped of their metaphysical connotation; they are not ontological entities, but pure, creative ideas. Primacy belongs to the concept of the infinitesimal, not to that of the monad; the latter should be understood in the light of the former as pure concepts. The concept of the infinitesimal may have been the ground on which the metaphysical conception of the *Monadology* was constructed by Leibniz. For Maimon, primacy belongs to monads as metaphysical entities; the conception of the monad as a metaphysical idea is the ground from which the concept of the infinitesimal is derived. He states explicitly that it was the metaphysics (*Monadology*) that led Leibniz to the conception of the infinitesimal. Like the idea of an infinite reason, the idea of an infinitely small entity is metaphysical. Maimon's idealism is thus grounded in

---

[18] *Ibid.*, p. 56.
[19] See H. Cohen, "Das Prinzip der Infinitesimalmethode und seine Geschichte," *Schriften zur Philosophie und Zeitgeschichte I*, Berlin, 1928. See particularly pp. 55 ff.

the assumption of metaphysical ideas, without which he could not overcome skepticism.

Furthermore, for Maimon, the capacity of our mind to conceive infinitesimals derives from the fact that our mind is a part of the infinite mind. For Cohen, the concept of the infinitesimal is purely methodological. In this concept, which is the foundation of modern science, there is manifest the nature of our cognition of reality. It shows that the basis of our cognition is not sense perception but pure ideas of understanding. There is no need to have recourse to a metaphysical idea of an infinite mind or to the conception that our mind shares in the infinite mind.

Since Maimon's conception of the infinitesimal is based on metaphysical assumptions, his idealism constitutes only one aspect, one phase of his thought, the other aspect being skepticism, and he vacillates between these two: skepticism and idealism grounded in metaphysical assumptions. It should be noted, however, that the doctrine of infinitesimals of sensation and the idea of an infinite mind, which are so prominent in his early writings, do not play such a salient role in his later work. It must also be pointed out that Maimon approaches a consistent critical position in his conception of the monads as fictions. For if we understand by fiction not a conscious falsehood but an idea of reason, the monads are no longer metaphysical entities, but are hypothetically laid down by the creative mind as principles generating reality.

Cohen's system of critical idealism stands on safer ground, for it is not dependent on metaphysical suppositions. The conception of infinitesimals as the fundamental principle in the construction of physical science constitutes for him the heart of transcendental (scientific) idealism, to which he adhered consistently throughout his philosophical career.[20]

---

[20] Even in Cohen's "Religion of Reason" (*Religion der Vernunft aus den Quellen des Judentums*, Leipzig, 1919) there is no retreat from his fundamental position of critical idealism, as some expositors have held. The concept of a correlation between man and God, which is central in his religious philosophy, is not to be understood in an ontological and transcendent sense, but in a purely immanent sense. This correlation is an immanent idea of consciousness; it is not a correlation of transcendent entities.

CHAPTER VII

LEVELS OF COGNITION

It is a persistent thought of Solomon Maimon, repeated several times by him in various connections, that while perception is a process occurring in time and subject to the mode of time, pure thought emerges instantly, at one stroke as it were, and is not a temporal process at all. In view of the prominence that Maimon gives to this distinction between perception and pure thought, two questions demanding elucidation necessarily arise. First, what is the source and origin of this idea? And second, what is the importance of this idea and its systematic place in Maimon's thinking as a whole? In answering these questions we may even gain clarification of Maimon's conception of *a priori* thought as distinct from sense perception.

In tracing the source of this idea we cannot be content with some casual reference to it in a philosophical work with which Maimon may have been acquainted.[1] Such a derivation would not explain satisfactorily the special significance that Maimon attributed to this idea and would not be commensurate with the prominence it commands in his system. We must herefore look for the origin of this idea, namely, the distinction between perception as a process occurring in time and pure thought as emerging instantly, in a thinker whom we know to have shaped Maimon's thought to a considerable degree. Such a thinker was Maimonides.

In dealing with the effective cause of the creation of a thing that has not existed previously, Maimonides says: "The series of causes of a certain phenomenon must necessarily conclude with a first causeless cause, always existing. As to the question, why is this thing produced now and not before, inasmuch as the cause has always existed, we can answer it in two ways: Either a certain relation between cause and effect has till now been absent, if the cause be corporeal; or, if the cause be incorporeal, the substance had not been sufficiently prepared... In physics it has been proved that a body acts upon another body either

---

[1] Cf. H. Bergmann, *Ha-philosophia shel Shlomo Maimon* (Hebrew), Jerusalem, 1932, p. 130, note 1, who refers to Judah Halevi, Kuzari 5, 12, as a possible source for Maimon's thought.

by direct contact with it or indirectly through the medium of other bodies... There are, however, changes which concern only the forms of things; they likewise require an effective cause. This cause is incorporeal, for that which produces form must itself be form... This can be explained only thus: All combinations of the elements are subject to gradual increase and decrease; their change takes place by degrees. It is different with forms; they do not change by degrees and are therefore not subject to motion. They appear and disappear instantaneously and are, consequently, not the result of the combination of corporeal elements... The effective cause that produces the form is indivisible... It is absurd to maintain that the action of this incorporeal agent is dependent upon its relation to the corporeal product. Since it is incorporeal, its action cannot depend on a relationship of distance; it cannot approach a body or recede from it... The same applies to the action of the intelligence. It is not the result of a force coming to it from the outside, nor does it affect at a certain distance, nor does it act at a certain time..."[2]

In his exposition of Maimonides' philosophy, Maimon presents this distinction between the effect of an idea, a pure form, and that of a material object in the following manner: "All that is possible, i.e., the potential that becomes real, must have an effective cause, a sufficient reason, in consequence of which the potential is transformed into a reality. This effective cause is either material or immaterial. Matter as such, however, is passive and cannot be an effective cause unless it is determined through a form. The immediate cause of a certain effect must again have a determining cause, and so on. But this cannot go on infinitely... All reality thus presupposes a first cause. The reason, however, why this necessary cause, which is eternal, is effective now, at a particular point in time, and not before, is to be found in the absence of an external relation between the immediate cause and the effect, a relationship that is necessary for the cause to become effective. This is the case when the cause is material. Otherwise, the cause may not be effective, owing to the insufficient preparation of the material object. The creation of a composite object requires the attraction of its component parts and their effect one upon the other. But this process presupposes a definite relation in space, since material objects mutually attract one another and have an effect one upon the other only at a certain distance. Forms, however, such as simple substances or powers, do not presuppose a certain relation in space, for there can be no spatial

[2] See *Guide*, II, 12.

relation between a simple and a component object. The effect of forms on matter is conditioned only by the necessary preparation of the material object. The cause of these forms must in itself be a form. But since these forms are simple substances, they cannot arise and disappear *in time*, i.e., their generation and disappearance cannot be a process occurring in time, but they emerge suddenly and instantaneously."[3]

Two ideas, which are mutually interdependent, are here set parallel to each other. First, a distinction is made between the manner in which a material object affects another material object, and the effect of a pure form, a simple substance. While the former is subject to the relation of space, since it can affect another object at a certain distance, the latter is not dependent on the relation of space. Second, the relation of time is tied up with that of space. The effect of a material object is a process occurring in time; it is subject to the relation of time as well as of space. The effect of pure form, however, is not spatio-temporal; it does not require an object to be at a certain distance in order to affect it, nor does it occur in time.

Maimonides is thus undoubtedly the source of Maimon's idea that pure thought is not a process occurring in time, but rather arises instantly, in contradistinction to sensuous perception, which is a temporal process. Since perception is the result of the effect of an object upon the senses, it is conditioned by the relation of space as well as of time; it therefore emerges gradually in time.

The fundamental distinction between propositions that arise gradually *in time* and propositions that arise not in time but instantaneously, to which Maimon refers again and again, is closely bound up with Maimon's skepticism regarding the reality of the hypothetical propositions in natural science. According to Kant, the hypothetical form of

---

[3] The italics are Maimon's. Cf. *S. Maimons Lebensgeschichte*, II, 83 f. Maimonides' last sentence is rendered by Maimon thus: "Die Ursache dieser Formen an sich aber kann nichts anderes als selbst eine Form sein. Und da diese Formen einfache Wesen sind, so können sie nicht entstehen und vergehen *mit der Zeit und nach und nach*, sondern plötzlich und auf einmal."

Maimonides' statement can be understood to imply merely that the divine intelligence does not affect "at a certain time" but flows continously, as is evident from the context and the whole tenor of Maimonides' argument. Maimon, however, interprets it to mean that the effect of the divine intelligence is not a spatio-temporal process and therefore not subject to the conditions of space and time. Maimon is correct in his conception of this idea, even though it is not an exact rendering of, but rather involves a step beyond, Maimonides; for the two aspects of this idea are closely interrelated, the one following from the other. The effect of the divine Intellect does not occur "at a certain time" because it is not a temporal process at all. Munk correspondingly renders the sentence thus: "... dans un temps plutôt que dans un autre temps," *op. cit.*, II, 101, which is in keeping with the original Arabic text.

propositions – when a thing A is given, another thing B must be posited – is grounded in a logical form of *a priori* thought, the reality of which cannot be doubted. Maimon, however, maintains that the reality of this form of thought in relation to objects of experience must be established by demonstrating its rightful application to definite objects of experience. But we cannot possibly deduce the reality of the hypothetical form of thought from experience, inasmuch as the connection between the phenomena of A and B following one upon the other can be explained by the association of the faculty of imagination (in accordance with Hume, who denies the reality of the hypothetical form of propositions, i.e., causality, and explained it as a mere consequence of habit and association).

A concept resulting from habit and continuous association of perceptions (and ideas) arises gradually and in time. Through the repetition of the succession of phenomenon B upon phenomenon A we acquire the notion of a necessary connection between them. This is merely a subjective necessity, since it is due to a repetition of the succession of the phenomena one upon the other in time. In short, subjective necessity is the result of a repetition of occurrences in time.

A proposition of understanding, however, such as A is A, arises not in time but instantaneously and spontaneously. Such a proposition does not require a repetition of experiential occurrences; it therefore possesses objective necessity.

The fundamental difference between Kant and Maimon with reference to the reality of the form of hypothetical propositions is reducible to Maimon's distinction between propositions derived gradually in time and propositions arising in the mind spontaneously and instantaneously. According to Kant, the hypothetical propositions are grounded in a logical form of thought. Like the logical form in which they are grounded, they arise instantaneously (according to Maimon's definition) and consequently command objective necessity. Maimon, on his side, holds that the hypothetical propositions in relation to definite objects of experience are the result of a repetitious observation of the phenomena of experience and of the continuous association of ideas; they arise *in time* and thus can command merely subjective necessity.[4]

The distinction between cognitions that arise gradually in time and cognitions that arise instantaneously served Maimon as a criterion for the characterization of sensuous and intellectual knowledge. It

Cf. *Bacon*, p. 217.

constitutes a *fundamentum divisionis* of the various kinds of cognition. It is defined by Maimon thus: "That aspect of a thing which is cognized by a process taking place in time constitutes an object of sensuous cognition, but that aspect of it which is conceived instantaneously constitutes an object of intellectual cognition. The cognition of forms of understanding is wholly intellectual, the cognition of the material of the objects is wholly sensuous. The cognition of an object as consisting of form and matter is a mixed cognition."[5]

With this criterion Maimon deviates from Leibniz in the formulation of the distinction between sensuous and intellectual knowledge. According to the school of Leibniz and Wolff, sensuous and intellectual cognitions do not differ from each other in essence, but merely in the degree of distinctness and clearness. While the former is confused and indistinct, the latter is clear and distinct. Kant objects to this classification by pointing out that while there are confused cognitions that can be made clear, sensuous cognition, such as the perception of the color red, for instance, can never be made conceptually clear and distinct. Kant therefore maintains that the distinction between them is one of essence; they constitute two essentially different kinds of knowledge.

On the whole, Maimon accepts Leibniz' characterization of the two kinds of knowledge as differing merely in degree. His objection to Kant is that if intuition and understanding were essentially different from each other, how could concepts of understanding be applied to objects of intuition? The question *quid juris* could then not be answered.

Maimon objects to the Kantian dualism of intuition (*Anschauung*) and understanding. According to him, the application of the forms of understanding (categories) to objects of intuition can be explained only if we assume with Leibniz that intuition and understanding are capacities of cognition differing from each other not in essence but only in the degree of clarity and distinctness. The question of *quid juris* can be solved only by the acceptance of the Leibnizian doctrine of the unity of human cognitive capacities.

However, in the evolvement of the distinction obtaining between cognitions derived from sensuous perceptions as arising gradually in time and intellectual cognitions as arising instantaneously, Maimon introduces a distinction in the cognitive capacities of man, which is an essential characterisation of the Leibnizian differentiation of the various degrees of distinctiveness. He offers his criterion, grounded in the very nature of the various kinds of cognition, for the character-

[5] *Logik*, pp. 120 ff.

ization of the essence of this distinction. Every sensuous perception (*Vorstellung*) of an object is a temporal process taking place in time. In order to imagine a line, one has to draw it gradually in thought, which is an act accomplished in time. But the concept of a triangle, under the assumption of the lines having already been constructed, is a thought conceived instantaneously. "Line is thus a product of sensuous intuition, even though it is *a priori* (since it is not 'given' but constructed by the mind). Triangle is, in respect to its matter, i.e., the lines, also a product of intuition. But in respect to its form, i.e., the synthesis of the three lines enclosing space into a unity of conciousness, it is a product of thought."[6] It is a concept arising instantaneously.

In order to understand fully the significance of Maimon's idea, that pure thought is not a temporal process but emerges instantly, and its bearing on his thought in general, we have to examine it in the various contexts in which it appears in his writings.[7]

In analyzing the process of thought, Maimon states that the essence of understanding consists in the presentation of the object of cognition as fluid and becoming, or, in other words, the understanding of an object implies comprehension of the mode of its generation.[8] Since the task of cognition is the production of unity out of the manifold, the understanding of an object consists in the presentation of the mode of its becoming, for only in this manner can the manifold be brought into unity. The act of cognition, therefore, does not consist of thinking the object as already given, but only as being generated. The particular manner of the generation of an object (e.g., mathematical objects) makes it a particular object. And the relation of objects to one another is reducible to the relation of the various modes of their generation.

---

[6] *Ibid.*, p. 121.

[7] In addition to the references in Maimon's writings quoted in the text, see his commentary on Maimonides' *Guide*, Chaps. 32 and 68, and *Philos. Wört.*, p. 63. In *Com.*, Chap. 32, Maimon discusses the idea that intellectual concepts are dependent on the perception of material objects and expounds it in the following manner. Rational concepts are *dependent on* the perception of objects, which is a process occurring in time, but they (the rational concepts) are not to be *derived from* the perception of objects. Since the origin of rational concepts lies in the mind, they arise spontaneously and instantly and are not conditioned by time. (Italics mine.) This distinction between being "dependent on" and "derived from" is reminiscent of Kant's differentiation between "beginning with" and "arising out of" with reference to the relation between cognition and experience. Cf. Introduction to the *Critique of Pure Reason*: "But though all our knowledge begins with experience, it does not follow that it all arises out of experience" (Englsih translation by N. K. Smith, p. 41). In the distinction between "beginning with" and "arising out of," properly understood in all its implications, is contained the very essence of the *Critique*. Cf. Hermann Cohen, *Kommentar zu Kants Kritik der reinen Vernunft*, pp. 8 f.

[8] See *Tr.*, pp. 33 f.

Maimon writes further that the understanding of an object requires, first, a given intuition (*Anschauung*) and, second, a general rule of understanding by which the manifold of the intuition is ordered and determined. This rule of understanding is not a process occurring in time, but something arising instantaneously. Intuition *a posteriori*, however, or the application of the general rule to a particular intuition, is a process occurring in time, and the object of intuition cannot be conceived otherwise than as becoming, as fluid. In the concept of *a posteriori* intuition Maimon makes use of his distinction between perception and thought to differentiate between the general rule governing the relation between the sides of a triangle, which is a thought arising instantly, and the application of this general rule to a particular triangle, which is a temporal process.[9]

In his treatment of the problem of antinomies, Maimon deals with the mathematical antinomy of an infinite series of all natural numbers. The human mind can produce an infinite series only through an infinite succession in time, as our perception is bound up with time. The finite and limited human mind is thus incapable of completing an infinite series. The infinite mind, however, which is not restricted by sensibility and not conditioned by time, conceives the thought of an infinite series simultaneously and instantaneously; it does not require for its completion a succession in time.[10]

Maimon introduces here the distinction between two different modes of thought with reference to the condition of time involved in order to bring into sharp relief the distinction that exists between the limited human mind and the infinite mind. As a corollary it follows that inasmuch as the human mind is in possession of *a priori* concepts, which are not the result of empirical experience, it is a part of the infinite mind, and as such it is not bound up with the form of time. The human mind, too, is capable of conceiving pure ideas, not by a temporal process, but spontaneously and instantaneously.

In dealing with Aristotle's concept of the active intellect as an immortal reason in contradistinction to the passive reason, which is temporal and mortal like any other bodily function, Maimon adds the following consideration. The thought of the active reason is indivisible, and only that thought is immortal which is conceived by the mind as an indivisible entity. Perceptions and associations, however, are processes occurring one after the other; they take place in time and thus

[9] *Ibid.*
[10] *Ibid.*, p. 228.

they are divisible. A logical proposition, A is B, for instance, cannot be conceived otherwise than as an indivisible unity. It occurs spontaneously and instantaneously. Such is the nature of every rational concept and proposition comprising a synthesis of a subject and a predicate. A true and indivisible unity is the product of logical inference, and as such it is not a process occurring in time.[11]

Here Maimon develops the distinction between pure thought as the function of the active reason and perception as the function of the passive reason, with reference to its bearing on the concept of immortality. The active reason, which is not restricted by conditions of time, is immortal in contradistinction to the passive reason, whose effect is divisible and conditioned by time. The distinction between the active and passive intellect, with reference to the idea of individual immortality, is fully developed by Maimonides. He conceives of the idea of immortality as a task, an ideal for man to attain by activating his reason. On the whole, Maimon follows Maimonides in his conception of the idea of immortality. It is possible for man to approach endlessly the ideal of immortality by constantly perfecting his mind and by extending his intellectual comprehension of reality, thereby transforming the individual subjective consciousness into a part of the general objective consciousness. Man's approach to the idea of immortality stands in inverse ratio to his subjective, individual, and empirical self-consciousness, and in direct ratio to his share in the objective, super-individual and super-empirical consciousness.[12]

In another context Maimon writes that in the capacity of thought we distinguish a higher and a lower faculty, and this is based on the following consideration. The perceptions of the manifold by the act of cognition are the result of a process similar to all physical processes, which are subject to natural laws. They occur in time and according to the law of causality. But the synthesis of this manifold as a unity of consciousness is an intellectual process, which differs fundamentally from the physical process and is not subject to natural laws, but only to purely intellectual laws. While the former is to be designated as a lower faculty, the latter is to be termed a higher faculty of thinking.[13] Thus the higher faculty of thought is not a temporal process.

This fundamental distinction, which Maimon makes between pure thought and sensuous perception, is bound up with his conception of

[11] Cf. *Bacon*, p. 213.
[12] See *Krit. Unt.*, pp. 244 f., 248 f.
[13] Cf. *Ibid.*, p. 233.

space as the form of the variety and heterogeneity of objects, and his conception of time as the form of the succession of objects one after another.[14] Since time and space are tied up with the perception of sensuous objects, they are not applicable to pure thought. Maimonides is mainly concerned with the metaphysical question of Creation, with the relation of God, as pure form, to the world. In dealing with the concept of space, he points out that material objects alone are subject to conditions of space, as material objects affect one another only at a certain distance. But the emanation of the divine intellect as pure form cannot be conditioned by elements of space, such as distance and proximity. It can be subject only to conditions of preparations of the material object. Maimonides then says of time that it, too, cannot apply to the divine emanation as a pure form. The question, why creation took place at a certain point in time, presents no problem in view of Maimonides' concept of time as an accident of motion. Time as an accident of motion is bound up with the perception of sensuous objects. Therefore, creation was not *in time* but prior to all time. Thus the divine emanation cannot be subject to the form of time and to its conditions.

Maimon's chief concern, however, is with the epistemological question, with the essence of cognition as distinct from perception. He takes up the Maimonidean idea of time as a concept that is inapplicable to pure form, i.e., to the divine emanation, and gives it another meaning by applying it to the process of cognition as such. He thus fills in the Maimonidean metaphysical idea with epistemological content, pointing out that pure thought is a process not occurring in time and not subject to the conditions of time, that human *a priori* thought arises suddenly and instantly in contradistinction to sensuous perception, which is a gradual process subject to temporal conditions.

Maimon's idea has its roots in Maimonides, but its scope is broader than that of Maimonides' concept, since its application is not only metaphysical but also epistemological. This thought of Maimon, moreover, is bound up with his concept of *a priori* and with his idea of an infinite mind of which the human mind is a part. It is thus not accidental with Maimon but occupies, rather, a pivotal place in his system of thought.

The very concept of *a priori* knowledge Maimon knew from Maimonides, even prior to his acquaintance with the Kantian philosophy. Maimonides defines the essence of God's knowledge as distinct from the knowledge of man. First, God's knowledge is one, even though it en-

[14] See *Str.*, pp. 260 ff.

compasses many different kinds of objects. Second, it is applied to objects not yet in existence, i.e., his knowledge embraces the future. Third, it comprehends the infinite. Fourth, it is unchanged, though it comprises knowledge of changeable objects. Fifth, God's knowledge of one of two eventualities does not deprive man of his freedom of action.[15]

The reason for these various distinctions between God's and man's knowledge is the following: "Our knowledge of things is derived from observation; therefore we cannot know the future or the infinite. Our knowledge increases in proportion to the things known by us. God's knowledge, however, is not derived from things as they come into being, but things are according to His knowledge, which is prior to the things' coming into existence... In His knowledge there is neither plurality, nor acquisition, nor change. By His knowledge of His own essence He knows all things..."[16]

Thus the finite knowledge of man is derived from and is dependent upon experience and observation of empirical objects, while the infinite knowledge of God is independent of and prior to all experience. To the former things must be given from without, to the latter nothing can be given. The infinite mind cannot be dependent upon experience; it must encompass the infinity of things prior to their existence.

Translating Maimonides' thought into Kantian language, we can say that while human knowledge is *a posteriori*, divine knowledge is in its very essence *a priori*. Thus, the metaphysical distinction of Maimonides concerning human and divine knowledge, of which Maimon is aware, contributed, in his study of Kant's *Critique*, to his comprehension of the epistemological distinction between *a priori* and *a posteriori* with regard to human knowledge. On the other hand, Maimon's philosophical apperception determines his own perception of the concept of *a priori* as distinct from that of Kant.

In his definition of the concept of *a priori* Maimon differs from Kant. Whereas for the latter, a concept that is logically prior to and independent of sensation and perception belongs to the *a priori* mode of

[15] *Guide*, III, 20.
[16] *Ibid.*, Chap. 21. Maimon renders Maimonides' last sentence thus: "God imagines the knowledge of His own self as the ground of all things. The imagination of all things is thus for God inseparable from the imagination of His own self." Cf. Maimon's *Lebensgeschichte*, II, 124. In its main features this is, of course, an Aristotelian idea. But Maimon knows it from Maimonides in the connotation Maimonides imputes to it and in his formulation. Furthermore, according to Aristotle, God, as the source of all forms, knows only the general forms of all reality, and knows the particulars only to the extent that they are presentations of the general forms, while for Maimonides His knowledge extends over the particulars as such.

cognition, for Maimon *a priori* is only that mode of cognition which precedes cognition of the object itself. Even the objects of mathematics, which are constructed by the mind and not derived from sensuous perceptions, are, in Maimon's view, not absolutely *a priori*, as their cognition is dependent on construction through intuition. For Kant, however, they are *a priori*, since according to him *a priori* is that mode of cognition which is derived from thought and is independent of all sensation; and mathematical objects are not derived from sensuous perceptions but constructed by the mind and its forms of intuition.[17]

A priori cognition is, for Maimon, related to objects in general, such as the propositions of logic, or to the mere relations of objects to one another, by which the objects are determined, as is the case in arithmetic. That mode of cognition is *a priori* which is concerned only with the relations between objects, independent of and prior to the cognition of the objects themselves. The principles by which such a mode of cognition is determined are the law of identity and the law of contradiction. However, when the cognition of objects must precede the cognition of their relations to one another, it is *a posteriori*.

It follows from this that the axioms of mathematics are not *a priori*, since the cognition of matehmatical objects by their construction – mathematical lines, for example – must precede cognition of their relation to one another. According to Kant, however, these axioms are *a priori*, since the mathematical objects are grounded in the forms of intuition, time and space, which are prior to perception and sensation.

Maimon illustrates his point of view by the following example. "Assuming I have no idea of a straight line and I am asked whether a straight line can, at the same time be not straight, I need not postpone my answer under the pretext that I have no idea of the object concerned until I have acquired a clear idea of a straight line, but my answer would be ready that such a thing is impossible," merely on the basis of the law of contradiction, that an object cannot at the same time be *a* and *non-a*. This illustrates the essence of *a priori* knowledge, which is based on the laws of identity and of contradiction and precedes the cognition of the object itself. "But if I am asked," writes Maimon, "whether a straight line is the shortest line between two points, my answer would correctly be, 'I do not know,' so long as I have no clear idea of a straight line."[18]

The laws of identity and of contradiction are the most general

---

[17] Cf. *Tr.*, p. 168.
[18] Cf. *ibid.*, pp. 169 f.

forms of every mode of cognition and are valid with reference to all objects as such, quite independent of their nature and content. Therefore, Maimon's first question can be answered definitely: An object contradicting the law of identity is impossible. However, in the case of the proposition that a straight line is the shortest between two points, we cannot know whether the proposition is correct so long as we have no clear idea of the object itself. Only if we define a straight line as the shortest between two points is the truth of the proposition determined by the law of identity.

Maimon's criticism of Kant is based on his conception of the *a priori* mode of cognition as analytical knowledge, solely determined by the laws of identity and of contradiction. In the present context it is of interest to note that in his definition of the *a priori* concept as knowledge that does not require a construction of the object in intuition and is prior to the intuition of the object and independent of its cognition, Maimon is influenced by Maimonides' distinction between infinite divine knowledge and finite human knowledge. In Maimonides' view, divine knowledge cannot be dependent on cognition of objects given from without or on intuition of objects, even though constructed by the mind. It must precede the objects and be prior to them; in other words, it must be entirely analytic.

In modern terms, Maimonides' thought can be expressed thus: Only God's knowledge is *a priori*, since it does not require any object of experience and is in fact prior to all experience of objects. Man's knowledge, however, which is dependent on cognition of objects of experience, is *a posteriori*. When Maimon, under the influence of Kant, conceives the possibility of an *a priori* mode of cognition for man, he places it under the same conditions as those by which Maimonides defines divine knowledge, namely, only that mode of cognition is *a priori* which is prior to the cognition of the object, i.e., cognition that is analytic and solely determined by the law of identity and that of contradiction which are related to objects in general, quite independent of their content and nature.

Maimon's criterion of the distinction between the subjective and objective necessity of a proposition also reveals the same trend of thought. Maimon writes: "The objects of perception presuppose a condition in the subject in order for us to conceive their relation to one another as necessarily true, while the objects of mathematics do not presuppose such a condition in the subject. Thus, when I think the straight line as necessarily the shortest between two points, this proposition commands necessity quite independently of whether I have repeated the presentation of a straight line several times or whether I have conceived it for the first time. The proposition, however, that fire melts wax becomes necessary only after perceiving it several times. This repetitious perception of the phenomenon may have been presented by accident or may have been purposely performed. But since the proposition is dependent on a certain condition of repetition, it commands merely subjective, not objective necessity."[19]

A priori knowledge must be independent of any condition in the subject, otherwise it cannot be objectively necessary. If we recall Maimonides' distinction between God's knowledge and man's knowledge and apply it to Maimon's distinction between subjective and objective necessity, Maimon's thought becomes clear. In relation to divine cognition it is unthinkable to require repetition as a condition of knowledge, because knowledge acquired through the repetition of a phenomenon is a mode of cognition subject to temporal conditions; it is a temporal process. Divine knowledge, however, is not subject to conditions of time.

Maimon thus derives his conception of pure thought as a mode of cognition that arises instantly and is not a process occurring in time from the Maimonidean definition of divine thought as a mode of cognition that is independent of temporal conditions.

In order to understand a philosophical idea properly, it is not sufficient to comprehend it as it stands by itself; it is necessary to strive to encompass exhaustively its relation to other philosophical ideas of the same author and thus to comprehend it as an integral part of his philosophical system as a whole. Philosophy is in its very essence systematic thinking. Consequently, the full comprehension of a philosophical idea can be attained only when we succeed in establishing its scope and systematic place in the totality of the author's thinking.

Thus far we have succeeded in establishing the relation to Maimonides' view of Maimon's distinction between sensuous perception and pure thought. Our task, however, is not yet finished. Our objective now is to strive for an understanding of the scope and systematic place that this fundamental differentiation occupies in Maimon's thought as a whole. It is obvious that this distinction is not an isolated idea with Maimon, but fulfills a certain function in his system of thought and constitutes an integral part of it. We must then consider this idea, not merely in its isolation and differentiation, but also in its integration.

[19] Cf. *Str.*, p. 193.

It seems to me that this distinction of Maimon is bound up with his concept of analytic and synthetic propositions and with his idea that the guarantee for the reality of synthetic propositions rests in the metaphysical idea of an infinite mind, in relation to which all synthetic propositions are dissoluble into analytic ones. Analytic propositions are based on the law of identity. For instance, the proposition that a body has extension (a Kantian example) follows necessarily from the law of identity, since the opposite statement is self-contradictory. The thinking of the law of identity is not a temporal process, but rather an instantaneous one. Synthetic propositions, on the other hand, having their basis in observation of natural phenomena, are grounded in the law of sufficient reason and are all the result of a process occurring in time. From the metaphysical idea of an infinite mind, in relation to which, according to Maimon, all our synthetic propositions are analytic ones, it follows that the thinking of the infinite mind is determined by the laws of identity and of contradiction. The law of sufficient reason of the limited human mind is thus dissoluble by the infinite mind into the law of identity. In other words, the relation of cause and effect in the realm of natural phenomena is transformed by the infinite mind into a relation of logical antecedent to logical consequent. The synthetic propositions in mathematics are governed by the law of logical inference, i.e., the law of logical antecedent and consequent, which is different from the law of sufficient reason governing physical phenomena. The synthetic propositions in mathematics need for their verification the mere construction of the objects and the analysis of their integral elements in their relations to one another. The synthetic propositions of natural science require for their verification experience and observation of physical phenomena. Synthetic propositions as such are thus conditioned by the forms of time and space. Both forms, however, are unthinkable in relation to an infinite mind, whose thought is governed only by the law of identity and the law of contradiction.

Since, however, the human mind is part of the infinite mind[20] and is capable of creative *a priori* thought, its pure thought must have the same qualitative distinction as that of the infinite mind, i.e., it must not be a process occurring in time but must arise instantaneously. As to the concept of pure thought which occurs instantly, Maimon is not explicit concerning whether it refers only to analytic propositions, which are determined by the law of identity, or whether it relates also to synthetic propositions. I am inclined, on the basis of the passage

[21] Cf. above, Chap. V.

quoted above, to interpret his concept of pure thought to refer first and foremost to propositions determined by the law of identity, i.e., analytic propositions, and then also to such synthetic propositions as can in the course of time be dissolved into analytic ones, such as the synthetic propositions in mathematics. But the synthetic propositions of natural science, the reality of which may legitimately be doubted by a follower of David Hume, since they are based on experience and observation of the physical phenomena, are, each and every one of them, the result of sensuous perception and thus subject to temporal conditions. With reference to the synthetic propositions in mathematics, even though the construction of mathematical objects is required for the establishment of the laws governing the relation of the objects to one another, this is merely preparatory to the emergence of the proposition itself; the actual emergence is instantaneous.

We must thus recognize with Maimon that there is a fundamental distinction, with reference to their certitude and general validity, between the synthetic propositions of mathematics and those of natural science. The laws governing mathematical objects and those governing the natural laws by which we try to master the realm of physical phenomena are not of the same quality. While the former justifiably claim general validity and universality, the validity of the latter, i.e., their reality, may be doubted on Humean grounds.

Every synthetic proposition that is universally valid must, in principle, be reducible to an analytic proposition. If we are not capable of performing this reduction, it is due merely to the limitations of the human mind. To the infinite mind they are all analytic propositions and determined by the law of identity and the law of contradiction. The possibility, in principle, of the transformation of synthetic propositions into analytic ones imposes a task on the human mind to strive for the attainment of this reduction, since ideal knowledge is cognition through analytic propositions determined by the law of identity, according to Maimon and all the rationalists of the seventeenth century, such as Leibniz, whom he followed.

Consequently, Maimon's attempt, by way of illustration, to dissolve a synthetic proposition into an analytic proposition is confined to mathematics.[21] He does not attempt a similar reduction in the realm

---

[21] See *Tr.*, pp. 65 f., where Maimon attempts to reduce the synthetic proposition that a straight line is the shortest line between two points to an analytic proposition on the basis of Wolff's definition of a straight line as a single line, i.e., the parts of which are in the same direction as the whole.

Maimon's intention is thus to prove that the proposition, a straight line is the

of natural science. The reason for the discrimination is simply this: Since the reality of the synthetic propositions in natural science can justifiably be doubted, there is no guarantee for the possibility of their reduction to analytic propositions. Only when the validity, the objective necessity of the synthetic proposition is well established and beyond any doubt, do we have to strive for its reduction to an analytic proposition and to the law of identity on which the latter is based. The certitude and objective necessity of the proposition is a sure guarantee of the possibility of such a reduction. In other words, only to the degree that the reality of the law is certain are we entitled to assume that the synthetic proposition is grounded in an analytic one and that its reduction to the law of identity becomes a task, a goal worthy of attaining.

Hence it follows that there is a fundamental distinction between the synthetic propositions of mathematics and those of natural science. Since the validity and objective necessity of the proposition must first be established before we assume its possible dissolution into analytic thought and its reduction to the law of identity, the striving for such a reduction is legitimate only with reference to mathematical propositions, the reality of which cannot be doubted. With regard to synthetic propositions in natural science, the reality of which may be doubted, we are not entitled to assume the possibility of their reduction to the law of identity, and to attempt their dissolution into analytic thought is illegitimate.

So far we have discussed Maimon's distinction between perception, which is a temporal process, and pure thought, which arises instan-

shortest line between two points, is not an axiom but is derived analytically from the definition of a straight line as a single line (Wolff). Maimon then adds in a note (*ibid.*) that even assuming that Wolff's definition can be shown to be rooted in a synthetic proposition, it should still be possible to resolve that synthetic proposition into analytic thought. Furthermore, Maimon admits that he is not quite satisfied with the Wolffian definition, but nevertheless maintains the possibility in principle of such a reduction.

It seems that Maimon added his note after having read Kant's letter to Markus Herz, containing a criticism of Maimon's doctrine by way of a refutation of Wolff's definition of a straight line. Kant writes: "As to the definition of a straight line, it cannot be defined as the identity of the direction of all its parts, since the concept of direction itself presupposes the concept of line." *Briefe von und an Kant*, ed. Cassirer, I, p. 420. Kant read Maimon's manuscript, *Versuch über die Transcendentalphilosophie*, which Herz sent him, and understood Maimon to imply a definite proof of a particular reduction of the synthetic proposition into an analytic one. On reading Kant's criticism Maimon felt constrained to add his note modifying his doctrine, namely, that his intention was not to propose a definite reduction based on a particular definition of a straight line, but merely to offer an illustration of a *possible* reduction, i.e., such a reduction must, in principle, be possible of attainment on the assumption that the synthetic proposition is grounded in analytic thought.

taneously. It is also important to point out the converse aspect of the same idea, namely, that whereas a proposition that is the result of a temporal porcess may claim merely subjective validity, a proposition that is not conditioned by time acquires the rank of objective truth.

In another context Maimon expresses the thought that a proposition arrived at through a temporal process is based on perception and is therefore subjective, while a proposition resulting from a thinking process, in which the element of time is merely a prerequisite for its pictorial presentation, may claim objective validity. In his correspondence with Reinhold, Maimon writes: "The objects of sensuous experience presuppose a condition in the subject for the cognition of their relation to one another, while the objects of mathematics do not presuppose such a condition in the subject..."[22] Thus a proposition that is the result of repeated experience is subjectively conditioned, and its reality can be doubted. We may go a step further, adding that a synthetic proposition that has no right to claim objective validity cannot be assumed to be rooted in an analytic proposition. However, a proposition that is not the result of repeated experience but rather derives from the pure conception of a single object, i.e., a proposition that arises instantaneously, may claim objective validity, and the assumption is legitimate that it is rooted in an analytic proposition.

Here lies the clue to the reason for Maimon's distinction between synthetic propositions in mathematics, which we may assume to be rooted in analytic propositions, and synthetic propositions in physical science, the reality of which can be doubted. The element of time is decisive in the determination of whether or not a proposition is, in principle, reducible to an analytic proposition. A proposition resulting from repeated experience occurs "in time" and is dependent upon subjective conditions; it cannot, therefore, claim objective validity. A proposition, however, that does not derive from repeated experience and in the conception of which the element of time is necessary only for its pictorial representation, as is the case with mathematical propositions, can claim objective validity, and hence the assumption that it is grounded in an analytic proposition is legitimate.

Only the metaphysical assumption of an infinite reason, of which our mind is a part, can give objective validity to our synthetic propositions in natural science. The assumption of such an infinite mind in relation to which all our synthetic propositions are analytic ones is a sort of guarantee that our propositions resulting from repeated experience are

[22] See above, p. 135, where the entire passage from Maimon is quoted.

real. The confirmed skeptic, however, who doubts the reality of experience cannot be refuted by epistemological reasons.

We sometimes find contradictions in Maimon's writings which require explanation. Maimon himself said of his method of writing that "the same problems are dealt with by me in a different manner on different occasions and in different connections."[23] Thus it sometimes occurs that Maimon's various treatments of one and the same problem contain apparent contradictions, to which he himself does not refer. For example, in his first philosophical work, Maimon seems to deny the synthetic *a priori* character of the mathematical propositions, while in his later works he is in accord with Kant that mathematics contains synthetic *a priori* propositions. Thus he writes in his *Transcendentalphilosophie*: "The proposition that the straight line is the shortest between two points may be the result of the fact that I have perceived it; its necessity may, therefore, be grounded in subjective experience."[24] Here Maimon doubts the *a priori* character of synthetic judgments in mathematics, while in the *Streifereien*[25] he writes: "That mathematics contains synthetic propositions is beyond any doubt, and I am astounded to see how one can dispute it.... But how is critical philosophy to prove that we are in possession of experiential synthetic propositions?" In other words, here Maimon doubts the reality of synthetic *a priori* propositions in natural science but not in mathematics.[26]

It seems to me that the contradiction is only apparent and not real. Maimon does not deny in his first work the presence of synthetic *a priori* propositions in mathematics. His main thesis there is that we have to assume that the synthetic propositions in mathematics are rooted in analytic ones and may in the course of time be dissolved into analytic thought. The last is the final goal and the ideal of cognition, which man should strive to approach. For an infinite mind our synthetic propositions are all analytic. Maimon himself undertakes to demonstrate how the synthetic proposition that a straight line is the shortest line between two points can be dissvoled into an analytic proposition. He admits the failure of his attempt, adding, however, that his particular mode of reduction is meant merely as an illustration of its possibility on the assumption, of course, that for the infinite mind such a reduction is a reality.[27] It is thereby implied that the reduction into analytic

[23] See *Logik*, Introduction, p. xxvi.
[24] *Tr.*, p. 173.
[25] P. 50.
[26] Cf. B. Katz, "Zur Philosophie Salomon Maimons," in *Archiv für Geschichte der Philosophie*, XXVIII (1915), 55 f., who pointed out this contradiction in Maimon.
[27] See *Tr.*, pp. 65 f., and above, note 21.

thought is the ideal and endless task of knowledge, giving direction and purpose to the process of human thought. Thus Maimon's attempt, in spite of its failure, is in keeping with the whole trend of his thinking, namely, that the human mind must strive to attain analytical knowledge. This alone – the knowledge of the infinite mind – is the absolute guarantee of truth.

When Maimon writes in the *Transcendentalphilosophie* about synthetic propositions in mathematics in the same tenor as he writes in the *Streifereien* about propositions resulting from repeated experience, saying that one may doubt the reality of both, he means merely to prove the necessity of the idea of an infinite mind. Without this idea even synthetic propositions in mathematics can be doubted.

There is no contradiction in Maimon, as some critics maintain,[28] but merely a different manner of presentation of one and the same philosophical viewpoint. This consists of the alternative: Either the reality of synthetic propositions can be assumed on the basis of the idea of an infinite reason or, lacking this assumption, there can be no answer to the skeptic. In the various works of Maimon one or the other aspect of this alternative predominates.

In this connection it is of interest to note the motto to the *Transcendentalphilosophie*, which Maimon took from Virgil, for with it Maimon gives expression to the alternative character of his philosophical viewpoint and to the whole tendency of his work: *Dextrum Scylla latus, laevum implacata Charybdis*. Critical philosophy is untenable by itself, and the question *quid juris* is insoluble; it must be supplemented by a metaphysical idea (Scylla) or we fall into the abyss of skepticism (Charybdis).

With regard to synthetic propositions in mathematics, Maimon tries to prove that they are rooted in analytic thought and that there is hope that the human mind may succeed in dissolving them into analytic propositions. The idea of an infinite mind with respect to the synthetic propositions in mathematics is not a metaphysical, transcendent idea, but rather an ideal, which the human mind should endlessly strive to approach. It is an intellectual perfection, which is, in principle, attainable by the human mind, even though the road to it may be endless. For there is an essential difference, with reference to the degree of certainty and objective validity, between synthetic propositions in mathematics, which require for their verification merely construction of the mathematical objects, and synthetic propositions in natural

---

[28] See above, note 26.

science, which require for their verification experience and repeated observation of the natural phenomena. Only the reality of the former can legitimately be assumed, not that of the latter. Should one reject the assumption that synthetic propositions in mathematics are rooted in analytical thought, he must become skeptical with regard to their reality.

Maimon's statement that the proposition that a straight line is the shortest line between two points may be the result of observation and experience is not to be understood as an expression of his definite and conclusive viewpoint. It is merely an argument in favor of the assumption that this proposition is rooted in analytical thought. For certainty and reality are to be attributed only to analytic propositions. Without this assumption even the reality of synthetic propositions in mathematics may well be doubted by a skeptic.

It cannot be said, then, theat Maimon in his *Transcendental-philosophie* denies the presence of synthetic propositions in mathematics. His only intention there is to prove the necessity of the assumption that synthetic propositions can, in principle, be reduced to analytical ones. If those who maintain that there is a contradiction in Maimon between his viewpoint as presented in *Transcendentalphilosophie* and that of *Streifereien* were right, we could on the same ground find the *Transcendentalphilosophie* itself self-contradictory. For in the beginning of this work Maimon tries to reduce the synthetic proposition that a straight line is the shortest line between two points to an analytical one, and later he maintains that the reality and objective validity of this proposition may be doubted on the basis of the consideration that it may be the result of subjective conditions, such as habit and repeated observation. In our view, this proves the correctness of our interpretation and understanding of Maimon.

We have tried to establish the fundamental distinction that exists, according to Maimon, between synthetic propositions in mathematics and those in natural science from the general tenor of Maimon's thought as well as from the fact that he attempts a reduction of the synthetic proposition to an analytic one only in mathematics. The foregoing analysis of Maimon's thinking now suggests the following question: If the synthetic propositions in the two realms are so fundamentally different, how can Maimon propose, even on the assumption of the metaphysical idea of an infinite reason, the possible reduction of synthetic propositions in natural science into analytic ones, similar to the reduction we hope to obtain in mathematics? In other words, how can the solution of the question *quid juris*, which is the main purpose of Maimon's philosophy as developed in his *Transcendentalphilosophie*, be attained even on the basis of the idea of an infinite mind? Whereas synthetic propositions in mathematics arise instantaneously, those of natural science are the result of observation and repeated experience and are based on temporal processes. The former can legitimately be assumed to be rooted in analytical thought but not the latter.

For an answer to this question we must return to the beginning of this chapter and to the reference in Maimonides concerning the distinction between the relation of cause and effect in material objects and in the realm of pure form. The concept of causality, establishing a connection between natural phenomena, involves, according to Maimonides, a time-relation as well as a space-relation. But the categories of time and space are necessary conditions of material objects; pure form is not conditioned by them. And just as the effect of pure form is not subject to the conditions of time and space, so the infinite mind thinks even of natural phenomena in purely logical-mathematical terms, and the relation of cause and effect is not a time-relation but a purely logical-mathematical relation. Hence, from the idea of the possibility, in principle, of a reduction of synthetic propositions to analytical ones in mathematics it follows that for the infinite mind, which thinks only in mathematical-logical terms, there is no difference between the realm of nature and that of mathematics. All propositions are for the infinite mind dissoluble into analytic propositions.

Furthermore, inasmuch as the physical sciences are based on mathematics, the synthetic propositions of these sciences are also dissolvable into analytic propositions. Maimon's theory of differentials, which is a sort of epistemological atomism or monadism,[29] follows from this. Its essence consists in the idea that the relations existing between objects of experience, which are derived from perception, are assumed to be rooted in relations existing between the first constitutive elements of reality, i.e., its differentials, which are mathematical objects. The thought of the infinite mind, however, proceeds in purely logical-mathematical terms and is, therefore, genuinely related to the differentials. While for the limited human mind the idea of differentials is arrived at by a long process of abstraction, for the infinite mind, which is creative and thinks intuitively, the differentials are realities constituting the genuine elements of its thought. While the thought process of the human mind goes from integrals to differentials, i.e., from relations

[29] Cf. *Tr.*, pp. 31 f., and at the end of Maimon's Introduction to his *Com. on the Guide*.

existing between objects of experience to relations existing between their differentials, the thinking process of the infinite mind ("process" is here to be understood in a figurative sense, since the thinking of the infinite mind is spontaneous and instantaneous) lies in the opposite direction, from differentials to integrals, i.e., from the relations that exist between the first constitutive elements of reality to those of the objects of experience.

In the light of this analysis of Maimon's distinction between the perception of objects of experience and pure thought, we understand the significance of Maimon's reference to mathematics as involving a thinking process by which we obtain an inkling of the essence of divine thought as distinct from human thought. Maimon writes: "God, as the infinite thinking capacity, thinks all possible objects by thinking of Himself as restricted in all possible manners, i.e., by limiting his infinity he thinks of a finite and limited object."[30] Just as man thinks of infinity by the abstraction of his limitations, so God thinks of limited and definite objects by the abstraction of his infinity. "God does not think discursively, which is the characteristic feature of human thought, but intuitively and creatively. His thoughts are at the same time presentations of real objects."[31] As to the objection that might be raised that we cannot possibly have an idea of a process of thought *toto caelo* different from our own, Maimon writes: "We are partly in actual possession of such a concept of thought in mathematics where all concepts are comprehended by us intuitively and at the same time through construction *a priori* they are presented as real objects. In mathematics we are thus godlike. This is the reason why the ancients held mathematics in such high esteem and considered it an indispensable prerequisite for philosophy."[32]

In other words, since in mathematics synthetic propositions are rooted in analytic thought, the construction *a priori* of mathematical objects is a presentation in reality of concepts conceived instantaneously and spontaneously, and it is here that the similarity between human and divine thought lies.

---

[30] *Str.*, p. 20.
[31] Cf. *Com. on the Guide*, Chap. 1, p. 10b.
[32] *Str.*, p. 20.

CHAPTER VIII

PRINCIPLE OF DETERMINABILITY

Maimon formulated the principle of determinability as a principle by which synthetic propositions are governed. Synthesis is an act of cognition through which a unity of manifold is established. The manifold is the material of the synthesis, and the unity is its form. The cognition of matter and form as separate concepts is bound up with Maimon's conception of symbolic cognition. The comprehension of the role and function of symbolic cognition is indispensable for the understanding of the workings of the human mind. Through the employment of symbolic forms man is capable of obtaining the highest abstractions and evolving new truths from the already known and immediately given perceptions.

A symbolic cognition is to be distinguished from an intuitive cognition. By the term "intuitive cognition" in this context, i.e., as opposed to symbolic cognition, we mean cognition of an object present to the mind either by means of perception or by means of imagination. What distinguishes the human mind is man's capacity to employ symbolic forms for the extension of the range of knowledge above and beyond the immediately and intuitively given. Even in the most elementary form of human cognition there is implied a transcendence of the immediately "given." The very essence of human cognition is the capacity to subordinate perceptions to concepts of thought, thus transforming the given into a conceptual order. In the perception of the succession of phenomena the mind applies a form of causality binding the phenomena into a unity of thought. The cognition of such a necessary truth as causality, for instance, is bound up with the perception of the phenomena presented to the mind. Through the symbolic forms the mind is capable of transcending the immediately given. By applying the form of causality the given phenomena are conceived as necessarily connected. Likewise, through the symbolic form the mind reaches out towards that which is absent, as, for example, in the conception of an infinite idea.

To be sure, the cognition of an infinite idea must have a basis in the cognition of some intuitively given object. Thus the idea of an infinite line or an infinite series is connected with the conception of a finite line. The conception of the idea of an infinite line is the result of the application of a symbolic mode of cognition by which the mind transcends the immediately given.

Through the proper understanding of the different kinds of symbolic cognition, their role and function, many difficulties can be resolved. The conception of form and matter is grounded in symbolic cognition. An object of cognition is a manifold synthesized into a unity by a concept of thought. The manifold is the material of the synthesis; its form is the concept of thought by which the manifold is brought into a unity. Thus, for instance, the concept of a triangle, which is space enclosed by three lines, is an object of intuition (*Anschauung*). Space and three lines constitute its material. This manifold material is connected into a unity in the form of subject and predicate: space, which is thinkable in itself, is the subject; being enclosed by three lines, which are not thinkable in themselves but only in connection with space, constitutes the predicate. We are thus in a position to recognize in the intuition of the synthesized object (triangle) the material in itself and the form in itself. But the form in itself can never be cognized apart from the synthesized object, nor can the material in itself be recognized separated from its form, except under the condition that the material of the object is in itself a synthesized object consisting of form and matter. Thus space, as the material of the synthesis, triangle, is in itself a formalized object, for space is, according to Maimon, a relational concept, i.e., the form of the variety and heterogeneity of objects. The idea of an empty space is therefore to be considered a fiction of the imagination. Only space as a relation between objects, as the form of the diversity of objects, can be cognized as real. But space as a relational concept is an object consisting of form and matter.[1]

Thus, matter and form can be cognized only in and through the object of the synthesis; they cannot be cognized in isolation from each other. Yet each of them must be thought of as real in itself, apart from its connection in the synthesis, otherwise their connection into an object cannot be accounted for. The synthesis of matter and form into an object of intuition renders their intuition possible in the synthesized object, but the reality of each of them separately is presupposed. We are compelled to think of something as real which cannot be presented in intuition. It can be presented only through a symbol. Matter and form are thus objects of symbolic cognition. We can now define the

[1] *Tr.*, pp. 271 ff.

essence of symbolic cognition thus: "The form or the mode in which an object of intuition is synthesized, detached from the synthesis and considered an object in itself, constitutes symbolic cognition."[2]

Maimon formulated his conception of matter and form as symbolic cognitions with reference to the Kantian conception of matter and form, i.e., matter is the manifold of perceptions, and form is the concept of unity by which the manifold is synthesized. But the conception of matter and form as symbolic cognitions can be applied equally to the Aristotelian doctrine of matter and form. According to Aristotle, any object of experience is always formed matter. Matter in itself and form in itself are beyond the limits of human experience. They are derived by a process of abstraction, and we ascribe to them metaphysical reality. In experience, however, matter and form do not exist in isolation from each other. Yet matter and form must be assumed as being separately real, otherwise it would be impossible to account for the reality of formed matter. Hence the ideas of matter in itself and form in itself can be defined as symbolic, in accordance with Maimon's conception of the essence of symbolic cognition. With Maimon matter and form are symbolic cognitions, since they cannot be perceived by the direct and immediate intuition of matter in itself and form in itself; their separate reality must, however, be assumed for a full explanation of the synthesized object. And the same applies to the Aristotelian as well as the Kantian conception of matter and form. In both instances they cannot be directly perceived in separation from each other but must be presupposed in order to explain formed matter (Aristotle) or an object of synthesis (Kant).

Since matter cannot be cognized in itself, the material element must be abstracted and sought for in the object of cognition. Now the material common to various objects can be found either by an analytic or by a synthetic process of thought. In the first case, we proceed by analyzing the objects in their essential characteristics and features, and we separate those elements by which the objects differ from one another from those elements that are common to them all. The element abstracted in this manner (which is found to be common to all the objects) is designated as matter. In this way, for example, we proceed in establishing the concept of body common to all bodily objects: we abstract the particular features of the singular bodies and retain only what is common to them all, namely, extension and solidity. This is the analytic method of arriving at the concept of matter.

[2] *Ibid.*, p. 272.

In the second case, i.e., the synthetic process, we proceed in the opposite direction. We begin with an aspect of the objects that can be thought of by itself and by adding to it various possible determinations, we derive simultaneously different objects as well as the element common to them all. So, for instance, the concept of space in general is determined by various specific determinations, as a triangle, a circle, etc. Space, which is common to all of them, is not abstracted from the various objects, but is rather presupposed, since the various geometrical objects are unthinkable without it. This is the synthetic method by which the concept of matter is derived.

In the analytic method, matter and form as cognized by us are not necessarily but only accidentally connected with each other. From the concept of body as extension and solidity we could not obtain the synthetic reality of gold, that is, the particular determination of the yellow color and its specific weight, which are the characteristic features of gold. We recognize these specific features of a particular object merely empirically. Their connection with one another in a specific object is merely accidental and not necessary.

Where the concept of matter is obtained by the synthetic method, however, the connection of matter and form is a necessary one and is *a priori*. Since the form "circle" is not thinkable in itself, but only in its connection with matter, "space," and since the concept of space is thought of as a subject, and "circle," its determination, is its predicate, the connection between circle and space is a necessary and an *a priori* connection.

Form and matter derived by the synthetic method can also be found by the analytic method, but the opposite process cannot always be applied. The idea of space, for instance, can also be obtained by abstracting it from various mathematical figures as the feature common to all of them. But we cannot possibly obtain the particular bodies through the synthetic method, i.e., by adding determinations to the general feature, extension, common to all bodies, in a manner similar to the derivation of mathematical objects from the general concept of space.

Maimon defines thus the distinction between the two methods of obtaining the material subject: While the synthetic method starts with the material subject, which can be thought of in itself and generates from it the particular objects by adding to the subject specific characteristics, the analytic method analyzes the many objects from which it abstracts the most common element. The matter derived synthetically is a *real* subject, since it is the basis of the reality of the various objects, as is the case with space, which is thinkable in itself and presupposed in the construction of the various geometrical figures. The material subject derived analytically is merely a logical object, for the various objects from which the material subject is derived must be presupposed. The conception, for instance, of a table as a square is merely accidental. Table and square are not essentially but only accidentally connected; they do not stand in a *real* relation to each other but only in a logical relation of subject to predicate. The logical relation of subject and predicate does not depend on whether their association is real or accidental. However, in the conception of the geometrical figure of a triangle (space enclosed by three lines) or quadrangle (space enclosed by four lines), triangle and space or quadrangle and space are connected essentially and not merely accidentally. Since space can be thought of in itself, and the lines of the triangle or the quadrangle cannot be thought of without space, space and lines do not stand in a merely logical relation to each other but in a real relationship of subject and predicate. Space as the necessary condition of the geometrical figures constitutes the material principle of these objects. The capacity of cognition produces its forms only in relation to a matter that is indispensable and necessarily presupposed.

In the light of the distinction between an accidental connection and a necessary connection of subject and predicate we understand the difference between a logical subject and a real subject. The former, which is derived analytically, is an accidental subject, while the latter, which is derived synthetically, is a necessary subject.

This analysis of Maimon's is bound up with his fundamental distinction between mathematical and experiential knowledge. Kant recognized the reality of synthetic propositions in mathematics and posed the question, "How are synthetic *a priori* propositions in mathematics possible?" along with the question, "How are synthetic *a priori* propositions in natural science possible?" Kant raised the first question in contradistinction to Hume, who considered the realm of mathematics grounded in analytic propositions. Now Maimon, on the one hand, sides with Kant, who holds that mathematics contains synthetic propositions, but on the other hand, he recognizes the fundamental distinction prevailing between synthetic propositions in mathematics and synthetic propositions in the natural sciences. While the former are real, the latter are merely accidental; the reality of the latter can therefore be doubted. Only on the assumption of an infinite mind in relation to which our experiential knowledge can be translated in terms of mathematical knowledge can the reality of experiential knowledge be guaranteed.

The test of the reality of synthetic propositions in mathematics lies in the possibility of their deduction from the "principle of determinability." This principle, which governs synthetic propositions in the same manner as the law of identity determines analytic propositions, can be applied only to synthetic propositions in mathematics. The material subject in a triangle, for instance, is here not derived analytically as the element common to many objects, but synthetically as the element which can be thought of in itself, such as space, and the predicate (such as being enclosed by three lines) as the determination of the subject.

We understand now the significance of Maimon's statement that God thinks of reality in terms of mathematics and that man is Godlike in his mathematical thinking and in his construction of mathematical objects. Man is capable of constructing synthetic propositions, according to the principle of determinability, only in the realm of mathematics; in its knowledge of experience, however, the human mind is capable of obtaining the material subject only by way of abstraction through the analytical method. But we can imagine an infinite mind as having the capacity to think of all synthetic propositions, including those referring to experience, in accordance with the principle of determinability. The material subject of all empirical objects is thought of by the infinite mind synthetically, that is, as that element which can be thought of by itself, and the prediactes, which cannot be thought of by themselves, are its determinations.

In the principle of determinability Maiman formulates a law by which synthetic propositions in mathematics are governed. Our knowledge of experience is accidental, and the synthetic propositions of experiential knowledge do not follow from the principle of determinability. We imagine, however, an infinite capacity of cognition as an ideal stage of cognition in relation to which our experiential knowledge can be translated in terms of mathematical knowledge and necessarily determined according to the principle of determinability. This principle governs ideal knowledge, i.e., synthetic propositions that can be logically deduced by positing the material subject as a subject thought of in itself and the predicates that cannot be thought of in themselves but only as determinations of the subject. An infinite mind, however, thinks all reality in the same manner .In other words, to speak in the language of Leibniz, for an infinite mind there can be no distinction between truth of reason and truth of fact; what is for the limited human mind truth of fact is for the infinite mind truth of reason; what is for us experiential knowledge is for the infinite mind knowledge determined by the principle of determinability. The question may be raised, however, What guarantee do we have that our konwledge of experience, which is merely accidental, is true in itself, and what right do we have to presuppose that an infinite mind is capable of deducing it from the principle of determinability? The truth of our experiential knowledge may be based on an illusion or on psychological habit, as Hume presupposes.

Herein lies the distinction between the first period of Maimon's thought and its later development. Whereas at first Maimon intended by the introduction of the idea of an infinite mind to guarantee the reality of experiential knowledge, at a later stage the emphasis of his thought is rather on skepticism, that knowledge based on experience may be due to psychological deception. But he differs fundamentally from Hume in that he maintains that in mathematics the reality of synthetic propositions cannot be doubted. The principle of determinability, which governs the synthetic propositions in mathematics, guarantees their reality; it is a principle of deduction, since the synthetic propositions are deduced logically from it. Only the reality of synthetic propositions concerning empirical objects of experience, which cannot be deduced from the principle of determinability but are accidental, can be subject to doubt. While for Hume the certainty of mathematics lies in the analytic character of its propositions, Maimon asserts the presence of synthetic propositions in mathematics, for the deduction of which the principle of determinability is introduced by him. In order to fully understand the significance of the principle of determinability, we must see it in terms of the context out of which it arose. We shall show its development against the background of the Kantian treatment of the problems with which this principle attempts to deal.

Maimon's principle of determinability rests on his criticism of Kant's deduction of synthetic *a priori* propositions. Maimon subjected the Kantian solution of the problem of the possibility of synthetic *a priori* judgments to the following criticism. The general question, How are synthetic *a priori* judgments possible? Kant subdivided into two questions, How are such propositions possible in mathematics? and, How are they possible in natural science? Each of these questions has been dealt with by Kant in a different manner corresponding to the material and the nature of the objects concerned.

The difference between analytic and synthetic *a priori* propositions is this: While the first can be demonstrated by the mere logical analysis of the subject-predicate relation of the proposition, for the second we must resort to the experience of a particular object. We can demonstrate the absolute necessity of an analytic proposition by the mere formal logical principle that no predicate can be ascribed to a subject in violation of the law of contradiction. The law of contradiction asserts that of no object can a statement be made in which the predicate is contrary to its subject. What is binding and valid for any object of thought must also be binding and valid for this or that particular object. The particular case is derived from a general logical principle, the validity of which extends over all objects or any object of thought quite independent of its content.

The case is totally different, however, with regard to synthetic propositions, which refer to definite objects and not to objects of thought in general. Synthetic propositions in mathematics are related to definite mathematical objects; they do not claim validity in relation to any object of thought, and they are not governed by the law of contradiction. The propositions of pure mathematics are valid only for such objects as can be subsumed under these mathematical concepts.

The question, for instance, as to why a geometrical rectilinear figure can be thought of only as being enclosed by three or more, but not by two lines, cannot be answered in the same manner as that used in determining analytic propositions, namely, by stating that no object as such can be thought of otherwise or, positively expressed, that any object must be thought of in this way. It can be answered only by realizing the impossibility of imagining these particular objects (i.e., rectilinear geometrical figures) otherwise than as enclosed by at least three lines. Thus the particular proposition concerning definite mathematical objects is not derived from a general logical principle governing all objects as such. Rather, it is deduced from the possibility of the construction of these definite particular objects.

The question, how are synthetic *a priori* propositions in mathematics possible? is solved by Kant, first, by proving that time and space, which are the underlying forms of the mathematical objects (arithmetics and geometry), are *a priori* forms of intuition, and then by demonstrating that the construction of mathematical objects by the imagination is impossible without the assumption of such propositions. We must attribute to the objects the predicates determined by the synthetic propositions, since mathematical objects as real objects could not be constructed otherwise. Their necessity is derived from the principle of the possibility of construction.

From the necessary conditions of constructon of mathematical objects Kant deduced the necessity of the synthetic propositions determining these objects. Construction, however, is a process of experience; it cannot, therefore, serve as a basis of *a priori* propositions. Kant did not give us a principle that could guide us in recognizing *a priori* whether an object can or cannot be an object of construction in intuition. Since it is necessary actually to perform the construction of the object in order to recognize its reality, and construction of an object of intuition is a phenomenon of experience, we are not in possession of a pure *a priori* principle from which to deduce the synthetic propositions *a priori* in mathematics, and therefore they cannot be considered as *a priori*.

Kant failed to establish a general logical principle governing synthetic propositions as such, from which the particular cases can be deduced. Factual construction is the presentation of an object in intuition. It is a medium by which synthetic propositions can be recognized, but it is insufficient as a principle for the deduction of synthetic propositions. With regard to analytic propositions, the law of contradiction in logic is itself an analytic proposition as well as a general principle governing all such propositions. We lack such a general principle for synthetic propositions. The possibility of construction, to which Kant refers, does not provide us with such a principle; it provides only a method for the factual presentation of synthetic propositions.[3]

Furthermore, with regard to analytic propositions, we can assert *a priori* of an object that it necessarily has such-and-such predicates even prior to the cognition of the object and its qualities, since the relation of the predicates to the subject is determined by the law of contradiction. This law is valid for any and all objects. The same must be demanded for synthetic propositions. The real meaning of the question of the possibility of synthetic *a priori* propositions in mathematics is: How can the relation of the predicates to the subject be recognized as a necessary relation determined by the form of cognition as such and not merely by and through the definite objects given to us, or by the principle of the possibility of construction?

The Kantian answer to this question, that the necessity is derived from the possibility of construction, is insufficient, for by construction merely the factual reality of these propositions is established, not their logical necessity. The necessity of synthetic *a priori* propositions as such must be deduced from a general principle. In order to prove the

---

[3] *Logik*, pp. 413 ff.

necessary nature of such propositions in relation to the particular objects,critical philosophy must,first and foremost, answer the question, "How are synthetic *a priori* propositions as such possible?" before it considers such propositions in relation to particular and definite objects.[4]

In view of this, Maimon tried to discover a principle of deduction of synthetic propositions that would serve the same purpose as the law of contradiction. Just as the law of contradiction is an *a priori* principle governing all objects of thought as such – no object can be thought of in defiance of this law – the principle governing synthetic propositions should be an *a priori* condition of real objects. Maimon considers that he discovered such a principle in the principle of determinability, which determines the reality of objects of thought just as the law of contradiction determines the thinkability of objects. This principle aims at establishing a general logical form of cognition, from which synthetic *a priori* propositions can be derived. It also serves as a controlling agency, for only those propositions that comply with this form of cognition are necessary propositions. Those propositions, however, that cannot be derived from this principle are merely empirical and experiential, the certainty of which is subject to doubt.

Now the question, "How are synthetic *a priori* propositions in natural science possible?" receives a different treatment by Kant from the question concerning mathematical propositions. The meaning of the question is, on what basis do we employ synthetic *a priori* propositions in relation to empirical objects in general, without qualifying the objects? The Kantian answer is that the ground of reality of such propositions resides in the consideration of the possibility of experience. Experience is an undeniable fact, and empirical objects can be objects of possible experience only on the assumption of such propositions. Thus, for instance, the concept of causality, which states that when A is given, B must follow, is such a proposition, without the assumption of which experience would be impossible.

Now Maimon says: When we think of two particular objects A and B as standing in the relation of cause and effect, that is, A is the cause of B, it is not because all objects in general must be thought of as related in this particular fashion, for, in fact, only A and B and not A and C are thought of as being thus related. Nor is this relation derived empirically from the objects given to us in such a relation, for if this were the case, the proposition, would be a mere experiential propositon and could not claim general validity and necessity. We apply a general

4 *Ibid.*, p. 414.

a priori principle, such as causality, to these particular objects because experience is itself possible only under the assumption that a relation of cause and effect generally exists between the objects. Maimon's objection to Kant's principle of the possibility of experience consists in the realization of the schism dividing the general principle of causality and its application to definite, particular objects.

According to Kant, there is a clear distinction between the deduction of synthetic *a priori* propositions in mathematics and the deduction of such propositions in physical science. To be sure, both of them cannot be derived from the law of contradiction; the thought that a geometrical figure enclosing space could have only two lines does not involve us in any contradiction. We cannot, therefore, state *a priori* that the construction of such a figure is in principle impossible. We must rather attempt the construction of such a figure in order to convince ourselves of its impossibility. The possibility of construction is thus the ground for synthetic propositions in mathematics.

Likewise, the idea that fire is the cause of warmth is not the result of the consideration that its denial would involve us in a contradiction. The relation of causality obtaining between the objects of experience must be assumed, otherwise the succession of warmth upon fire would be a mere accidental perception, not a scientific experience. From the fact of experience, that is to say, from the assumption of the reality of scientific experience as grounded in general and necessary laws, Kant deduces synthetic propositions in natural science. Kant thus applies an analytic method, since the fact of scientific experience has to be assumed from which the synthetic propositions are deduced.

The Kantian principle of the "possibility of experience" is unthinkable without the assumption of the reality of scientific experience. The reality of experience as grounded in general and universally valid laws and principles has to be assumed prior to the deduction of these principles. This is an analytic process of thought, as the fact of experience is assumed from which the validity of the principles is deduced. This mode of thought cannot convince a skeptic who is doubtful about the very assumption of the reality of experience. The Kantian *Critique* has thus, in Maimon's view, jumbled together various doctrines (the deduction of synthetic propositions in mathematics and in natural science,) each having a different meaning. The Kantian solution of the problem cannot, therefore, satisfy the critical mind.[5]

Maimon's criticism of the Kantian deduction of synthetic *a priori*

[5] *Ibid.*, p. 417.

propositions is rooted in his monistic tendency, which manifests itself throughout his writings. Maimon searched for a general principle governing synthetic *a priori* propositions as such, while Kant made the deduction of such propositions dependent on the material of these propositions, employing a different method of deduction with reference to synthetic propositions in mathematics and with reference to such propositions in physical science. The dualism of Kant reveals itself in the division of forms of sensibility (Aesthetic) and concepts of thought (Analytic), in the distinction between noumena and phenomena, i.e., things-in-themselves and appearances, and in the distinction between the theoretical and the practical reason. And this dualism is to be detected in the Analytic itself, namely, in the various methods of deduction used by Kant for synthetic propositions in mathematics and for such propositions in physical science. Maimon's criticism of Kant is thus consistent with his monism in general. The same monistic tendency is revealed in Maimon's criticism of Kant's dialectics: instead of various ideas of reason, as proposed by Kant, Maimon posits one idea, namely, the idea of an infinite mind, from which all other ideas are to be deduced.

Kant comes under further criticism from Maimon for failing to give a criterion of cognition, i.e., thought in relation to real objects (*reales Denken*). The *Critique* defines cognition as the unification by a form of thought of a manifold material given through sensibility. It fails, however, to establish a criterion *a priori*, by which it is possible to distinguish one given manifold which can, from another manifold which cannot, be brought into unity and recognized by a certain form of thought. For not every manifold lends itself to objective unification in the form of a relation of subject and predicate. Thus, for instance, a rectilinear figure and three lines can be cognized and brought into a unity of thought in the form of an affirmative proposition, since the construction of a geometrical figure enclosed by three lines is a possible object. Likewise, a geometrical figure enclosed by two lines can be brought into a unity of thought in the form of a negation as an impossible object. But "figure" and "virtue" cannot be brought into any unity of thought, either in the form of affirmation or in the form of negation. It is meaningless to say of a figure that it is virtuous or that it is not virtuous. There must, therefore, be an *a priori* criterion by which we can distinguish a manifold lending itself to unification by a form of relation of subject and predicate from a manifold that cannot be brought into such a relation. Kant has failed to establish such a criterion of *real thought* (*reales Denken*); he did not even search for such a criterion, for he did not see the need for it.

Maimon sees the reason for Kant's failure in his method, which consists of "the complete and strict separation between general logic and transcendental philosophy, the former standing by itself and serving as a basis for the latter."[6] For Maimon, on the other hand, the laws of formal logic cannot be separately formulated without taking into consideration the capacity for cognition of objects of reality by the logical forms of thought. General logic, which deals with forms of thought, must be treated in conjunction with transcendental philosophy, the subject matter of which is the cognition of objects of reality by the forms of understanding. Only by analysis of the application of logical forms to real objects shall we be able to arrive at formal principles of thought. The logical forms have meaning and significance only when they are considered in their function of cognizing objects of reality.

Consequently, general logic does not precede transcendental philosophy, as Kant thinks, but, on the contrary, the latter must precede the former. This is what Maimon means by insisting that "the logic itself must be subjected to a critique of the capacity of cognition."[7] General logic deals with the mere forms of thought; the subject matter of transcendental philosophy is the possible cognition of real objects by the logical forms. Now, Kant treats the first separately and independently of the latter; he presupposes general logic as a basis of transcendental philosophy. Maimon, however, insists that general logic must be subjected to an investigation concerning its capacity for cognition of objects of reality; that is to say, only on the basis of, and in conjunction with, transcendental philosophy will it be possible to arrive at a formulation of the general logical forms.

Here, too, we see Maimon striving for greater unity of the various functions of thought. In his reversal of the relationship obtaining between general logic and transcendental philosophy, and in his conception that the logical forms should not be abstractly treated as entities *per se* but must be arrived at through an analysis of their application to the process of cognition of objects of reality, Maimon again reveals himself as the critical monist.

Every synthesis consists of a union of concepts. Since not all the possible concepts lend themselves to a process of unification – there are concepts that cannot possibly be brought into a unity – there must

6 *Ibid.*, p. 418.
7 *Ibid.*, p. 419.

be a law by which we can determine *a priori* the possibility, i.e., reality, or the impossibility of a synthesis. The possibility or the impossibility of a synthesis should not be derived from mere observation or analysis of the facts of experience but must be established by a principle determining the relation that exists between the concepts forming the synthesis. The determination of the possibility of a synthesis can be designates as an *a priori* determination, since it follows from the analysis of the relationship obtaining between the concepts constituting the unity.

Now, according to the principle of determinability, two or more concepts form a real unity only when the connection of the concepts follows a certain law and order. A synthesis defining an object is real only when the constituent concepts of the synthesis stand in a definite and unequivocal relation to each other. This occurs when one of the concepts can be thought of by itself, independently of the other, while the other concept cannot be thought of by itself but only in connection with the first. Thus, for instance, the concept of a right angle or of a rectangular triangle constitute real objects and not merely logical objects of thought, since the elements of synthesis follow the law governing the relation of the concepts constituting the synthesis. For the concept "angle" can be thought of by itself without its qualification as being "right," but the concept "right" (i.e., in relation to the angle) cannot be thought of by itself, independent of the concept "angle." Hence, "angle" is the determinable and "right" is its determinant. Likewise, a triangle can be thought of by itself, but rectangular cannot be thought of otherwise than as the determination of a triangle. Hence "triangle" is the determinable; "rectangular" is its determinant. While the determinable can be thought of by itself, the determinant can be thought of only in connection with the determinable. Not the intuition and the possibility of construction, as Kant maintains, but the principle of determinability is, according to Maimon, the principle of objectivity and of reality.

In connection with a possible source of the principle of determinability as formulated by Maimon, it has been suggested[8] that it appears to have its origin in the observation of a simple phenomenon that must have astonished the one who first came upon it. This phenomenon can be defined as the possible compatibility of predicates. Why can we, for instance, say, "A line is straight," but not "A line is sweet," or "A line

---

[8] Cf. Friedrich Kuntze, "Salomon Maimons theoretische Philosophie und ihr Ort in einem System des Kritizismus," *Logos*, III (1912), p. 286.

is black?" Or why can we say, "A triangle is rectangular," but not "A triangle is virtuous"? In each case an immediate sense of evidence compels the judgment as to which of the particular predicates is and which is not a permissible predicate of the respective subject.

It seems to me, however, that such an observation is insufficient to serve as a source of Maimon's logical principle. A psychological observation like this may do for ordinary experience, which is directed and determined by an immediate sense of evidence. But it does not suffice for transcendental philosophy, which is concerned with logical principles determing reality. We have, therefore, to search for an objective ground of this subjective phenomenon.

The origin of Maimon's principle of determinability cannot be the mere observation of a certain type of proposition, which our subjective mind determines as unpermissible. For the question would still remain, first, How did Maimon come to observe this phenomenon? and then, How did he come to consider it a philosophical problem of such importance and central significance? We must therefore search for the roots of this principle as a logical and philosophical idea, not in the realm of subjective experience and observation, but in the realm of logic and the history of thought.

As we follow this path, it becomes apparent that the origin of Maimon's principle of determinability is to be found in Maimonides. The principle as formulated by Maimon is, of course, not explicitly stated by Maimonides, but a critical analysis of Maimonides' thought leads to the idea involved in it. Maimon could not read an author without recreating the author's ideas and adding his own spirit to them. He always tried to penetrate into the depth of another system of thought, interpreting and assimilating it for his own purposes. The first part of Maimonides' *Guide for the Perplexed* is devoted to the investigation of the meaning of Biblical terms in their application to God. The purpose of this investigation is to prove that terms implying corporeality cannot be applied to God as an incorporeal being. These terms must be understood as homonyms. That is to say, these terms, employed with reference to God, have a meaning totally different from that which they have when applied to corporeal objects. The idea of the presence of homonymic terms in Scripture constitutes for Maimonides a key to the solution of certain central metaphysical and theological problems. The determining factor in the conception of a term as a homonym is the realization of the impossibility of applying a term implying corporeality to an incorporeal subject. Thus the logical question of the possible compatibility of predicates with the subject forms the heart and soul of Maimonides' doctrine of homonyms.

We can now translate this doctrine in the light of Maimon's principle of determinability thus: The corporeal terms, i.e., the predicates that cannot be attributed to an incorporeal subject, are predicates incompatible with the subject. These terms do not comply with the conditions required by the principle of determinability. The definition of the subject as incorporeal determines the incompatibility of the predicates with the subject. They do not stand in a relation of determinability to each other. Thus the idea that there are predicates which are incompatible with the subject was suggested to Maimon by Maimonides. This led Maimon to the realization of the need for a general logical principle determining *a priori* the compatibility or the incompatibility of the predicates with the subject.

Maimon's conception of infinite propositions as a separate class of logical judgments, which is closely bound up with the principle of determinability, was also suggested to him by some ideas of Maimonides, as we shall try to prove. This does not mean to say that Maimonides was fully aware of the concept of infinite judgments in the sense of Maimon's conception and formulation of it. But Maimonides' conception of the *via negativa* led Maimon to his idea of infinite judgments, which is one of important contributions to philosophy in general and to logic in particular.[9]

Every judgment, positive as well as negative, forms a unity of consciousness, for it establishes a definite relation between two concepts,

---

[9] Cf. Friedrich Wilhelm Joseph Von Schelling, *Sämtliche Werke,* Stuttgart und Augsburg, 1856, *Erster Band,* p. 221, who writes: "As far as I know, it was Maimon until now who specifically urged the distinction between the infinite judgment and positive and negative judgments." It is of interest to note the explanation and the examples that Schelling adduces to illustrate this distinction. According to him, the negative judgment merely takes the subject out of a definite sphere of reality, but it does not place it in another sphere. Thus, the negative judgment; "A circle is not rectangular," does not place the subject "circle" in another sphere of reality. The denial of rectangularity does not preclude the possibility of the circle being quintangular or multiangular. What Maimon calls the infinite judgment Schelling designates as a "thetic-negative" judgment. "Thetic" is derived from the Greek verb *tithemi,* which means to put, to posit. A "thetic-negative" judgment is thus a judgment which, in denying a predicate, places the subject in another sphere of reality. Such a judgment is not only negative; it also has a positive function. For instance, the judgment, "A circle is not sweet," not only denies the predicate "sweetness," but places the subject "circle" into another sphere of reality, where neither sweetness nor any other predicate of the same kind is applicable. In the negative judgment the negation is placed before the copula (A is–not B); in the thetic-negative judgment, which also has a positive function, the negation is placed before the predicate (A is not–B). Schelling's examples illustrating the distinction between infinite (thetic-negative) and negative judgments are similar to Maimon's.

that of the subject and that of the predicate. As infinite judgment implies a denial of any possible relationship between the subject and the predicate, it does not constitute a unity of consciousness. By unity of consciousness is to be understood unity of the manifold. The manifold can form a unity either positively (A is B) or negatively (A is not B). But the exclusion of B from A in the infinite judgment, "A line is not sweet," by which the incompatibility of the predicate with the subject is implied, does not constitute a manifold amenable to unification by an act of consciousness.

The negation of the predicate in the infinite judgment is not determined by the law of contradictions, as is the case with analytical propositions, for line and sweetness do not contradict each other. The elimination of the predicate as a possible determination of the subject does not result from the fact of other determinations of the subject, with which the attribution of the predicate would involve a contradiction. Its negation is also not the result of the impossibility of construction, as is the case with mathematical propositions, such as "There is no triangle in which the sum of the two sides equals the third." Thus neither the law of contradiction nor the impossibility of construction is the ground of the negation in the infinite judgment.

Infinite judgments are totally different from positive and negative judgments; they constitute, according to Maimon, "a class in itself" of propositions with an entirely different meaning. While the positive judgment attributes a definite predicate to a subject, and the negative judgment, conversely, withdraws a certain predicate from a subject, the infinite judgment implies that there is no possible relationship between the subject and the predicate, that is to say, there is no ground whatsoever in the subject either for the affirmation of the predicate or for its denial. The attribution of the predicate to the subject, as well as its denial, do not constitute a possible determination of the subject. For instance, such judgments as "Virtue is not triangular" or "A line is not sweet" are infinite judgments. Being triangular or not being triangular does not constitute a possible determination of virtue. The predicate "triangular" and its denial are possible determinations of space, which have nothing in common with virtue. Similarly, sweetness is not a possible determination of a line. Neither the predicate nor its denial is attributable to the subject.

The negation of the infinite judgment is *sui generis*. It is not a logical negation determined by the law of contradiction, neither is it a negation of construction as is, for example, a decahedron, the construction of which is impossible. The negation of the infinite judgment arises from the incompatibility of the predicate B with the subject A. That is to say, neither B nor its opposite, not-B, can be attributed to the subject. This kind of negation follows from the principle of determinability. It is just as impossible to say of the stone, it is blind, as it is to say, it is not blind (in the sense of an ordinary negative proposition). Both statements can be used only in the sense of an infinite judgment, that is, the predicate "blindness" is not compatible with the subject "stone"; the two do not stand in a relation of determinability with each other. Likewise, it is incongruous to say of virtue, it is rectangular or it is not rectangular.[10]

This very example (the stone does not see) seems to have been suggested to Maimon by Maimonides. The latter employed a similar one (the wall does not see) for the purpose of defining his doctrine of the negative attributes.[11] Maimon comments on this passage in Maimonides: "That is to say, the negation of the predicate is not only a negation of its reality but of its possibility." This is in harmony with Maimon's conception of the infinite judgment, that its negation is due to the incompatibility of the predicate with the subject.

The negation of the possibility of a predicate with reference to a certain subject means that the affirmation as well as the negation of the predicate is inapplicable. This is the case when the subject and the predicate do not stand in a relation of determinability with each other, which is the distinguishing mark of the infinite judgment. By his commentary on this passage in Maimonides' *Guide* Maimon has clearly shown the relationship of his principle of determinability to Maimonides' doctrine of the negative attributes as formulated and illustrated by the example, the wall does not see.

Narbonne[12] comments on this passage in the *Guide*: "You know from logic that there are two kinds of negatives. One is a particular negation, such as "Balaam does not see," and this is a true negation; the other is an absolute negation, i.e., a negation of a predicate with reference to a subject, the nature of which is not susceptible to such a predicate, as in the proposition, the wall does not see. This is a general or an absolute negation. A general negation thus means not the denial of a quality that naturally belongs to the subject, as 'seeing' with respect to a man, but the denial of its possibility. That is to say, the subject is not susceptible to a determination by such a predicate. Neither the

---

[10] *Kat. d. Arist.*, p. 236.

[11] *Guide for the Perplexed*, I, 58.

[12] Moses ben Joshua Narbonne, philosopher of the fourteenth century, wrote commentaries on various treatises of Averroes and on the "Guide" of Maimonides.

affirmation of the predicate nor its denial are compatible with, or applicable to, the subject."[13]

Narbonne goes on to say that by employing with reference to God propositions involving a particular negation, or by applying to God positive attributes with the understanding that they imply the negation of privation, it is intimated that God is in principle determinable by the predicates involved. For instance, the denial of impotence or ignorance with respect to God implies that God is determinable by the affirmation of omnipotence and omniscience. Maimonides therefore explains that we have to understand the negative attributes as general or absolute negations. In this sense the negative attributes can be applied to God. In other words, the general or absolute negation implies the impossibility of determining God by such predicates. Not only the affirmation of the predicate but its negation is denied in relation to God. The general or absolute negation, which is a denial of the possibility of the determination of a subject by a certain predicate, has a positive function. In it is implied the recognition of the incompatibility of the subject with the predicate. This is a positive statement. A new idea has accrued to our knowledge of the subject by the realization of its incompatibility with a certain predicate or attribute.

Now, the negation of the possibility of a predicate with reference to a subject because of their incompatibility is the very essence of Maimon's conception of the infinite judgment. Maimon was acquainted with Narbonne's commentary on the *Guide*. He quoted Narbonne in his own commentary on Maimonides and in his autobiography. The idea expressed by Narbonne lends itself to translation in terms of Maimon's concept of the infinite judgment. And in the light of Narbonne's interpretation of the passage quoted, we cannot dismiss the likelihood that Maimon received from the study of the *Guide* the impulse to his doctrine of the infinite judgment.

A distinction should be made between two kinds of negation: negation that follows from the law of contradiction and negation that follows from the incompatibility of the predicates with the subject. The first is a logical negation, which is analytically derived. A logical negation implies that the opposite of the negation can be predicated of the subject. The proposition, *A* is not *B*, means that the opposite of the negation is true. Thus from the proposition, a triangle can have no side which equals the sum of the other two sides, there follows necessarily

---

[13] Cf. *ibid.*, Narbonne's comment.

the non-equality of the one side with the other two sides. But the infinite judgment, such as, a triangle is not virtuous, does not imply that the opposite of the negation can properly be predicated of the subject.

The distinction between the two kinds of negation, i.e., particular and general, underlies Maimon's conception of the infinite judgment as a separate and distinct class of propositions. It seems, however, that Maimonides conceived of the second kind of negation as following from the law of contradiction, just as does the first kind of negation. This may be inferred from the context in which the example (a wall does not see) appears, as an illustration of the doctrine of negative attributes. That no positive attributes of God are possible follows analytically. Since God, by the very definition of the concept, is the all-perfect being, no composition and no limitation of His being is thinkable. Positive attributes would imply both, composition and limitation. Hence positive attributes must be ruled out.

But the negation of positive attributes is equally impossible. To say that God is not omniscient or not omnipotent contradicts the concept of God as an all-perfect being, just as does the proposition, God is omniscient and omnipotent. We can properly attempt a definition of the attributes of omniscience and of omnipotence only in terms of negation of privation, that is (to use the examples cited), God is not not-knowing, God is not not-omnipotent. Since the application of our conception of knowledge and omnipotence would imply a limitation with reference to God, we can speak of God only in terms of not not-knowing or not not-omnipotent. By negating the imperfections, a "nothingness" is attained in which the most perfect reality (*ens realissimum*) is grounded. For by the negation of not-knowing the attribution of knowledge as the human mind understands it is not implied. As our knowledge and the divine knowledge are essentially different from each other, knowledge as a positive attribute cannot be ascribed to God; only not-knowing can be denied as to Him. In this connection Maimonides refers to the possibility of denying, with reference to a subject, such predicates of which it is not susceptible, such as, a wall does not see. Thus, knowing as well as not knowing is denied as to God, for God has no relation to the kind of knowledge known to us, and the predicate is one to which the subject is not susceptible. But the negation of not-knowing as well as of knowledge follows analytically from the idea of God as the all-perfect being; it is thus determined by the law of contradiction.

This is well pointed out in Narbonne's statement, which shows that the distinction between a particular negation and a general negation is a gradual distinction. That is to say, both negations are of the same kind, except that the latter is more inclusive than the former. They are both grounded in the law of contradiction.

For Maimon, however, the infinite judgments constitute a class in itself. The difference between the infinite and the negative judgments is not a difference of degree but of essence. The root of Maimon's conception of the infinite judgment is in Maimonides' distinction between two kinds of negation. The conception, however, of the infinite judgment as a unique class and the role Maimon attributes to this kind of judgment is his own.

Furthermore, the following passage in the *Guide* of Maimonides, (I, 52), seems to have suggested to Maimon the idea that a synthetic proposition presupposes a certain relationship between subject and predicate as a necessary condition for the formulation of a synthesis. "There is no correlation between God and His creatures... As God has absolute (i.e. necessary) existence, while all other things have only possible existence, there cannot be any correlation between God and His creatures.... It is impossible to imagine a relation between intellect and sight, although the same kind of existence is common to both. But how could a relation be imagined between any creature and God, who has nothing in common with any other thing, for even the term existence is applied to Him and other things as a pure homonym (i.e., the term 'existence' applied to God means something totally different from its meaning with reference to other things).... When two things belong to different species there is no relation between them. We therefore do not say, this red compared with green, is more, or less, or equally intense, although they both belong to the same class-color. But when they belong to different *genera*, there is no relation whatsoever between them. Thus between a hundred cubits and the heat of pepper there is no relation whatsoever, the one being a quantity, the other a quality. Likewise, there is no relation between wisdom and sweetness, or between meekness and bitterness, although all of them belong to the class of quality. How, then, could there be any relation between God and any of His creatures, considering the essential difference between them in respect of true existence...."

This idea of Maimonides is explained by Maimon in his commentary (*Giv'at Hammoreh*, chaps. 56, p. 50b, and illustrated by the same examples which he employs in the formulation of the principle of determinability. He writes: a triangle is space enclosed by three lines, 'space' being the determinable, 'enclosed by three lines' being its determination. The former [which can be thought of by itself] is a general presentation, the latter [which cannot be thought of by itself] is its limitation. [The former is the subject, the latter is the predicate]. It is impossible to formulate a synthesis of the concept 'line' with that of sweetness; we cannot imagine a sweet line.... But we can imagine a straight line. Line is more general than straightness. We can think of a line in itself; hence it is the subject. Straightness, however, cannot be thought of by itself but only as a determination of a line; hence it is the predicate.

Maimon has here formulated the principle of determinability in connection with Maimonides' conception of God's existence as a totally different kind of existence, from which there follows the impossibility of any proposition implying a relation between God and other things. Maimon illustrates the requirement of a relationship between subject and predicate as a necessary condition for a synthetic proposition by the examples of a "sweet line" and a "straight line." There is no relationship between "sweetness" and "line". This is analogous to Maimonides' examples of a proposition connecting two concepts which are not related to one another, such as "intellect" and "sight", or "wisdom" and "sweetness". The similarity of the examples used by both Maimonides and Maimon amply demonstrates the dependence of the latter on the former.[14]

---

[14] Cf. Friedrich Kuntze, *Die Philosophie Salomon Maimons*, p. 293, who refers to Maimon's relation to Maimonides, the latter being the origin of Maimon's conception of the principle of determinability. Kuntze, however, does not state explicitly the source in Maimonides which may have suggested to Maimon the main idea implied in his principle. But the passage of Maimonides we quoted and Maimon's explanation thereof with the illustration by examples similar to those used by Maimonides clearly show the root of Maimon's principle to be in the *Guide* of Maimonides.

See also Curt Rosenblum, *Die Philosophie Salomon Maimons in seinem hebräischen Kommentar Gibath-Hammoreh des Maimonides*, Berlin, 1928, p. 13 f., who searches for a reference by Maimon to the principle of determinability in his commentary to Maimonides. Rosenbloom has overlooked the passage in Maimon's commentary to which we referred, in which not only the main idea of Maimon's principle is clearly expressed, but its relation to Maimonides is amply demonstrated.

CHAPTER IX

TIME AND SPACE

Rhetorical figures of speech are a common occurrence in language. We employ them consciously as such. There are also philosophical figures of speech, which can be recognized by analysis. By philosophical figures Maimon understands imaginary ideas or fictions that are represented by concepts, to which they do not adequately correspond, but which are applied only by virtue of an act of imagination. These concepts were originally formed with reference to objects for which they were adequate. They are real only in relation to the objects constituting their original domain; they are imaginary when abstracted from these objects and transferred to other objects by an act of the imagination. Philosophical figures differ from rhetorical figures merely in that their origin is more difficult to determine. It is the task of philosophy to demonstrate the illusory nature of the "fictional" character of these concepts by discovering their true origin.

The ideas of time and space as forms of sensibility are such philosophical figures. An analysis of the origin of the idea (*Vorstellung*) of space will show that it is closely associated with perception of the variety of objects. The idea of space presupposes the diversity and heterogeneity of objects and is predicated upon and closely connected with the perception of the variety and heterogeneity of objects. Space is not a quality inherent in things, as Kant conclusively proves against the dogmatic philosophers. Space is also not a transcendental form of intuition of external objects in general, as Kant proposes. According to Maimon, space is the transcendental form of the variety and diversity of objects. It is impossible for the human mind to imagine and to comprehend the variety of sensuous objects, differing from us and from each other, without imagining them at the same time as being in space beyond us and beyond each other. Space is thus the necessary and indispensable condition of the apprehension of a variety of objects. It is an illusion to consider space a separate entity, abstracted from the variety of objects with which it is necessarily associated, or as a pure transcendental form of intuition of external objects.

The idea of space is, in its origin, essentially the form of perception of the variety and diversity of sensuous objects. Since however the concept of space is not dependent on a particular variety of definite objects, but is related to the diversity of external objects in general, the human mind is inclined to conceive of it as independent of the variety of objects altogether. It is a known mode of the operation of the imagination that ideas that were originally bound up with certain objects are transferred to other objects, which stand in some relation to the former. By a further process of the imagination it is possible to detach the ideas from the objects altogether and to consider them as separate entities. Space, as the form of perception of the variety of objects, is closely bound up with the perception of the diversity of objects. But since we can legitimately abstract space from a particular variety of definite objects, we have, by an illusion of the imagination, abstracted it from the objects altogether. The idea of space abstracted from objects altogether is an illusionary idea or a philosophical figure, or, in the words of Maimon: "Space is originally the form of the variety and diversity of external objects. That is to say, it is impossible for the human mind, owing to its constitution, to comprehend and to imagine sensuous objects as differing from itself and from each other, without imagining them at the same time as being in space beyond the mind and beyond each other."[1]

The Kantian doctrine of space as a pure transcendental condition and form of the intuition of external objects as such is grounded in the conception of the originality of the idea of infinite space. As a matter of fact, Kant deduces the *a priori* transcendental character of space from the realization of the idea of infinite space as prior to the perception of partial spaces; the former is the necessary condition of the latter. Maimon, however, tries to prove that the origin of the idea of space resides in the perception of the diversity and the heterogeneity of sensuous objects; partial space is thus prior to the idea of infinite space. In maintaining that the idea of space abstracted from all objects and the idea of infinite space are imaginary ideas, Maimon deviates fundamentally from Kant.

From the concept of space as a form of thought of the variety and heterogeneity of objects, it follows that a unitary object can be conceived as being in space only because of its relation to other objects. For instance, a river as a unit is perceived as being in space owing to the mode of operation of our imagination. If there were no other sensuous objects besides the river, it would not be an object imaginable

[1] *Str.*, p. 261.

in space. Since, however, besides the river there exist objects on the bank which, because of their variety, are imagined in space, the imagination transfers the idea of space from them to the river itself. Hence we imagine the river not only as distinct from and outside of the objects on the banks, but we imagine that its homogeneous parts, because of their different relations to those various objects, are distinct from and outside of each other.

In the same manner, according to Maimon, time is the form of the diversity and heterogeneity of internal intuitions. It is not a pure form of intuition in general, as Kant states; it is the form of the variety of internal intuitions, just as space is the form of the variety of external objects. If there were no variety and diversity of the internal intuitions, there would have been no notion of temporal succession. Thus, time and space as forms of intuition are closely bound up with the perception of the variety of objects, internal as well as external. The forms of space and time originate in our consciousness with the consciousness of the variety and diversity of objects. Time and space may be considered the conditions indispensable for the perception of the variety of objects.

Here the opportunity is presented for Maimon to address himself to a problem, the solution of which is possible only on the basis of his doctrine of time and space as forms of intuition of the variety and diversity of objects. This is the problem of the possibility of a comparison between various notions and perceptions. Considering that various notions cannot be present simultaneously in one's consciousness and that every proposition about the relation of objects to each other presupposes an idea of each of them individually, the following problem arises: How is a comparison between different notions possible? That is, how can we logically account for a proposition concerning the difference between perceptions and notions? Let us consider the evident proposition that red is different from green. This presupposes the notions of red and green as separate entities. On the one hand, these notions preclude each other in the consciousness, as they cannot exist simultaneously; on the other hand, the proposition stating the difference between them refers to both of them simultaneously. Some psychologists try to explain the possibility of such a proposition by the traces left in the mind by the impressions of these objects. Yet this does not resolve the problem, since the traces of the impressions are just as difficult to imagine simultaneously as the notions themselves.

The problem can be solved on the basis of Maimon's doctrine of time and space as the forms of variety, for as such they are the conditions of the possibility of a comparison between the sensuous objects, i.e., the possibility of a proposition concerning the relation between the objects. The proposition about the difference between various impressions can be explained only with the help of the idea of temporal succession, that is, the form of variety with which the intuition of time is bound up. Succession in time is a unity of the manifold. The preceding point of time as such is different from the succeeding one. Two points in time, which are bound up with the internal intuitions, are not analytically the same, yet they are imagined together to constitute a synthetic unity. The idea of temporal succession is thus a necessary condition for the possibility of a proposition concerning the difference between various objects. Without temporal succession, a comparison between the various perceptions and notions cannot become an object of cognition. On the other hand, objective heterogeneity is a necessary condition for the possibility of temporal succession, since time is the form of the variety and heterogeneity of internal intuitions. Variety and temporal succession are thus in a mutually necessary relation to each other. "If red and green were not different in themselves we would not be in a position to imagine them in temporal succession. If, however, we had no idea of temporal succession, we could not recognize them as different and heterogeneous objects."[2]

The same relation obtains between the form of heterogeneity and diversity and the imagination of objects being apart-from-each-other in space. The latter cannot arise without the former, and the former cannot be recognized without the latter. Critical philosophy has, according to Maimon, not sufficiently defined the notions of time and space; it has determined neither the scope nor the limitations of these forms. According to critical philosophy, time is the form of the inner as well as the external intuitions, and space is the form of the external intuitions alone. From Maimon's deduction of these forms it follows that time and space are not the forms of inner and external intuitions, but rather the conditions for the propositions concerning the variety and heterogeneity of objects.

A synthesis of a manifold brought into a unity cannot be effected unless the elements of the synthesis are imagined separately and apart from each other. And when the synthesis refers to sensuous objects, the constituent elements of the synthesis must be thought of as being apart from one another in space. Synthesis thus presupposes the difference between and the variety of the objects synthesized. However,

[2] *Ibid.*, p. 264.

a manifold that is being comprehended into a unity can be imagined in a succession of time. Thus a synthesis of a substance with its concomitant accidents presupposes the accidents as being different and apart from one another. The concept of substance in itself, however, which implies duration of existence in time, in contradistinction to the accidents which are transitory, can be imagined through temporal succession. The concept of substance is a manifold brought into an analytic unity; it does not presuppose the elements synthesized as being apart from each other; it implies merely the continuous existence in time of a bearer of the transitory accidents; it can thus be imagined through temporal succession.[3]

The conception of the extension and divisibility of space *ad infinitum* is an imaginary idea, an illusion. Since the idea of space is bound up with the concept of the variety and heterogeniety of objects, space is real only with reference to the perception of objects of diverse experience. Infinite space, abstracted from all sensuous objects and conceived as an entity in itself, is not an object of experience and is therefore unreal. Limited space filled with objects is recognizable only because of the comprehension of the diverse objects. Hence, the concept of infinite, empty space is not a real concept, but a fiction of the imagination. Likewise, the concept of the endless divisibility of space can be understood only as a fiction. Endless divisibility is a possible concept only on the assumption that the idea of space is an entity in itself, i.e., a continuum. But on the basis of the conception of space as the form of the variety and diversity of objects, endless divisibility of space is not a real concept; it is, rather, like infinite space, a fiction of the imagination. According to Maimon, these imaginary ideas can also be defined as transcendental fictions of our imaginative faculty. These ideas, considered as real objects, are the result of an illusion. The same reasoning applies to the idea of the infinity of time and to the idea of the endless divisibility of time.

The conception of these ideas as fictions, however, does not in any way depreciate the value of mathematics, which employs these concepts with great success. As a matter of fact, Maimon, as we have noted, shows in another context the important place fictions occupy in science, and accordingly proposes that metaphysical concepts be considered fictions. The inquiry leading to the exposition of certain ideas as illusions, as in the case of infinity of space and time and their endless divisibility, does not detract from the scientific value of the branches of science that

[3] *Ibid.*

are based on these illusions. Its purpose is rather to enlarge the scope of philosophic investigation, to discover and bring to our consciousness the roots and sources of a certain category of notions, and to reveal the particular faculty of cognition in which these ideas are grounded.

Maimon maintains that it is the task of critical philosophy to expose the imaginary nature and the fictional character of certain concepts that dogmatic philosophy takes for real objects. This is also the case with the concept of the thing-in-itself, which, according to dogmatic philosophy, is a transcendent reality having an existence of its own, while, according to Maimon's conception of critical philosophy, it is a fiction of the imagination. Maimon thus compares the concepts of infinite extension and endless divisibility of space and time with that of a thing-in-itself. Just as he demonstrates by incisive analysis the dogmatic nature of the concept of a thing-in-itself as a transcendent reality behind the phenomenon, so he shows that the notion of the infinity of extension and of endless divisibility of time and space is not a concept of a real object; they are all illusions and figments of the imagination.

The same reasoning holds for the concept of absolute motion, which presupposes empty space. Empty space is not the immediate intuition of the form of sensibility, as Kant maintains; it is an imaginary idea derived by a process of abstraction. The concept of space as such is the form of the diversity of objects; it is directly conceived together with the diverse objects. By a process of abstraction, however, it is possible to imagine that if there were no objects in the world, space would nevertheless remain. This result rests on a peculiar illusion of our imaginative faculty. It follows from taking something that is not dependent on a particular condition for something not dependent on any condition whatsoever. Since the idea of space is not dependent on any particular diversity of objects, we are inclined to imagine that it is altogether independent of the diversity of objects. Space is an idea arrived at, not with the perception of certain definite objects, but with the perception of diverse objects in general (*überhaupt*). By an illusion of our imagination, however, we conceive the idea of space independently of sensuous objects altogether.[4]

According to Maimon's deduction of the concept of space, empty space is unreal, and no real concept can be had of it as an object. And since the concept of an absolute void is based on an illusion, absolute motion, which cannot take place except in an absolute void, is likewise

[4] *Ibid.*, pp. 266 f.

an illusion. All motion that becomes an object of cognition is relative. Absolute motion, like absolute empty space, is due to an interchange of the two meanings of the term "absolute" or unconditional: it may mean not being dependent on a particular condition, and it may imply not being dependent on any condition whatsoever. This imaginary idea is the result of a confusion of the two meanings of the term "unconditional."

As an illustration, let us consider the following: A boat moves from the coast into the sea. We ascribe absolute motion to the boat, while to the coast we ascribe merely relative motion. This is because the boat changes its place not only in relation to the coast but in relation to all other objects as well; the coast, however, changes its place in relation to the boat alone. But to maintain that the boat changes its place with regard to all objects is presumptuous, since we can have no knowledge of its relation to all objects. Thus all motion is relative, as it takes place only in relation to other objects. However, since the motion of an object is not dependent on its relation to particular objects, for in their stead we can imagine other objects, our imagination makes the leap from being independent of particular objects to being independent of objects altogether.

Thus, by an illusion of the imagination there arises the idea of absolute motion implying the idea of motion in empty space, as if it is independent of objects altogether. But the idea of absolute motion should actually mean the motion of an object in relation to "all" possible objects. Since the motion is independent of particular objects, it is imagined as changing its place in relation to "all" possible objects. But we can have no precise concept of locomotion except in relation to definite objects. Hence, the idea of absolute motion is a fiction of the imagination.

The capacity of the imagination is, in Maimon's view, an intermediate capacity between sensibility and understanding. Whereas through the faculty of sensibility we perceive sensuous qualities of objects without relating them to each other and without bringing them into an order of unity in our consciousness, through the capacity of understanding the sensuous qualities are related to one another and brought into unity of consciousness in accordance with certain rules and principles. The faculty of imagination, however, is the capacity to impart figurative force, sensuous significance, or an image to the relations of the understanding, thus giving them existential and objective import.

Time and space are such forms of the imaginative faculty, or two modes of perception by which sensuous objects are related to one another in externality; they are images of the variety and the differentiation of objects. Assuming that two sensuous objects are given to us, such as red and green. Our understanding relates them to each other under the form of differentiation and thinks of them as different from each other, without thinking of their relation to each other in space or time. Our understanding conceives of their difference in the same manner as it thinks of the difference between two mathematical figures, such as a triangle and a circle. The two objects form a unity in our consciousness, as our mind thinks of both of them simultaneously. This unity, however, is merely subjective, as it is an immanent process confined to consciousness. It acquires objective import by relating the unity to external objects. This can be attained only through the operation of the faculty of the imagination, presenting the objects as existing at different places, one outside the other in space, or as occurring at different points in time. By this process the form of differentiation acquires a sensuous signification or an objective image and presentation. This process of objectivization is grounded, on the one hand, in the form of understanding (differentiation and heterogeneity) and, on the other hand, in the sensuous objects themselves in relation to which the forms of the understanding are applied.[5] The operations of the imagination are thus partly grounded in the sensuous capacity and partly in the capacity of the understanding.

While the law of identity, like its counterpart the law of contradiction, is the *conditio sine qua non* of thought in general and the basis of all analytic propositions, the form of differentiation and diversity is the necessary and universal transcendental *form* of all real thought (*reales Denken*). Objects must first be generally thought of as diverse and different before the particular kind of diversity and difference can be determined.

The necessary conditions of all real thought, i.e., objects thought of as real, are thus the "given" objects, the forms of understanding and the capacity of the imagination. Without the given material, to which a form of the understanding is applied a consciousness of the form cannot be obtained. Without a form of understanding, the given material is chaotic, and the faculty of the imagination cannot give it an objective image. And without the given material and the imagination, the understanding can apply the form of diversity only to objects that are the products of the mind, such as mathematical objects; it cannot apply

---

[5] *Philos. Wört.*, pp. 14 f.

the form of diversity to objects of reality, which cannot be produced by the mind.[6]

Maimon's statement, that the "given" objects are a necessary condition for the thinking of objects as real, should not be understood as a reference to objects as things-in-themselves given to consciousness. The thing-in-itself as a *noumenon* underlying the *phenomena* of experience is an incongruous concept in a critical system of thought. The "given" should not be considered the effect on our sensibility of a thing-in-itself, for the reason that since the relation of cause and effect is subject to the *schema* or form of time, and time is a subjective constitutive form of consciousness, the concept of causality cannot be applied to a transcendent thing-in-itself outside consciousness. By the "given" is meant, therefore, not the effects of a thing-in-itself on our sensibility, but those immanent elements of consciousness with reference to an object, of which neither the cause nor the manner of their generation is known to us. In other words, those elements of our consciousness concerning an object of which we have no clear and distinct conception, i.e., the irrational elements of consciousness, are to be designated as the "given" object. Hence, Maimon's reference to the "given" objects must be understood as referring to those phenomenal aspects of the objects that are not categorized and synthesized into a unity of consciousness. In this sense the given objects, combined with the form of the understanding (diversity) and the faculty of the imagination, are the necessary conditions for the apprehension of objects as real.

If all sensuous objects were homogeneous, we would have no concept of diversity, which is the form of time and space. We have the capacity to imagine a homogeneous, sensuous object in space only through its relation to other different objects. The imagination of something that is enduring in time is likewise possible only because of its relation to other objects and occurrences in time. For time and space are the forms or modes of perception of the relation of objects to one another; they are the images of the variety and the discreteness of objects.

It may seem, at first thought, that in Maimon's doctrine of time and space there is implied a conception of a reality as a heterogeneous manifold, for the form of diversity as a form of understanding, which is the mode of time and space, must correspond to the material, sensuous world, otherwise, the application of this form to reality could not be accounted for. One may be led to such a conception by Maimon's

[6] *Ibid.*, p. 16.

words: "If all sensuous objects were indistinguishable and indiscernible, we would have no concept of differentiation, and consequently we could not obtain an image of sensuous objects, nor would we have an idea of time and space, which are the forms of differentiation and discernibility."[7]

Heinrich Rickert, a modern Neo-Kantian philosopher, has also defined reality as a heterogeneous continuum. "We can define reality," he writes, "as a heterogeneous continuum in contradistinction to the abstract, unreal homogeneous continuum of mathematics."[8] Since it is impossible for the human mind fully and completely to portray the discrete, heterogeneous continuum of reality, Rickert holds that the task of science is either to transform reality into a homogeneous continuum or into a heterogeneous differentiation or discretion. While the former is the method of the natural sciences, the latter is the method of the historical disciplines.

The natural sciences based on mathematics strive to master reality through the transformation of the inexhaustible manifold reality into a series of general and universal concepts embracing a variety of objects. They try conceptually to conquer reality by the establishment of unity and order. This can be accomplished only by the establishment of general laws and concepts, ignoring the endless variety of the individual characteristics of the objects. On the other hand, historical and humanistic disciplines aim to describe the individual phenomena; their purpose is to bring into relief the singular features of the phenomena rather than the general and universal laws and concepts. The historical sciences divide and cut into segments the continuous historical flow of events for the purpose of emphasizing their heterogeneity and their individual characteristics. While natural sciences search for the general as a unifying principle and ignore the heterogeneous, the historical sciences emphasize the heterogeneous and ignore the general.[9]

It seems to me, however, that in Rickert's definition of reality as a heterogeneous continuum there is implied a metaphysical assumption of a thing-in-itself as having a definite nature. In a critical system of thought consistently developed there can be no place for an idea of a transcendent reality of a definite nature existing in itself outside con-

---

[7] *Ibid.*

[8] Cf. *Grenzen der Naturwissenschaftlichen Begriffsbildung*, 4th edition, Tübingen 1921, p. 28.

[9] Cf. Rickert, *Kulturwissenschaft und Naturwissenschaft*, 2nd ed., Tübingen, 1910, pp. 32 f.

sciousness. The thing-in-itself can be understood only as a problem, an unknown X, which is fundamentally different from Rickert's definition of it as a heterogeneous continuum. Even the conception of reality as a heterogeneous continuum is impossible without concepts of thought. A heterogeneous continuum should not, therefore, be posited as a transcendent reality, separated and abstracted from thought and existing by itself outside consciousness.

Maimon, however, in accordance with his conception of the thing-in-itself and with his conception of the "given" in an immanent sense as those irrational elements of our consciousness whose generation is unknown to us, also conceives of the manifold of reality and the differentiation of the objects as "given" to us in a purely immanent manner. That is, the perception of the variety of objects is due to the form of differentiation, which is a form of thought.

There is a striking similarity between Maimon's conception of time and space as the forms of diversity and heterogeneity of internal and external intuitions and Schopenhauer's conception of time and space as forms of the individualization of objects of reality. Of Kant's twelve categories, Schopenhauer considers the category of causality as the only determining principle in our comprehension of the phenomena. The forms of sensibility, time and space, and the form of the understanding, causality, are not to be separated from each other. All together, according to Schopenhauer, determine our conception of the appearances of reality. The individual objects of the spatio-temporal world are distinguished from one another by their place in space and their position in time. Space and time are thus for Schopenhauer the principles of individuation, resembling Maimon's designation of space and time as the forms of the diversity and heterogeneity of objects. Both of them agree that time and space are not pure forms of intuition in general, as Kant proposes. While for Kant time and space as forms of pure sensibility constitute an area of consciousness separate from the realm of understanding, for Maimon time and space are closely bound up with the perception of the various objects, internal as well as external, and for Schopenhauer time and space together with the form of causality constitute the forms by which the comprehension of the individual objects of the phenomenal world is achieved. Thus, for Maimon as well as Schopenhauer, time and space are tied up with the conception of the various individual objects of reality.

In view of the agreement between some aspects of their conception of the forms of time and space, the possibility that Maimon had a direct influence on Schopenhauer is not excluded. As a matter of fact, Schopenhauer knew of Maimon's works and had the opportunity to become acquainted with at least the main trends of his thought. Friedrich Kuntze[10] reproduces evidence showing that Schopenhauer owned one of Maimon's main works, *Versuch einer neuen Logik*. Schopenhauer took as a motto for his *Parerga* the Latin phrase, *Vitam impendere vero*, which Maimon had used for his *Philosophisches Wörterbuch*.

Despite the similarity of their conceptions of the forms of time and space and of their criticisms of some doctrines of Kant, Schopenhauer and Maimon come to entirely different conclusions. Schopenhauer's departure from Kant results in the construction of a metaphysics of the will that is the complete opposite of the critical idealist position. Maimon, on the other hand, remains within the boundaries of critical thought, even though he embraces some metaphysical ideas. For him the forms of diversity are immanent forms of consciousness, as the "given" is not the result of an effect of a thing-in-itself. Through time and space, as forms of diversity, we perceive the objects of reality, for phenomena constitute the only reality known to us, there being no *noumena* behind them; we have no idea of the *noumena* to make any conjectures about them.

[11] See *Die Philosophie Salomon Maimons*, p. 499. See also Wilhelm Gwinner, *Schopenhauers Leben* (2nd ed., 1878), p. 112, where a letter of Schopenhauer to the library of the University of Jena is reproduced. A list of books requested by Schopenhauer for consultation includes Maimon's *Versuch über die Transcendentalphilosophie*. All this suggests the likelihood of Maimon's direct influence on Schopenhauer.

CHAPTER X

ANTINOMIES

i

Maimon lived in an intellectual climate totally different from that of Maimonides; his philosophical interests, therefore, revolved around a different center. Yet many aspects of his thought can be traced to the influence of the twelfth-century philosopher. In his philosophy of language and in his ethics the impress of Maimonides is particularly manifest. It is my prupose to discuss here Maimon's treatment of the problem of antinomies, his interpretation and criticism of Maimonides, and to trace his relationship to the latter in his criticism of Kant's approach to this problem, as well as in his own solution of it.

Maimon recognizes the influence that Maimonides exerted on the shaping of his thought.[1] He speaks of three periods, corresponding to three phases in his life, during which he was under the spell of three philosophers.[2] He calls these phases revolutionary periods, for they represent sudden and intense changes in his thinking. From Maimonides he learned to distinguish between literal and figurative forms of speech. We can trace the path from the differentiation between the various forms of speech to the distinction between the different modes of knowing, that is, between perception and cognition, between a lower and a higher form of knowledge, between a posteriori and a priori judgments. The world of thought is more extensive and much wider than the domain of language. Hence we oftentimes employ the same terms, such as knowledge and cognition, to designate essentially different kinds of knowledge. Moreover, Maimon's distinction between different kinds of negation, that is, between negative and infinite forms of judgment, has its root in Maimonides' philosophy of language.[2a]

Of the pre-Kantian philosophers, the first that Maimon had occasion to study was Christian Wolff. From him he learned the formal, logical distinction between confused and clear and distinct concepts. This knowledge led to an urge to redefine and re-examine the concepts he had accumulated, in accordance with the new requirements.

[1] *Lebensgeschichte*, II, p. 3.
[2] See "Salomon Maimons Geschichte seiner philosophischen Autorschaft in Dialogen, aus seinen hinterlassenen Papieren," *Neues Museum der Philosophie und Literatur*, hrsg. von Friedrich Bouterwek (1804), Teil I, p. 137.
[2a] See Maimonides, *Guide for the Perplexed*, part I. See above, p. 163. f.

In the final stage, he learned from Kant to distinguish between merely formal and real thought. The former is governed by the laws of logic, the laws of identity and contradiction, but the reality of objects cannot be determined by it.

In this chapter we have set ourselves the task of presenting, first, Maimon's conception of Maimonides' treatment of the problem of creation, which was for both Kant and Maimon an antinomy of human reason; second, Maimon's criticism of Kant's treatment of the antinomies, and, finally, Maimon's own conception of the antinomies, especially that of creation.

In his exposition of the philosophy of Maimonides, Maimon presents Maimonides' arguments against the Aristotelian proofs of the non-creation of the world. These proofs are based on the process of becoming as it is experienced in nature, which is always the coming into existence out of some previous reality. Maimonides concedes that all becoming in the world is not a becoming out of nothing, but it is nevertheless wrong to draw conclusions as to the origin of the world as a whole from the process of becoming exemplified in nature. The creation of the world *ex nihilo* cannot be refuted on the basis of our knowledge of nature, i.e., experience, in which there can be no coming into existence from absolute non-existence, since the origin of the world is beyond the limits of given nature and transcends the sphere of experiential knowledge.[3] Maimon then states Maimonides' further thought thus: "Should Aristotle or his followers argue against us, writes Maimonides, since we hold that the properties of the universe as it exists at present prove nothing as regards its creation, how could you prove the creation of the world out of nothing? To this our answer is, this is not our intention at all. We desire merely to show that this problem cannot be solved on the basis of natural experience. The creation of the world out of nothing is at least problematically possible; this is what we intend to prove."[4] The basis for his thought is in the *Guide*, II, 17, where Maimonides clearly says that *now* his intention is not to prove creation, but merely to demonstrate its possibility; later on, however, he proposes to prove creation.[5] Maimon, however, ignores the word "now," which he does not render at all; and then he renders the original phrase referring to the "possibility" of creation (i.e., of the world) as stating that creation is "problematically" possible.

[3] Maimon, *Lebensgeschichte*, II, 94 ff.
[4] *Ibid.*, pp. 97 f.
[5] Maimonides, *Guide*, II, 19, 22.

Maimon's method of presenting Maimonides' thought is revealed by Maimon's following remark: "The thinking reader who is acquainted with modern philosophy will recognize some similarity between Maimonides' arguments against Aristotle and Kant's refutation of dogmatic philosophy. Kant proves that the dogmatic philosophers are not entitled to argue from the nature of the world as a phenomenon to the nature of the world as a thing-in-itself. In the same manner Maimonides argues that Aristotle is not entitled to conclude from the nature of the world as it is in actual existence as to the nature of the origin of the world as a whole."[6] Maimon thus interprets Maimonides' arguments against the Aristotelians in the spirit of the critical philosophy of Kant, namely, that the problem of the creation of the world is an antinomy, that is to say, it cannot in principle be solved on the basis of arguments derived from the experience of the process of becoming in the world.

There was a time when the writer understood Maimonides' arguments against the Aristotelians in much the same way that Maimon does, without knowing of Maimon's interpretation.[7] On further consideration, however, we must recognize that a whole world divides the arguments of Maimonides from the Kantian method. For while Maimonides tries merely to show that a given set of arguments for non-creation is not conclusive, the critical method of Kant points out the impossibility in principle of employing natural phenomena as appearances in order to arrive at conclusions with respect to the nature of the world as a thing-in-itself. Whereas Maimonides' refutation of the Aristotelian proofs is merely a factual one, i.e, it demonstrates that the existing proofs are not conclusive, the Kantian refutation of metaphysics is, on the other hand, systematically based on the principle that metaphysical problems, such as creation *ex nihilo* and the existence of God, cannot be solved by means of a method whose validity is confined to the realm of experience. In other words, antinomies, such as the problem of creation, are a manifestation of the fundamental limitation of human reason. Maimonides, in his criticism of the Aristotelian arguments for non-creation, does not employ the method of critical thought. The similarity

[6] *Lebensgeschichte*, II, p. 98.
[7] Cf. my essay, "The Philosophy of Maimonides and Its Systematic Place in the History of Philosophy," *Philosophy, The Journal of the British Institute of Philosophy* (January, 1936), p. 64: "In this problem of *creatio ex nihilo*, Maimonides follows a course similar to the critical method of Kant. He does not try to prove the creation of the world in opposition to Aristotle. He tries only to disprove the eternity of the world. He has transferred the problem of *creatio ex nihilo* from the sphere of theoretical knowledge to the sphere of faith, of practical ethics..."

between Kant and Maimonides is, therefore, illusory and misleading.

In this connection it is of interest to note Maimon's fundamental distinction between different kinds of skepticism. He maintains that there are two kinds of skepticism, one negative and the other positive.[8] The first arises when two opposing views lack cogent and conclusive proofs. The second arises when two opposing propositions have equally valid arguments in their favor. The first implies a recognition of ignorance with reference to the material of the proposition; the second is the result of an equilibrium between two opposing views, as is the case, for instance, with the antinomies of pure reason, where the thesis and the antithesis are supported by equally valid arguments.

In the light of this distinction of Maimon's, as applied to the problem of creation, it would seem that Maimonides' treatment of the arguments against creation leads to a skepticism of the first kind, i.e., a negative skepticism, while the result of Kant's treatment of the problem leads to a positive skepticism. This distinction follows from the consideration that Maimonides, in trying to show the inconclusiveness of the argument for non-creation, merely refers to a matter of fact, while the Kantian position is, rather, that metaphysical problems concerning the thing-in-itself cannot, in principle, be solved by means of reason, which is the very definition of antinomy. The distinction between the two kinds of skepticism amounts, as it were, to the difference between contingent and necessary truth. Whereas Maimonides' refutation of the Aristotelian arguments leads to a negative skepticism and to a contingent, factual truth, the Kantian conception of the problem of creation as an antinomy involves a positive skepticism and a necessary truth.

Maimon, however, seems to have understood Maimonides as not merely rejecting a certain group of arguments, but as proving that, in principle, it is impossible to establish the eternity of the world on the basis of becoming as it is experienced in existing nature, thus treating Maimonides' refutation of the arguments for non-creation as implying an antinomy. He seems to have overlooked the fundamental difference between refuting certain arguments and maintaining that the problem of creation is, in principle, insoluble.

There is, however, another passage in the *Guide*, in which Maimonides comes nearer to the conception of the problem of creation as an antinomy. Maimonides was critical of the Muslim theologians, who tried to prove the existence of God on the basis of the creation of the world, and he rejected their method of making the thesis of the creation of the world

---

[8] *Philos. Wört.*, p. 217.

the premise from which to derive the existence of God as the creator. He writes: "For it is well known to all clear and correct thinkers who do not wish to deceive themselves that this question, namely, whether the universe was created or is eternal, cannot be measured with absolute certainty; here human intellect must pause." The thesis of the creation of the world should not, therefore, be taken as a necessary premise for proving the existence of God.

Maimon interprets the phrase "the intellect must pause" (*Maamad Sichli*) in the *Guide* as *Stillstand des Verstandes wegen Vorurteile.*[9] The expression *Stillstand des Verstandes* would seem to imply that Maimon intends to emphasize the impossibility in principle of attaining a final solution to the metaphysical problem of creation, i.e., whether the world had a beginning in time or has existed eternally. On the other hand, the expression, *wegen Vorurteile*, because of prejudices, would seem rather to imply that the reason for not having found a solution to this metaphysical problem is historically conditioned. It is because of certain prejudices, which are as a matter of fact historically given, that man has been unable to solve this problem. Or perhaps the prejudices to which Maimon here refers are to be understood in a more fundamental and basic sense. Not merely the historically given prejudices of men at a certain period in the development of human thought, but the prejudices inherent in man are meant. This latter interpretation is possible in view of the fact that man's thought in general is related to experience by its very constitution, and it is therefore impossible in principle for man to transcend the limits of experience.

Maimon leaves us in the dark as to his exact meaning. However, from his remark on Maimonides' theory of creation we gather that he interprets Maimonides in the critical spirit, i.e., he holds that the metaphysical problem of creation cannot in principle be solved because of the limitations inherent in human reason and because of the impossibility of the human mind to transcend the realm of experience.

In another context[10] Maimon views Maimonides' thought as stating that the problem of creation *cannot* be decided one way or the other by means of rational proofs. In support of this conception he quotes the Kantian distinction between the world as appearance and the world as a thing-in-itself. With regard to the latter, creation as well as non-creation can equally be proved, and the problem is, therefore, an antinomy.

---

[9] *Com. on the Guide*, p. 74b.
[10] *Lebensgeschichte*, II, 88.

The following considerations, however, make it legitimate to interpret Maimonides in the critical sense, that the problem of creation is an antinomy and not merely a statement of the historical fact that up to the present the problem of creation has not been solved. The expression Maimonides employs with reference to the problem of creation, that it is *Maamad Sichli*, i.e., "the human intellect must pause" (in Arabic, *Mukaf Akkal*), seems to imply that creation is a problem that is beyond the limits of our rational capacity.[11]

On the other hand, Maimonides continues to show the preposterousness of the Kalam method by pointing to the fact that for thousands of years philosophers have debated whether the world was created or has existed eternally and have not reached a final and decisive answer to this problem. The state of the problem is thus the result or the manifestation of the historical fact that no solution to it has been finally established. If this is the correct meaning of the phrase "the human intellect must pause," it is still not an antinomy in the Kantian sense, the very essence of which consists of the argument that our thought and logic have validity only with reference to objects of experience, and metaphysical problems, which are beyond the realm of experience, cannot in principle be solved by means of logic.

However, if we take into consideration the Scholastic spirit of Maimonides, to which the concept of the progress of human thought was unknown, then it must be said that any problem that has not been solved until now will never be solved. The very essence of Scholasticism consists of the investigation of the literary sources of the great minds of the past on the assumption that the human mind has, as it were, exhausted itself; no fundamentally new truths can be discovered. The only purpose of philosophical investigation is to understand and expound the truths presented exhaustively by the great minds of the past. Consequently, any problem that has not been solved till now – for which I would suggest the designation "historical antinomy" – acquires the status of a fundamental and systematic antinomy, for a problem that has not been solved by the philosophers of the past has no chance

---

[11] The phrase concerning the problematic nature of the question of creation is expressed in the original Arabic in the passive imperfect. Ibn Tibbon, however, renders it by the active imperfect, implying that the philosophers cannot answer this question with certainty. He has caught the right spirit of the original by translating it in this way. Furthermore, the Arabic expression *mukaf akkal*, translated as *maamad sichli* in Hebrew, meaning that the human intellect must pause here, is similarly translated by Munk, *Le Guide des égarés*, I, 347: "C'est un point où l'intelligence s'arrête." This statement implies the impossibility of a solution of this problem, that is, a solution on the basis of logical reasoning.

of being solved in the future. Even assuming that Maimonides' intention was merely to establish a historical antinomy on the basis of the historical situation of the problem, we can say that in view of the Scholastic spirit of his thought, a historical antinomy attains the validity and dignity of a systematic and fundamental antinomy. Maimon is thus correct in interpreting Maimonides' refutation of the Aristotelian arguments in the spirit of the Kantian concept of antinomies.

Maimonides is not satisfied with a mere refutation of the Aristotelian arguments; he produces an argument of his own for the creation of the world from the heavenly bodies. If the existence of the world, Maimonides argues, is to be fully explained on the basis of natural and necessary laws, as the Aristotelians maintain, the order of all phenomena will have to be deduced from these necessary and permanent laws. But while the phenomena of the sublunary world are sufficiently explained according to the laws of cause and effect, the movements of the heavenly bodies, the differences in their velocity and direction, cannot be logically derived from these laws. We must, therefore, assume that all superlunar phenomena are the result of design rather than of the necessity of the permanent laws of nature. Unless we assume the existence of design, it is impossible to find a sufficient cause that determines the number of stars and their respective orbits, the various distances between them, and their individual motions. According to the theory of creation, however, all these can easily be explained. For we say that there is a Supreme Being who determined the direction and velocity of each sphere and has endowed each of them with its peculiar properties.[12]

Maimon adduces this proof by Maimonides and adds the following modifying remark: "With this Maimonides intended to weaken the Aristotelian conception of the necessity and eternity of the world."[13] Thus Maimon holds that Maimonides does not consider it a definite proof but merely an attempt to weaken the Aristotelian arguments. He then offers the following comment: "I must note here that Maimonides' objection to the opinion of Aristotle is based on a fallacy. The world may be definite or indefinite in point of time, i.e., it may have a beginning in time or not. In any event, all phenomena resulting from the highest wisdom must be explainable on the basis of the law of sufficient reason. This is a requirement of reason. How far we can go with the process of rationalization is quite irrelevant. What Maimonides

---

[12] *Guide*, II, 19.
[13] *Lebensgeschichte*, II, 98.

considered inexplicable in view of the state of astronomy in his time may well be explained on the basis of the new discoveries and especially in accordance with the natural system of Newton. The concept of the highest order of law in the constitution of the world is a necessary idea of reason which, in the application of our understanding with regard to the objects of experience, we can constantly and steadily approach, but never fully attain. For there will always remain phenomena that we shall not be in a position to deduce rationally, even though we have to assume that the phenomena are subject to the general laws prevailing in nature... Even in Newton's system there are gaps. For there are unsolved problems which cannot be explained according to the laws of general attraction. They suggest, therefore, the necessity of discovering natural laws of a higher order and of greater generality, to which the unexplained phenomena as well as the laws of attraction are subordinated and by which a greater unity is established. But it is fallacious, on the basis of the *argumentum ad ignorantiam*, to argue either for or against the creation of the world."[14]

In order that the validity of Maimon's criticism of Maimonides may be appreciated, we shall demonstrate the role that an exception to a natural law may play in contributing to the discovery of new scientific phenomena. Whenever an exception to a natural law is encountered, it may turn out to be illusory rather than real. The following example, famous in the history of science, will illustrate the point. The astronomer Bessel doubted the validity of the Newtonian law of gravitation because of the observed irregularity of the course of Uranus. It was then discovered that these irregularities are due to another planet (Neptune), the existence of which had been previously unknown. The astronomer Leverrier deduced the existence of Neptune, prior to its discovery through direct observation, on the basis of the Newtonian law of gravitation and the irregularities of the course followed by Uranus. Thus the observed "irregularities" of the path of Uranus not only did not refute the law of gravitation but, on the contrary, proved to be a confirmation of the law of gravitation, with the help of which the existence of another planet was deduced and the correct explanation of the "irregular" course of Uranus was discovered. Thus, when we encounter exceptions to a natural law, when we experience phenomena that cannot be explained in accordance with the natural laws known to us, the problem always arises as to how they are to be interpreted,

---

[14] *Ibid.*, pp. 103 ff. The translation is mine.

for what appears at first as an exception to a law may in the course of time prove to be a confirmation of the law or a stimulus for a discovery of new laws.

No exception may be considered final by the finite, limited mind; each must be dealt with as a mere problem. Therefore no exception to a natural law as conceived by man is to be treated as proof of the existence of design in nature and of the creation of the world by God. Only to the infinite mind, which encompasses infinity, can there be, in principle, real exceptions to a law. On the other hand, the infinite mind may be in possession of a system of natural laws by which all phenomena without exception are explained. Moreover, the very idea of the infinite mind implies an absolute and ideal reason in relation to which there is absolute identity of thought and reality, and all reality is deducible from its thought. It is, therefore, not permissible to assume exceptions to laws conceived by the infinite mind. Even though real exceptions to a law are in principle possible only in relation to an unlimited mind, which embraces infinity, the very idea of the infinite mind, out of whose thought all reality is deducible, does not permit the assumption of the reality of exceptions. It is self-contradictory to assume the reality of exceptions to laws conceived by the infinite mind. In relation to a restricted, finite mind, however, all exceptions to laws should not be taken as definite and real, but must be treated merely as problems posed by reality for further investigation. Thus Maimon's criticism of Maimonides' argument for creation is bound up with his critical concept of the world as an endless task and with his fundamental distinction between a finite and infinite reason.

This basic distinction, which is pivotal in Maimon's system of thought, can be interpreted in a methodical and critical sense. The idea of the infinite reason, as introduced by Maimon, can be understood, not as a dogmatic assumption of a reality existing in itself, but as an idea, a method by which the limitations of the finite, limited human mind are brought into relief. Just as the Kantian concept of an *intellectus archetypus* does not imply a positive and dogmatic assertion of the reality of such an intellect, but merely an idea introduced for the purpose of describing the limitations of the human mind, so Maimon's idea of the infinite reason can perhaps be interpreted in the same way. But we have already shown that this is not so. Maimon seems to have thought of the idea of the infinite mind as having ontological status.

Maimon introduces the idea of the infinite mind through epistemological considerations. In the present context it is of importance to note the bearing of the distinction between a finite and an infinite reason on the problem of antinomies in general and on the method of the interpretation of an exception to a natural law. According to Maimon, it is not permissible, on the basis of phenomena that cannot be explained in accordance with the existing system of laws, to conclude the existence of design in the universe and consequently the creation of the cosmos. Since the limited human mind is always in the middle of the road in its striving for unity, those phenomena that cannot be deduced from natural laws are to be considered solely as tasks and as stimuli for further investigation.[15] Maimon's criticism of Maimonides' proof of the creation of the world corresponds with his conception of miracle and his criticism of dogmatic theology, which is based on miracles. "To the extent that revealed religion is based on miracles," Maimon writes, "its validity can be doubted. For even though the fact of miracles as such may be verified and they are not subject to doubt, yet it is not excluded that they may be explained by natural laws unknown to us. A miracle is a phenomenon that cannot be explained by natural laws as known to us, but since our knowledge of nature and of its laws is limited, we are not entitled to declare an occurrence to be a miracle, for it is possible that at a later date a law will be discovered by which the occurrence will be explained."[16] Thus, with respect to a phenomenon that we are unable fully to explain, we are entitled to declare only that it is a problem for our limited, finite mind.

Only the infinite mind, to which all laws – present, past, and future – are known, may state that an extraordinary occurrence is a miracle. Just as a miraculous occurrence should be considered merely a problem, so a natural phenomenon that cannot be deduced from the present system of natural laws should not be taken as proof of the existence of design, but rather as a problem for further investigation.

For Maimonides, however, as well as for all scholastics for whom the system of laws prevailing in nature and known to us has the character of finality, an exception to the natural law is not apparent and temporary, but real and final. Consequently, in their view, we are entitled, on the basis of such inexplicable phenomena, to assume the existence of design and the creation of the world by a Supreme Being, who for some purpose has endowed the individual heavenly bodies with their singular and particular characteristics. Thus Maimonides' proof

---

[15] As Maimon points out: "The world in its totality as the result of the highest wisdom must be explainable according to the law of sufficient reason." *Lebensgeschichte*, II, 103.
[16] *Philos. Wört.*, p. 218.

of creation as well as Maimon's criticism are to be viewed in the light of their general outlook and as integral parts of their respective systems of thought.

ii

The antinomies of Kant are the creation and non-creation of the world; the existence and non-existence of simple substance; freedom and absolute causality; and the existence and non-existence of an absolutely necessary being. Whenever we not only employ principles of understanding for the purpose of comprehending objects of experience, but venture to extend these principles beyond the realm of experience, we involve ourselves in the dialectical difficulty that both the positive assertion and its negation can be confirmed by rational methods. The positive assertion in the realm of metaphysics (thesis) is free from contradiction, and one may find a rational basis for its necessity in the very nature of reason, but its negation (antithesis) can be equally maintained and proved on grounds just as valid and convincing. Positive assertions concerning metaphysical objects, such as the creation of the world, the existence of simple substance, freedom and God (the theses), are, according to Kant, transcendental ideas and the results of a process of thought that posits an absolute, unconditional principle for the conditional judgment. The idea of the world as a whole expresses the full and complete series of the conditions of a given phenomenon. In each particular phenomenon a conditioned magnitude, a conditioned matter, a conditioned effect, and a dependent reality are given. Consequently, the cosmological idea demands the complete series of the conditions of a particular given phenomenon. Since there are various kinds of logical propositions – categorical, hypothetical, and disjunctive – it follows that there are necessarily corresponding ideas, which are categories embracing totality: absolute subject, absolute cause, and totality of the world. In the forms of logical conclusions lies the root of the antinomies. i.e, the conflict of reason with itself.

Maimon extends the sphere of ideas and the scope of antinomies and thus demonstrates that they require a much more general solution than that offered by Kant. According to Maimon, antinomies are to be found not only in metaphysics, but also in physics as well as in mathematics. This fact proves that antinomies are not merely the result of certain logical forms of judgment, but express an inherent quality of human thought as such. This consists in that our reason can be considered under two aspects, first, as an absolute reason, not limited by sensibility and its laws, and second, as our own limited and restricted understanding, subject to the laws governing sensibility.

The theory of infinity in mathematics and infinite objects in physics necessarily involve us in antinomies. The complete series of all natural numbers is not an object of intuition and perception, but an idea through which continuous progress into infinity is considered an object. We involve ourselves in a conflict by considering something an object that can never be such. The solution of this antinomy consists in the following: We cannot possibly produce an infinite series except through an infinite succession in time, for our perception is bound up with the form of time. And since an infinite succession in time can never be fully completed, an infinite series can never be produced as an object. An infinite reason, however, which is not restricted by forms of sensibility, can conceive an infinite series at one stroke without a process extended in time. What is thus for understanding in its restricted, limited form a mere idea is for the absolute reason a real object.[17] We have here a clear illustration of Maimon's concept of the infinite reason as an explanation of the thinking process of man. Our thinking can be considered under the aspect of an absolute, unlimited reason owing to the fact that it is part of the infinite mind. And just as, in relation to the infinitesimals and with reference to the problem of *quid juris*, the idea of the infinite reason explains the process of human thought and its relation to real objects,[18] so the problem of antinomies is solved by Maimon with the help of the idea of an infinite, absolute mind, of which the human mind is a part.

The idea of an infinite reason, which plays such a prominent role in Maimon's philosophy, we have traced to the influence of Maimonides. For the present discussion we will recall Maimon's exposition of Maimonides' idea: "There are two distinct modes of thought; one is a process from *a priori* to *a posteriori*, and the other is a process from *a posteriori* to *a priori*. This distinction is valid only with respect to a finite reason, such as the human intellect, for which the existing objects are given and are not the result of its own thought, i.e., the concepts revolve around the real objects. But with respect to the infinite reason, the distinction between these two processes of thought has no meaning,

---

[17] Cf. *Tr.*, p. 228: "Daher ist das, was der Verstand seiner Einschränkung nach, als blosse Idee betrachtet, seiner absoluten Existenz nach ein reelles Objekt." The expression "seiner absoluten Existenz nach" refers to the infinite mind of which the human mind is a part.

[18] Cf. *ibid.*, pp. 27 ff., 64 ff., and *Com. on the Guide*, end of the preface.

as there can be no objects given to it, and the real objects must be the product of its thought. Consequently, the thinking of infinite reason can only be *a priori.*"[19]

Now, an intellect can conceive of itself or the universals that constitute the essence of reality, but it cannot comprehend existents, for they are not rational. Infinite reason can thus conceive of a limited intellect by imagining itself in a finite manner, i.e., by a process of limitation with regard to its own infinite reason it arrives at a finite reason. Likewise, a finite reason can imagine infinite reason by a process of the negation of its own limitations. "Finite reason and the infinite reason are thus of the same kind; they differ only in degree."[19a]

The relation between the finite and the infinite Logos and the method of arriving at one from the other can be thought about in two ways. In one the process is from the finite to the infinite Logos by the method of abstracting the limitations of the finite human mind. Through the intensification of a predicate of the human domain, such as the rational faculty, and by raising it to an absolute dimension, we attain the idea of an infinite reason. This is the *via eminentiae.* The other way leads from the infinite Logos to the finite by the method of restrictions, that is, by imagining the infinite Logos as restricting itself to the level of the limited human mind. This is the *via restrictionis.*

Maimon has elaborated and reformulated an idea taken from Maimonides, which has its roots in Aristotle. Artisotle conceived the idea of the resemblance between the divine *nous* as pure *Energeia,* and the human *nous* as restricted by necessary suppositions, such as sensibility; there is a unity of the *nous poietikos* and the human perception. Though the human mind is conditioned by sense data, it can attain the level of the *nous poietikos* by the method of abstraction.

Maimonides' conception of a resemblance between the finite and infinite Logos should be understood in the sense of *analogia mentis,* that is to say, the finite and the infinite mind are neither of the same kind nor entirely different. The term "mind," in connection with the finite and infinite Logos, is neither univocal nor equivocal. Each of the two alternatives involves far-reaching implications. The supposition that they are identical in essence, differing only in degree, is dogmatic. This is the position of speculative idealism, which was expounded by Hegel. The supposition that they are entirely different must lead to agnosticism and to the denial of the possibility that man may have any

---

[19] *Com. on the Guide,* p. 9b.
[19a] *Ibid.*

idea of divine attributes and that the idea of God has a function in our life. Maimonides was aware of the difficulties implied in the unequivocal assumption of any of the two alternatives. He therefore developed a doctrine of a kind of *analogia mentis*, according to which the relation between the finite and infinite Logos is to be understood neither as identical nor as entirely different in essence. While he proposed the resemblance between them with a view to expounding the possibility of man's comprehending the forms of being and the ethical attributes of God in a positive manner, he demonstrated the essential difference between them by denying the possibility of positive attributes with regard to the essence of God and by pointing out the impossibility of man's comprehending the infinite Logos. Maimon, however, here emphasizes the resemblance between the finite and infinite Logos as being of the same kind, differing only in degree.

But let us return to our original exposition. Maimon writes that the human mind is in a position either to substitute objects for ideas or, conversely, to dissolve objects into ideas. This is the case with infinite convergent series. We are in a position to find their exact numerical value; on the other hand, definite numbers can be converted into an infinite series.[20]

There are ideas, however, that continuously approach the objects but can never reach them, and therefore the objects can never be substituted for the ideas. This is the case with irrational roots. Through infinite series (according to the binomial theorem) we are able to approach the objects, but their definite value can never be ascertained. We have here an antinomy, since reason, on the one hand, prescribes the rule by which definite numbers must be found, and, on the other hand, proves the impossibility of accomplishing the task. These are examples of antinomies in mathematics.[21]

In addition to the mathematical antinomies, we encounter antinomies in physics; the concept of motion, especially, leads to a conflict of reason with itself. This antinomy arises as a result of the relativity of motion. The motion of a body is the change in its place in relation to another body in space. This relation between objects is merely a subjective idea, which should not be attributed to the objects as such. Consequently, motion, which concerns the relation between objects, should not be attributed to one object more than to another. In order that this subjective idea of the relation between objects may attain objective

[20] *Tr.*, pp. 227 ff.
[21] *Ibid.*

validity, we must ascribe to object *a* another motion, apart from the change in its relation to object *b*, which is reciprocal. We maintain that object *a* is in motion and not *b*, because *a* has changed its relation not only with regard to *b*, nut also with regard to *c*, while *b* has changed its relation only with regard to *a* and not with reference to *c*. But since the relation between *a* and *c* is in its turn also reciprocal, we are not entitled to ascribe motion to object *a* more than to object *c*. Moreover, the relational, subjective character of motion has not been eliminated by introducing a third object *c*, but merely shifted from *a b* to *a c*. We shall have to introduce another body *d*, in relation to which *a* changes its place and not *c*, and so *ad infinitum*. We are thus unable to ascribe motion to object *a* without thinking of its relation to an infinity of objects, which is impossible to accomplish. Yet reason demands (for the purpose of experience) the assumption of absolute motion. We have here an antinomy; we unjustifiably ascribe absolute motion to an object, whereas motion is merely a subjective, relational concept.

Another antinomy is, according to Maimon, the idea of the actual existence of the infinitely small. When a wheel revolves on its axis, all its parts move at one and the same time. We can imagine the wheel as consisting of an infinite number of circles. The nearer a circle is to its center, the slower is its motion, since it covers less space than the wider circles. It follows that there is in nature, as an actual reality, an infinitely small motion, a motion that is *omni dabili minor*. We have here an antinomy, for an infinitely small motion must be thought of as a reality, whereas it cannot be thought of as an object of experience. Maimon then deals with the problem of the motion of a circle. It will suffice for us here to refer only to his conclusion, namely, that we must assume the reality of the infinitely small magnitude, not merely as a mathematical infinity, i.e., the possibility of division *ad infinitum*, but as an actually existing infinity, as the constitutive element of finite magnitudes. Here arises an antinomy, for, on the one hand, reason demands that the process of the division of a definite magnitude never stop, so that we can never arrive at an infinitely small element, but on the other hand, there are cases in which we must assume the reality of such an element.

It follows from all the examples cited that the infinite, in relation to our capacity for producing it, is a mere idea. Nevertheless, the infinite is to a certain extent an actual reality. These antinomies require a solution just as the Kantian antinomies did, and they cannot be solved by the Kantian method. For Kant's solution refers to antinomies re-

stricted to the metaphysical realm and does not apply to antinomies in
the realm of physics. By positing the idea of an infinite reason, Maimon
claims that his approach to the problem of antinomies and its solution
is more inclusive. He conceives of our capacity of comprehension as
having two aspects: a limited understanding bound by the laws of
sensibility, and a reason sharing in an unlimited absolute reason that
is capable of conceiving objects beyond the realm of sensibility and the
laws to which it is subject and of transforming relational subjective
concepts, as in the case of absolute motion. Thus Maimon's solution
of the problem of antinomies is closely connected with this concept of an
infinite reason, of which the human reason is a part.

It is of interest to note that in another connection[22] Maimon speaks
of absolute motion as a fiction of the human imagination, a term
that he applies also to the concept of infinity, while here Maimon proves
on the basis of these concepts the antinomical character of human
thinking. To my mind, this proves that Maimon understood by fiction,
not a conscious falsehood, but ideas of reason that are the product of
the imagination. In the fictions as well as in the ideas there is manifest the infinite character of human thought and imagination.[23]

Maimon's treatment of the problem of antinomies in his *Kritische
Untersuchungen über den menschlichen Geist*[24] must be interpreted in the
same way, namely, that antinomies are the result of different aspects
of human thinking. He deals with transcendental antinomies, not as a
separate phenomenon, but in close connection with mathematical
antinomies, for in both is manifest the same characteristic of the human
mind. The thesis and the antithesis have their roots in a different emphasis: While the first stresses the actual cognition of an object, the
second emphasizes the mere process of the thinkability of an object.
The thesis is bound up with sensibility and its laws; the antithesis is the
result of the imaginative faculty of the human mind, which is capable
of transcending the realm of sensibility. Herein lies the reason for
Maimon's parallel treatment of transcendental antinomies and mathematical antinomies.

As the forms of intuition, i.e., space and time, are the basis of
mathematics, Maimon prefaces the problem of antinomies in general
with the observation that time and space as intuitions, as dealt with in

---

[22] *Str.*, pp. 226 f. Cf. also *Anfangsgründe der Newtonischen Philosophie von Dr.
Pemberton* (Berlin, 1793). Vorrede von S. Maimon.
[23] As a matter of fact, Maimon defines the metaphysical ideas as fictions. See, for
instance, *Str.*, p. 30; *Logik*, p. 206.
[24] Pp. 221 ff.

mathematics, can be obtained only through a process of thinking *ad infinitum*. Time and space, as concepts of succession and of the discreteness of objects, cannot be conceived in themselves but are bound up with the perceived objects.

The mathematicians, however, who think of time and space as divisible and capable of being extended *ad infinitum*, deal with the forms of space and time as produced by the imagination, which conceives these forms as entities in themselves, not as relational concepts bound up with the perceived objects. They thus presuppose time and space as consisting of infinite series of simple elements, i.e., mathematical points.

The transcendental antinomies, placed parallel to the mathematical ones, are dealt with by Maimon after the mathematical antinomies.[25] There are four mathematical antinomies. The first concerns the problem of whether or not a given number or magnitude presupposes an element, a unit, as the beginning of its synthesis, for every given number or magnitude is nothing other than an aggregation of such units. The former cannot exist without the latter. The antithesis asserts that every given number or magnitude has no beginning for its synthesis but can be divided as well as increased endlessly. Since every number can be increased as well as decreased endlessly, every given unit is subject to the process of further increase or decrease.

The solution of this antinomy consists in the following: The term "unit" is used in the thesis and in the antithesis in two totally different senses. The antithesis speaks of an arbitrarily taken unit, which can be recognized as a magnitude in intuition, while the thesis speaks of an absolute unit, which cannot be recognized in intuition but merely thought of as a concept.

The same reasoning applies to the second antinomy, which concerns the problem of divisibility. The thesis maintains that through the process of the division of a given magnitude we arrive at a magnitude that is smaller than any other given magnitude. The antithesis argues that each given magnitude consists in turn of smaller magnitudes which likewise can be divided. It is, therefore, impossible through the process of division to arrive at a final magnitude. Here, too, the solution of the antinomy lies in the different meanings of the term "magnitude" as used in the thesis and in the antithesis. The thesis understands magnitude in an absolute sense (as *omni dabili minus*), which can only be thought of but not given as an object of intuition. The antithesis,

---

[25] See *Krit. Unt.*, pp. 223–230.

however, understands magnitude as an object of cognition and intuition (i.e., as *quovis dato minus*); consequently, no final magnitude can be obtained. We can think of the smallest magnitude, but we cannot construct it in intuition, for every magnitude constructed by our intuition may be subject to still further division.

The third antinomy deals with the problem of the greatest number. The thesis maintains that in the series of possible numbers, which begins with one and increases by one, there can be no greatest number. Assuming that N is the greatest of all possible numbers, we can still add to it some of the others, or all of them, so that the sum total will be greater than N. Therefore, N cannot be the greatest of all possible numbers. The antithesis maintains that in the series of all possible numbers there must be one which is the greatest. If we assume that there is no greatest number, then it will be possible to find a greater number than any given number. There must, therefore, be a number which is greater than a given N, and since N stands for any possible given number, there must be a number which is the greatest of all possible numbers. Here, too, the solution is to be found in the distinction between the "given" and the "thought." Any number that can be constructed cannot be the greatest; the greatest number can only be thought. In other words, the antithesis speaks of the construction of the greatest possible number as *quovis dato majus*, which can never be attained. The greatest number as a concept can be thought of only as *omni dabili majus*.

The fourth antinomy concerns the concept of a curved line. The thesis maintains that a curved line, as an object of geometry, cannot consist of indivisible parts or points. The antithesis claims the opposite, namely, that a curved line consists of points. The solution of this antinomy lies in the same distinction between the "given" and the "thought" as that above. A curved line is an object of geometry only when conceived as a geometrical place. For the construction of this object only a number of points are definitely given. The other points are merely "thought" and added for the purpose of making this object a single whole, which the concept of a geometrical place presupposes.

Just as Maimon proposed the mathematical antinomies for the purpose of demonstrating a larger scope for the problem of philosophical paradox, so he introduced two transcendental antinomies of his own.

The thesis of the first of Maimon's antinomies maintains that succession of phenomena one upon the other presupposes the concept of time, and their separation from one another presupposes the concept of space. Since succession means the conception of phenomena occurring at different points in time, and separation from one another means the conception of the objects situated at different places in space, time and space must, therefore, be presupposed. The antithesis maintains the opposite: Time and space presuppose succession and separation from one another, respectively. Time and space are *quanta*, for they imply a manifold of similar parts. It is possible to conceive this manifold of similar parts as being at different points in time and at different places in space; consequently, time and space presuppose succession and discreteness.

Maimon's second antinomy concerns the concept of line. The thesis maintains that the concept of line presupposes the idea of space. Since a line is space determined through a concept, line and space are related to each other as the determination and the determinable. The antithesis maintains the opposite, that the idea of space presupposes the concept of line. For if space were the determinable, it would be more general than line, its determination. The features of space must then also be attributed to line. The fact, however, is that the three dimensions are attributed to space rather than to line.

The solution of the transcendental antinomies lies in the following. The succession of objects and their discreteness can be directly perceived with the objects. Time and space, however, as continuous and infinite entities, can be imagined indirectly only by conceiving a continuity and endlessness of objects. Thus, transcendental antinomies, like mathematical antinomies, have their root in the distinction between empirical knowledge and abstract or reflective thought. Space and time, as mere ideas of thought, are the conditions of the possible discreteness of objects as well as their succession one after another, and they are considered as such in the thesis. The thinkability of time and space is presupposed in the conception of objects. However, as directly conceived and recognized objects of cognition, time and space are conditioned by the discreteness of the objects; as the antithesis maintains, they are cognizable only through and with the objects.

This solution of the problem of antinomies applies as well to the mathematical antinomies of Kant,[26] of which Maimon cites only the first as an example. The proposition that the world has a beginning in time means that the series of the past successive situations of the world

---

[26] Kant designates the first two antinomies as mathematical, as distinguished from the last two, which he labels dynamical. While the mathematical transcendental ideas synthesize the homogeneous, the dynamical may connect the heterogeneous. Cf. *Critique od Pure Reason. The Transcendental Dialectic*, Book II.

and consequently also the past time, which is recognizable through these situations, are both finite. This proposition, however, is not quite correct. One should say rather: The world has a beginning *with* time, not *in* time, for "in time" implies time prior to the world, but time as such, abstracted from the object, is not an object of cognition.

Here, too, Maimon follows Maimonides, who speaks of time as an accident of motion. Maimonides writes: "Time also belongs to the created things... Therefore, in the proposition: God was prior to the existence of the world, the term 'was,' which is a temporal determination, and also the assumption of God existing an endless time prior to the existence of the world are to be understood in an imaginary sense. It is not real time but fictional time."[27]

The antithesis maintains the opposite. The world has no beginning in time. Here time and space are considered as concepts of thought, and as such they can be thought of as endless, for to every number of given situations more can be added. The proposition that the world has no beginning in time means that the given series of past situations of the world may be finite, but our thought may add an infinite number of possible situations to the series. Time as the condition of these possible situations is also infinite, since we think here of time and space as conditions, not of given intuitions, but of all possible intuitions.

The solution of the problem of antinomies takes on another form with Maimon in his *Philosophisches Wörterbuch*.[28] There he states that there are two functions of the faculty of the imagination. One is apprehension, which aims at the immediate perception of the world of objects; the other is association, which grants to the imagination the faculty of extending the application of its concepts, such as causality, to objects beyond the limits of the objective world. The first and second antinomies of Kant are to be solved thus: While the thesis one-sidedly emphasizes the rightness and the limited force of the function of apprehension, the antithesis emphatically defends the legitimacy of the function of association and recognizes the capacity of the faculty of imagination to break out of the limits of experience.

There is, however, no essential difference between Maimon's treatment of the problem of antinomies in his *Wörterbuch* and the manner in which

---

[27] Cf. *Guide*, II, 13. Cf. also Maimon's *Autobiography*, English transl. by J. Clark Murray (1888), p. 104: "As little could I conceive that, before the world had been created, a time had passed, as I knew from the *Moreh Nebochim*, that time is a modification of the world, and consequently cannot be thought without it."

[28] Pp. 18 f.; cf. Hugo Bergmann, *Ha-philosophia shel Shlomo Maimon* (Hebrew) (Jerusalem, 1932), pp. 154 f.

he deals with it in other works. The two functions of imagination, apprehension and association, actually correspond to the distinction between empirical experience and abstract thinking, or between cognition and pure thought. While the function of apprehension encompasses the realm of experience, the function of association is capable of transcending the sphere of empirical knowledge and of embracing the realm of thought. Through association the human mind applies the categories of understanding to mere objects of thought. The function of apprehension, which is applied only to objects of possible experience, corresponds to that aspect of the human mind which is limited by the bounds of sensibility; the function of association corresponds to that aspect of the human mind which is part of infinite reason.Both functions are thus manifestations of the two aspects of human thought: the limited, restricted understanding within the boundaries prescribed by the laws of sensibility, and the infinite reason, which is not subject to the laws governing the sensuous world.

In his *Logik*[29] Maimon subjects the arguments of Kantian dialectics to a detailed analysis and criticism. Since Kant ascribes to reason the conception of the totality of the application of the forms of understanding, reason is led into a conflict with itself. But surely, objects Maimon, it must be an "unreasonable" (*unvernünftige*) reason if it can become involved in a conflict with itself.

Kant's first antinomy is this: The thesis maintains that the world has a beginning in time and is also limited as regards space. "If we assume that the world has no beginning in time, then up to every given moment an eternity has elapsed, and there has passed away in the world an infinite series of successive states of things. Now, the infinity of a series consists in the fact that it can never be completed through successive synthesis. It thus follows that it is impossible for an infinite world-series to have passed away and that a beginning of the world is therefore a necessary condition of the world's existence."[30]

Maimon's objection to this argument is that Kant here employed the ambiguous terms "elapsed" (*abgelaufen*) and "passed away" (*verflossen*) without clearly defining their exact meaning. "Elapsed" and "passed away" do not have the same connotation as the past; their relation to each other is that of the species to the genus. The past merely implies direction of time, which can be indirectly perceived in intuition as distinct from the opposite direction in the future as well as from the

[29] Pp. 200 ff.
[30] See *Critique of Pure Reason*, English transl. by Smith, p. 397.

present, which is the connecting link between the two opposite directions. We distinguish the past from the present and from the future without considering it a definite magnitude. While the term "past" implies direction solely, the expression "passed away" implies a definite magnitude. When we say that time has "passed away," we imply not only the direction it has taken, but that a definite and distinct amount of time has gone, which must have a beginning and an end. Thus, when we assume that the world has no beginning in time (thesis), we are not entitled to state that up to any particular point in time an eternity has "elapsed" and "passed away," since the passing away of time implies a definite amount of time, which must have a beginning. Kant thus substituted for a concept of direction a concept of quantity. Further, Kant says that the infinity of a series consists in that it can never be completed through successive synthesis. But how can we begin such a successive synthesis in order to demonstrate that it can never be completed? We cannot start it from the beginning, since we assume now that the world has no beginning. We must therefore start this successive synthesis from the present and proceed backward into the past. We shall find, then, that we cannot complete it, and this is contrary to the thesis. And how do we disprove the antithesis? If we project past time into the future, and proceed to make the successive synthesis from the present point of time continue into the future, we can never complete it, which proves rather the antithesis, that the world has no beginning.

Furthermore, Kant presupposes the concept of infinite time in the concept of an infinite series, and vice versa. The concept of an infinite series is such that it can never be completed through a successive synthesis. This "never" means only that the successive synthesis cannot be completed in a finite but only in an infinite time.[31]

The antithesis maintains that the world has no beginning. Let us assume that it has a beginning. Since the beginning of a thing means the coming into existence of something that is preceded by a time in which the thing was not, there must have been a preceding time in which the world was not. i.e, an empty time. Now, the coming into being of a thing is impossible in an empty time, because no part of such a time, as compared with any other, possesses a distinguishing condition

---

[31] Cf. *Logik*, pp. 213 f. The same critique of the arguments of the thesis is made by Bertrand Russell, who writes: "When Kant says that an infinite series can 'never' be completed by successive synthesis, all that he has even conceivably a right to say is that it cannot be completed in a finite time. Thus what he really proves is, at most, that, if the world has no beginning, it must have existed for an infinite time." B. Russell, *Our Knowledge of the External World*, p. 171.

of existence rather than of non-existence; and this is true whether the thing is supposed to arise of itself or through some cause. Many series of things can, indeed, begin in the world; but the world itself cannot have a beginning and is therefore infinite in relation to past time.[32]

Here Maimon objects to Kant's definition of the term "beginning" as the starting of existence, prior to which there was an empty time in which the thing (world) was not in existence. This definition is arbitrary and too narrow, since it does not fit the beginning of time and all that begins simultaneously with time. Kant in his argument assumes that time is infinite. Maimon, however, considers time as bound up with reality as a form of succession. Empty time as such has no reality but is the result of an act of the transcendent capacity of the imagination. Before the existence of the world there was no time either. The expression "before," designating a temporal determination, does not in our case actually refer to a reality of time but to an imaginary idea, such as the square root of -a in algebra ($\sqrt{-a}$).

In this Maimon follows Maimonides, who adopts the Aristotelian concept of time as an accident of motion, and therefore emphasizes the impossibility of applying the concept of eternity to the existence of God. Eternity is a temporal determination, and as such it can apply only to objects which are subject to motion. Of God we can say only that he is timeless or supratemporal, but not that He is eternal. Therefore, the term "first" (*Rishon*) applied to God belongs to the negative attributes and implies merely a denial of causality. Although Maimon does not follow Maimonides in the particular concept of time as an accident of motion, nevertheless, for Maimon, too, time is bound up with objects, since it is the form of the succession of objects following one after another.[33]

"Beginning of existence" is, therefore, according to Maimon, to be defined, not as existence prior to which an empty time has passed, but rather quite independently of the notion of empty time. "Beginning" is a point in time that is the last in the synthesis going backward from any given point of the existence of an object, so that, by forming a synthesis of the past and all its situations from any given point of time of the existence of the world, we shall arrive at a point at which this synthesis will be completed.

In the second antinomy, the thesis maintains that every composite substance in the world is made up of simple parts and that nothing

[32] *Critique of Pure Reason*, p. 397.
[33] Cf. above, note 27.

exists anywhere save the simple or what is composed of the simple. The antithesis asserts the opposite: No composite thing is made up of simple parts, and nowhere in the world does anything simple exist. "Assume that a composite thing (as substance) is made up of simple parts. Since all external relation, and therefore all composition of substances, is possible only in space, a space must be made up of as many parts as are contained in the composite that occupies it. Space, however, is not made up of simple parts, but of spaces. Every part of the composite must therefore occupy a space. But the absolutely first parts of every composite are simple. The simple, therefore, occupies a space. Now, since everything real, which occupies a space, contains in itself a manifold of constituents external to one another and is therefore composite; and since a real composite is not made up of accidents (for accidents could not exist outside one another, in the absence of substance) but of substances, it follows that the simple would be a composite of substances, which is self-contradictory."[34]

Maimon maintains that we are justified in stating merely that the existence of the absolutely simple cannot be deduced from experience and that the absolutely simple is a mere idea, the objective reality of which can never be presented in any possible experience. The antithesis implies, however, that since an absolutely simple object can never be given in any possible experience and the realm of perception and intuitions constitutes the totality of all possible experience, there can be nowhere a composite made up of simple parts. This part of the antithesis maintains much more than we are entitled to, for we cannot, just from the unawareness of such an object, make an inference as to its impossibility. For while the first part of the antithesis states only that no composite object of experience is made up of single parts, and the simple cannot be presented in intuition, the second part of the antithesis goes much further in asserting that nowhere in the world does anything simple exist. This should have been deduced not from the concept of a given object in intuition, i.e., the concept as a matter of experience, but on the basis of its relation to any object of possible experience in general.[35]

The whole antithesis is rooted in the concept of space as an infinite continuum, as the imagination conceives it. According to Maimon, however, space is not the form of intuition and sensibility, as Kant taught, but rather the form of the discreteness and variety of sensibility.

[34] *Critique of Pure Reason*, p. 403.
[35] Cf. *Logik*, pp. 217 f.

Therefore, the objects that fill space may consist of simple elements, which correspond to the simple parts of extension, and the simple parts of space correspond to the simple elements of the objects occupying it. Since the simple parts of space correspond to the simple elements, which are not conceived in their variety and discreteness, they are not necessarily spaces, as Kant maintains.

The first part of the antithesis, that no composite is made up of simple parts, is thus also not conclusively proved. The argument of the antithesis is bound up with the Kantian concept of space as a form of intuition, but it has no validity in the basis of Maimon's concept of space.

The space of the mathematicians is an endless continuum, as the faculty of the imagination conceives it. Mathematics is not concerned with the question of the origin of the idea of space. This is the task of transcendental philosophy, which is not concerned with space as such, but with the relation of space to the objects occupying it. Space in the transcendental sense is the form of the variety and discreteness of sensibility, and therefore it is not an endless continuum; there is discreteness in matter, not in endless continuum. There are as many parts of space as there are various perceived parts of matter occupying it. Space as a continuum is the result of the function of the capacity of the imagination. Since space is the form of the discreteness of sensibility, the parts of matter that are not perceived as discrete are not in space.

We cannot say of the simple parts that they are not discrete. This would be an unwarranted metaphysical statement. We can say only that they are not perceived as discrete. Since they are beyond the realm of possible perception, they can be conceived only by the mind, and the concept of the variety and discreteness of perceived objects does not apply to them. The imagination, however, fills out the gaps of space by placing parts of matter in some relation to other heterogeneous and discrete material objects and thus imagines them in space. The imagination can always find the occasion and the opportunity for such relations and can imagine every point of space filled with matter, which stands in various relations to other parts of matter. Thus arises the idea of space as an endless continuum.

Of the third antinomy Maimon remarks merely that the proof of the thesis is based on the necessary idea of totality, which is for Kant an idea of reason, while in Maimon's view it is an idea of the transcendent capacity of the imagination.[36]

The fourth antinomy is concerned with the idea of a necessary being.

---

[36] Cf. below, p. 215 ff.

Maimon observes, with respect to the argument of the thesis, that the proof of the existence of a necessary cause in general is again based on the idea of totality, which is for him not an idea of reason but an idea of the transcendent imaginative capacity.[37] As for the proof that this necessary cause is immanent, not transcendent, i.e., that the necessary cause belongs to the sensible world, Maimon maintains that it is predicated on that concept of beginning by which Kant understands an existence before which a time has preceded in which the thing that begins did not yet exist. For the proof of the thesis runs as follows: "For if it [the necessary cause] existed outside the world, the series of alterations in the world would derive its beginning from a necessary cause which would not itself belong to the sensible world. This, however, is impossible. For since the beginning of a series in time can be determined only by that which precedes it in time, the highest condition of the beginning of a series of changes must exist in the time when the series as yet was not (for a beginning is an existence preceded by a time in which the thing that begins did not yet exist). Accordingly, the causality of the necessary cause of alterations, and therefore the cause itself, must belong to time and so to appearance – time being possible only as the form of appearance."[38] Maimon, however, understands by the concept of beginning the complete synthesis or the end of the synthesis of the imagined existence of an object, starting from any given point of time and going backwards. According to this concept of beginning, the proof of the thesis loses its logical validity.[39]

In other words, with Kant, owing to his conception of "beginning," the necessary cause (in order to fulfill its function as a cause for the beginning of the world) must be in time and a part of the sensible world. For Maimon the first, necessary cause cannot be conceived as being "in time" preceding the beginning of the world. Therefore, the concept of a necessary, first cause can be thought of as transcending the sensible world. The first cause as the unconditioned condition of the world makes the synthesis of the totality of the world complete. Furthermore, for Kant the concept of causality, i.e., cause and effect, is bound up with time, as the hypothetical judgment, when *a* then *b*, refers to phenomena of experience that are in time. With Maimon, however, the concept of causality as such is the connection between ground and consequence in a purely logical sense, as is the case with mathematical

[37] See *ibid*.
[38] *Critique of Pure Reason*, p. 416.
[39] Cf. *Logik*, pp. 221 f.

objects, which are not in time. Hence Maimon's skepticism with reference to the hypothetical judgment regarding objects of experience.
Consequently, the first unconditioned cause is not necessarily a part
of the sensible world. It can be thought of as transcendent, not immanent
to the world of sensibility.

To the antithesis Maimon offers the following criticism. The antithesis
maintains that it is a contradiction to suppose that the series of alterations in the world is contingent and conditioned in all its parts, and yet,
as a whole, has no beginning and is absolutely necessary and unconditioned. Maimon, however, does not see any contradiction in the
assumption that the series of the phenomena of the world as a whole
is unconditioned and necessary, while its parts are conditioned and
contingent. We have examples of this kind of manifold, in which the
parts are separately conditioned while the whole as a collective is
necessary. A three-sided figure, for instance, is in itself not necessary,
nor is the three-angled figure necessary. But both together are necessarily connected in a unity of consciousness. A three-sided figure necessarily has three angles and vice versa. Thus, the necessary reality
of the series of the world as a whole may determine the contingent and
conditioned reality of its parts.

Maimon also objects to Kant's statement that the assumption of an
absolutely necessary cause outside the world must lead to a contradiction. The causality of such a cause will by no means be in time and
therefore will not belong to the totality of the phenomena of the world.
The antithesis says: "If we assume that an absolutely necessary cause
of the world exists outside the world, then this cause, as the highest
member in the series of the causes of changes in the world, must begin
the existence of the latter and their series. Now this cause must itself
begin to act, and its causality would therefore be in time, and so would
belong to the sum of appearances, that is, to the world."[40]

But if we assume with Maimon that time and the world are finite,
and posit causality through a freedom whose source is outside time
and the phenomenal world, then this act of freedom does not begin
to act *in* time but rather creates time itself. Here, too, Maimon's relationship to Maimonides is manifest, for since time is bound up with motion,
the category of time does not apply to God. Therefore, the act of creation
of the world by a free agent (God) was not *in* time.[41]

[40] *Critique of Pure Reason*, p. 416.
[41] Cf. above, note 27, It is of interest to note that Fichte expresses the same thought
thus: "When we posit the appearance of the absolute [i.e., God appearing through
the act of creation of the world] at a certain point in time, we thus presuppose the

iii

According to Maimonides, who follows Aristotle in the conception of time as an accident of motion, the assumption of the creation of the world out of nothing implies that time, too, was created. Since time is bound up with motion, i.e., with change in general, it follows that the existence of time is dependent upon the existence of the world. On the other hand, when we maintain that the world was created at a point in time, we posit the existence of time prior to the existence of the world, and the eternity of time implies the eternity of substance, since time as an accident of motion cannot be thought of without substance. Consequently, the proposition, "God existed before He created the world," in which the words "existed" and "before" imply that time is independent of matter, is to be understood in a fictional (*erdichtete*), not in a true sense.

Maimon presents this argument of Maimonides and remarks: "Kant has in our time demonstrated that time is neither a substance nor an accident, but the form of our intuition of the appearances. To the world as a thing-in-itself the concept of time does not apply."[42] In other words, the world as a thing-in-itself does not exist in time. The Maimonidean antinomy concerning the concept of time, which, on the one hand, is an accident of motion and thus bound up with the existence of objects, and, on the other hand, is a reality independent of matter, as the concept of creation assumes, is to be solved, according to Maimon, in the following manner: The world as a thing-in-itself does not exist in time; only the appearances are perceived by us through the form of time.

Here Maimon gives the solution of the antinomy of creation in accordance with Kant's concept of time as a form of intuition. Maimon himself, however, conceives of time as a form of successive perceptions, and thus his concept of time is bound up with the perception of sensuous

reality of time in which, before creation of the world, God did not appear. This is generally assumed to be the meaning of the concept of creation. But this is logically incomprehensible... for neither God nor his appearing is in time. The truth is rather the opposite; in the appearance of the world time arose..." (Fichte X, 345). Quoted from A. Messer, *Fichtes religiöse Weltanschauung* (1923), p. 129.

[42] *Lebensgeschichte*, II, 87 ff. Maimon rendered Maimonides' expression *sheur zman, o dmuth zman* in relation to time before creation (*Guide*, II, 13), as "figment" of the imagination or "fictional time" (*erdichtete*). Perhaps Maimonides was the source for Maimon's concept of fiction, which played such an important role in his thought. Maimon's own concept of time and space is similarly derived. Time and space, as conceived directly with the various objects, are a true image of the form of differentiation. When detached from the objects of perception, however, time and space are mere figments of the

objects. In this he is nearer to Maimonides' concept of time as an accident of motion than he is to Kant's. But he follows Kant in the basic distinction between the thing-in-itself and the appearances. There are, therefore, elements of both, Maimonides and Kant, in Maimon's solution of the antinomy of creation.

In his Commentary on the *Guide* Maimon presents the antinomy of creation in the light of his concept of time, in a manner similar to his definition of the Maimonidean antinomy,[43] and offers a solution to it on the basis of the fundamental distinction between the thing-in-itself and the appearances.

Time, as we know, is the form of the succession of perceptions, in their following one after another, and space is the form of the discreteness and heterogeneity of objects. While for Kant time and space are pure forms of intuition, for Maimon they are forms of discreteness of objects and of succession of phenomena; as such they are bound up with the perception of objects.[44]

Since time is the form of the successive perception of objects, there can be no time without objects of perception. Consequently, when we assume creation of the world, we also posit creation of time, since time is necessarily bound up with the perception of sensuous objects. On the other hand, the concept of creation implies the coming into being of a world that did not exist before. It thus necessarily presupposes the existence of time prior to the existence of the world. This proposition, however, contradicts the previous one, which is based on a concept of time as a form of sensibility, i.e., as the form of successive perceptions. Maimon follows Maimonides here in presenting the antinomy of creation as a concept contradicting the concept of time.[45]

Maimon's formulation of the antinomy of creation in this manner is entirely different from the Kantian formulation. For while Kant tries to show that the thesis of creation and its antithesis are logically equally valid, Maimon's endeavor is to demonstrate that the assumption of creation must involve us in a contradiction concerning the concept of time.

According to Maimon, the solution of this contradiction is to be found in the distinction that must be made between the thing-in-itself

---

imagination. As fictions, time and space arise when we imagine them, not as a form of differentiation and the heterogeneity of objects, but as entities in themselves, abstracted from the objects in connection with which they occur.

[43] *Lebensgeschichte*, II, 99.
[44] Cf. above, Chap. IX.
[45] *Com. on the Guide*, p. 96.

and the appearance. The concept of the world in its totality is subject to this basic distinction. The world as a thing-in-itself does not have a beginning in time nor is it eternal. Creation as well as non-creation are temporal determinants and presuppose time, which by its definition as a form of successive perceptions of sensuous objects can apply only to objects of experience. Hence, creation, or its opposite, is logically inapplicable to the world as a thing-in-itself. The world as appearance, however, simultaneously admits of the possibility of creation as well as non-creation. Potentially, the world has no beginning in time; since time is a form of sensibility, it is impossible to conceive of time without the existence of a world of objects, for we cannot think of time abstracted from sensuous objects. Consequently, as far back in time as our imagination can reach, time must always be associated with the existence of objects. On the other hand, it is impossible to conclude the series of causes and thus to obtain a concept of the world in its totality; therefore, our concept of the world is always finite and as such must have a beginning. This concept, however, is not of the world in its totality, but of an arbitrary part of it.[46]

In Maimon's formulation of the problem of creation as an antinomy, as well as in his solution of it, there are elements of both Maimonides and Kant. While in the formulation Maimon follows Maimonides, his solution of the antinomy is based on the Kantian distinction between the thing-in-itself and the appearance.

It is of interest to compare Maimon's views on the problem of creation as presented by him in different contexts. Whereas, in connection with the antinomy of creation, Maimon maintains that in relation to the world as appearance both creation and non-creation apply equally, in another context he develops the idea that in relation to the world as appearance neither the concept of creation nor that of eternity is applicable. The former does not apply because it presupposes the existence of time prior to the existence of objects; the latter does not apply because time as a form of sensibility is always limited to the series of successive perceptions that one can imagine.[47]

There is no contradiction between Maimon's two presentations of this antinomy. In both cases, his intention is to point out the difference between the world as a thing in itself and the world as appearance. The world as the absolute totality of appearances, which is beyond the capacity of our imagination, is a thing-in-itself in relation to which

[46] Cf. *ibid.*
[47] Cf. *ibid.*, p. 103.

neither creation nor eternity applies. However, with regard to appear-ances which we can imagine, the concept of creation as well as non-creation equally applies, depending on whether the series of successive perceptions is limited or not. In the case of the absolute totality of appearances, we are dealing with an arbitrary part of the world, not the world in its totality. The statement that "the concept of non-creation as well as creation does not apply to the sensible world," refers to the appearances of the world in their totality, which constitute a thing-in-itself.

While Kant formulates the antinomies in a positive manner, that is, the thesis as well as the antithesis can be proved with equal cogency, Maimon defines the antinomy of creation in a negative form, that is, in such a way that both the thesis and the antithesis can be disproved. The reason for Kant's formulation resides, so it seems, in the considera-tion that though metaphysical problems are insoluble by rational meth-ods, they must be possible as articles of faith. For Kant, faith transcends the rational realm, but it must not contradict reason; belief in a supreme being and in creation must be rationally possible. The antinomies are thus formulated in a positive form; the thesis of creation and the thesis of a supreme being can be rationally justified, though not conclusively proved; and the belief in creation and a supreme being is a rationally possible belief as it does not contradict reason. If the antinomies had been formulated in a negative manner, that is, in such a way that the thesis and the antithesis would be shown to be rationally untenable, the belief in the theses of creation and of a supreme being would have contradicted reason. The thinking, prevalent in contemporary theology, which emphasizes the paradoxical nature of faith, that is, that the realm of faith is in its very essence contrary to reason, is incompatible with the Kantian formulation of the antinomies. It is in harmony rather with the conception of these theses as rationally untenable.

In another connection Maimon refers to the concept of creation out of nothing as transcending the limits of experience.[48] Creation out of nothing would seem to be a metaphysical idea lying entirely beyond the realm of experiential knowledge. On further consideration, however, Maimon maintains that creation out of nothing is not a transcendent concept, for we can derive it out of our own self, as our understanding, with its *a priori* forms, is capable of comprehending objects of experience as an ordered world of phenomena. Since the ordered world is not "given" as a matter of fact, but is rather the result of the application

[48] Cf. *Philos. Wört.*, p. 31.

of forms of thought *a priori*, we realize the possibility of creation by an analysis of our thinking process and of its function in establishing order in the world. The forms of thought as ordening principles have a creative function, and by realizing this function we obtain an idea of creation.

Also through the pure capacity of imagination, which supplies the forms *a priori* with the corresponding material and thus presents them as real objects, we experience an act of creation. "The material *a posteriori*," writes Maimon, "must be given, but through the forms of thought *a priori* and the pure capacity of the imagination we have partially a concept of creation out of nothing. We can thus in our thought steadily and endlessly approach an absolute concept of creation, which would embrace the creation of matter out of nothing as well."[49] Thus the possibility of the metaphysical idea of creation of the world is bound up, according to Maimon, with the critical concept of the world as a creation of the human mind.

To a critical philosopher, who conceives the ordered world, i.e., scientific experience, as the result of the creative process of human thought, the concept of creation as such is not entirely beyond the realm of human experience, since in the thinking process of man we experience creation. The idea of a divine, absolute act of creation is in harmony with the critical concept of the world, which emphasizes the creative character of man. We become aware of this creativity through an analysis of our process of thought in relation to objects of experience.

It must be pointed out, however, that Maimon does not think that the forms *a priori* themselves spring out of the human mind, in the course of the thinking process, as it struggles with the problems of reality. In our opinion, it is possible to conceive of the forms *a priori* as creations of the human mind rather than as constant and abiding forms that make up the changeless pattern of thought. The concept of *a priori* as eternal forms constitutive of the mind is subjective. The concept of *a priori* as emerging forms emphasizes the creative character of the human mind, i.e., the forms *a priori* are not constitutive of the subject, but are creations of the thinking process. According to such a critical concept of *a priori*, the forms of thought are actually creations out of nothing. Maimon, however, does not state explicitly that *a priori* forms are creations of the human mind. He seems to have considered *a priori* forms of thought as constitutive elements inherent in the subject. His reference to the "*a priori* given"[50] might be understood to mean

---

[49] Cf. *ibid.*
[50] Cf. Emil Lask, *Fichtes Idealismus und die Geschichte* (1912), p. 46, n. 2.

that *a priori* forms are constitutive elements of the human mind, forming
the abiding and constant principles of thought. But is is possible to
understand the "*a priori* given" as referring to the manifold that is in
itself the result of a synthesis. A synthesis establishing a unity is *a priori*,
as it is an act of thought unifying a manifold. The manifold to be
synthesized is "given *a posteriori*" when it is an object in itself and not
the result of a synthesis. The manifold is "given *a priori*" when it is in
itself the result of a synthesis.[51] Thus, for example, the concept of space
as an endless entity is a result of the synthesis of limited spaces into
infinity. This act of extension is a synthesis. But the manifold of limited
spaces synthesized into a unified intuition of a single infinite space, is
a priori given, for the limited spaces are in themselves the result of a
synthesis *a priori*. Limited space, even the infinitely small, is possible
only through an act synthesizing it into a unity. This is an "*a priori*
given" manifold. But the manifold contained in the concept "body,"
that is, extension and solidity, is "given *a posteriori*." Extension and
solidity are the conditions of the concept of body.[52] Hence the "*a priori*
given" does not have to imply that the forms of thought are "given."

Maimon, moreover, does not consider the subject as a thing-in-itself.[53]
The concept of subject as a creative agent, not as a metaphysical entity,
is compatible with the conception of *a priori* forms as creative functions,
not as constant metaphysical entities. While his doctrine of the subject
is critical, that is to say, the subject is in flux as a creative agent and
not a thing-in-itself, Maimon's conception of *a priori* forms is ambiguous. The possibility is not ruled out that he may have conceived
of the forms of thought as subjective principles. In his conception of the
subject Maimon grasps something new, which he does not follow
through to its final conclusion with reference to forms of thought. He
thus leaves open the possibility of the conception of forms of thought
as constitutive principles inherent in the subject.

All the same, even according to a subjective concept of forms *a priori*,
forms of thought have a creative function in relation to the manifold
"given" to which they apply. For it is only by these categories and forms
a priori that the manifold of perceptions is synthesized into objects
of reality.

It must be admitted, on the other hand, that the creation of the
thinking process is not a creation out of nothing, since the material

[51] Cf. Kuno Fischer, *Geschichte der neueren Philosophie, Sechster Band, Dritte Aufl.*
Heidelberg, 1900, p. 78 f.
[52] See *Krit. Unt.*, pp. 141 f.
[53] See above, Chap. IV.

a posteriori must be "given" to it from the outside. It would seem that Maimon's intention is to point out that we can imagine an absolute act of creation on the basis of our experiential knowledge of relative creation. The transition from limited and restricted creation (creation out of something) to absolute creation (creation out of nothing) is a gradual one, and the concept of absolute creation can be attained by a continuous and gradual process of elemination of those limitations implied in the relative acts of creation as experienced by man; or, in Maimon's words, we can in our thought steadily and endlessly approach an absolute concept of creation.

Just as the idea of an infinite reason can be obtained through a continuous process eliminating the limitations of the finite reason,[54] so can we obtain an idea of absolute creation through a continuous process of thought eliminating the limitations involved in the creative thinking of man. In the material *a posteriori* "given" to our thought inhere the limitations of creation. By a process of abstraction eliminating the "given" elements we shall arrive at a pure and absolute act of creation, i.e., creation out of nothing.

Furthermore, in the conception of mathematical objects, nothing is "given" to us from without; mathematical objects are wholly produced by our mind. In the *a priori* construction of objects of mathematics we are like God, "who produces the objects of nature in a manner similar to the method by which we produce the objects of mathematics through real thought, i.e., through construction."[55]

The fundamental difference between dogmatic and critical philosophy lies in the fact that the former conceives the world as being and the latter as becoming. In the classic distinction between the Eleatics, who conceived reality as constantly abiding and changeless being, and Heraclitus, who conceived the essence of reality as perpetual change and ceaseless becoming, there lies the basic distinction between dogmatic and critical philosophy. To this fundamental distinction between being and becoming all systems of thought are reducible. The more dogmatic a system of thought is, the more it stresses the concept of changeless being, and the more critical a system of thought is, the more it emphasizes the concept of becoming as the fundamental essence of reality. The conception of becoming in Hegel's system is not becoming at all, but rather another mode of being, since the process of becoming is determined by a rigid logical principle.

[54] Cf. above, p. 94.
[55] *Str.*, p. 36.

With the Copernican revolution of Kant in philosophy the idea of becoming gained prominence and was placed in the center of philosophical thought. The world is an endless process; nothing is given as final, but merely as a task. The thing-in-itself is not a substance bearing the appearances, a noumenon behind the phenomena, but rather an idea, i.e., an ideal which the human mind constantly strives to approach. The final solution of all problems, which is an ideal, a goal toward which to strive, is designated as the thing-in-itself. Maimon was the first to promulgate such a concept of the thing-in-itself.[56] In recent times it was Neo-Kantianism which conceived of the thing-in-itself as a limiting concept, that is an idea of complete unity which is an endless goal.[57]

In a world outlook which conceives of synthesis as the ground of reality, the concept of creation has its legitimate place, since the world as an ordered cosmos is a product of the creative process of the human mind. The more problems we are capable of solving and the closer we come to establishing the unity of the world, the more the creativity of the human mind is manifest. Since the thing-in-itself presents the ideal of the final solution of all problems, which can be hoped to attain by an endless process, with the attainment of this ideal maximum creativity will be realized. With God all objects are the result of His thought. As we approach the thing-in-itself by constant and ceaseless striving toward the final solution of all problems, we too come nearer to that state in which all objects are the result of our thought. It seems to me that there is a necessary connection between Maimon's doctrine of the thing-in-itself and his concept of creation as an idea known to us through an analysis of our thought in relation to mathematics and to objects of experience.

It is true that the creation of the human mind is limited and restricted, since material *a posteriori* must be given to it, and we have no experience of an absolute act of creation, i.e., creation out of nothing. But by eliminating the limitations of the restricted human act of creation, we arrive at an idea of an absolute act of creation. The limited human act of creation is absolutized, and thus the idea of an infinite act of creation, i.e., creation out of nothing, is deduced. The same method that Maimon employed for the deduction of an idea of an infinite reason is to be discerned in his concept of absolute creation, and the function of the idea of an infinite mind as well as that of an absolute creation are to be understood in the light of his concept of the thing-in-itself as an idea.

---

[56] Cf. *Philos. Wört.*, p. 162; *Krit. Unt.*, pp. 7–15; and see above, chap. II.
[57] Cf. H. Cohen, *Kants Theorie der Erfahrung*, 3rd ed. (Berlin, 1916), pp. 638 ff.

All these doctrines of Maimon form integral parts of a single whole, i.e., of his critical outlook on the world as a constant process of becoming, by which, owing to the creativity of the human mind, we can asymptotically approach absolute unity.

iv

The ideas of reason, which Kant confines to the realm of speculative metaphysics, are accorded much wider scope by Maimon. According to the latter, they have their roots in the faculty of the imagination, whose field of action is much broader than the range of the Kantian ideas of reason. Maimon writes: The striving after the highest perfection in general, including the conception (*Vorstellung*) of the totality of our knowledge (which is the basis of metaphysical ideas, according to Kant), is not a function of reason, as Kant assumes, but of the transcendent imaginative capacity, which comes into conflict with reason. "The striving after totality of comprehension, that is, the continuous approach to it, is an undeniable fact and is not confined to the capacity of cognition, but is characteristic of all human faculties. The conception of this totality with regard to cognition is absolute, unconditioned truth; with regard to the human will it is the highest good; with regard to aesthetic feeling it is the highest ideal of beauty. In all these realms, however, the striving is the same. The idea of totality is the aim of this striving... The transcendent imaginative capacity [*Einbildungskraft*] unjustifiably transforms this idea into an object that does not have reality as such ... but is indispensable as a goal, as an aim toward which to strive."[58]

Thus ideas have reality merely as manifestations of the striving after totality, not as conceptions of totality as an object. Kant severely limits this striving after totality, as he considers it to be merely a function of reason, while, according to Maimon, it is common to all human faculties, ethical and aesthetical as well as theoretical, and the urge to attain the highest perfection must be presupposed as the root and basis of this striving after totality.[59] Here Maimon deduces the ideas of reason from a deeper source in man, his striving after the highest perfection, from which flow not only metaphysical ideas of the totality of cognition, but also ethical as well as aesthetic ideas of totality.

Maimon differs fundamentally from Kant in his explanation of meta-

[58] *Logik*, p. 225.
[59] *Ibid.*, p. 226.

physical ideas or in their "deduction." For while Kant ascribes to reason the idea of the totality of the application of the forms of understanding, Maimon considers that the source of this idea, such as the whole series of causes leading to a first cause, is the productive imaginative faculty, which is capable, by means of fictions, of transcending the realm of experience. In the conception of man striving after perfection as the root and basis of ideas of totality, Maimon was influenced by the Enligtenment which regarded the pursuit of ethical and rational perfection as the highest goal of man.

Hegel, like Maimon before him, criticizes Kant for enumerating only four antinomies corresponding to the four categories. Hegel sets out to show the larger scope of the antinomies, that they are not merely manifestations of the conflict of reason with itself, but rather of the very essence of human thought as such. But he goes much further than Maimon in maintaining that the antinomies are due, not to reason or to the imaginative faculty, which seeks to comprehend the essence of the world in its totality, but to the world itself, to thought and reality as such, reality and thought being identical for Hegel. The contradictions, the antinomies, are manifestations of the dialectical movement of thought. To comprehend an object is to be conscious of it as a concrete unity of opposed determinations. "The true and positive meaning of the antinomies is this: that every actual thing involves a coexistence of opposed elements."[66]

Before Kant it was assumed that when cognition lapses into contradiction, it is to be attributed to some subjective mistake in argument. Kant's merit consists in acknowledging that the antinomies are not due to mere aberrations of thought; whenever thought seeks to apprehend the infinite, the thing-in-itself, it must involve itself in contradictions or antinomies. Kant does not explain the positive reason of the antinomies. The result of his doctrine is negative, i.e., our reason has necessary limitations, and whenever thought strives to transcend its limits, contradictions are the outcome. Maimon, however, is not satisfied with the mere negative result of Kant's doctrine of antinomies; he tries to penetrate to the root of antinomies and to find a positive reason for this phenomenon. In enlarging the scope of the antinomies and in searching in a more positive sense for a basis for them in our consciousness, Maimon anticipated Hegel.

While Kant's analysis of the antinomies leads only to the negative result that the thing-in-itself is unknowable, the result of Maimon's

[66] Cf. *The Logic of Hegel*, English transl. by William Wallace, 2nd ed., pp. 100 ff.

conception is positive, i.e, the human mind, as an aspect of an infinite mind, can think of objects creatively and positively. With Maimon the field of action of the antinomies is much wider than it is with Kant. Antinomies are to be found not only in the realm of metaphysics, but also in physics and mathematics. He thus strives to discover their real and positive meaning. According to him, they manifest the infinite aspect of our mind, since through imagination it is capable of comprehending objects in a manner transcending the experiential. The human striving for totality of knowledge is the result of man's striving for perfection, which is an endless goal. Man is aware of his relation to infinity in his striving after perfection. In the idea of perfection as well as in the idea of an infinite reason, which we obtain by a process of negating the limitations of the finite reason, there is manifest the infinite aspect of the human reason. In the infinite aspect of the human mind the root and basis of the antinomies are to be found.

While Maimon enlarges the scope of the antinomies in order to find their true basis, Hegel tries to demonstrate that the true nature of all thought is antinomical in character. Maimon thus stands between the critical position of Kant and the speculative position of Hegel. Maimon, by demonstrating the larger field of action of the antinomies, by showing that they are not confined to the cosmology of the old metaphysical systems, and by seeking a positive basis for the phenomenon of antinomies in the very nature of the human mind, prepared the ground for the conception that contradictions are constituent elements of the process of thought as such. According to Hegel, reality as well as thought are subject to the dialectical process, the essence of which consists in reconciling the contradictions into a synthesis. The very nature of thought as synthesis requires two opposing elements, i.e., a contradiction, an antinomy, as the necessary material for the process of synthesis. The concept of synthesis has thus changed: it is no more a synthesis of a manifold, as with Kant, but a synthesis of opposites. The thesis and the antithesis are sublated in the synthesis; the contradiction between the thesis and the antithesis is a necessary condition for the synthesis.

This does not mean that Hegel was aware of Maimon's conception of the antinomies. We intend only to point out the various stages in the development of the doctrine of antinomies from the critical method of Kant to the speculative-critical doctrine of Maimon and to the dialectical, speculative-dogmatic construction of Hegel. The transition from one to the other is thus made continuous.

Maimon's influence on the philosophy of Fichte has been established by many thinkers.[61] It is the philosophy of Maimon, not that of Jacob Siegmund Beck, that constitutes the transition between Kant and Fichte.[62] Fichte's system led to that of Schelling and Schelling's to that of Hegel. The development of the three systems of thought represents a continuous growth, to be treated as a unit, each of them representing an indispensable element of an organic whole. In this continuous line of thought the link formed by Maimon is not to be ignored.

---

[61] See Willy Kabitz, *Studien zur Entwicklung der Fichteschen Wissenschaftslehre aus der Kantischen Philosophie* (Berlin, 1902), p. 78; Emil Lask, *Fichtes Idealismus und die Geschichte* (Tübingen und Leipzig, 1902), pp. 116, 121 ff., 131; Friedrich Kuntze, *Die Philosophie Salomon Maimons* (1912), pp. 307, 325 ff., 347 ff.; Ernst Cassirer, *Das Erkenntnisproblem* (Berlin, 1923), III, 16 ff.; Richard Kroner, *Von Kant bis Hegel*, I, 326 ff., 497; M. Gueroult, *La Philosophie Transcendentale de Solomon Maimon* (Paris, 1929), pp. 71 ff., 141 ff., and in his *L'Evolution et la structure de la doctrine de la science chez Fichte* (Paris, 1930), pp. 110 ff.; Bergmann, *Ha-philosophia shel Shlomo Maimon*, pp. 149 f.

[62] Cf. Wilhelm Dilthey, *Gesammelte Schriften*, Leipzig und Berlin 1921. IV, *Band*, p. 319 f.

CHAPTER XI

PHILOSOPHY AND MATHEMATICS

i

In his orientation towards mathematics and in his conception of the role mathematics has to play in philosophical investigations Maimon follows in the great tradition of the seventeenth century represented by Descartes, Spinoza, and Leibniz, a line of thought of which Kant constitutes the last link. We have seen that Maimon reinterpreted various of Leibniz' doctrines to suit them more to his critical bent by transforming metaphysical ideas conceived by Leibniz as transcendent entities into critical ideas, that is, as methodical principles. But in his attitude towards the place of mathematics and the role it has to play in metaphysical speculations and in epistemological investigations Maimon remained a true follower of Leibniz.

The association between mathematics and philosophy is of ancient origin. The Pythagoreans were the first to discover the tremendous importance of mathematical thought for metaphysical speculation. With them began a new trend in the development of philosophical thought as well as in the physical sciences. The reduction of physical objects to mathematical relations, which forms the basis of modern physics, was first conceived intuitively by the Pythagoreans. The idea that the essence of all things is to be expressed in mathematical terms – for numbers are the heart and core of all things – took on with the Pythagoreans a poetical and mythological form. Only in the Renaissance, with the rise of the new physics, did the idea that the essence of all things consists in mathematical relations, to which the physical objects are to be reduced, acquire an exact scientific form. A poetic intuitive idea was transformed by the new physics into an exact scientific concept. The progressive development of modern physical science down to our own day testifies to the fruitfulness of this concept. And it was the association of mathematics and physics that made this progress possible.

The Aristotelian physics, dominant until the rise of modern science, was static for almost two millennia. It was unfortunate for the development of science and philosophy that the Pythagorean trend was superseded by Aristotle, whose physics and philosophy predominated generally throughout the ages until the Renaissance. Aristotle's thinking was oriented towards biology, the scientific explanation of which is based on the teleological principle, as the organic form strives to realize itself, to attain its purpose, i.e., the completion of the organism. Hence physical phenomena were explained by the teleological principle, and where teleology reigns as the method for explaining natural phenomena, there is no place for the conception of mathematics as a basis of physical science.

Plato fully realized the importance of mathematics for philosophy and science, but this aspect of Platonic thought did not have much effect on the history of scientific thought. In the rise of the new physics, however, the mathematical method came into its own and placed the investigation of physical phenomena on a different basis. The new trend in physical science was bound up with the abandonment of Aristotelianism in favor of Platonism, especially that aspect of Plato's philosophy which recognized the importance of mathematics for philosophy and science. The teleological principle, which was the basis of the old physics, gave way to the mechanical principle grounded in the deductive mathematical method.

The Pythagoreans, who discovered the uniqueness of the mathematical process of thought, were intrigued by the exactness of its logical deductions, by the precision of its method, and by the extraordinary regularity of its relations. Such a method, which is both exact and independent of empirical material and yet can be applied with absolute confindence to the explanation of empirical objects, the Pythagoreans considered the insignia of the divine. Hence the great, almost uninhibited enthusiasm with which the ancients greeted any new mathematical discovery. It was a religious enthusiasm, because they saw in such a discovery a revelation of divine thought. Maimon attributes the excessive enthusiasm of the ancients over the formulation of the famous Pythagorean theorem, not so much to the ingenuity of the theorem itself as to the discovery of the systematic unity implied in it and the consequences flowing from it.

The Pythagoreans sensed in the rules and principles governing mathematical relations the inspiration of a supreme divine intelligence; they regarded the comprehension of mathematical principles and rules as a gift of God, since these rules are not derived from the observation of empirical objects and are not grounded in sense-data, but are pure creations of the sovereign independent mind. In the creative spontaneity of the human mind man experiences the divine in him. And Maimon follows in the Pythagorean, Platonic tradition when he epitomizes his conception of mathematics in the statement that in mathematics man is Godlike.

Plato held that in the essence of mathematical concepts there is revealed the ideal pattern of pure being; and all forms of being, physical as well as ethical, have their roots in an ideal reality analogous to the pure ideal mathematical reality. The new philosophy beginning with Descartes again recognized the close association between mathematics and philosophy. The orientation toward physical science became paramount for philosophy, and mathematics was the driving force in the progressive development of modern physics, which is characterized by the quantification of physical objects, i.e, the dissolution of objects into mathematical relations. Hence the deductive method of mathematics came to be considered the ideal method, which philosophy had to emulate. Descartes and Spinoza employed mathematics, i.e., the geometrical method, in their metaphysical constructions. And Leibniz was so captivated by the mathematical method that he attempted to construct a logic according to the mathematical pattern of thought, by which the whole universe could be explained: man and God, nature and culture, the sensuous and the super-sensuous, the immanent and the transcendent. Descartes and Leibniz were creative in both fields, mathematics and philosophy. The two realms of thought fructified each other. Metaphysical constructions led to mathematical concepts, and mathematical ideas led to philosophical doctrines. It was Maimon who recognized the close relation between Leibniz' metaphysical doctrine of the monads and the conception of the infinitesimals, the basis of calculus.

ii

The importance of mathematics for philosophy lies, according to Maimon, not in the mathematical method, which is to be applied in philosophy, as was the case with Spinoza, but in the fact that the science of mathematics constitutes the only area in which synthetic propositions are governed by the principle of determinability, a principle of "real thought" (*reales Denken*), i.e., thought in relation to definite and real objects. Moreover, the problem of the possibility of synthetic *a priori* propositions, which is the central philosophical question, is, in Maimon's formulation, the question of the possibility of real thought. Formal thought, which is the subject matter of general logic, is governed by the laws of identity and contradiction, which refer to objects of thought in general, inasmuch as any object of thought independent of its contents is subject to these laws. A synthetic proposition, however, establishes a synthesis concerning a definite object of reality; it is thus real thought or thought of reality. It requires a law of its own, which Maimon formulated as the principle of determinability. The law governing synthetic propositions was derived by Maimon through the analysis of mathematical objects. The only area, however, in which synthetic propositions are determined by this principle, thus deriving objects of reality from a principle of thought, is mathematics.

Bound up with the preceding analysis is Maimon's orientation to mathematics in the construction of transcendental logic. In the conception of the relation between logic and mathematics Maimon differs fundamentally from Kant as well as from Hume. The connection of mathematics and logic is, according to Maimon, not due to the fact that mathematical propositions are all analytic propositions, as Hume proposed and as Bertrand Russell and A. N. Whitehead in our time have tried to demonstrate. Maimon held with Kant that the science of mathematics is grounded in synthetic propositions.

Maimon shares with the whole line of philosophers of the seventeenth and eighteenth centuries, the last of which was Kant, the appreciation of the particular place of mathematics in the realm of science and in the conception of the special value of mathematics for the work of philosophical analysis. The distinguishing marks of mathematics are the generality and universality of its propositions, the certitude and apodictic character of its principles. These characteristic features of the science of mathematics are for Maimon an established fact not subject to any doubt. With respect to the certitude of its propositions mathematics is comparable to the science of logic. The certitude, apodicticity, generality and universality of logical propositions, however, are due to the fact that logic is a formal science. Its propositions and rules refer to objects of thought in general, since any object of thought must be thought of in accordance with the principles and rules of logic; this is why logical propositions are analytic and *a priori*.

However, mathematics is a "material" science, as definite objects constitute its subject matter. Mathematics as a science is not as pure as logic, according to Maimon's conception of purity. The purity of a science is determined, first, by the distinctness and clearness with which the objects are subsumed under its rules, and second, by the fact that its propositions are independent of the scrutiny and investigation of individual and particular objects. The less a science is dependent on the analysis of definite objects in the formulation of its propositions, the purer it is. Now, the science of logic deals with the thinking of objects in general. It formulates principles with which any object of thought, regardless of its content, must comply. Transcendental philosophy, which is the science of the possibility of an object of experience in general (*überhaupt*), also is purer than mathematics, for the latter deals with definite objects; its propositions refer to determinable objects.

And yet mathematical propositions command certitude, generality, and general validity – all qualities characteristic of the formal science of logic. This is due to the distinguishing feature of mathematics which is the possibility of construction of its objects. The science of mathematics is governed by a method by which the objects constituting the subject matter of its propositions can be constructed by the capacity of the imagination. Geometrical figures, for instance, can be produced by construction according to a mathematical principle. Construction of mathematical objects is thus a sort or "verification" of mathematical propositions. It is a kind of experience fundamentally different from the experience derived from the observation of occurrences taking place in nature. While the construction of objects according to a principle is an experience of creation, the consideration of phenomena repetitiously occurring in nature, which is the basis of the natural sciences, is an experience of observation.

Because of the possibility of construction of mathematical objects, which is an active, creative experience, in contradistinction to the empirical experience of the observation of natural phenomena, another characteristic feature of mathematical science can be accounted for, namely its ability to proceed from the particular to the general as well as from the general to the particular. Maimon writes: "Mathematics may ascend from the particular object to the general concept or descend from the general principle to a particular object; it attains always certainty of its propositions and secures the reality of its objects through construction."[1]

Even though the construction of a mathematical object, such as a triangle, presents only an individual object, the general concept of which the object is a representation is universally valid. The construction serves the purpose of granting objective reality to the concept. "Every construction of a mathematical object is an individual construction, but the concept derived from it is generally valid."[2] The construction

---

[1] *Str.*, p. 15.
[2] *Krit. Unt.*, p. 23.

of the individual object is produced by the capacity of the imagination. But the understanding abstracts it of its individual features and recognizes in and through the individual construction the concept in its generality. "This can justifiably be designated as a construction *a priori*, inasmuch as the generality of the concept is not given in the construction itself but is an *a priori* thought of our understanding."[3]

Furthermore, mathematics as a science is distinguished from all other sciences in that its objects arise simultaneously with the scientific propositions concerning them .The objects of a science generally precede the particular science that deals with these objects. Not so in mathematics, in which the subject matter arises simultaneously with the science itself. Its object, numbers, and figures, as well as the science concerning these objects, namely, the relations obtaining between them, are determined *a priori*. The objects, therefore, cannot precede mathematical science, since they are determined as real objects by the very propositions constituting mathematical science. In this respect the science of mathematics constitutes an exception from all other sciences. "Logic, which is a formal science dealing with the laws determining the thinking of any object, and transcendental philosophy, which is the science of the possibility of an object of experience in general, though *a priori* sciences, cannot be compared with mathematics in this respect. Empirical objects, which are subsumed to the general principles of logic and of transcendental philosophy, precede these sciences, just as is the case with sciences dealing with experiential objects in which the objects precede their respective sciences.[4] The objects *a priori* of logic and transcendental philosophy, which constitute the propositions of these sciences, are only the forms of thought as such, and they are not real objects at all.

According to Kant, this distinction of mathematics is due to the *a priori* character of time and space, which are forms of intuition underlying the science of mathematics. Synthetic propositions *a priori* in mathematics are possible because the objects themselves are produced and created by the mind, for time and space are *a priori* forms of intuition, Maimon follows Kant in his emphasis on the simultaneous origination of mathematics as a science with its objects.

But a proper understanding of critical philosophy together with a consistent comprehension of the Copernican revolution in philosophy must lead to the same conclusion with reference to the science of

---

[3] *Ibid.*, p. 24.
[4] *Kat. d. Arist.*, pp. 42 f.

physics. According to critical idealism, in physical science also the objects arise simultaneously with their science. Synthetic propositions *a priori* are possible in physical science because of the *a priori* character of the concepts of thought in which the possibility of scientific experience is grounded. The general laws and principles of the science of physics constitute its subject matter, and these general laws, which are the objects of physical science, arise simultaneously with the science itself; they are the result of the creativity of the human mind just as much as mathematical objects. If it were otherwise, according to Kant, the possibility of synthetic propositions *a priori* in physical science could not be accounted for. The Kantian position is: "We comprehend in the objects as much as we put into them." Consequently, in physical science as well as in mathematics the objects of the science arise simultaneously with the respective science. Maimon, however, here parts with Kant; he recognizes the presence of synthetic propositions *a priori* in mathematics but not in physics. This position is bound up with his skepticism concerning the possibility of deriving experience from the general concepts of thought *a priori*. Even granting the validity of transcendental philosophy, which determines the general principles of thought as necessary conditions of experience in general, since without them experience as such would be impossible, it is still not possible to prove the application of a general concept of thought to a particular object of experience. According to Maimon, one cannot surmount the difficulty of proving the transition from transcendental philosophy to physics as an experiential science by demonstrating the application of general concepts of thought to a particular objects of experience. Unlike mathematics physics is a domain in which the objects precede the science, for the objects are presented as problems for scientific investigation.

In view of the creative character of the science of mathematics, i.e., its objects arise simultaneously with the science concerning these objects, we understand the full import and significance of Maimon's statement that "in mathematics we are Godlike." For the idea of God as an infinite mind implies absolute creativity. Nothing can be "given" to it from without. "We can thus," writes Maimon, "problematically assume an intelligent being whose relation to all objects of nature is similar to the relation of our capacity of cognition to the objects of mathematics."[5] The idea that nothing can be presented to the infinite mind from without but the objects of reality must be thought of as

---

[5] *Magazin zur Erfahrungsseelenkunde, herausgegeben von Karl Philipp Moritz und Salomon Maimon*, X, (Berlin, 1793), p. 61.

arising simultaneously with its thought is thus expressed by Maimon:
"The representations [*Vorstellungen*] of an infinite mind are at the
same time presentations [*Darstellungen*], that is to say, by the very act
of representing an object by the conception of its idea it attains objective
reality outside the mind."[6]

In Maimon's view mathematics was the basis for Plato's metaphysical conception of the world. Mathematics was held by Plato in such
high esteem because through it he was led to the construction of his
world view. According to Plato, the world of real things was produced
by God after an ideal pattern. This ideal pattern is to be considered as
the best of all possible worlds. Since the world is a coherent unity,
everything in it, as a part of the whole, must be in accord with the ideal
of the whole. The objects of mathematics consist of form (concepts of
understanding) and matter (intuitions *a priori*, i.e., time and space).
Our understanding produces the objects of mathematics through
construction *a priori*, namely, by the connection of a form of understanding with an intuition *a priori*, i.e., pure space and time. Both
elements are necessary for the production of a mathematical object.
The form alone without the construction of the object in space has no
objective reality. Thus, for instance, the discursive concept of a regular
solid decahedron is a logically correct concept, since it involves no
contradiction. However, the construction of such an object is impossible; that is to say, such a concept has no objective reality. The
mere logical possibility of an object does not insure its objective reality.
It acquires objective reality only when the material of the concept,
namely, space, lends itself to the construction of the object corresponding to the concept. Logical possibility implies only an object of thought,
not an object of cognition (i.e., a real object). Thus the decahedron
clearly demonstrates that a logically coherent concept, i.e., a concept
that does not involve a contradiction, is merely an object of thought
as long as the construction of the object is impossible.

Just as the mere possibility of formal thought is insufficient to insure
objective reality, so intuition alone does not make an intellectually
coherent reality. The intuitive capacity, not conjoined with a concept
of understanding, cannot grant us coherent and comprehensible objects.
Both form and matter are necessary for the cognition of mathematical
objects and neither takes precedence over the other.[7]

---

[6] *Ibid.*, p. 62.
[7] *Str.*, pp. 34 f.

Understanding without the help of intuition (*Anschauung*) is thus incapable of attaining objective reality. Only such concepts of thought as can be constructed in intuition can grant us mathematical objects having objective reality. The distinction between thought and cognition is clearly brought out here. Thought is governed by the formal laws of logic. For cognition of mathematical objects, however, formal thought is insufficient, but the possibility of construction of the objects is indispensable. In the construction of the objects by intuition a material element is added to the formal. The concept of a decahedron is a logically possible concept. The material of intuition, namely, space, resists the construction of a decahedron; the concept therefore has no objective reality.

Furthermore, the possible constructions are not all alike in their nature but are subject to various degrees of perfection. Thus, with regard to precision, one object may possess greater perfection than another, if the rule of its construction does not contain anything superfluous; with reference to purity one object may be purer than another, if it does not presuppose anything empirical, such as motion. Finally, an object may attain greater perfection with reference to its scope, if it encompasses a greater content.

The perfection of the presentations and the constructions with reference to the purity, completeness, and the scope of the concept corresponds to the degree of perfection of the mind producing them. An infinite mind is perfect; any other mind can attain various degrees of approximation to the ideal of the infinite mind.

Plato applied the same method in explaining the manner in which God produced the world beyond Himself. For the production of a real object two elements are necessary, a concept and matter. In infinite reason there are only ideas, not concepts. Only with reference to a finite mind does a distinction obtain between concepts of understanding and ideas of reason; the former are confined to objects of experience, the latter transcend the limits of experience. In infinite reason, which cannot be thought of as being restricted by anything beyond itself, concepts are identical with ideas. As to matter, which is necessary for the presentation and the realization of the concepts, it should be understood, in relation to an infinite reason, not as an empirical matter, but as a pure intuition of the infinite capacity of the imagination. "God produces the objects of nature in the same manner as we produce the objects of mathematics through *real thought*, namely, through construction. These objects are produced according to the ideal of the highest perfection, compatible with the material in which they are presented."[8]

In the same way Maimon interprets the system of Leibniz. The infinite reason of God encompasses all possible things or worlds. In relation to God, however, the possible is also real; what is logically possible for the infinite mind is also real, and what is not real must also be logically impossible. Only in relation to the limited human mind is there a distinction between the possible and the real and between the ideal and the material. Pure concepts constitute the realm of the possible, and the presentation of concepts in the realm of matter constitutes the real. Owing to the restrictions posed by matter upon the concept, the possible is presented through the material in a restricted manner. The world of real objects is thus, for the human mind, nothing other than a presentation of the possible in a restricted and limited manner. Of the totality of all possible concepts only so much is conceived by the human mind as real as matter (i.e., our own restriction) permits. And inasmuch as not all that is possible is made real for the human mind, we may say that matter resists the finite mind of man.

There is, according to Maimon, a parallelism between logic and mathematics in that the various modes of thought employed in the former are to be found also in the latter. Mathematics provides a pattern for the classification of the various modes of logic.

Kant divided the science of logic into the general and the transcendental. Both deal with objects of thought in general irrespective of their contents. They ignore the particular characteristics of the objects to which they are to be applied; their attention in the formulation of principles governing the objects of thought is directed exclusively to the possible thinkability of the objects. The difference between general and transcendental logic consists in the following. The former is concerned with the possibility of the thinking of undetermined objects; its subject matter is solely the possibility of a relation of thought obtaining between the objects, irrespective of the possibility or impossibility of the reality of these objects. The latter, on the other hand, is concerned with principles of thought relating to objects of possible reality. The concepts of transcendental logic acquire validity as necessary conditions of possible experience. The transcendental method as formulated by Kant consists in the assumption of the reality of scientific experience as an undeniable fact from which concepts of thought are derived as necessary conditions of the fact of experience. The validity of transcen-

8 *Ibid.*, p. 36.

dental logic is grounded in the possibility of scientific experience. Since without transcendental concepts the facts of experience would be impossible, the reality of these concepts is assured as necessary and indispensable conditions of the reality of experience. Transcendental logic is thus closely bound up with the transcendental method, which is the essence of philosophy oriented on scientific experience. They are mutually dependent; hence the distinctive character of transcendental logic. Its concepts of thought are related to objects of possible experience; they refer to the possible reality of *a priori* determinable objects.

A similar division of modes of thought can be found in mathematics. The general theory of magnitudes (*arithmetica universalis*) treats of mere relations of magnitudes to one another; it does not deal with empirical objects or *a priori* determinable objects of pure mathematics. Even such a concept as the square root of minus one, $\sqrt{-1}$, the application of which leads to an impossible magnitude, belongs to the general theory of magnitudes. It thus corresponds to general logic, which formulates principles of the thinkability of objects, irrespective of the possibility or impossibility of the reality of these objects.

However, the pure theory of magnitudes, in contradistinction to the general theory of magnitudes, deals with magnitudes of possible construction, such as geometrical figures. Magnitudes of possible construction constitute its subject matter. Just as transcendental logic defines the concepts that are necessary conditions of scientific experience, so the pure theory of magnitudes deals with mathematical objects whose construction is possible. The concepts of transcendental logic and of the pure theory of magnitudes are related to objects of reality; *a priori* determined objects constitute the subject matter of both.

From the consideration of the affinity of some modes of thought in mathematics to those of philosophical speculations and in view of the fact that modern physics is grounded in mathematics, it necessarily follows that a philosophical understanding of mathematics is of significance for a philosophical analysis of thought and its relation to reality. Maimon therefore chides his contemporaries, who claim to be followers of Kant, for, among other things, their lack of appreciation of the importance of mathematics for philosophy. They ignore completely examples from the realm of mathematics that illustrate their philosophical views. "And when they descend from their high speculative position to quote examples for an illustration of their ideas, instead of using simple concepts and propositions from the realm of mathematics (as the great Wolff almost always did), they use examples which obscure the issue rather than clarify it." "In speculative matters," Maimon writes, "examples are indispensable... and only examples from the realm of mathematics are suited for this purpose, since the objects of mathematics can be constructed in intuition through concepts in a precise manner."[9] Of the many examples from mathematics that Maimon employs for an illustration of philosophical ideas, the following frequently occur: the straigth line as the shortest distance between two points; the triangle and its qualities; the circle and the relations obtaining between its parts.

For an illustration of the idea that a logically correct concept (i.e., a concept that does not involve a contradiction) may not be real, as its construction is impossible, Maimon frequently uses the example of a regular decahedron which is a solid figure having ten equal sides. This concept does not involve a contradiction, yet its construction is impossible. Maimon explicitly states that in employing this example he follows Leibniz.[10]

The method of fictions by which Maimon explains some central metaphysical ideas, such as the concept of the thing-in-itself, and the idea of absolute space, has been formulated by him in light of the significance of the method of fictions in mathematics. Above all, Maimon's doctrine of the infinitesimals of sensation, which plays such a central role in the first period of Maimon's writing, namely, in the *Transcendentalphilosophie* and in his commentary to Maimonides' *Guide*, is entirely patterned after a mathematical concept. The mathematical theory of infinitesimals, invented by Leibniz and Newton, is employed by Maimon for an analysis of sensations and perceptions. By this method he interprets Leibniz' conception of the difference between thought and perception as being merely a difference in degree, not in essence, thus arguing against the Kantian doctrine of the essential difference between understanding and intuition (*Anschauung*), i.e., between thought and perception.

The value of mathematics for philosophy does not consist, according to Maimon, in the application of the mathematical method to the investigation of philosophical problems. The mathematical method is a method of progression; as such, it may lead from error to error just as much as from truth to truth. It is not the progressive method as such that is of value for philosophy. But by an analysis of mathematical

[9] Introduction to *Krit. Unt.*
[10] *Ibid.*

thought we can gain clarity about the principles of human cognition in general. For in the construction of mathematical concepts and their relation to one another there is revealed the process of understanding and of reason as such.[11]

Here is clearly manifest Maimon's negative attitude toward the Spinozian mode of philosophizing, which consists in the application of the mathematical method to philosophy (*more geometrico*). This is not a reliable basis for attaining certitude. It is a progressive method grounded in certain assumptions, i.e., definitions, which are laid down dogmatically. Even if we assume that the process of thought is consistently developed, since the basic assumptions may be wrong, the method will lead from error to error instead of from truth to truth. The value of mathematics for philosophy consists, not in the progressive method as such, but rather in the analysis of mathematical concepts from which we can gain clarity about the essence of synthesis, about the method of fictions, about the true nature of the concept of infinity, about the various kinds of infinity; in short, about all the concepts that are of major importance in philosophy.

The definition of a synthesis as an act of thought by which a unity of a manifold is established may be illustrated by an example of a physical object, such as a golden ball, in which the various perceptions of the object – its yellow color, specific weight, roundness, etc. – are comprehended in one concept, which is its unity. Such an example, however, writes Maimon, would give an incomplete, even a wrong conception of the essence of a synthesis. For a synthesis means essentially a necessary unity of the manifold. In the case of a golden ball the unity of the manifold is merely an accidental unity. The yellow color and the specific weight are thought of as united in the object only because we have always perceived them together in time and space. Their connection with one another is neither necessary nor natural, but only accidental, inasmuch as it is derived from the perception of the togetherness of the manifold and not from a law determining by necessity the connection of the manifold into a unity.

The essence of a synthesis can best be illustrated by an example from mathematics, such as a triangle, which is space enclosed by three lines. In the geometrical figure, triangle, space is thinkable in itself without the determination of "being enclosed by three lines." However, three lines, which constitute the determination, are not thinkable in themselves without space as their determinable. Space as a subject of

[11] *Tr.*, p. 285.

certain predicates, such as infinite divisibility, is thinkable in itself, but three lines are not thinkable in themselves without space, since a line is a certain modification of space. Here we have an example of a true concept of a necessary synthesis.[12]

Thus only mathematical examples are suitable for the illustration of philosophical ideas. This is due to the fact that mathematical objects are constructions of the mind and do not contain anything superfluous or accidental. And therein lies the reason for the essential difference between a synthesis of a mathematical object and a synthesis of a physical, material object.

Kant has defined the essence of cognition as consisting, not in a portrayal or depiction of the objects as they are, but in an act of synthesis. Every act of cognition of an object is a synthesis, establishing the unity of a manifold of perceptions. In this Maimon follows Kant. But Maimon stresses the essential difference between an act of synthesis with reference to mathematical objects and a synthesis with regard to material objects. The ideal synthesis is for Maimon a synthesis that complies with the principle of determinability. According to this principle, which governs synthetic thought just as the laws of identity and contradiction govern formal logical thought, a synthesis is that unifying act of thought in which one element of the synthesis (i.e., the determinable), is thinkable in itself, while its other element (i.e., the determination) is not thinkable in itself, but only in connection with the determinable.

iii

According to Maimon, there are three degrees of truth: first, there is subjective truth, that is, a cognition of a particular thinking subject; second, there is subjective truth which is also metaphysically true, that is, a cognition determined by the constitution of the human mind as such, with its particular forms of sensibility and understanding and the capacity of the imagination; and third, a concept recognized by the mind as a truth for any thinking subject is objective truth in an absolute sense. When Maimon speaks of mathematical propositions as subjective truth, he means the second kind of truth. Our sensuous intuitions, i.e., forms of time and space, are merely subjective, for it is possible to imagine other thinking subjects endowed with different forms of sensibility and imagination. These forms therefore have merely

[12] *Ibid.*, pp. 283 f.

subjective reality, even though they are *a priori*. The same is true also
for the forms of understanding. There may be other thinking subjects
with different forms of understanding, by which the appearances, i.e.,
the phenomena, are synthesized into objects of thought.[13]

Maimon considers the forms of sensibility and the forms of understanding as of equal rank; the objectivity of the cognitions determined
by these forms is limited to the human mind. But a clear distinction
must be drawn between the forms of cognition, comprising sensibility
and understanding, and the logical forms of thought. While the former
are valid and objectively true only for the human mind, the latter are
objectively true for any thinking subject. Maimon's intention is to
show the fundamental difference between the forms of sensibility and
of understanding as applied to objects of experience, on the one hand,
and the logical forms of thought, on the other. Only the former, that is,
forms of sensibility and understanding, are subjective in the second
sense of subjectivity, i.e., their validity is confined to human thought;
the logical forms are objective in an absolute sense, their validity is
necessarily binding for any thinking subject. From this follows the
fundamental difference between formal thought, comprising the laws
of logic, i.e., the laws of identity and contradiction, which are binding
for any object of thought and for any thinking subject, and real thought,
i.e., thought referring to determinable objects of experience, which are
valid for the human mind with its definite forms of sensibility and
understanding.

"If I should prove," writes Maimon, "a mathematical proposition
by demonstrating that its opposite involves a contradiction, and some-
one should raise the objection that the argument is convincing for us
only because of our forms of sensibility and understanding, but there
may be other thinking subjects with different forms of cognition, I
would answer that the proposition is actually valid only for us, but not
for those other thinking subjects."[14] This skepticism concerning the
objectivity of our cognitions refers only to those notions that are
grounded in our forms of sensibility and understanding, but not to
the formal laws of logic, i.e., the laws of identity and contradiction;
the latter must be considered valid for any thinking subject. In raising
the question, "Perhaps there are thinking subjects with totally different
forms of cognition," it must be admitted that those thinking subjects,
inasmuch as they are thinking subjects, must have something in common

[13] *Ibid.*, pp. 151 f.
[14] *Ibid.*, p. 152.

with the human mind.[15] Since thought as such is unthinkable in defiance of the formal laws of thought, the laws of identity and contradiction must be considered binding for any thinking subject. Hence, truth derived from these forms of thought is objectively true. Only the truths derived from the forms of sensibility and understanding may be subject to skepticism concerning their objective reality in relation to other thinking subjects, but not the truths grounded in the formal laws of thought in general. Thought in general connotes the subsumption of a manifold under a unity. And even if this were the only aspect of thought common to the human mind and to other minds, the process of unification as such is unthinkable in defiance of the law of contradiction. Even if it were certain that for other minds the manifold and the unity are of a kind different from the manifold and unity known to the human mind, the very act of subsumption of a manifold under a unity presupposes the laws of identity and contradiction.

From the very start of Maimon's argument it is clear that his intention is to prove the objectivity of logical principles and their binding validity for any thinking subject. But the mathematical axioms that are necessary assumptions for the human mind with its particular and definite forms of intuition cannot claim such objectivity. These axioms are subjective because they are bound up with the forms of sensibility and the capacity of the imagination of the human mind; yet they are not arbitrary assumptions that can be replaced at will by others. For human thought, however, the axioms are objectively valid. The consideration that for other thinking subjects with different forms of intuition other axioms are possible does not deprive the axioms grounded in the forms of sensibility of the human mind of their objectivity and validity for us. Since the use of the axioms and their truth are only for us, "it cannot be maintained that they are objectively true, but only that they are real, i.e., they are useful for the cognition of truth and its use."[16]

The term "useful" with reference to truth should not lead us to associate truth with the concept of usefulness in the sense of modern pragmatism. In the pragmatic definition of truth the usefulness of a proposition in the biological sense is its determining factor, whereas for Maimon an idea is "useful" when it fits into a systematic unity of thought. Maimon's purpose is rather to emphasize the reality of the cognitions grounded in the forms of intuition and understanding of

---

[15] *Ibid.*, pp. 152 f.
[16] *Ibid.*, p. 406.

the human mind. Even though these cognitions are not necessary for thinking subjects with other forms of intuition, their truth and reality for the human mind is of an objective nature; in the usefulness (i.e., application) of these cognitions for the human mind lies their true reality. And herein is the ground for the characterization of the Euclidean axioms as "metaphysically true."[17] Metaphysical truth does not mean necessary truth for any thinking subject, but necessary truth for the human mind as it is constituted.

Concerning a deeper understanding of the essence of logical truth in its relation to reality, Maimon writes: "Logical truth consists in the act of connecting the objects of thought, i.e., the concepts, according to the laws of understanding. The axioms are elements of truth but not truth itself. Also, the products of thought resulting from the connection of the axioms are effects of true thought but not truth itself. For, according to my view, truth consists only in the process of thought or in the legitimate manner in which the thinking process takes place. But neither the principles, i.e., the axioms, from which the thinking process started, nor the consequences resulting from these axioms can be designated as truth. All assumptions, even metaphysically false ones, can serve as principles of logical truth... Under the assumption that false principles are true, definite results must necessarily follow. In such a case, the products of thought as well as the principles will have no practical use, but for the definition of truth only the use of the principles for the process of thought is decisive. Had Euclid started his system from false axioms, instead of metaphysically true ones, I am convinced that he would have given the world a work no less consistent than that we now possess. If I assume, for instance, that the exterior angle of a triangle is not equal to the sum of the opposite interior angles, but is equal to one and a half times the sum of these angles, it will necessarily follow that the angle in the center of the circle is not twice (as it actually is), but three times as large as the angle on the periphery. And similarly, when we assume that a part is larger than the whole, results will necessarily follow which will be totally different from those following from opposite axioms..."[18]

Consequently, Maimon divided principles and propositions into real and non-real instead of true and false. The latter, the non-real principles, require at least one real principle, namely, the law of contradiction, which is indispensable for the process of thought. By assuming

---

[17] *Ibid.*, p. 149.
[18] *Ibid.*, pp. 148 f.

different axioms (i.e., non-real, according to Maimon's definition) and proceeding consistently according to the laws of identity and contradiction, the thinking process sa such is true. This opens up new prospects for the operation of thought, namely, that we may discover a new mathematics.[19]

Here Maimon gives a definition of "logical truth," which consists only in the thinking process according to the laws of thought, independent of the content of the objects of thought and of the reality or non-reality of the axioms. The concept of truth is applicable only to the thinking process in harmony with the laws of identity and contradiction. Or, to define Maimon's idea of truth in terms of his own principle of determinability, we may say that the predicates "true" and "false" and the thinking process stand in a relation of determinability to one another. We can say of the thinking process as the determinable that it is true or false. The axioms, however, stand in a relation of determinability to the predicates "real" and "unreal," not to those of "true" and "false."

Maimon refers to Wolff's definition of truth as implying correspondence between a proposition and its object, and this is logical truth. As an example Wolff refers to the proposition, "A triangle has three angles." Maimon's objection to the correspondence theory of truth in general and to Wolff's designation of a mathematical proposition as a logical truth in particular is of importance for the understanding of Maimon's doctrine of truth and his conception of mathematics. The laws of logic are binding for any object of thought, and the *objectum logicum* is the idea of an object of thought in general (*überhaupt*). A logical truth can be only a proposition that can be predicated of any object of thought as such; it does not have a definite content. Therefore, a proposition concerning the relations between the elements of a triangle, which is an object with a definite content determined by conditions *a priori*, such as the form of space, is not a logical truth. The proposition, "A triangle has three angles," is not a logical truth, since the "three angles" are predicated of a particular geometrical object and not of an object in general.[20] Only a proposition like "A triangle is identical with itself" can be designated as a logical truth, since any object must be thought of as identical with itself by any thinking subject.

In addition, Wolff's definition of truth determines only truth of speech, not truth of thought. When we say, "A triangle has three

[19] *Ibid.*, p. 150.
[20] *Ibid.*, p. 400.

angles," we speak the truth because we actually can think of such an object. The opposite statement is false because the object cannot be imagined. But with regard to the thought of a triangle, the predicates "true" and "false" are not applicable; only the predicates "real" and "non-real" can be applied to it. Since we can think of a triangle only with three angles, when we try to think of one with more or less angles, there is no reality to this thought. Thus the idea of a triangle is either real or not real, but not true or false.

Furthermore, "the principles of an object are not the object itself, otherwise the object would be presupposed prior to its formation [*Entstehung*]. The principles of a surface, for instance, are not the surface itself, and the principles of a line are not the line itself. In the same manner, the principles of truth cannot be truth itself."[21] Consequently, the predicate of logical truth cannot be applied to the principles of mathematics, i.e., the axioms, which are the principles of mathematical objects. In this connection, Maimon again characterizes the synthetic propositions of mathematics as subjective truths. The verification of synthetic propositions in mathematics lies in the possibility of construction of the mathematical objects, and construction is dependent on the form of intuition of space, which is subjective. We can well imagine the existence of a thinking subject endowed with a different capacity of intuition of space, who would construct mathematical objects having a totally different form from those of our mathematics.[22] The concept of a regular decahedron, for instance, does not involve a logical contradiction, from the point of view of logic it is a possible concept, yet a regular decahedron, i.e., a solid body having ten equal sides, does not lend itself to construction. It is therefore not a real object for us. However, we can imagine a mind with a different intuitive capacity, that could construct a decahedron. The laws of logic, i.e., those of identity and contradiction, are binding for any thinking subject. No thinking process as such is possible in defiance of these laws. But the synthetic propositions, even in mathematics, are binding only for us. "Mathematical propositions," writes Maimon, "are objectively true, but only on the supposition of the objectivity of the fundamental assumptions, i.e, the axioms... This, however, does not deprive them [mathematical propositions] of their legitimate use, since their usefulness and their truth are only for us. Consequently, it is not correct to say of a mathematical axiom that it is objectively true, but only that

---

[21] *Ibid.*, p. 406.
[22] *Ibid.*, p. 151.

it is real. That is to say, it is useful for the cognition of truth and its use."[23]

The application of the predicates "real" and "not real" to mathematical axioms, instead of the predicates "true" and "false," is bound up with Maimon's doctrine that truth is determined by coherence and logical consistency.

Maimon strives to replace the correspondence theory of truth with a systematic coherent conception of truth. The first is realistic and dogmatic, for it is grounded in the concept of substance in its realistic and dogmatic sense; Maimon's concept of truth, on the other hand, is functional and critical, for it is grounded, first, in the idea of substance as a relational concept and secondly, in the idea that the criterion of truth is the systematic and coherent unity of thought. The correspondence theory of truth maintains that an idea of an object is true when it corresponds with the object. This notion is untenable when we realize that we can only compare one set of ideas with another set of ideas, but it is beyond our ken to compare an idea of an object with the object itself.

Maimon's anticipation of the possibility of the discovery of a new mathematics by assuming axioms different from the Euclidean axioms seems to imply that Maimon conceives of axioms as mere assumptions or hypotheses. The axioms in themselves are not metaphysically true but are presuppositions, the verification of which lies exclusively in their function for the construction of a consistent mathematical system of propositions.

By assuming axioms different from the Euclidean axioms, a system of different mathematical propositions would necessarily follow. And such a system would be of equal value with regard to truth as Euclidean mathematics. Some have seen in Maimon's conception of the axioms an anticipation of non-Euclidean geometry.[24] Also, a comparison has been made between Maimon's conception of mathematical axioms and the modern theory of the axioms as a logical system of forms of possible scientific constructions.[25] According to the latter doctrine, axioms in themselves are empty forms; they do not refer to ontological existence, i.e., the shape and reality of space. The verification of the axioms lies exclusively in their function and usefulness for the construction of a system of mathematical relations. The task of the geometrician does

---

[23] *Ibid.*, pp. 405 f.
[24] Cf. Kuntze, *op. cit.*, p. 375, and Richard Kroner, *Von Kant bis Hegel*, I, 345.
[25] Cf. Hugo Bergmann, "Salomon Maimons Philosophie der Mathematik," *Isis*, No. 49, Vol. XVI[2], p. 223, who refers to H. Weyl, *Philosophie der Mathematik*, p. 21.

not consist in the search for the ontological truth of the axioms in themselves. Rather, his task is confined to the evolvement, on the basis of certain assumptions, of a coherent and consistent system of mathematical relations. In other words, the main concern of the mathematician should not be ontology, i.e., the reality and nature of space, but merely the deduction of a system of mathematical propositions, their relations to one another, and their interconnections. Axioms as formal assumptions constitute merely a point of departure for the deduction of such a system. All systems of axioms themselves are of equal value with reference to truth, inasmuch as any system of axioms can serve as a basis for the construction of a coherent system of mathematical propositions.

It seems that Maimon anticipated the conception of geometry as a science dealing exclusively with relations. The early discoverers of non-Euclidean geometry, in abandoning the axiom of parallels, believed that they had finally found the true nature of space. Janos Bolyai held that through the new geometry a clue had been discovered to the theory of the true nature of space. Hence the name of his book, *The Science of Absolute Space*.[26] Thus the new geometry led to an ontological conception concerning the nature and reality of space. It was Felix Klein who opposed these conclusions. He maintained that mathematics is a science dealing exclusively with relations; hence from the assumption of axioms different from the Euclidean no conclusion can be drawn as to the ontological reality and nature of space. There is no path leading from the axioms as assumptions to the ontological existence of space and its nature.[27] In this sense, the implication in Maimon of the possibility of the discovery of a new mathematics can be understood as an anticipation of the conception of the axioms as assumptions. His reference to them as being "subjectively true" could be taken to mean that they are presuppositions.

In fact, however, there is a tremendous difference between the modern conception of the axioms as assumptions, hypotheses, or empty forms, and Maimon's conception of them as being "subjectively true." They are "subjective," in Maimon's view, because they are grounded in the forms of our intuition of space, and a mind is imaginable with different forms of intuition. But for the human mind with its particular forms of intuition the Eucledian axioms are subjectively true. The term

---

[26] It was published in 1832 as an appendix to a book of his father and had the title "Appendix scientiam spatii absolute veram exhibit."

[27] Cf. Ernst Cassirer, *The Problem of Knowledge* (New Haven: Yale University Press, 1950), pp. 28 f.

"subjective," employed by Maimon to designate the nature of the axioms, does not mean that they are "arbitrary," or that they have the character of hypotheses, for which another set of axioms could be substituted with equal cogency. It implies merely the distinction between the axioms and the principles of logic. While the latter are necessary for any thinking subject, the former are true only for the human mind endowed with particular forms of intuition.

Maimon's anticipation of the possible discovery of a new mathematics must be viewed in the light of his attempt to reduce synthetic propositions in mathematics to analytic propositions. Even though he did not succeed in accomplishing such a reduction, as he himself resignedly admits, it remained for him an ideal goal for which to strive. The attainment of such a reduction is, in principle, possible.[28] Moreover, the dissolution of synthetic thought into analytic thought, which constitutes for the human, finite mind a mere possibility, is for the infinite mind an actual reality.

The very idea of an infinite mind implies an ideal goal of cognition for the human mind. Should we succeed one day in attaining such an ideal stage of cognition, i.e., the synthetic propositions in mathematics are dissolved into analytic ones, we shall no longer be dependent on intuition and on the construction of mathematical objects. Mathematical propositions will be completely deduced from the logical principles of identity and contradiction. They will be pure, for they will no longer be grounded in the forms of intuition; they will also be *a priori* in the absolute sense of the term, i.e., not because of the possible construction of mathematical objects in intuition, which is the Kantian concept of *a priori*, but because of the possible deduction of mathematical propositions from the logical principles of thought and *prior* to the construction of the objects through intuition and independent of the analysis of these objects. This in Maimon's view of *a priori* in an absolute sense.

Now, since the ideal goal of cognition consists in reducing synthetic propositions to analytic ones, this ideal has meaning and reality only on the assumption that the axioms, upon which synthetic propositions are based, are real and metaphysically true. If they were mere hypotheses and arbitrary suppositions, instead of which other axioms could equally be posited, the striving for a dissolution of synthetic propositions into analytic ones would lose its basis. In order to entertain the hope and the belief in the possibility of a continuous transition from subjective truth (i.e., truth grounded in the subjective forms of our intuition)

[28] See above, p. 138 f.

to objective truth (i.e., truth grounded in principles valid for any thinking subject), it must be assumed that the subjective forms of intuition are not mere assumptions but are metaphysically true and real even in relation to an infinite mind. The metaphysical idea of an infinite mind implies the possibility of the reduction of synthetic propositions into analytic propositions. This idea can fulfill the function for which it was conceived only on the assumption of a certain affinity and relationship between the finite mind and the infinite mind, so that the very same synthetic propositions of the human finite mind can be dissolved into analytic ones by the infinite mind. Hence the axioms of Euclidean geometry must be considered as real and metaphysically true axioms, otherwise the idea of the dissolution of our synthetic propositions into analytic ones by an infinite mind would have no basis, nor could such a dissolution be for us an ideal goal after which to strive.

The anticipation of the possibility of a discovery of an entirely new mathematics is, to my mind, incompatible with the assumption of the possibility and the striving for a dissolution of synthetic propositions into analytic ones and with the idea of an infinite mind in relation to which such a dissolution is an actual reality. The former is grounded in the conception of the axioms as mere assumptions, hypotheses, or empty forms; the latter presupposes the axioms to be metaphysically true.

Consequently, mathematics based on axioms as mere assumptions and hypotheses cannot claim with regard to its truth-value to be of the same rank and dignity as Euclidean geometry, which is based on axioms grounded in the capacity of our imagination and in our forms of intuition of space. Maimon was aware of the distinction in the gradation of truth between the Eucledian axioms and any other system of axioms posited as mere assumptions. "If Euclid," Maimon writes, "had presupposed false axioms instead of his metaphysically true ones, etc." While the Euclidean axioms are defined as metaphysically true, any other set of presupposed axioms are designated as false. And again Maimon writes in one of his letters to Reinhold: "I would have esteemed the work of Euclid, with reference to its theoretical value, not less, if it were established on false axioms, than his present work."[29] The axioms are thus not mere assumptions or empty forms, but they are either true or false. And the Eucledian axioms are true. Any other set of axioms upon which a system of geometry could be constructed would be false. Such a scientific construction would equally command our

[29] *Str.*, p. 218.

admiration because of its theoretical excellence, which is the result of the harmony and the coherence of its propositions with one another and with its basic principles, thus forming a unified system of thought. Since, however, the fundamental principles are false, a system built upon such principles would be of no use.

Alongside the conception of space as a concept of thought, i.e., as a form of heterogeneity and diversity of objects, Maimon retains the view that space is grounded in our forms of intuition. The former is based on Leibniz' view of space and the latter on the Kantian doctrine of space. While the Leibnizian conception of space is employed by Maimon in relation to objects of experience, the Kantian conception of space is valid in relation to the construction of mathematical objects. A synthesis of Leibniz and Kant is here clearly discernible, as it follows from the whole trend of Maimon's thought. However, the ideal goal that Maimon envisioned consists in the replacement of the forms of intuition by concepts of thought. As long as the comprehension of space is grounded in the forms of intuition, our mathematical propositions are not *a priori* in the absolute sense of the term, since we are dependent on the actual construction of the mathematical objects and on the analysis of these objects for the derivation of the laws and principles governing them. Nor can our aspiration for a dissolution of synthetic propositions in mathematics into analytic ones ever be realized, as long as we cannot dispense with our intuitions, and the system of mathematical relations is contingent upon the construction of mathematical objects.

iv

Maimon held that mathematical propositions are synthetic, but since they are derived by a process of analysis of the objects constructed, their *a priori* nature is modified. The capacity of cognition produces the mathematical objects according to certain rules, of which we become aware through an analysis of the objects produced. Thus, for instance, the concept of space enclosed by three lines does not contain within itself the concept of a geometrical object with three angles; only analysis of the object constructed shows that space enclosed by three lines produces a triangle. Prior to its construction it cannot be known that space enclosed by three lines produces a triangle. Herein lies the difference between mathematical propositions and analytic propositions, such as "a thing cannot at the same time be and not be," which are derived from the principle of contradiction, for synthetic propositions in mathematics are dependent on and posterior to the objects. The latter are akin to experiential propositions *a posteriori*, with this difference, however, that the material of mathematical propositions is produced by the mind, while the material of synthetic propositions relating to objects of experience is given from without.[30]

In both cases, however, the propositions as such are *a posteriori*. The mind conceives the idea of a mathematical object, such as space enclosed by three lines, and the imagination produces such an object. Upon the construction of the object it is discovered that it has three angles. Thus the concept of space enclosed by three lines does not necessarily contain the concept of three angles. The connection between the two concepts is not analytically derivable; it is therefore not a necessary connection. The human mind here makes a virtue out of necessity by stating that space enclosed by three lines must have three angles, as though our mind were the lawgiver of this connection. In fact, the mind is here compelled to obey a law given to it from without. Analysis of the object produced demonstrates that the two concepts are connected, but it is unwarranted to assume the objective necessity of the proposition connecting the two concepts. As it is not analytically derivable, the possibility cannot be ruled out that some mind may in principle be able to enclose space by three lines without necessarily producing a triangle. Since the idea of such an object does not contain a logical contradiction, the conception of its impossibility is merely subjective, being grounded in experience. It is a truth of fact, not a truth of reason. "It can only gradually approach objective necessity through greater induction. The more we observe and comprehend triangles, the more we become convinced that space enclosed by three lines can have only three angles. But since induction can never be completed, the subjective necessity can continuously approach objective necessity, but never fully attain it."[31]

The same reasoning applies to all propositions concerning objects of experience. We observe that fire produces warmth and melts wax. Two impressions following each other in time are connected in a proposition of cause and effect. It is an experience of sensation, which is merely subjective. An experiential proposition can approach objective certitude only through induction. Since induction can never be com-

---

[30] *Philos. Wört.*, pp. 174 f.
[31] *Ibid.*

pleted, we can only gradually approximate objective necessity but never fully attain it.

Maimon thus differentiates between three classes of propositions: analytic propositions, which are governed by the law of contradiction; synthetic propositions concerning objects of experience; and synthetic propositions concerning objects of mathematics. Though the latter are *a priori*, in that they are produced by the mind, the rules to which they are subject are not *a priori*, since they are dependent on the analysis of the objects "given," i.e., given from within. Synthetic propositions in mathematics, like synthetic propositions concerning objects of experience, can approach objective necessity only through induction.

The following objection may, however, be raised against Maimon's contention. The causal nexus between phenomena occurring in time is indeed dependent on induction. The logical connection between two concepts in the form, "When A, then B," is a principle of thought not bound up with time. In order to subsume phenomena of experience following each other in time under the logical principle of causality, the aspect of time must be overcome. That is to say, the experience of a succession of phenomena in time must be brought into a causal connection of logical necessity. This can only be approximated through progressive induction. But with regard to mathematical objects, which are not phenomena occurring in time, the establishment of a rule governing them is not dependent on induction. Thus, for example, the proposition that the enclosing of space by three lines results in an object having three angles is dependent on analysis of the object produced, but it acquires objective necessity by analysis of a single object. It is not dependent on the observation and analysis of additional objects. Since there is no need to subordinate phenomena occurring in time to a logical principle, the analysis of a single mathematical object is sufficient for the establishment of the rule by which it is governed. Mathematical objects are ideal objects, therefore the analysis of one object is sufficient for the establishment of a universal rule.

In another context Maimon defines mathematical propositions as *a priori* but not pure. Pure cognition consists of such concepts as are exclusively the product of the understanding unsullied by any sensibility; pure concepts are also *a priori*. But the reverse cannot be maintained, as there are *a priori* cognitions that are not wholly pure. This is the case with mathematical concepts. The concept of a circle, for instance, is *a priori*, as it is wholly produced by the understanding and is not due to the perception of an object given from without. However, it is not

pure, since it is grounded in the intuition of space, which is not the product of the mind but is given from elsewhere. The concept is *a priori* as
it is a product of the mind, but it is not pure, since it is not independent
of the forms of sensibility.[32]

According to this definition of pure cognition, only logical principles,
which are entirely independent of any intuition, comply with the
requirements of purity. Logical principles, however, are formal and
constitute only a negative criterion of cognition, that is, a *conditio sine
qua non*, in defiance of which no object of cognition is possible. But they
do not grant positive knowledge of objects. Hence the objection may
be raised that we have no pure cognition at all, as there are no objects
of knowledge that fulfill the demands of purity as defined. Recognizing
the consequence of his conception of pure cognition, Maimon points out
that with reference to objects of experience our understanding can only
posit hypothetical propositions. Propositions that are not wholly pure
are sufficient for the cognition of objects of experience. "Moreover,
from the generality of the propositions, as verified by experience, we
are entitled to assume their necessity by supposing that our synthetic
propositions are analytic with reference to a higher reason."[33] That is
to say, cognitions that are for us not wholly pure are for a higher reason
absolutely pure.

The question concerning the possibility of synthetic propositions
a priori was solved by Kant in accordance with his understanding
of the meaning of *a priori*. Kant considers the cognition of an object
to be *a priori* when the object itself is grounded in the forms of the
cognitive capacity. When the object itself is deduced from the forms of
sensibility and understanding, the propositions concerning its particular
characteristics are *a priori*. Kant did not require the deduction of the
relation between subject and predicate from a general principle the
validity of which is not dependent upon the analysis of the object. He
considered synthetic propositions in mathematics as *a priori*, since the
objects are grounded in the *a priori* forms of sensibility.

According to Maimon's understanding of the meaning of the concept
a priori, the cognition of the relation between the subject and the
predicate of a proposition must be deduced from a general principle
preceding the construction of the object. Even though the object itself
is the product of *a priori* forms of cognition, the cognition of the particular characteristics of the object may still be *a posteriori*, for it is depen-

[32] *Tr.*, p. 56.
[33] *Ibid.*, pp. 359 f.

dent on the analysis of the "given" object. A synthetic proposition can attain the rank of an *a priori* cognition only if it can be deduced from a general principle conceived independently of and prior to the rise of the object.[34]

Another formulation of the various kinds of *a priori* consists in the distinction between formal and material *a priori*. *A priori* in the formal and absolute sense of the term applies to those propositions which precede the cognition of objects. They are propositions governed by the laws of identity and of contradiction and refer to objects of thought in general. Mathematical objects, which are the product of our cognitive capacity, are materially *a priori*. But cognitions concerning the characteristic features of these objects are *a posteriori*, since they are dependent on an analysis of the objects. The distinction between objects in general, which are *a priori* in a formal sense, and propositions that follow the cognition of a given object can be illustrated thus: "Assuming I have no idea of a straight line and the question is put to me: Can a straight line be at the same time not-straight? I cannot, by claiming ignorance of the nature of the object, postpone my answer until I have obtained a clear idea of a straight line. My answer will be ready at hand that such a possibility is excluded. If, however, the question is put to me, Is a straight line the shortest? my answer may be, I do not know until I have obtained a clear idea of a straight line. The reason for this distinction is that in the first case my answer is determined by the law of contradiction, which is the most general form of thought; it is valid for all objects of thought independent of their nature. But in the second case, the proposition that a straight line is the shortest between two points does not follow necessarily from the notion of straight line (unless a straight line is defined as the shortest distance between two points). Hence, as long as we have no clear idea of a straight line, we cannot know whether it is the shortest."[35]

Now, the purpose of Maimon's doctrine, formulated as the principle of determinability, is to provide a criterion of synthetic propositions. It fulfills a function for synthetic propositions similar to that of the law of contradiction for analytic propositions. This principle is the preceding cognition conceived independently of and prior to the existence of the objects; it is the criterion of synthetic propositions.

According to the principle of determinability, the subject is defined

---

[34] Cf. *Bacons von Verulam Neues Organon. Mit Anmerkungen von Salomon Maimon*, p. 216. There Maimon refers to his essay in *Berlinisches Journal für Aufklärung*, 9 Band, Stück III.

[35] *Tr.*, pp. 169 f.

as the concept that can be thought of by itself, while the predicate is the concept that cannot be thought of independently but only in conjunction with the former. Thus, in the proposition, "Space can be enclosed by three lines," "space" is the subject, as it can be thought of by itself, while "enclosed by three lines" is its predicate, as it cannot be thought of otherwise than in connection with space. However, the proposition, "Space enclosed by three lines forms a triangle," does not comply with the principle of determinability prior to analysis of the object. To be sure, "triangle" presupposes space of which it is a modification, but it does not presuppose space enclosed by three lines before the object is analyzed. It is therefore a synthetic proposition resultung from an analysis of the object "given," but it is not *a priori*. This seems to be the import of Maimon's conception of mathematical propositions as not strictly *a priori*. As the proposition is dependent upon the analysis of a given object, even though the object is the product of the creative capacity of cognition, there is a formal incompleteness in our cognition, the absence of which is the hallmark of *a priori* cognition. Furthermore, "we encounter also a material incompleteness in our cognition of mathematical objects when the construction of the object cannot be attained except by a process of thought *ad infinitum*."[36] This is the case, for instance, in the consideration of a circle as a polygon with an infinite number of sides. This can be attained only by an infinite process. The drawing of a circle is the product of the imagination, not of thought. Its conceptualization by considering it a polygon with an infinite number of sides can never be completed. "There arises thus the following antinomy. On the one hand, reason demands the possibility of the construction of the object as a necessary condition of its reality, for if it cannot be presented by construction, its reality is problematical. On the other hand, reason demands the conceptualization of the object, that is, its deduction from thought, and is not satisfied with its mere construction by the imaginative faculty."[37]

In the consideration of a circle as a polygon with an infinite number of sides, the mind's quest for conceptualization is manifest. But the completion of the object is impossible to attain except by an infinite process.

The possibility of synthetic propositions *a priori* in mathematics is, according to Kant, deduced from the fact that mathematical objects are grounded in the forms of intuition *a priori*. The propositions are

[36] *Bacons von Verulam Neues Organon*, p. 217.
[37] *Ibid.*, p. 218.

a priori, since the objects are the product of our thought in accordance with the laws and principles determining their construction. Maimon, however, holds that such propositions cannot be considered *a priori* in the strict sense of the term, since they are dependent on the consideration and the analysis of the objects produced.

Maimon's definition of *a priori* in this sense is a return to the concept generally held by the scholastics and the pre-Kantian rationalists. Kant, however, introduced a new concept of *a priori*, which can be defined as the genetic-transcendental *a priori*. By "transcendental" is meant the necessary condition of an object. The *a priori* concept is not transcendent but immanent to our consciousness, and it is the necessary condition of the generation of the object. Hence the definition "genetic-transcendental." Propositions concerning mathematical objects are *a priori* even though the objects must first be constructed and presented for analysis, since these propositions establish the necessary conditions of the reality of the objects.

CHAPTER XII

MAIMON'S CONCEPTION OF PHILOSOPHY

Maimon is a true follower of Kant in that he has drawn the conclusions of critical philosophy with a systematic consistency unsurpassed by any of his contemporaries. In addition, he follows in the tradition of Leibniz, apparent not only in his adoption of certain of Leibniz' doctrines, but also in his realization of the close connection between philosophy and the natural sciences. Of his contemporaries only Beck can be classed with those rationalist thinkers whose philosophic orientation was towards mathematics and the natural sciences; the great speculative system-builders of the post-Kantian period were oriented towards the humanistic branches of knowledge.

The close association between philosophy and the natural sciences, the hallmark of the philosophy of the seventeenth and eighteenth centuries, especially the continental branch, was completely loosened in the metaphysical speculations of the nineteenth century. The rise of historical consciousness was the characteristic feature of that century, and this is evident in speculations of the representatives of the philosophy of that time. While philosophy's gain in that period was the acquiring of a new orientation towards the historical and humanistic sciences, this was achieved at the cost of losing contact with, or giving up its orientation towards the natural sciences.

The relation of philosophy to natural science is of paramount importance for critical philosophy. It resides in the conception of philosophy as consisting of an investigation of being as presented in a system of laws and not of being as perceived by our senses. In other words, the essence of being as defined and formulated by scientific thought, and not being as given to our ordinary, natural consciousness, is the subject matter of the philosophic inquiry. This is best illustrated in the Kantian questions: How are synthetic propositions *a priori* possible in mathematics and in natural science? To be sure, philosophy is concerned with the ultimate questions concerning the essence of being. But the critical method consists in the consideration of being resulting from scientific thought, that is, the phenomena of experience presented by a system of laws as the subject matter of a philosophic investigation. Not the "brutal facts" of natural experience, but the "facts" of reality as conceived and presented by the exact sciences constitute the essence of being. These are the facts resulting from scientific thought which is based on principles *a priori*. The process of scientific thought is not a passive ordering of "given" facts. It is, rather, a creative process which consists in evolving hypotheses and concepts originating in pure thought, on the basis of which the phenomena are explained and ordered in a unified system of laws. By realizing the creative and active character of scientific thought, the phenomena of experience, i.e., scientific experience, will be understood, not as "given" facts, but as facts that have their root in creative "acts." And the task of critical philosophy is to show how the "facts" are grounded in "acts." Herein consists the significance of the relation of philosophy to scientific thought.

This relation is brought out in an essay by Maimon, which we shall now analyze in detail. In 1792 the Academy of Sciences in Berlin set the problem, "What progress has metaphysics made since Leibniz?" ("Was hat die Metaphysik seit Leibniz für Progressen gemacht?") as the subject of a literary competition for that year. A year later, in 1793, Maimon wrote an essay (not competing for the prize) dealing on the whole with the same problem but under a different title: "On the Progress of Philosophy."[1]

In this essay Maimon is critical of the formulation of the problem by the Academy for the following reasons. The Kantian who accepts the conclusions of critical philosophy cannot consider the task posed by the Academy as a problem worthy of investigation. The follower of Kant must deny the very possibility of metaphysics as a science dealing with the "thing-in-itself." Therefore, the science of metaphysics, whose subject matter is "things-in-themselves," cannot possibly have made any progress at all. However, the problem as formulated by the Academy is predicated upon the assumption of the possibility of metaphysics as a science. The anti-Kantian, who does not despair of a possible solution of metaphysical problems, must, before attempting to answer the specific question of the Academy, try first of all to solve the general problem: Is metaphysics as such possible? This is the broader question, which must naturally precede the specific question concerning the progress of metaphysics since Leibniz. By ignoring the general problem concerning the possibility of metaphysics as a science, says Maimon, one only reveals his total disregard of the new state of

---

[1] *Über die Progressen der Philosophie.* It forms the first part of *Str.*, pp. 3–58.

philosophy brought about by Kant. It is therefore proper to transform the question of the Academy into a more general problem: What progress, if any, has philosophy made since Leibniz? To attempt to solve this problem is a worthy undertaking in itself, and not merely as a preliminary to a solution of the problem with regard to metaphysics.

Maimon here sets the focus of the essay, which is to prove the close connection and interrelationship between philosophy and the natural sciences. Science and philosophy can influence each other fruitfully and thus benefit from each other. In this Maimon follows in the path of Leibniz, whose whole work is an attempt at comprehensive synthesis of all the aspects of the human spirit.

The solution of the question concerning the progress of philosophy not only is of vital importance for the establishment of the essential subject matter of philosophy, but it is of relevance for the work of science as a whole, its possibility and scope, its limitations and the certainty of its methods. Since the core of the task is the progress of philosophy as a science, the object of which is, according to Maimon, the establishment of the form of all sciences, the results of such an investigation has a bearing on all sciences. It is of the greatest importance for all sciences that they be conscious of the contributions of philosophy to the clarification of the essence of cognition, the possibility and scope of human knowledge. Furthermore, the consideration of the development of philosophy in a certain period, the investigation of the causes of its progress as well as of its retrogression, may help to discover means for its advancement as well as remedies for the causes of its relapse.

The period chosen by the Academy is of particular importance for the following reasons. The reformation or revolution undertaken by Kant with respect to the philosophy of Leibniz and Wolff is well known. After the appearance of Kant's first *Critique* the philosophical world was divided between two schools, those who accepted the conclusions of critical philosophy and those who followed Leibniz and Wolff. It is therefore fitting to try to determine what philosophy has gained since Leibniz.

"It must, however, be pointed out," writes Maimon, "that a purely historical solution of the problem will not suffice. A mere account of the various works written in this field in their historical order and an exhaustive report of the manifold applications of this philosophy to various realms of human endeavor, in order to determine its progress, will not contribute much towards a successful solution of this all-important question, as I understand it. A 'pragmatic' history of philosophy, of which the solution of our problem constitutes an integral part, must be written under the aspect of an *a priori* principle. The human spirit is, in its essence, always the same. The modes of its progress toward perfection and of its aberrations are, on the whole, at all times and in all climes the same."[2] It must therefore be possible to determine by an analysis of the constitution of the human mind the various methods and modes of its growth and development.

Maimon thus demands that the essence of philosophy as well as of philosophical principles should be determined *a priori*, in view of the insight into the essence of the human mind and as a consequence of the understanding of the constitution of the human spirit. In other words, an appeal is here formulated for the application of the transcendental method to philosophy itself. This method, which is the very heart and soul of critical philosophy, has established certain *a priori* principles on the basis of which scientific experience is possible. Philosophy as a science is likewise possible only under the assumption of certain *a priori* principles. The order and classification of the various philosophical systems can be performed only on the basis of a certain *a priori* principle. By the term "pragmatic" Maimon means a systematic and coherent presentation of the various modes of philosophical thought, as he explicitly states: "A pragmatic history of philosophy should not present various opinions of philosophers but modes of thought, neither should it describe works but methods, nor set forth a conglomeration of individual and ingenious ideas but coherent systems of thought."[3]

As a matter of fact, the application of the transcendental method to philosophy itself is already pointed out by Maimon in his first work, *Versuch über die Transcendentalphilosophie*, where the question is raised: "How is philosophy as a pure *a priori* science possible?" This is analogous to the main questions with which Kant's *Critique of Pure Reason* is concerned: "How is pure mathematics possible?" and "How is pure science possible?" In like manner, a systematic presentation of the progress of philosophy must be bound up with some *a priori* principle, otherwise we can only apply the method of induction and present a conglomeration of individual ideas, not a "pragmatic history of philosophy." Inasmuch as a systematic presentation of the progress of thought is a science, the essence of which is a coherent entity and an ordered body of ideas, it cannot be the result of a haphazard induction of single facts and of a loose and random recording of ingenious ideas.

[2] *Ibid.*, p. 6.
[3] *Ibid.*

The single facts and the individual ideas must be subordinated to a unifying principle conceived by the mind *a priori*.

As a consequence of his conception of philosophy as the science of the form of all sciences, Maimon subdivides the question concerning the progress of philosophy since Leibniz into the following separate questions:

1. In what sense can the growth of a science in general take place?
2. What is the essence of philosophy in general?
3. What is the essence of the philosophy of Leibniz?
4. In what sense is the growth of philosophy possible and by what means can it be achieved?
5. What has philosophy gained since Leibniz, and what are the new insights that philosophy has acquired through the influence of Leibniz and its followers?

In this division of the problem into various separate questions we observe the method of considering first the general and then the particular. Maimon's aim is thus to establish the general principles from which the particulars follow. Consequently, he considers first the various aspects of the possible growth of science in general, and then he applies the principles governing the growth of science in general to the development of philosophy in particular.

As far as the first question is concerned, Maimon defines the possible growth of science as taking place in the direction of extension as well as intension. Science can gain in extension by the widening of the scope of the application of it principles. For example, pure mathematics was highly developed by the ancients; in antiquity it had attained astounding results. But the extensive application of its principles has been developed only in modern times. The connection between an arithmetic series and a geometric series, which is the basis of logarithms, was discovered first, it took however a considerable length of time before the logarithms were actually devised. The method of fluents, i.e., variable quantities considered as continuously increasing or diminishing, was used as a scientific method before the discovery of calculus. It took some time, however, before Newton and Leibniz gave to this method a generally applicable form. The science of algebra is no more than the general application of the particular relations obtaining between entities as established by arithmetics; differential calculus is grounded in a clear concept of the limits of relations which Archimedes had already employed.

Here modern science has not invented entirely new principles; it has only extended the limits of the area of application of principles already known. Science can also develop by extension through the discovery of a new principle or the improvement of a principle already known.

With respect to intensity, the growth of science is possible through the acquisition of a principle from which the objects with which it is concerned can be deduced in a systematic form. It is a great advantage for science to be able to deduce these objects from a unifying principle, thus acquiring formal unity. The astronomy of Ptolemy explained the phenomena of the universe satisfactorily. What, then, has astronomy gained by the contributions of Copernicus, Kepler, and Newton? Nothing but a principle of greater unity, from which the various objects of the universe can be deduced.

The general principle, from which the particular objects can be deduced, may be defined as a "real" principle. A general principle is in itself an ideal concept; it attains reality only when the "real" particular objects can be deduced from it. Newton's law of gravitation is a "real" principle, since particular natural phenomena are explained by it and deduced from it. Natural laws grounded in "real" principles, which is the attainment of modern science, have granted to natural science a systematic form and unity it did not possess previously. Science gains in intension through the discovery of a necessary and universally valid principle and by the invention of a method appropriate for the particular science. "Thus natural science as well as psychology, ethics, and aesthetics gain in intension, i.e., strength of conviction [and unity], when it can be shown that various phenomena of a particular science, which are given a posteriori, can be determined a priori," that is to say, they can be deduced from a general principle.[4]

Without entering into a detailed discussion of the concept of philosophy in general, Maimon emphasizes the essential distinction between pure and applied philosophy. This distinction has not been properly or adequately recognized, just as the various philosophical methods have not been fully acknowledged. One may open the best history of philosophy only to find in it mental products of various types and methods, all presented under the title of philosophy, without a proper distinction being made between the characters of each of them. Yet who does not observe the essential difference between Thales, who did not recognize an intellectual, but only a material principle of all things, and Anaxagoras, who acknowledged the necessity of assuming two heterogeneous principles to explain all things, namely, an intellectual principle as an

---

[4] *Ibid.*, p. 10.

efficient, formal, and final cause and a material principle as a material cause?[5] Or who does not see the fundamental distinction between the method of Thales, who, in his search for a principle of all things of reality, did not go beyond the world of material phenomena, but conceived of water, a material object and not an intellectual abstraction, as the principle of all things, and the Atomists, who, though they did not rise above the physical world, yet transcended the limits of the sensuous in their search for a principle of all being? While the atoms are material elements, they are conceived by a process of abstraction of the sensuous; they are thus the result of pure thought and intellectualization. Yet all these various doctrines, arrived at by divers methods, are presented as products of the same science, the same category of knowledge, i.e., philosophy.

Now, philosophy in general, like mathematics, can be divided into a pure, an applied, and a practical science. A pure science considers its object as it is in itself, in its pure form, abstracted from the various qualities with which it may be associated. So, for instance, the object of pure geometry is space in all its possible determinations. A parabola as a geometrical figure is considered in geometry a pure quantity abstracted from body and motion. An applied science deals with an object actually possessing different qualities but considered only with reference to that quality which is the subject matter of the particular science. So, for instance, the consideration of the line, forming an oblique angle, that is described by a moving body thrown through the air, i.e., a parabola, is an object of applied mathematics. This is in accordance with the law that determines the motion resulting from a combination of the force of gravitation and the force imparted to the body by throwing it in a certain direction. The body, possessing various qualities, is considered here only with reference to the geometrical line it describes under certain conditions. A parabola as such is an object of pure geometry. The consideration of the movement of a body under certain conditions resulting in the formation of a parabola is an object of applied geometry.

Now, it is possible to assume that a different relation exists between the force of gravitation and the force imparted to a trajected body, that its movement actually describes a hyperbola instead of a parabola. If this assumption were made, the proposition that the body describes a parabola would be false with respect to its practical use. However, it would still remain a true proposition of applied mathematics, provided

[5] *Ibid.*

it is formulated as a hypothetical proposition: If the relationship of the force of gravitation to the force imparted to the body by trajecting it into space were such and such, its movement would describe a parabola. Since this is actually the case, i.e., the statement that the movement of such a body describes a parabola is of practical use, the proposition can be stated in a categorical instead of a hypothetical form, thus: The movement of a body thrown into the air at an oblique angle will describe a parabola owing to the law determining the relation of the force of gravitation to the force imparted to the body by throwing it in such a manner.

The distinction between an applied science and a practical science has been overlooked to the detriment of the expansion of the scope of our knowledge. We have to think of natural laws formulated in mathematical terms as possible laws; when pure laws are applied to objects of experience, they become propositions of applied mathematics. "The subject matter of science as such is the merely possible." For an explanation of this statement by Maimon the following must be borne in mind. By the concept of "possibility" we have to understand here the logically possible. Through its application to an object of experience the possible attains "reality." Natural laws in their pure, ideal form are not derived from experience but are conceived by the mind for the purpose of explaining the phenomena of experience. In actual reality we can perceive the phenomena of experience only as approximations to pure, ideal laws, but never as their full and adequate manifestations.

As ideal laws, natural laws refer only to the "possible"; only by means of subsidiary hypotheses explaining the deviations of the phenomena of experience from the ideal law is the possible related to the real; and the ideal becomes practical. Natural laws in their pure, ideal form express only "possible" relations. So, for instance, the Newtonian law of gravitation in its ideal form was not derived from experience but conceived as an ideal relation. As such it expresses only a possible relation, as it does not contradict the laws of logic, and its application to objects of reality is possible. In another connection Maimon writes that Newton's fundamental principle, that a body persists always in its present state of rest or motion (inertia) until the force of another body changes its present state, cannot be derived from experience, for we do not find a body that always remains in the same state. And yet this fundamental principle is real as an idea; it can be presented in intuition (*Anschauung*) through approximation *ad infinitum*. Now, this fundamental principle, which is real as an idea, refers only to a possible and not an actual reality. This pure and ideal principle can be presented in experience only through approximation *ad infinitum*. That is to say, the possible can refer to actual reality and the ideal can become real only by a process of approximations. In order for the possible to become real, i.e., to correspond to an object, a process of synthesis is required by means of which that which is thought as merely possible is recognized as real.

Notwithstanding the different views concerning the essence of philosophy, the following must be considered as its general characteristics. First, philosophy is a science; its principles are necessary and command general validity, the two characteristic features of all exact sciences. Second, philosophy is the science of all sciences. All branches of knowledge acquire the rank of science only through philosophy. As long as the phenomena of nature are treated merely in a historical fashion, they do not constitute a science. Only when the objects of investigation are treated philosophically, i.e., are ordered into a system according to principles, do they acquire the rank of a science.[6]

The distinction between "historical" and "philosophical" is to be understood in the following manner. The first is a haphazard, random description of natural objects without ordering them into a unified system; the second implies the establishment of an ordered system by means of which the objects are explained according to principles. The latter refers to natural science based on mathematics, and this is entirely in accord with Kant's remark that there is as much science in a branch of learning as there is mathematics in it.

On the basis of the preceding considerations Maimon defines the essence of philosophy thus: Philosophy is a science, the subject matter of which is the form of science in general (*überhaupt*). Philosophy as a whole comprises a pure science, an applied science, and a practical science. Logic is the science of the forms of thought in relation to any object, or to an object of thought in general (*überhaupt*); transcendental philosophy is the science of the forms of thought in relation to an object of experience as such in general. Thus, the concept that no phenomenon occurs without a cause is a concept of transcendental philosophy. Both constitute pure philosophy. The subject matter of moral science is man as a rational being; only the rationality of man, abstracted from all other human impulses, is taken into consideration in the formulation of a moral principle of conduct. Moral science is thus an applied science. Whether it is also a practical science is a question, the solution of which

[6] *Ibid.*, p. 12.

depends on whether we hold that man is actually determined in his conduct by the moral law or whether other motives and impulses shape his actions. The science of psychology, which tries by way of induction to establish general laws of association from which particular cases of human reaction can be deduced, is a practical science.[7]

Maimon's definition of the concept of philosophy is entirely in the spirit of critical philosophy. Philosophy and science supplement and complement each other; one is impossible without the other. Maimon's statement that philosophy is an exact science possessing necessary and universally valid principles can be understood only with reference to the transcendental method of Kant, according to which *a priori* concepts of thought are deduced from the factual reality of science by the principle of the possibility of experience. The reality of scientific experience is taken for granted. From the consideration that without the supposition of *a priori* concepts of thought experience as such would be impossible, necessarily follows the reality of *a priori* concepts. Thus the "possibility" of mathematics and natural science, i.e., physics, is proved by the transcendental method by the deduction of the *a priori* forms of intuition, time and space, and *a priori* concepts of thought. By proving the "possibility" of science, the "possibility," i.e., the actuality, of transcendental philosophy is *ipso facto* established. Likewise, by proving that science possesses necessary and universally valid principles, it is *ipso facto* established that philosophy, too, is in possession of such principles, for the principles of science are deduced by the transcendental method, which is the very heart of critical philosophy. Hence the possibility of transcendental philosophy is proved by the same method by which the possibility of mathematics and natural science is demonstrated.

As a matter of fact, Maimon explicitly points out that by solving the questions, "How is mathematics possible?" and "How is natural science possible?" with which the first section of the *Critique of Pure Reason* is mainly concerned, Kant has established the "possibility" of transcendental philosophy. Maimon writes: The question is this: How is philosophy as a pure cognition *a priori* possible? The great Kant posed this question in his *Critique of Pure Reason* and himself solved it by demonstrating that philosophy must be transcendental... that is to say, it must be related to objects of esperience in general. This is the meaning of the term transcendental philosophy. It is a science the subject matter of which is objects in general, which are determined

---

[7] *Ibid.*, p. 13.

by conditions *a priori*, not by particular conditions of experience *a posteriori*. Herein is transcendental philosophy distinguished from logic, the subject matter of which is undetermined objects in general, for any object of thought must comply with the laws of logic. Transcendental philosophy is also distinguished from natural science, the subject matter of which is the objects as determined by experience.[8]

The following examples will illustrate the distinction between transcendental philosophy and logic, on the one hand, and transcendental philosophy and natural science, on the other. The proposition, *A* is *A*, or a thing is identical with itself, is a proposition of logic. *A* signifies here a thing in general. That is to say, any object, be it an object of experience *a posteriori* or an object of thought *a priori*, must comply with the law of identity. However, the proposition, snow is white, belongs to natural science, because the subject (snow) and the predicate (white) are objects of experience. But the proposition, every contingent, i.e., accident, is necessarily connected with something constant and permanent in time, i.e., substance, does not belong to logic, because the subject and the predicate of the proposition are not undetermined objects as are the objects of logic. The subject is here determined as something constant and permanent in time, and the predicate is determined as something accidental and provisional. Neither is this a proposition of physics, since the objects here are not determined by experience *a posteriori*, but by determinations *a priori*, such as time, which is an *a priori* form. Hence this proposition belongs to transcendental philosophy. The same reasoning applies to the concept of causality. The principle that every phenomenon of experience is governed by the law of cause and effect refers to objects of experience in general; it is thus not derived from experience *a posteriori*, which can determine the qualities of only this or that particular object, but not of objects of experience in general. A proposition concerning every phenomenon, or all phenomena, of experience can be grounded only in a proposition *a priori*. Such a proposition is a proposition of transcendental philosophy.

To sum up: The principles of transcendental philosophy are thus necessary concepts, without which scientific experience is impossible. Transcendental philosophy is founded on the principle of the possibility of scientific experience. Hence, by proving the validity of synthetic propositions in science, the validity of the principles of transcendental philosophy is *ipso facto* demonstrated.

On the basis of his definition of the essence of philosophy, Maimon

[8] *Ibid.*, p. 13 ff.

proceeds to present an answer to the question: In what respect and in what direction can the progress of philosophy take place? Pure philosophy can gain by an increase in its intensity, that is to say, by acquiring a definite clarity of its principles. In this respect logic reached the highest point of perfection at its very beginning.[9] The establishment of transcendental philosophy is due to Kant; it is, according to Maimon, also completed. The accomplishment of transcendental philosophy consists in the discovery of certain principles of thought *a priori* that are necessary and indispensable for our cognition of the phenomena of reality. In this respect Kant's achievement cannot be surpassed. Only with reference to the application of the general principles of thought does Maimon raise critical objections to Kant.

Applied philosophy, i.e., philosophical principles in their application to objects of reality, can gain in intensity by proving, to the extent that this is possible, that its objects are grounded in the general principles of pure philosophy. The ascent from mere comparative certainty, which is the result of induction, to more general certainty and universal validity is the ideal to which science aspires. This can be attained only by proving that the laws established by induction are rooted in the general principles of thought established by pure philosophy. Only thus can the philosophy of nature acquire universal validity. But again this is only an ideal to which scientific knowledge aspires. In reality, the general principles of pure philosophy, which command universal validity, refer only to objects of experience in general (*überhaupt*) and not to this or that particular object.

By proving that objects of experience in general are impossible without the assumption of general principles of thought, we have not yet established that this or that particular individual phenomenon is determined by this or that general principle of thought. A great distance separates the area of objects of experience in general, which is a mere abstraction, and the area of concrete individual objects of experience; and the application to the latter of the pure principles valid for the former can be accomplished only by means of induction, which can grant us only comparative, not absolute, certainty. In spite of the unbridgeable gap existing between the recognition of the necessary assumption of pure concepts of thought, without which experience

---

[9] *Ibid.*, p. 13. Maimon here adopts the Kantian view of logic as expressed in his statement that logic has not made any progress since Aristotle. However, his own contribution to the science of logic is the best refutation of this statement. It is sufficient merely to recall here Maimon's conception of an infinite judgment as a particular class of logical propositions, which in itself is an important contribution to logical science.

in general is impossible, and the rightful practical application of pure concepts to particular individual objects (in the cognition of this gap lies the essence of Maimon's criticism of Kant), the acknowledgment that experience as such is grounded in certain pure principles of thought is a great advancement in philosophic thought. The assumption of pure concepts of thought transcendentally determines the phenomena of experience in general, for it is a necessary condition for the possibility of experience. It is, however, empirically impossible to determine each individual case of experience by applying to it a pure concept of thought, for it is subject to doubt whether the particular object falls under this or that specific general principle and is determined by it. Nevertheless, through the cognition of the necessary connection existing between experience and pure concepts of thought, natural science acquires systematic order; it may also rightfully claim necessity and universal validity for its principles, which are transcendental conditions of experience.[10]

We have already referred to the fact that Maimon holds that transcendental philosophy was completed by Kant. Maimon is a true follower of Kant in his recognition of the necessity of the assumption of certain a priori principles of thought. His criticism of Kant, which results in his skepticism, consists not in doubting the reality of these general principles of thought, but in questioning the legitimacy of the application of these general concepts to particular objects of experience. The essence of transcendental philosophy, the recognition of the assumption of general a priori concepts of thought as necessary conditions indispensable for scientific experience, is not the target of Maimon's criticism. His criticism is directed, rather, against the possibility of deducing individual cases from general concepts, that is to say, against critical philosophy as a practical philosophy. So, for instance, from the general principle of transcendental philosophy, that everything must have its cause, cannot be deduced the particular cause of an individual phenomenon in view of the multitude of causes operating in nature. That all phenomena of nature are subject to the principle of causality and determined by it is a necessary and fundamental principle of transcendental philosophy, but with the multitude of causes operating in nature, how can we possibly conclude as to the particular cause determining an individual case? That the relation of cause and effect obtains is a necessary assumption without which science is impossible;

[10] *Ibid.*, p. 14.

it is an *a priori* concept indispensable for the very reality of experience. But from this general and necessary assumption there does not follow the character and nature of the particular cause of this or that phenomenon. For the determination of the particular cause operating in each individual case we must resort to induction, i.e., observation, analysis, and experimentation. However, principles derived from induction can never possess general necessity and universal validity, only probability and comparative certainty. Hence the practicability of principles of critical philosophy is doubtful.

Only in mathematics can we deduce with absolute certainty the individual case from the general principles. The reason for this difference between mathematics and natural science lies, according to Maimon, in the following. Mathematics may ascend from the particular to the general or descend from the general to the particular; it assures the certainty of its concepts with the help of construction. In mathematics the human mind creates the objects according to its own principles. Since mathematical propositions are verified by construction, no repetition of the presentations of the object is necessary for its verification. A proposition concerning a phenomenon of experience, however, requires for its verification the observation of a repetition of the same phenomenon. The repeated perception of a phenomenon may occur by accident or may be done purposely. But since the proposition is dependent for its verification on the repetition of the observed phenomenon, it commands merely subjective and comparative certainty, not objective and absolute certainty.[11]

This criticism of critical philosophy as formulated by Kant, Maimon sums up thus: "Philosophy has not succeeded in establishing a bridge, i.e., a safe passageway that makes feasible the transition from the pure transcendental to particular individual cases. One is on safe ground in his assumption of *a priori* principles as long as he remains within the limits of the transcendental sphere."[12] One must recognize that the supposition of certain forms of thought *a priori* as the general conditions of the possiblity of experience is a necessary assumption. But when one leaves this safe ground of transcendental forms of thought as conditions of experience in general (*überhaupt*) and ventures into the sphere of the particular objects of experience, that is, when one tries to apply the general forms of thought to this or that particular object, one can use only induction, analogy, and probability. Induction, however, can grant

[11] Cf. *ibid.*, p. 193.
[12] *Ibid.*, p. 16.

us only comparative certainty, never general validity and objective necessity.

Maimon's criticism of critical philosophy is directed against the application of general forms of thought, which are of a transcendental nature, to the particular objects of experience. He formulated his skepticism in the question *"quid facti,"* that is to say, how can we maintain with absolute certainty that this or that particular experiential object is determined by this or that general transcendental form, otherwise than by induction, analogy, and probability?

Kant has correctly shown the possibility of synthetic *a priori* propositions by proving the necessary assumption of certain forms of intuition, time and space, and certain transcendental forms of thought, the categories, without which no experience is possible. But Kant has shown only the possibility of synthetic cognition *a priori* in general, not its actual reality. Satisfactorily answering the question *"quid juris"* does not solve the question *"quid facti"*; it is still necessary to prove that the application of general transcendental forms of thought to particular empirical objects is not merely a possibility but an actuality.

CHAPTER XIII

MAIMON'S SKEPTICISM AND ITS RELATION TO CRITICAL AND DOGMATIC PHILOSOPHY

i

The question we now have to consider is, What is the specific feature of Maimon's skepticism? It would seem at first thought that Maimon's conception concerning the application of the principle of causality to particular phenomena of experience as being based on induction, which can lead only to probability, does not supersede the skepticism of Hume, who maintains that any statement as to a causal connection between phenomena is nothing other than the result of habit and custom. In what sense, then, is Maimon's skepticism different from that of Hume, and what is its relation to the various schools of skepticism as they have evolved in the history of human thought? The consideration of this question has relevance for contemporary thought. "Logical positivism" and cognate schools of thought prevalent in our time maintain that any statement of a causal connection between the phenomena of experience, and for that matter, any synthetic proposition, can claim only probability, no certainty. In what sense, then, is Maimon's skepticism different?

For an answer to this question we must recall again Maimon's view of the relation obtaining between applied philosophy and practical philosophy. Applied philosophy, which constitutes the heart of transcendental philosophy, is a pure science *a priori*; its subject matter is the pure concepts of thought with reference to their application to objects of experience in general. That is to say, the general principle of causality determining the relation of objects of experience in general is a logical concept of thought *a priori* and not a psychological phenomenon resulting from repeated observation of experience. The concept of causality as such in relation to objects of experience in general, implying the assumption that there is a necessary connection between the phenomena of nature, is a necessary concept not subject to doubt. In this respect Maimon is a pure rationalist and a follower of transcendental philosophy. He is skeptical only with reference to the actual application of the general principle of causality to particular objects, *A* and *B*.

The subsumption of these particular objects under the transcendental principle of causality may be due to a psychological illusion. There is no guarantee that these particular objects, whose succession one upon the other was observed, are a manifestation of the transcendental principle of causality. This principle implies only that objects of experience in general are conjoined with one another by a causal connection. But how can we possibly know that these particular objects are actually a realization of or a manifestation of the general transcendental principle except by observing that the objects habitually follow one upon the other. Observation, however, can yield only probability, greater or smaller, according to the number of facts observed. This is the question *quid facti*, the essence of which consists in doubting the reality of practical philosophy but not that of applied philosophy.

Maimon was conscious of the wide gap separating practical philosophy from applied philosophy; he realized that the assumption of the reality of a concept of thought *a priori* in relation to objects of experience in general is no proof of its reality in relation to particular objects *A* and *B*. From the assumption of the former it does not necessarily follow that the given facts of experience are actually determined by it. Being a transcendental idealist with reference to the principle of causality in relation to objects of experience in general does not imply acceptance of its practical application to particular facts of reality.

While for Hume, who considers causality the result of habit and custom, the idea of causality as such is not a legitimate logical concept at all, but a mere psychological phenomenon, for Maimon it is a legitimate logical concept. Maimon doubts only the practical use of this concept in relation to particular facts. But since the concept as such is not an illusion resulting from habit, but a legitimate logical concept *a priori*, grounded in creative human thought, a continuous approximation to it is possible through observation and comparison of the facts of experience, i.e., induction. Through observation of the repetition of the same phenomena following upon each other in time we attain probability concerning the causal connection between them, and the greater the probability the closer the approximation to the transcendental principle of causality. With the attainment of greater probability by means of induction, the gap between applied philosophy and practical philosophy can be narrowed down continuously.

Maimon's attitude toward induction is fundamentally different from that of the various positivistic schools of thought, which maintain that the very concept of causality is nothing but the result of induction. If their position is correct, the concept of causality may be an illusion, since induction can lead only to probability, not to necessity. These schools of thought, however, are incapable of explaining satisfactorily the rise of the idea of necessity, which is implied in causality. Since induction can give only greater or lesser probability, how does the notion of necessity as such arise in our mind?

Thus, according to Hume, the observation of a repetition of the succession in time of the phenomena A and B results only in mental habituation, that is to say, expectation of the reoccurrence of the phenomenon B following upon A will be more confident in the future. But such an observation can never bring closer an actual connection between the two phenomena in reality. According to Hume, we may say that by greater induction the probability of the order of experience observed will increase, but it will never lead to the recognition of a necessary causal connection between the objects. This means actually that more exact and more numerous observations of the order of the phenomena will increase our expectation of its recurrence, but not the reality of the connection between the phenomena. The idea of causality is to be explained psychologically; the transformation of a habit into a logical concept is due to a psychological illusion, and a psychological phenomenon can never approach reality or approximate a real logical concept, i.e., a logical concept having a relation to reality. Or, to paraphrase a Kantian remark, causality, which is, according to Hume, a legitimate child of psychology, can be transformed into an offspring of logic only by way of an illusion, but it can never approximate logical legitimacy through the increased repetition of the observation of the same experience.

With Maimon, however, who considers the principle of causality as such to be a legitimate principle of transcendental philosophy, through induction by repetitious observation of the same facts of experience, the regular sequence observed may properly be thought of as endlessly approaching the transcendental principle of causality. Our skepticism concerning practical philosophy is likely to be mitigated by induction through repetitious observation of the same order of phenomena. The attainment of greater probability with regard to the order and connection of certain facts of experience through greater induction does not mean, according to Maimon, greater habit or greater expectation, on the part of the subject, of the recurrence of the same experience in the future; it does mean a continuous approximation to the logical concept of causality, which is a legitimate transcendental principle. Thus, through a progressive induction leading to greater probability concerning the order to which the natural phenomena are subject, we may continuously approach the attainment of a recognition of a causal connection between the objects of reality; and causality as a law governing the relation of the objects to one another means a necessary connection between the phenomena.

The difference between Hume and Maimon can be expressed in the following way. For Hume the distinction between a concept grounded in habit and custom, which is a psychological phenomenon, and causal nexus, which is a logical concept, is one of essence. A subjective psychological reaction to impressions and a logical concept of necessity are entities of a different order. The gap between them cannot be narrowed by means of induction. The distance between them cannot be bridged by repetitious observation of phenomena following each other. Increase in the observation of the phenomena results in habituation, not in the attainment of greater logical probability. For Maimon, however, the difference between applied philosophy and practical philosophy is not a difference of essence. The concept of causality as such is a transcendental principle by which objects of experience in general (*überhaupt*) are determined. Since without the assumption of the concept of causality experience would be impossible, the fact of experience guarantees the reality of the concept of causality as a transcendental principle. We are in doubt, however, as to the right application of the principle, that is, the subordination of the particular phenomena, A and B, to the general transcendental principle of causality. Here repeated induction, i.e., more numerous observations of the same phenomena following each other, will result in greater logical probability, which can continuously and gradually approach necessity. Since causality is a principle of transcendental philosophy, referring to objects of experience in general, frequent induction will narrow the gap between applied philosophy (i.e., the transcendental principle) and practical philosophy (i.e., the particular instances observed). Only a distance between entities of a different order, such as a subjective psychological reaction and an objective logical concept, cannot be diminished by increased induction. But the distance between a transcendental concept referring to objects of experience in general and particular objects of experience can gradually be closed by greater induction; and by the repetitious observation of the same phenomena following upon each other we may approach objective necessity and certainty.

ii

Maimon's skepticism thus differs fundamentally from Hume's. Maimon speaks of his position as a new kind of skepticism. There are various kinds of skepticism, all of which share a common characteristic feature: the denial of rational principles. Maimon, however, accepts on the whole the results of the Kantian *Critique,* which prove the indispensability of *a priori* concepts. Hence he does not follow a dogmatic skepticism, unaffected by the doctrines of the *Critique.* On the other hand, he does not adhere to Kant dogmatically.

In order to understand the relation between skepticism and critical philosophy, it is necessary, according to Maimon, to analyze the essence of Hume's skepticism and that of critical philosophy with regard to the latter's claim to have refuted the former. Kant and his followers believe that the *Critique* undermined Hume's arguments for skepticism. Maimon, however, maintains that Kant did not completely succeed in this. To be sure, Hume's skepticism as he presents it was shaken by Kant, but the claims of critical philosophy that it has refuted skepticism altogether are also not justified. Maimon therefore proposes a method of philosophizing, which is his own form of critical philosophy leading to "rational skepticism."[1] In explanation of this term it should be said that the adjective "rational" is in opposition to Hume, who denies the reality of rational principles of thought not derived from sense impressions, and the noun "skepticism" is in opposition to Kant, who maintains that experience is wholly derivable from *a priori* principles of thought.

What is the essence of "rational skepticism," how does it differ from Hume's skepticism, and what is the path that leads to it? Maimon develops his position through questions and answers. He puts to the followers of critical philosophy various questions, the answers to which will indicate the way to the kind of skepticism he calls "rational skepticism."

The first question: Do we have pure concepts and principles of cognition *a priori* that are related and applicable to objects of thought in general (*überhaupt*)? The answer: Yes. Following is the reason for this affirmative answer. There are pure *a priori* concepts that are the necessary conditions of thought as such. Such conditions are indispensable for the thinking of any object. General logic demonstrates that the formal laws of identity and contradiction are the necessary forms of thought as such, for no object is thinkable in defiance of these laws. These principles of general logic are *a priori,* as they are not derived from the observation of objects of experience. They are prior to all experience and are applicable to any object of thought, be it experiential

---

[1] "Vernünftiger Skeptizismus," *Logik,* pp. 224 f.

or pure, *a posteriori* or *a priori*. Hence it follows that we are in possession of pure concepts *a priori*, which are applicable to objects of thought in general.

The second question: Do we have pure concepts *a priori* that are applied to an object of cognition *a priori*? The answer: Yes. Cognition, in contradistinction to thought, determines an object as real outside of thought. The question before us presupposes as a fact that we have objects cognized as real outside of thought, i.e., in intuition, which are determined by thought. The question, however, is whether we have pure concepts *a priori*, prior to the process of cognition, that are applied in the determination of these objects. The answer is affirmative, as pure mathematics demonstrates. Mathematics contains synthetic propositions *a priori*. The objects of mathematics cannot be derived analytically from the general laws of logic, as Hume held. Let us now recall Maimon's doctrine of real thought (*reales Denken*), which is governed by the principle of determinability and which is exemplified by the objects of mathematics. A real object, i.e., an object of thought as real, is possible only when the manifold components synthesized in it stand in a relation of determinability to each other. This is the case when one component, the determinable, can be cognized as the subject, that is to say, when it can be an object of consciousness by itself, and the other component, the determination, can be cognized as the predicate, that is to say, when it can be an object of consciousness only in connection with the subject and not by itself. This is the criterion of *real* thought. All thought that is not in accordance with this criterion is merely formal or arbitrary. The objects of mathematics are governed by this principle. Now we may see that the answer to our question is affirmative because the objects of mathematics presuppose the pure concepts of the determinable, the determination, and the principle of determinability. Thus *a priori* concepts are employed in the cognition of mathematical objects.

The third question: Do we have pure concepts *a priori* that are employed in the cognition of an empirical object *a posteriori*? The answer is: No. In his negative response to this question Maimon differs from Kant, who answers it in the affirmative. Kant's answer is based merely on the assumed facts of experience. We say, for instance, that fire warms the stone, i.e., fire is the cause of the warmth of the stone. In like manner we look for the cause of every phenomenon. The concept of causality is assumed, and the general principle that every phenomenon must have a cause is likewise presupposed. The difference between

Maimon and Kant lies not only in the answer to the question, but in the formulation of the question itself. Kant asks not "whether there are" synthetic propositions *a priori* in natural science, but "how" are they possible? He takes for granted the reality of such propositions in the scientific cognition of empirical objects. Maimon, however, puts the reality of these facts under question, for the assumed facts may be due to an illusion or they may be grounded in the capacity of our imagination. The concept of causality is truly *a priori*, but it has no other application than to objects *a priori*, i.e., mathematical objects.

For an explanation of Maimon's position the following distinction must be considered. In mathematics the idea of a necessary connection between two concepts implies a relation of reason and consequence, not that of cause and effect. With reference to empirical objects, however, the principle of a necessary connection between two phenomena implies a relation of cause and effect. In the conception of a necessary relation between mathematical objects a concept *a priori* is applied to objects *a priori*. But in the conception of a necessary relation between empirical objects a concept *a priori* (causality) is applied to experiential objects, and this is subject to doubt. The transformation of the idea of a necessary connection between concepts in the sense of reason and consequence, as it is in mathematics, into an idea of a necessary connection between empirical objects in the sense of cause and effect cannot be justified.

Further, the concept of substance is not to be understood in an empirical sense as something constant and abiding, but in a purely logical sense as a concept that can be thought of by itself. The concept of substance is commonly understood to imply something enduring, unchangeable, and existing in itself, while accidents are changeable and cannot exist by themselves, only as adhering to a substance. Maimon's conception of substance, however, is not of something existing in itself, but of something that can be an object of consciousness by itself, while accident is a concept that cannot be an object of consciousness by itself, but only in connection with substance. This is the basis of Maimon's "rational skepticism." The concepts of causality and substance are *a priori*, and their application is limited to objects *a priori*, i.e., mathematical objects; their application to empirical, *a posteriori* objects is unwarranted. The transformation of the idea of a necessary relation of reason and consequence between two mathematical objects, which are *a priori*, into the conception of a necessary connection of cause and effect between empirical objects can be attributed to an illusion, to an aberration of the human mind, or to the capacity of the imagination.

Likewise, the pure idea of substance as a concept that can be an object of consciousness by itself is entirely different from the conception of substance as a reality existing in itself, constant and unchanging, i.e., as a bearer of changeable accidents. The pure concept of substance is derived from an analysis of the very nature of thought; it is applicable to objects of mathematics. The conception of substance as something consisting in itself, independent of accidents, implies the reality of something transcending experience. In experience we perceive and cognize only phenomena that are composed of accidents. The reality of substance as a metaphysical entity, always existing and not subject to change, may legitimately be doubted.

The fourth question is concerned with the problem of the justification of the connection of pure concepts *a priori* in the cognition of a real object *a priori*. To explain this question we must recall that with Maimon all cognition of an object proceeds in the form of a subject-predicate relation. An object is cognized as real when two concepts are conjoined and brought into a relation of subject and predicate. Thus, in the cognition of a straight line, for instance, "line" is the subject and "straight" is the predicate. The question now arises, What justification is there for thinking of line as the subject and of straightness as the predicate and not the reverse? Further, why can we not think of line and sweetness in such a relation, thus determining a sweet line as a real object?

It is clear that not all concepts can be brought into this relationship to each other. In order to connect two concepts in the form of a subject and a predicate, they must apparently be in some way compatible with each other. If the compatibility of the concepts were derived from empirical experience, all synthetic propositions in the form of a subject-predicate relation would be experiential propositions *a posteriori*. But we are seeking *a priori* cognition. To demonstrate the possibility of synthetic propositions *a priori* in mathematics, the compatibility of the concepts must be recognized by the test of a logical *a priori* principle such as the principle of determinability. This principle provides a criterion of the compatibility of concepts, by which we can determine in advance which concepts can and which cannot be brought into a subject-predicate relation. This criterion consists in the following. Only when the subject can be an object of consciousness by itself, and the predicate can be an object of consciousness only in association with the subject and not by itself, can they be brought into a subject-predicate relation and thus determine a real object. "Line" can therefore be thought of as subject and "straightness" as predicate because line can be an object of consciousness by itself but straightness can be an object of consciousness only in association with line, as a modification thereof, but not by itself. Line and sweetness, however, can be objects of consciousness by themselves, independent of each other. Consequently, they cannot be conjoined in consciousness; and the thought of them in a subject-predicate relation is not *real* but arbitrary thought.

Every cognition of an object necessarily involves the following conditions: a determinable concept, a concept of determination, and a particular relation of the two concepts to each other as defined by the principle of determinability. These conditions are *a priori* concepts indispensable for cognition, for without them there can be no determination by thought of an object as real. The reality of these conditions is thus deduced from the fact of the reality of cognition *a priori*. If one doubted the reality of this fact, the supposition of these conditions would have no basis .The fact, however, is that in mathematics we have cognition of objects *a priori*. This proves the reality of those conditions, that are necessary and indispensable for such cognitions.

The fact that mathematics contains synthetic propositions *a priori* is thus maintained by Maimon, and this is the basis for his principle of determinability. Herein he differs fundamentally from Hume, who doubts the reality of cognition altogether and considers mathematics as exclusively analytic. It is this difference that forms the basis of Maimon's rationalism. His skepticism is directed only at synthetic propositions in natural science. Here the fact of the reality of cognition *a priori* is subject to doubt. The application of concepts *a priori* to empirical objects cannot be demonstrated. Kant has presupposed the fact of cognitions *a priori* in natural science, and from this assumed fact has derived the necessity of the application of *a priori* concepts to empirical objects of experience, since without these concepts it would be impossible to account for the fact. Maimon, however, maintains that the fact of cognitions *a priori* in natural science cannot be considered certain even though its possibility is not excluded. Hence the Kantian method has validity only in a hypothetical sense. That is to say, assuming the fact of the reality of cognition *a priori* in natural science, the question arises, How and why can we apply pure concepts *a priori* to empirical objects of experience? The solution of the question will follow the same line as that laid down for the cognition of mathematical objects, i.e., it will be arrived at in accordance with the principle of determinability. So long as the fact is not established, however, the critical method has no application. And this is the import of Maimon's "rational skepticism."

Now, it seems to the writer that Maimon's rational skepticism differs from Hume's skepticism in a more decisive respect in that it renders the metaphysical idea of an infinite mind possible. Maimon admits the possibility of cognitions *a priori* in natural science and of the application of *a priori* concepts to empirical objects; he doubts only the certainty of the application. The reality of such cognitions cannot be certain; it is merely assumed by Kant as a fact. But its possibility is not excluded. The admission of such a possibility opens the way for the metaphysical assumption of an infinite mind comprehending the empirical objects in a manner similar to our comprehension of mathematical objects, i.e., by the application of *a priori* concepts to empirical objects in accordance with the principle of determinability. If our human mind were completely devoid of such a mode of cognition, such an idea would have no basis whatsoever in experience.

According to Hume, the idea of necessity is confined to analytic propositions, but all cognition of objects by synthetic propositions is the result of impressions received by the senses, and the very idea of a necessary connection between objects is an illusion arising from habit. The reality of necessary cognitions, or synthetic propositions *a priori*, not only is doubtful because unprovable, but it has to be denied because there is no basis in our experience for such a mode of cognition, since our very concept of a necessary cognition may be an illusion resulting from habit. Hence the idea of a mind cognizing all empirical objects by *a priori* concepts has no basis whatsoever in our experience. In Maimon's view, however, mathematics is governed by precisely such a mode of cognition; the possibility is therefore not excluded that it may also be real with regard to empirical objects. Through extension of a form of knowledge known to us we can, by removing the restrictions of our limited human mind, imagine a mind, i.e., an infinite mind, which cognizes all empirical objects in a way similar to our cognition of mathematical objects. This is not a fancy; it has a basis in our knowledge. The fact of the reality of *a priori* concepts determining mathematical objects and the admission of the possibility of *a priori* concepts in relation to empirical objects provides a real basis for the idea of a mind possessing such a mode of cognition in an infinite measure. This aspect of rational skepticism, though not explicitly stated by Maimon, seems to be implicit in the whole tenor of his thought.

iii

Maimon's philosophical point of view can best be understood by considering its relation to Kant and Hume. With Kant he accepts (1) the impossibility of metaphysics as a science, and (2) the transcendental character of the forms of our understanding. On the other hand, he does not agree with Kant as to the factuality of science. Only such *a priori* forms of thought as identity and contradiction must also apply to objects *a posteriori* because their validity extends to all objects in general (*überhaupt*). These forms have reality even prior to their application in the thinking of real objects. Other forms, however, have no validity before their application to objects of experience. They gain validity only through their employment with objects; consequently their factual application must first be established before they can be said to have *a priori* validity. And when one doubts with Hume the reality of the application of forms of thought to objects of experience, one is entitled to doubt even the very reality of these forms in themselves, unless one can prove their reality with regard to *a priori* object of mathematics.

By way of challenge to the anti-Kantian, dogmatic philosophy as well as to the followers of Kant, Maimon tries to show the irrefutability of this standpoint.[2] To the dogmatic, anti-Kantian philosophers he says: You will, I believe, admit the following propositions: (1) Concepts concerning the relationship of objects (*Verhältnisbegriffe*) are merely logical forms or modes of thought by which objects are brought into relation with one another, but are not themselves real objects. (2) We know no objects other than sensuous ones. (3) Sensuous objects consist of matter and form, that is to say, something in relation to which our thinking faculty is merely passive, inasmuch as the thing is given to thought and not produced by it, and of an active element in our thinking capacity, inasmuch as our thought produces and bestows upon the given a form of its own. (4) To be able to form valid propositions concerning reality, i.e., to think of our logical forms as having a necessary application to real objects, the objects themselves must be generated by our thought *a priori* (like the objects of mathematics), otherwise we cannot know them, as they do not necessarily lend themselves to logical formulation. This is so, for that which exists by itself and has been produced independently of the subject possesses a reality of its own and is determined by laws unknown to us; it may not be subject to the

---

[2] See *Philos. Wört.*, p. 21 ff.

rules and forms of thought and be dependent on them. In other words, we can only know what we ourselves produce. (5) The subject matter of metaphysics (God, soul, etc.) is not sensuous objects of experience.

On the basis of these premises Maimon concludes that the dogmatic philosophers have no right to consider the objects of metaphysics as real objects and to ascribe to them certain forms, such as substantiality and simplicity to the soul. They must either let these objects be deduced from the forms, which is impossible, since forms can never become objects, or they must ascribe these forms to entirely unknown objects, which is illegitimate. The conclusion must necessarily follow that metaphysics as a science is impossible.

To the follower of Kant Maimon says: I hope you will admit the following propositions: (1) In order to explain the reality of an object, it is not sufficient to demonstrate its possibility, this being merely the lack of inherent contradiction. Nor is it enough to point to the fact that such a thing is really being thought of. It is necessary to show that the mode of its possibility is the mode of its generation, as, for instance, the manner by which Euclid showed the possibility of parallel lines or of an equilateral triangle. (2) The logical forms, such as the forms of identity and contradiction, are related to any and all objects without qualification and without conditions. But the forms of understanding, such as the concepts of causality and substance, are applicable to objects or occurrences. These forms are recognized in the objects through temporal relations (like succession in time, or endurance). (3) When a phenomenon is explicable by means of a known principle, recourse does not have to be taken to an inknown principle. (4) The law of association is a known principle, by which it is possible to explain the mode of the generation of concepts concerning objects. (5) A vicious circle is not permitted as a method of explanation.

Now, the *Critique of Pure Reason* has shown the impossibility of metaphysics and the possibility of mathematics and science. Maimon subscribes to the first on the basis of the foregoing. But to the second Maimon offers the following objections. Regarding mathematics, the explanation of the possibility of its fundamental concepts and propositions consists merely in the demonstration of its logical self-consistency, not in proving their real existence. This is sufficient for mathematics, as its objects are creations of our mind. It is different, however, with the natural sciences, where our thinking is related to real objects. Here we can prove only the necessity of the logical forms of identity and contradiction, which are principles *a priori* employed even for objects *a posteriori*, as their validity is general, extending over all objects. They have reality even before their use in the thinking of real objects. Only with respect to mathematical science do they suffice for a complete deduction of their objects; for the natural sciences, however, additional cognitive forms, such as causality and substance, are required to establish the reality of their objects. These forms have no reality before their employment in relation to definite objects. They attain reality only through actual use. Their use, however, must first be established as a condition for the deduction of their actual reality. Thus, when one follows David Hume in doubting the actual use of these forms, their very reality is placed in doubt. It is quite possible to explain the process by which we come to think of causality and substance, namely, through the process of association. We are therefore not justified in assuming the *a priori* character of these forms.

Finally, we become involved in a vicious circle of explanation if we follow Kant in declaring these forms of thought to be necessary conditions of experience, which we assume as an actual fact, for we have to assume experience as an actual fact in order to deduce the reality of these forms. The follower of Kant must first prove the inadequacy of the law of association to explain the mode of our attaining these forms. Furthermore, the Kantian must convince us that these forms have reality in our mind *a priori*, or that we actually employ them in relation to objects of experience. Only in this way it is possible to show the invalidity of skepticism. So far, however, critical philosophers have convinced us neither of the former nor of the latter.

Maimon manifests a total disregard for the position of his opponents when he demands that dogmatic philosophers concede that concepts concerning the relation of objects are merely logical forms or modes of thought and not real objects. Does he mean that the dogmatic philosopher should admit that the concepts of substance and causality as relational concepts are only modes of thought and not real? If so, then he is asking for too much, for this constitutes the very dispute between dogmatic and critical philosophy. The same applies to Maimon's declaration that "that which exists by itself and has been produced by something other than myself... cannot be subject to the rules and forms of thought and dependent on these forms." The very essence of dogmatic rationalism is that we can know things in themselves and not only that which we ourselves produce. Similarly, when Maimon says that "we know no objects other than sensuous ones," he is positing too much, and the anti-Kantian will not accept this statement without challenge, for the very essence of dogmatic rationalism is the proof of the possibility of knowing reality in itself and not only our perceptions.

Objections can also be raised to Maimon's criticism of Kantianism, as it is here formulated. The law of association is insufficient to explain the existence of the forms of thought, since it presupposes causality as principle. Even in the explanation of the origin of the cognitive forms as resulting from the habit of experiencing a regular succession of phenomena, which is the very essence of the law of association, the concept of causality is already assumed. The attempt thus to explain the generation of the concept of causality is impossible without the application of the logical form whose explanation it seeks. With Hume Maimon endeavors to deny the logical validity of causality and substance and to show their psychological origin. But we cannot explain a phenomenon on psychological grounds without the logical forms. Since the logical concepts are indispensable for any kind of explanation, the priority of logic to any other science, including psychology, must be conceded. In other words, the logical forms constitute the very basis of all scientific experience, and psychology is no exception to this rule. Consequently, we cannot adequately explain the genesis of the principle of causality by the law of association. The law of association itself rather assumes causality as a principle of thought, for without the application of the principle of causality we are not in a position to demonstrate the necessary connection between habit, i.e., the succession of the phenomena, and the concept of causality.

The crux of Maimon's criticism of Kantianism, however, lies in his reference to the vicious circle implied in it. Kant declares, on the one hand, that the forms of thought are *a priori* and necessary conditions of experience and consequently considers their reality established; on the other hand, he has to assume experience as an actual fact in order to deduce the reality of these forms. Kantianism is thus conditioned on the assumption of the factuality of scientific experience, the reality of which can be doubted.

Neo-Kantians will have to admit the validity of this criticism and will, therefore, have to modify critical philosophy so as to emphasize that its very essence is the transcendental method, which is dependent on the factuality of scientific experience. Since, however, scientific experience in itself is a historical process and in constant flux, the logical forms deduced from a stage of this process cannot claim absolute validity for the historical process of experience as a whole. The Kantian criteria for *a priori* forms of thought, their necessity and their universality, will have to be modified accordingly in the sense that these forms are necessary and universally valid for the given particular stage of the scientific process. Every period in the development of the scientific process will have to be examined anew and the transcendental method applied to it, in order to discover those *a priori* forms which make it possible, i.e., which are necessary and universally valid for the particular stage of experience. It is not precluded that new transcendental *a priori* forms may, in the course of time, evolve and emerge out of the human mind.

Thus, it is true that critical philosophy is dependent on the factuality of scientific experience. The results of scientific experience, however, are never final – they are subject to constant change and development – and the *a priori* forms of thought deduced by the transcendental method from a given period of scientific development can claim necessity and universal validity only for this particular sphere of experience and not beyond it. The requirement of critical philosophy not to transcend the realm of experience is valid also with reference to the development of scientific experience itself. Since the validity of these *a priori* forms is limited to experience, and since these forms cannot transcend the realm of experience and be applied to the realm of metaphysics, they must also be limited to a given period of scientific development. They cannot, therefore, transcend the temporal boundaries of a given realm of experience and extend themselves to scientific experience as a whole.

CHAPTER XIV

CONTEMPORANEOUS PHILOSOPHY

Kant, who set himself the task of reconciling empiricism with rationalism, retained a certain dualism in his thought, that was fully overcome only by the philosophy of identity. The whole period between Kant and Fichte, the first representative of the post-Kantian speculative metaphysics, which culminated in the philosophy of identity, was dominated by the struggle against this dualism and by the attempt to replace it with a monism. The given object (thing-in-itself) and pure thought (*a priori* thought), matter and form, receptivity and spontaneity, *a posteriori* and *a priori*, the empirical and the intelligible, nature and man, causality and freedom – these are the characteristic features of Kantian dualism. It is true that Kant emphasized the priority of the second element in his dichotomy, i.e., form over matter, pure transcendental subjectivity over thing-in-itself, *a priori* over *a posteriori*, and so forth. Nevertheless, the first element – matter, thing-in-itself, and *a posteriori* – was not, so it seemed to the first interpreters of Kant, entirely discarded by the master but retained a definite and legitimate place in his system.

The systematic development of philosophy in the period immediately following Kant's *Critique* takes place around the four main points, which are closely connected with one another: the thing-in-itself, the "given," the deduction of the categories, and the problem of consciousness. The *Critique of Pure Reason* seems to assume the reality of things-in-themselves as essences existing in themselves beyond our consciousness. At least the contemporaries of Kant so understood Kantianism. In recent times Neo-Kantianism has attempted to show that Kant never meant the thing-in-itself as a real entity but as a mere idea. But for the first Kantians things-in-themselves were understood as underlying entities affecting our ego and determining the content of our perception and cognition of the objects. Thus the relation between things-in-themselves and our conscious perception is that of cause and effect. This assumption, however, does not agree with the fundamental doctrine of the *Critique* concerning the theory of causality as a category of thought, limited in its application to the realm of appearances, i.e., experience. Furthermore, the positing of things-in-themselves as existing realities assumes something that cannot in principle be proved and demonstrated; it is an assumption that cannot be deduced.

To solve this inconsistency in Kant, the thinkers of that time tried different approaches. One school of thought attempted to disprove the Kantian doctrine because of the contradiction involved in the concept of thing-in-itself (Aenesidemus-Schulze and Jacobi); another school of thought endeavored to show that Kant himself never assumed the reality of things-in-themselves (Fichte). Maimon occupied a different position. He differed from Fichte in that he understood Kant as having maintained the reality of things-in-themselves; and he disagreed with Aenesidemus-Schulze and Jacobi in that he gave a new interpretation to the concept of the thing-in-itself, thus showing its legitimate place in critical philosophy.

The second main problem with which the philosophy of that period was concerned was that of the "given," the manifold of intuition and its forms, space and time. The concept of the "given" as employed by Kant has something in common with that of the thing-in-itself. Both concepts imply the limitations in the process of "deduction." What is given is an irreducible fact. Because of its very nature it cannot be deduced; only that which belongs to the form of knowledge is deducible, not its matter. Only those elements constituting the form of cognition can be objects of deduction. This is the reason why, according to Kant, time and space do not lend themselves to "deduction." In the factual constitution of our intuition are contained the forms of space and time. Instead of a cognitive deduction and logical foundation of the forms of space and time, we must be satisfied with the mere fact of our awareness of their presence in our intuition. Consequently, the sharp distinction between form and matter in cognition must be retained, i.e., the distinction between the thought form and the given content, between the forms of understanding and the forms of intuition; the former is logically deducible, the latter is merely given. And in order to justify the assumption of the "given" we have to deduce it from the very essence of cognition, i.e., cognition as such is impossible without the assumption of a given (Reinhold). There is, however, another possibility, namely, that of eliminating the distinction between matter and form altogether by trying to deduce matter and form, space and time, as well as the categories of thought.

To be consistent, critical philosophy must do away with this dualism of the forms of intuition, which are factually given, and the categories of thought, which are logically deducible. In fact, Neo-Kantianism of the Marburg school has dropped the distinction between given forms of intuition and logical concepts of thought and has conceived of space and time as concepts of thought like the other categories. It has extended the transcendental method to embrace space and time and has endeavored to deduce them from scientific experience just as the other categories. It was also the aim of Fichte and Hegel to abolish the distinction between given forms of intuition and logical concepts of thought, between *a posteriori* and *a priori*, between the undeducible "given" and the deducible concepts, and thus bring idealism to its completion.

The two attitudes toward the problem of the "given" correspond to the two solutions to the problem of the thing-in-itself. One can try to justify the concept and the assumption of the thing-in-itself and the "given" by analyzing the essence of cognition as such, and thus deduce this concept from the very process of cognition, or one can discard completely the concept of the thing-in-itself and the "given." Reinhold and Beck follow the first method, Maimon and Fichte the second.

These two possibilities, however, are not absolutely opposed to each other; there is a gradual transition from one to the other. When Beck or Reinhold try to demonstrate that the concept of the thing-in-itself is deducible from the very process of cognition, the thing-in-itself is deduced from, and posited by the understanding instead of being assumed as a reality behind and beyond understanding. The step is thus made toward an idealistic conception and a complete elimination of the concept of the thing-in-itself. The same applies with reference to the concept of the "given"; for if the "given" as such, not its specific content, is deducible from the very process of thought, the "given" is to a certain extent transformed into an *a priori* concept and a beginning is made toward a relativization of the distinction between *a priori* and *a posteriori* – a process of thought that is later completed by Hegel. We thus see that in both cases post-Kantian philosophy aims either at an elimination or at a justification of the concepts of the "given" and the thing-in-itself, which are present in Kantian philosophy and which do not harmonize with the main tenets of critical idealism. For critical idealism does not permit the assumption of a reality outside the realm of thought and the state of mind without a logical deduction from the very essence of cognition.

The same task arises with respect to the problem of the categories. The twelve categories appear in the Kantian system as haphazardly and arbitrarily collected; there is no necessary deduction of the number twelve or of the particular categories. Kant deduces the categories from the table of judgments of traditional Logic. He thus presupposes the table of judgments. The critical thinker, however, can not be satisfied with such an assumption. It is the very essence of the transcendental method not to accept facts of culture merely as given but to deduce them i.e., to find their root and source in the creative process of thought. Knowledge of a phenomenon is completed when it is derived from the process of thought as a function of the mind or its creativity. The deduction of the categories must lead to a deduction of the table of logical propositions. Furthermore, Kant assumes the validity of the laws of logic. The validity of the law of contradiction, on which analytical propositions are based, presents no problem for Kant. His concern is with the synthetic propositions *a priori*, which constitute the foundation of pure mathematics and pure science. However, a consistent idealism must extend its inquiry to the laws of logic.

The extension of the critical inquiry to logic and its principles brings about, as a necessary consequence, the transformation of the essence of the transcendental deduction. The fundamental principle of the Kantian deduction consists in the principle of the possibility of experience, the possibility of the scientific cognition of objects as presented in natural science. The law of causality is the necessary condition of the possibility of experience, for without it experience is altogether impossible. It must therefore be valid for all possible objects of experience. The principles of logic have a much wider scope. They are valid not only with reference to objects of experience, but with reference to objects of thought in general. Consequently, they must be deduced from the possibility of thought, i.e., consciousness in general, and not only from the possibility of mere experience.

The forms and laws of thought must be developed out of the pure self, that is, the transcendental apperception. But as a consequence of this task a new difficulty arises. According to Kant, experience consists of two elements, matter and form, i.e., the given manifold of intuition and the forms of thought. This duality constitutes the foundation of the deduction. The analysis of the forms of thought applied to the manifold of our intuition presents the possibility of deducing the fundamental principles. From the combination of the manifold as presented in the form of intuition with the form of thought of the categorical judgment (which is a connection of two concepts, such as S is P), the fundamental principle of substantiality is deduced. Likewise, the principle of causality is deduced from the combination of the manifold as presented in the form of intuition with the form of thought of the hypothetical judgment. The deduction thus consists of an analytical process, as the fundamental principle is deduced from a mode of cognition, which itself contains a manifold of elements.

The case is different, however, with regard to the realm of thought and consciousness separated from its application to the manifold of sensibility. The concept of thought, of consciousness, is in itself a simple concept, not a compound one, and yet we find in the post-Kantian philosophy attempts to deduce the various forms of thought from consciousness. Here also two approaches to the problem are possible. Either we seek in the apparent simple concept of consciousness a variety of components closely connected with one another, or we endeavor to find a method of deduction that does not consist in a mere analytical solution of a compound, but tries to show how, out of the simple concept of consciousness, another new simple element is necessarily generated. This is the method adopted by Hegel. Reinhold introduces the first method in that he attempts to show the manifold components of consciousness. By analyzing the phenomena of consciousness he discovers the following necessary components: the cognizing presenting subject with its functional unities, the presented object, and the presentation (*Vorstellung*) which is related to both. And Maimon, while critical of Reinhold's principle of consciousness, likewise tries to deduce the various forms of thought from an analysis of consciousness and its various manifestations, as formulated by his principle of determinability and deduction of categories. A synthetic judgment is real when one component of the proposition can be thought of by itself (determinable) and the other component can be thought of only in connection with the former (determination). Herein Maimon also employs a method of analysis by which the various components of thought are brought forward.

Thus the fourth problem with which post-Kantian philosophy is concerned is the concept of consciousness. For the philosophy of the pre-Kantian period consciousness in its various manifestations is a simple idea not requiring any deduction. The rationalists as well as the empiricists, who disagree about the genesis and the origin of our ideas, take the concept of consciousness as such for granted. Consciousness is defined as non-spatial; it is not subject to any deduction. Only because of its simple nature can consciousness, thought, be declared by Spinoza to be an attribute of God. For post-Kantian philosophy, however, the concept of consciousness presents a problem for further analysis and determination. Owing to the centrality of the concept of consciousness, the epistemology of the post-Kantian period is no longer oriented exclusively to the facts of mathematical and natural sciences, but to a more general and wider concept of cognition, i.e., consciousness as such.

(a) MAIMON AND REINHOLD

The *Critique of Pure Reason*, with its dualism of intuition and understanding and its seeming inconsistency with respect to the concept of the thing-in-itself as a subject-bearer of the appearances, provoked a series of criticisms from contemporary philosophers. These strictures later determined the development of the speculative metaphysics of Fichte, Schelling and Hegel. The early critics of Kant – Jacobi, Reinhold, Aenesidemus-Schulze and Maimon – all agree on the apparent inconsistencies and the lack of unity in the critical system of Kant. They differ fundamentally, however, in their tendencies and in their attempts to reconcile the difficulties involved. While the work *Aenesidemus* of G. E. Schulze reveals a skeptical tendency, pointing out that critical philosophy must lead to skepticism, Reinhold tries to give the Kantian system a foundation by deducing the dualism of object and subject, the thing-in-itself and appearances, from the very essence of consciousness itself. By an analysis of consciousness he tries to deduce the necessity of this dualism, arriving at the same results as Kant by a different method. His approach thus results in a total vindication of Kantianism, which he interprets as a sort of "critical realism." While Kant's transcendental method consists of the analysis of the objects of scientific experience, Reinhold's starting point is the analysis of consciousness itself. Reinhold thus fails to grasp the very essence of the Copernican revolution, which is the transcendental method, that is to say, that the starting point of the philosophical account should be neither the subject *per se* nor the object *per se*, but the objects of scientific experience, which are grounded in objective thought. Or, to interpret Kant in a more realistic spirit, the objects of scientific experience are the function of both some "given" elements and creative spontaneous thought. Subject *per se* and object *per se* are but mere abstractions. Only the object of scientific experience is real, and this object is the function of the "ideal," creative, and spontaneous subject and the material "given" through the forms of sensibility.

The correlate of the objects of scientific experience cannot be considered the individual subject, but scientific thought as such, that is, consciousness in general (*Bewusstsein überhaupt*). In pre-Kantian philosophy, dogmatic rationalism as well as empirical sensualism, on the whole, consider subject and object separate entities, and the question concerning the correlation between them is the relationship between the individual subject and the concrete objects of reality. Kant's transcendental method starts its investigation with the objects of scientific experience, instead of with the objects of sensuous empirical experience. This is the meaning of the question: How are synthetic *a priori* propositions in natural science possible? The counterpart of objects of scientific experience is scientific thought in general. While the correlate of objects of sensuous experience is the individual psychological subject, the correlate of objects of scientific experience is the subject of thought in general.

Reinhold, however, tries to deduce his principle of the relation of subject and object from an analysis of consciousness as experienced by the individual subject and by reflection on the individual act of consciousness. His method is thus a return to pre-Kantian dogmatic philosophy.

In their criticism as well as in their attempt to modify critical philosophy, the contemporary critics of Kant were, on the whole, influenced by tendencies alien to the spirit of that philosophy. In his deduction of the principle of consciousness Reinhold displays a psychological dogmatism. He begins his analysis with the subject of consciousness leading to the recognition of the reality of objects presented in the act of cognition. His phenomenology of consciousness results in a realism. The course of the procedure initiated with the act of consciousness of the individual subject involves a subjective dogmatism, as the point of departure, the reality of the individual subject as a self-sustaining entity, is taken for granted. Jacobi's criticism of Kant and his appeal to faith in the reality of objects manifests an objective dogmatism, inasmuch as the reality of objects as things-in-themselves are to be taken for granted. Aenesidemus-Schulze's skepticism likewise involves a dogmatism and suffers from inconsistency. On the one hand, Schulze tries to vindicate Hume's skepticism; on the other hand, he believes in the possibility of metaphysics as a science. That is to say, by the progress of philosophical thought it is possible to approach metaphysical knowledge, i.e., cognition of objects transcending experience.

Maimon stands out from his contemporaries in retaining the critical

position. Even when he finds himself compelled to introduce a metaphysical idea to explain reality and scientific experience, he presents it,
not dogmatically, but merely as a possible alternative. He realizes that
without the assumption of an infinite reason it is impossible to account
for the possibility of experience consisting of synthetic propositions.
Skepticism is the only alternative to the assumption of this metaphysical idea. Maimon himself characterizes the difference between his
position and that of Reinhold thus: While Reinhold's method is "dog-
matic-critical," his own is "skeptic-critical."[1] Both methods are critical,
for they recognize the need for analysis of the concepts of thought as
the transcendental conditions of cognition of experience. But inasmuch
as Reinhold's method of analysis of the act of consciousness is psychological and leads to the cognition of the reality of the objects represented
in this act, it is dogmatic.

Maimon regards Reinhold as surpassing all his contemporaries in
depth of thought and originality.[2] He agrees with him on the following
basic principles: A philosophical account of the content and scope of
knowledge must be preceded by a critical analysis of the capacity of
cognition itself. The Kantian *Critique* is neither the only possible nor
the best critical analysis of the cognitive capacity.[3] Thus Maimon
understands Reinhold's interpretation and exposition of the Kantian
philosophy as an attempt to demonstrate a new method by which the
main thesis of the *Critique of Pure Reason* is to be deduced.

Reinhold endeavors to overcome the inherent dualism of the Kantian
system, namely, the dualism of *phenomena* and *noumena*. This is the
purpose of his "first fundamental principle," out of which Kant's
doctrine of the relation between subject and object, between the thinking
capacity and the "given" follows with logical cogency. Reinhold calls
this principle the principle of consciousness. (*Satz des Bewusstseins*).
He does not attempt to prove or deduce this principle; he considers it
to be a self-evident and fundamental fact of consciousness. Just as the
Euclidean axioms, on the basis of which the system of geometry is
developed, are not proved but posited, so this principle of consciousness,
from which critical philosophy is to be deduced, must be posited as self-
evident and undeniable. Hence Reinhold's designation of this factor
of consciousness as a "fundamental" and "elementary" principle.

The following is the import of this principle: The presentation or idea

---

[1] *Str.*, p. 217.
[2] *Logik*, p. 323.
[3] *Ibid.*

(*Vorstellung*) of an object in our mind is an act of consciousness in which there is a distinction between the presentation itself, and the presented object and the presenting subject, to both of which the presentation is related.[4] In other words, in the very act of consciousness a relation between the subject and the object is necessarily and analytically contained.

Criticising Reinhold's doctrine of consciousness, Maimon writes that the act of consciousness that relates an idea (*Vorstellung*) to an object and a subject is not a single and irreducible phenomenon; it is an act made up of various components: consciousness of the subject, of the object, of the idea, of the act relating all three components to one another, and, finally, consciousness of the particular mode in which they are related to each other. Each of these components can be subsumed under the general mode of consciousness. Even though in actual experience all of them are closely connected and inseparable from one another, it is possible by a process of analysis to separate them in thought and to think of them as different from one another.[5]

Consciousness as such is thus a general attribute that can be ascribed to various manifestations of the thinking process. "Consciousness is the most comprehensive form of the activity of the soul. It is comparable to extension as the most comprehensive form which can be predicated of various corporeal objects."[6] Extension in general is an all-embracing form, the modification of which are the particular corporeal objects. The general form must be thought of as different from its particular modifications. Likewise, consciousness in general is the most comprehensive form embracing various kinds of specific consciousness. We have thus to consider the specific, particular modifications of consciousness as superadditions to its general form. Consciousness in general, therefore, cannot be defined without taking into account its particular kinds of manifestations. Since the various kinds of consciousness participate in the general form of consciousness, a definition of the latter abstracted from the former is a *circulus vitiosus*.[7]

Thus the consciousness of the relation of the idea (*Vorstellung*) to an object and a subject is not, as Reinhold proposed, a necessary and constitutive feature of consciousness as such, but rather a characteristic feature of a particular kind of consciousness. Maimon holds, therefore,

---

[4] "Die Vorstellung wird im Bewusstsein vom Vorgestellten und Vorstellenden unterschieden und auf beide bezogen."
[5] *Magazin zur Erfahrungsseelenkunde*, 9 Band, 3 Stück, pp. 8 f.
[6] *Ibid.*, p. 9.
[7] *Ibid.*

that Reinhold's definition of the fundamental principle of consciousness suffers from the confusion of a particular with a general.

The analytical deduction of the principle of consciousness can be maintained only if it can be shown that it is analytically contained in consciousness as such. For what is necessarily inherent in consciousness in general cannot be denied, just as consciousness itself is an undeniable fact. Since, however, the components of the principle, that is, the presentation, the presenting subject, the presented object, and their relation to one another, are not contained in general consciousness but are the characteristic features of a particular kind of consciousness, this interrelationship cannot be considered a fundamental principle, as are the axioms of geometry. What belongs to a special kind of consciousness is derivative and secondary, as are laws governing a particular geometrical object. What belongs to a particular object cannot be considered a fundamental principle, for it is not the result of an analytical deduction; it may be due to subjective perceptions, the reality of which may be doubted.

Now Maimon's comparison of consciousness in general with extension in general, both of which constitute the underlying ground for their specifications, has its roots in Spinoza's conception of extension and thought as the two attributes of substance. Particular objects in space and particular ideas of the mind are modifications of the attributes of extension and thought. For Spinoza these attributes constitute the underlying metaphysical reality of their modifications in particular objects. Of course, for Maimon consciousness and extension are not metaphysical entities, but immanent ideas constituting the foundations for their modifications in particular objects. Nevertheless the comparison between general consciousness and extension was suggested to Maimon by Spinoza.

G. W. Bartholdy, in a letter to Reinhold dated Berlin, March 26, 1793,[8] writes that he has advised Maimon not to publish his correspondence with Reinhold,[9] in which they set out their different philosophical views, since this correspondence was not originally intended for publication. He then adds that there was never a philosophical discussion conducted on such a high level as this one. It was easy to

---

[8] *Karl Leonhard Reinholds Leben und Literarisches Wirken, herausgegeben von Ernst Reinhold*, Jena 1825, pp. 369 ff.

George Wilhelm Bartholdy collaborated with Maimon in publishing a German translation of "Bacon's Von Verulam Neues Organon"; the translation is by Bartholdy and the notes are by Maimon.

[9] The correspondence between Reinhold and Maimon appeared as a section of *Str.*, pp. 179–244 under the title, "Philosophischer Briefwechsel."

recognize that the term presentation (*Vorstellung*), which constituted the axis of the whole discussion, was understood by each of them in a totally different manner.

It is difficult, writes Bartholdy, to grasp the meaning of Maimon's concept of consciousness in general (*Bewusstsein überhaupt*), i.e., a consciousness that cannot be said to consist of definite ideas referring to objects, since it is not a consciousness of objects at all. Maimon seems to understand by this concept a consciousness in which there is absolute identity of subject and object. Such a consciousness seems to Bartholdy to be self-contradictory, just as motion without space involves a contradiction. Then he adds that Maimon's contention that the dualism of subject and object in any act of consciousness is an illusion is, in his opinion, "tantamount to an abrogation of the possibility of consciousness altogether." Bartholdy maintains that the necessary condition of any clear consciousness is realization of the self-sameness, i.e., the identity of the subject, on the one hand, and the various modifications of the object on the other. The realization of this dualism is a necessary presupposition of every act of consciousness. That is to say, a presenting, imagining subject and a presented, imagined object, to both of which the presentation, the idea (*Vorstellung*), is related, must be presupposed. In the consciousness of an idea of an object there is implied a relation of this idea to the thinking subject, on the one hand, and to the thought object on the other. Hence, the dualism of subject and object is a necessary and indispensable condition of every act of consciousness of an object.

Bartholdy has correctly grasped the core of the matter constituting the bone of contention between Reinhold and Maimon, though he seems not to have noticed the implications of the different conceptions of consciousness held by them; nor does he intimate the bearing their different views of consciousness have on their respective systems of thought as a whole.

The essential difference between the two systems is reducible, it seems, to the radical distinction between critical idealism and critical realism. In Maimon's concept of cognition as determining the object there is unity of thought and being. A thing "is" for us as it is determined by our knowledge of it. Reinhold's conception of cognition presupposes a metaphysical dualism between subject and object. By the analysis of the act of consciousness as necessarily consisting of the following components, an imagining, thinking subject, an imagined thought object, and an idea or presentation related to both the subject and the object, Reinhold has evolved an essential metaphysical dualism.

This analysis of consciousness reminds one of the various realistic trends of thought in recent times, with their emphasis on the "intentional" character of cognition.[10] From the very nature of thought as "intentional," that is, being directed toward an object, the reality of the object is deduced. According to Reinhold's interpretation of critical philosophy based on this conception of consciousness, the problem of the thing-in-itself arsises with greater acuteness. For if the very act of consciousness consists essentially of a presenting subject, a presented object, and the presentation, the idea of the object as related to both the subject and the object, the reality of a thing-in-itself is presupposed. This is the reason for our designation of Reinhold's system of thought as critical realism. It is critical because its point of departure is the analysis, not of reality, but of consciousness and thought from which the reality of objects is derived.

But the question naturally arises, how can such a position be consistently maintained and justified in a critical system of thought whose basic and central doctrine is that the object is the result of the synthetic act of thought, not its cause. The presentation of the object is the result of the act of synthesis. It is neither "directed" nor "related" to the object; rather, it generates, produces the object as a unified object of knowledge. Synthesis is an act of objectification, and an act of objectification presupposing the object is self-contradictory. The idea of an object, a thing-in-itself, abstracted from the concepts of thought constituting the synthesis, in unimaginable.

Maimon therefore strives for the complete elimination of the assumption of a thing-in-itself. Ideal cognition is, for him, the attainment of identity of thought and being. That is to say, the complete solution of an object, *viz.* an object of knowledge, in logical and mathematical relations is the ideal knowledge, in which nothing is "given" but all is thought. Such an ideal stage of knowledge would be impossible to strive for if the very constitution of our thinking capacity (consciousness, in the language of Reinhold) were characterized by its being directed to and related to an object outside consciousness. In order to make this ideal *qua* ideal possible, the presupposition of a metaphysical dualism of subject and object must be discarded, and the *locus* of the thing-in-itself must be placed in the mind itself and not outside consciousness. That is to say, the irrational, uncategorized components

---

[10] For example, Edmund Husserl, Max Scheler and Nicolai Hartmann.

of an object constituting a problem for our cognition comprise the thing-in-itself.

According to Bartholdy, Maimon's position in practical philosophy, i.e., ethics, is more convincing. Maimon does not deny the moral imperative as a law of theoretical reason. He does not entertain any doubt as to its origin, it is grounded in pure reason. But he is skeptical with regard to practical reality, i.e., the application of the moral law. The assumption that the moral imperative, which is conceived by pure reason, is the incentive determining man's actions is subject to doubt; the belief that man's conduct is the effect of the moral imperative may be due to an illusion and self-deception. Man's decisions and actions in practical life can be explained as determined by empirical incentives and motives and not necessarily by the pure moral imperative. One must admit, writes Bartholdy, that this position is difficult to refute either by means of theoretical considerations or with arguments from practical experience.

Here again Bartholdy fails to notice the relation of Maimon's skepticism in the realm of ethics to his skepticism in the realm of theoretical philosophy. In both Maimon is concerned with the question: *quid facti* that is, the relation of pure concepts to phenomena of experience. Even if we concede that the concept of causality is a pure transcendental principle *a priori*, it is still possible to doubt its applicability to particular phenomena of experience, i.e., facts of reality. This is Maimon's skepticism in the theoretical realm. Similarly, in the ethical realm the question is whether the pure ethical law is real in the practical conduct of man. The gap between the pure and the practical is unbridgeable, and the realization of the distance between them constitutes the core of the question *quid facti*.

Bartholdy then explains Maimon's polemical methods as remnants of the training he received in his youth. "He is dragging you into the public arena," Bartholdy writes to Reinhold, "because of his great respect for you. Though you continuously repeat in your letters that you do not understand him, he does not give up hope of making himself understood by you and does not get tired explaining his position. Maimon admits that Eberhard and others do not understand him because their way of thinking is entirely different from his, but he feels that your way of thinking is so much akin to his that he refuses to believe that you cannot understand him."[11]

Bartholdy sees clearly the affinity between Maimon's and Reinhold's

[11] See *Reinholds Leben und Literarisches Wirken*, pp. 369 ff.

systems of thought. Their philosophical positions are rooted in a common ground, *viz.* the *Critique of Pure Reason*; both men are concerned with understanding the essence of critical philosophy. Reinhold's position can be defined as dogmatic Kantianism. He tries to deduce logically the dualism of *phenomena* and *noumena* as necessary components of consciousness. This deduction he formulated in his fundamental principle of consciousness. Maimon, however, sees clearly the conflict between the spirit and the letter of the *Critique of Pure Reason*, realizing that in a consistent system of critical philosophy the reality of the *noumena*, things-in-themselves, cannot be maintained. In this respect Maimon anticipates the position of critical idealism evolved a century later in the school of Hermann Cohen and Paul Natorp. And the philosophical discussions between Reinhold and Maimon concerning the relations between *phenomena* and *noumena* foreshadow the various conceptions of Kantianism in recent times. Just as the position of Hermann Cohen and Paul Natorp is akin to that of Maimon, so the point of view of Alois Riehl and Friedrich Paulsen is similar to that of Reinhold.

According to Reinhold, the dualism of subject and object follows as a necessary consequence from the very definition and analysis of consciousness, and the thing-in-itself as the counterpart of the subject is a necessary concept derived logically and analytically. This view runs counter to Maimon's conception of the thing-in-itself as an immanent idea. Maimon's criticism of Reinhold's principle of consciousness is thus bound up with his conception of the thing-in-itself and with his understanding of critical philosophy in a fundamentally different way from that of Reinhold.

According to Maimon, the consciousness of the relationship of the idea (*Vorstellung*) to a subject and to an object is rooted in a dualism, the origin of which can be explained psychologically. This relationship is not a necessary ingredient constitutive of the very essence of the idea, as Reinhold maintains, but it has a psychological origin. The mind is accustomed to relate every perception to other perceptions with which it is usually associated. Through the habit of experiencing the coexistence of various perceptions the inclination arises in the imagination to associate them with, and relate them to something beyond themselves. We frequently perceive the color yellow in association with the specific weight and the solidity of gold or in association with the qualities of wax. The human mind then gradually transforms this subjective experience into a relation to a transcendent reality, namely, the color yellow must belong to some object beyond consciousness. Thus there arises the fictional (*fingierte*) idea of an object existing independent of the thinking capacity, i.e., an object that has reality in itself apart from its possible relationship to a subject. This object in and by itself is not only indefinite but indefinable.[12]

We mean by an indefinite object one that is not fully mastered by the mind. The possibility of its complete comprehension is, however, not excluded. It is thus an object for a thinking subject with its forms of thought and apperception. An indefinable object is an object in and by itself, without any possible relationship whatever to a subject.

Maimon's concept of a thing-in-itself refers to those uncategorized, not yet rationalized elements of consciousness regarding an object that constitute a problem and a task for our thought. Such an object stands in a possible relation to a subject, and it can be designated as an indefinite object. Hence, only the indefinite, undetermined manifold that stands in a possible relationship to a thinking subject (for it can and may be brought into a unity of understanding and mastered by the mind) is the thing-in-itself. But the indefinable, undeterminable object, i.e., the thing in and by itself, which does not stand in any possible relationship to a mind, is an impossible and incongruous concept.

Maimon recognizes with Reinhold that the presentation of an object is clearly discernible in our consciousness as distinct from, and related to, the thinking, presenting subject and the presented object. He maintains, however, that this is not an original and primary act of consciousness, but rather a derivative and secondary phenomenon. It is grounded in an illusion, the origin of which can be defined on the basis of psychological laws. Just as Hume explained the concept of causality as a psychological phenomenon arising in accordance with the law of association, so Maimon shows the psychological illusion that gave rise to the dogmatic concept of the thing-in-itself as a transcendent object existing beyond and outside the mind.

We have to realize the difference between presentation (*Darstellung*) and representation (*Vorstellung*). Presentation refers exlusively to the ideas present in the mind with reference to an object. "Presentation" and "present" (as a verb) have the same philological root in English, indicating a close relationship between these two terms. They refer to the act of conceiving an object without implying the transcendent reality of the object.

Representation, however, implies a relation to something objective

---

[12] *Mag. z. Erfahrungsseelenkunde*, 9 Band, 3 Stück, pp. 8 f.

beyond the mind. Now the thing-in-itself is nothing else but the full and complete comprehension of the object of our thought, that is, its full presentation. In our perception of things we cognize some features of the objects, realizing, however, that we have not comprehended the whole. The cognized features, which constitute only a partial presentation of the thing, we regard as representing the whole. The same applies to scientific knowledge. The difference between our conception of a thing at a particular stage of scintific development and complete comprehension of the thing in its totality is the difference between a partial and a complete presentation. As our knowledge at any stage of scientific experience is not complete and final, we are always in possession merely of a partial presentation of the things. And since we realize that our knowledge is not complete, we accept the partial presentation of a thing as its representation.

The conception of a partial presentation as a representation is due to the recognition that there are aspects of the object not fully presented in our consciousness. "The continuous activity of the reproductive capacity of our imagination represents objects as existing beyond our mind. This is because our imagination is not capable of presenting fully the features of an object. We consider therefore those ideas presented as representing the object in its totality..."[13] As we do not know how to relate those features of the object that are not comprehended, we ascribe them to imaginary objects beyond our presentations. Thus there arises the illusion that all objects of our consciousness of which we have only a partial presentation are representations of objects, as though these objects were the originals to which our presentations are related. "The truth is, however, that the so-called representations are nothing other than the objects given to our consciousness."[14] That is to say, the objects are not given from without, as ready made, but rather by formulating them as tasks for their complete comprehension, they are given from within consciousness. Our thinking capacity sets itself the task to bring the partial presentation to completeness and thus to dispel the illusion that the presentations are representations of objects in themselves existing outside our consciousness. The thinking of the subject and its self-identity is a necessary and indispensable condition of the possibility of thought. But the thinking of a transcendent object (not as an object of consciousness given as a task for thought) is an entirely unnecessary assumption. The process of thought can take

---

[13] *Logik*, p. 242.
[14] *Ibid.*

place without it.[15] In explanation of this idea it may be added that we are entitled to a minimum of suppositions that are necessary and indispensable for an understanding of the process of thought; any additional supposition is superfluous. And the assumption of a transcendent object is superfluous for the understanding of cognition.

As the concept of a thing-in-itself is a fiction, according to Maimon, and a fiction is the product of an illusion, we must consider Maimon's definition of an illusion and his conception of the cause of its rise in our consciousness. He defines an illusion as "an idea of an object taken for the object itself."[16] A subjective connection of ideas, determined by the psychological laws of association, is often taken as an objective connection inherent in the object itself. This is the source of all illusions. In sensations themselves there can be no illusion; only in the judgment relating the sensations to the object is there the possibility of illusion.

The meaning of the question whether the senses deceive us must accordingly be redefined. It cannot intend to ask whether the sensations affected by the objects are to be found in the objects outside us, since sensations as such are not features of an object but arise in the subject as a result of the effect of an object on the senses. Nor does it query whether the sensuous features of the idea of an object are essential to the idea, since the senses cannot decide the matter in any case. The illusion is not grounded in sensuous perceptions as such, only in the mind's judgment relating the sensation to a thing of reality. The illusion of a judgment is thus the result of a confusion of subjective ideas and presentations of a thing with the objective features of the same. An illusion arises when the former is taken for the latter.

We have here an explanation of the rise of the illusion of the concept of a thing-in-itself in its dogmatic sense, namely, as an object underlying phenomena. Every object is the result of a synthesis of understanding connecting subjective ideas and presentations into a unity. By considering the subjective ideas of an object as manifestations of their connection in a transcendent reality there arises the illusion of a thing-in-itself.

Maimon understood Reinhold's principle of consciousness as being grounded in reflection, which must be distinguished from abstraction. The difference between the method of reflection and that of abstraction is of fundamental importance for the understanding of Reinhold's principle as well as of Maimon's principle of determinability. As will be shown, it amounts to a distinction between psychological subjectivism

[15] Ibid., pp. 242 f.
[16] See Mag. z. Erfahrungsseelenkunde, 10 Band, 3 Stück, pp. 123 f.

and phenomenological objectivism. While by mere abstraction we may attain empty and arbitrary concepts, the method of reflection aims at the attainment of a clear consciousness of the concrete and objective concepts of reality.

In defending Reinhold against the accusation that his principle of consciousness is abstract and empty, Maimon says: "the principle of consciousness is not abstracted from manifestations. It is derived by the method of reflection and not by that of abstraction..." Abstraction takes place when the objects from which the separation of the general concept is to be made are deprived of their individual distinctiveness, as is the case with the features of empirical objects. In order to form general notions by abstraction from particular instances, the special features of the objects must be subdued. "That, however, which is recognized as the conditions of the possibility of a thing, is not derived by abstraction but is determined by reflection as its necessary condition. The principle of consciousness is valid, according to Reinhold, not because it is to be found in all manifestations of consciousness, but because it must be there as the necessary condition of all phenomena of consciousness."[17]

The distinction between abstraction and reflection consists in the following: In abstracting an element common to many objects and considering it as the general concept to which the objects belong, the individual characteristics of the objects are entirely ignored. The objects in their individuality are eliminated. The general concept derived by abstraction is not a necessary connection between the things, since other more or less general concepts may be constructed arbitrarily by abstraction. Abstraction thus leads to arbitrary and empty concepts. They are arbitrary because the feature common to various objects can be replaced by other features, which may embrace more or less objects. They are empty because they are the result of the elimination of the individual characteristics of the objects. We arrive at a general concept by abstracting it from particular things, ignoring their individual concrete features. Reinhold, on the other hand, aims at the recognition of the necessary conditions of the phenomenon of consciousness in its concreteness. Hence, the difference between the method of abstraction and that of reflection lies in the fact that while the former leads to psychological subjectivism, the latter aims at phenomenological objectivism.

The purpose of the principle of consciousness is to show the necessity

17 Logik, pp. 316 f.

of the Kantian doctrine of the relation of subject to object. Reinhold considers it to be a self-evident and unifying principle; just as the Euclidean axioms are posited as such without being demonstrated, so philosophy too must posit this principle as a self-evident, fundamental fact from which critical philosophy is to be deduced. The capacity of presentation is the central function of the human mind. Every presentation contains a material element and a formal element, that is, the act of presentation consists of receptivity and spontaneity. The former is the passive function of receiving material given from without; the latter is the active function of giving form to the material of the presentation.

The function of receptivity presupposes the capacity to be affected, which necessarily leads to the assumption of some thing that affects. From this there follows the reality of objects outside the mind. This is just as certain as the reality of the presentation itself. The starting point of the analysis is the self-evident fact of presentation, i.e., *cogito*, which leads to the reality of the objects. These objects are things-in-themselves. Even though things-in-themselves cannot be definitely presented in our mind or imagined, their reality as such is necessarily deduced from the very act of presentation. The reality of the thing-in-itself is thus more certain with Reinhold than with Kant, who considered the thing-in-itself a problematical concept. The term "problematical" in this context can be understood in two ways. It may mean, first, a reality, the nature of which is unknown, i.e., an X. It may also mean that the very assumption of such a reality is open to question. This ambiguity is inherent in Kant. The meaning of "problematical" in this connection will be determined by the philosophical position one holds. But with Reinhold the reality of the thing-in-itself is deduced from the very act of presentation. For him it acquires a positive and definite significance.

However, Reinhold has neither solved nor clarified the difficulty that arises: How can the thing-in-itself, which admittedly can be neither definitely presented nor clearly imagined, have the capacity of affecting the receptive faculty of the mind. How can the totally unknown, unimaginable transcendent thing stand in a relation of cause and effect to our perceptions and thus be subject to the principle of causality. Since the principle of causality, like all categories of thought, is confined to the realm of experience, it cannot be applied to a metaphysical entity, which is beyond the limits of experience. Reinhold maintains, however, that he has succeeded in transforming the factual dualism of Kant into a necessary dualism of principle analytically derived from the fundamental self-evident fact of consciousness.

In a recent publication, Alfred Klemmt[18] tries to show that Reinhold's *Elementarphilosophie* in general and his principle of consciousness in particular are to be understood in the spirit of Husserl's "phenomenology." A phenomenology of pure consciousness is not a psychological analysis of the individual act of consciousness, but a logical investigation of pure consciousness in general. Such an analysis is confined to the immanent realm of consciousness. It does not lead to the reality of objects existing outside consciousness, but to essences immanent to consciousness.[19] Pure phenomenology is concerned with essences, not with existence. Husserl was the pre-eminent opponent of the view that psychology is the basis of epistemology; his work was dedicated first and foremost to the task of differentiating between the psychological act of cognition and its pure logical content. In the analysis of the act of consciousness one has to distinguish between the act as a psychological phenomenon that occurs in time, here and now, and its pure cognitive content, which is directed toward the comprehension of a pure essence transcending time.

Klemmt sets himself the task of rehabilitating Reinhold's philosophy. He endeavors to discover in Reinhold the strict epistemologist and systematizer. Thus the object that Reinhold deduces by means of the principle of consciousness is not a thing-in-itself, a transcendent reality existing outside consciousness, but an essence immanent to consciousness. Klemmt rejects the prevalent conceptions about Reinhold as misinterpretations grounded in a misunderstanding of the true meaning of the principle of consciousness.[20]

This interpretation of Reinhold runs counter to the way in which he was understood by his contemporaries as well as by the historians of philosophy. To be sure, it is quite legitimate to give a new interpretation to a philosophical system, provided it can be justified and supported by the whole tenor and general spirit of the particular system. The history of philosophy should be not only history but also true philosophy, and philosophy means the re-creation of a philosophical system of the past in the light of new ideas. However, in dealing with the reaction of a contemporary thinker, such as Maimon, to the philosophy of Reinhold, we have to consider the latter's position as it

---

[18] Alfred Klemmt, *Karl Leonhard Reinholds Elementarphilosophie*, Verlag von Felix Meiner (Hamburg, 1958), "Vorwort," p. xi.

[19] However, some ontologists (chief among them Max Scheler and Nicolai Hartmann) employed the phenomenological method to deduce the existence of transcendent entities, essences, and values.

[20] See Klemmt, *op. cit.*, pp. xii f.

was understood by his contemporaries, and all of them understood Reinhold as maintaining the transcendent existence of things-in-themselves on the basis of the analysis of the component ingredients of the act of consciousness. The presented object of cognition, i.e., the thing-in-itself, is an indispensable element of the very act of consciousness of an object. The transition from the essential element of consciousness to the transcendent existence of an object is clearly implied in Reinhold. He also did not distinguish between the individual psychological subject and the general logical subject. His derivation of the principle of consciousness is grounded in the analysis of the act of consciousness of the individual subject, which is a psychological act.

The analysis of the act of consciousness in modern phenomenology is grounded in various suppositions and principles. Apart from the distinction between the psychological and logical subject, its conception of *a priori* is fundamentally different from the Kantian, critical conception of *a priori*. By the method of "phenomenological reduction," which eliminates the particular psychological characteristics of the act and retains its pure essence, withholding all reference to the existence of the object, it is possible to attain the "phenomenon" in its logical purity. The act of cognition in its logical purity is *a priori* in an objective sense, not because there are no objects of cognition except for a cognizing subject (as is the case with critical idealism), but because the pure act of cognition comprehends the real essences. Instead of *a priori* concepts being creative functions of the cognitive act, they are manifestations of the objective essences. In the comprehension of the essence of a phenomenon there is a correspondence between the pure act of cognition and the pure essence.

That the *a priori* concepts are objective and not subjective is also the view of critical idealism. The *a priori* forms of cognition are constitutive of objects, since objects as cognized objects are impossible without them. The doctrine of the objective *a priori* is not a point of contention between critical philosophy and phenomenology. They differ, however, in the conception of the ground of this objectivity, that is to say, where the priority of the *a priori* concepts is to be placed, whether in the essences of things or in the creative function of the mind. While phenomenology considers the essences of objects as the primary ground of the objective nature of *a priori* concepts, according to critical philosophy this objectivity is due to the creative function of cognition.

The objective *a priori* follows, according to phenomenology, from the "intentional" character of thought. That is to say, the very nature of thought is to be characterized by its being directed toward an object. "Intentional" implies direction. Reinhold's analysis of the presentation of an object as implying a presenting subject and a presented object, to both of which the presentation is related, can be translated in terms of modern phenomenology, in which the concept of "intention" is central. An idea of an object implies intention and direction toward an object. As intention is analytically contained in the very idea as such, i.e., in the presentation of an object, the reality of the object toward which the idea is directed follows necessarily, otherwise the "intentional" character of the idea could not be accounted for.

Such an interpretation of Reinhold is in principle possible. But the historical data at our disposal point to a psychological derivation of the presented object, the presenting subject and the idea as related to both the subject and the object. If it were otherwise, then not only Schulze but even Fichte completely misunderstood the very essence of Reinhold's elementary philosophy. Aenesidemus attempts to show the inner contradictions of Kant's *Critique* and the untenability of the elementary philosophy of Reinhold, which endeavors to give a solid basis to critical philosophy. Fichte subjects Aenesidemus' criticism to a thorough analysis in a lengthy and exhaustive essay.[21] Of the influence of the work of Aenesidemus on his thought Fichte writes: "Through the study of Aenesidemus I became confused for a considerable time. Reinhold's position became untenable. I became suspicious and skeptical with regard to Kant, and my own system was undermined."[22] Thus Fichte considers the criticism of Aenesidemus as having succeeded in demonstrating that Reinhold's principle of consciousness cannot be accepted as the first and fundamental principle. Consequently a new foundation must be sought from which the philosophy of idealism could be evolved.

In the Introduction to the first presentation of the *Wissenschaftslehre* (1794), Fichte attributes to the effect on his thought of the writings of Aenesidemus and Maimon his conviction that philosophy has not yet acquired the rank of a science commanding certainty. That is to say, he acknowledges the validity of their criticism. And the criticism of Reinhold is based on the understanding of the act of presentation of an object as a psychological act of consciousness of the individual subject. It follows, then, that Reinhold's contemporaries were of one

---

[21] See J. G. Fichte, "Recension des Aenesidemus...," in *Sämtliche Werke*, Vol. I (Berlin, 1845).
[22] See *Fichtes Leben und Briefwechsel* (2d ed., 1826), pp. 511 f.

mind in their conception of the characteristic feature of Reinhold's elementary philosophy as well as of his principle of consciousness. An entirely new interpretation of Reinhold, as proposed by Klemmt, may have its merits and is surely of value for the followers of modern phenomenology, for it shows that the motives and results of the latter can be discovered in a system of thought to which an analysis of the act of consciousness as such is central. However, it cannot invalidate the criticism leveled against Reinhold by Maimon. Reinhold's position is to be determined by the effect it had and the influence it exerted on the philosophical thought of his time and of the generation immediately following, and here the interpretation of his contemporaries should prevail.

(b) MAIMON AND AENESIDEMUS-SCHULZE

In Maimon's arguments against Aenesidemus-Schulze propounded in letters from Philaletes (Maimon) to Aenesidemus (Schulze), he discusses Hume's position as it is presented by Schulze and with which the latter identifies himself.[23]

Hume maintains that our ideas, the presentations (*Vorstellungen*), derive from the effects of the objects upon our senses, and the reality of the ideas is thus grounded in the reality of the objects. The ideas are, so to say, copies of the original objects existing outside us. Hence the concepts of causality, power, capacity, activity, passivity, connection and necessity must also be derived from impressions and effects upon our mind of objects existing outside.

Maimon tries to show that the conception of presentations as copies of original objects outside us must be understood "figuratively." Presentations cannot be copies of originals in the same way as impressions made by a seal (*Siegel*) on wax. For how can an idea, a mental image, be a copy of a material object existing in space? The conception of presentations as copies of originals can only mean that the particular components of ideas, which cannot be derived from the general forms and laws determining the essence of the process of presentations as such, are designated by us as objects outside our mind. A distinction has to be made between the general forms and laws that determine the essence of the process of presentation in general and the incidental aspects of the presentation that are the result of the accidental elements and circumstances of the particular object. The idea we have of an object

[23] *Logik*, pp. 293–438.

is grounded, first, in the general forms of thought and presentation, without which the conception of an idea is impossible and, second, in the incidental peculiarities of the particular object. The former constitute the essence of presentation in general, the latter constitute its material. The material of a presentation cannot be derived from the general forms that determine the essence of presentation in its generality. And it is the particular elements of the presentation that do not belong to its essence which are attributed to an object outside us.[24]

As an illustration let us consider the presentation of the pen in my hand. The general forms of this idea are: the space the pen occupies, its various qualities of color, hardness, etc. Without these general concepts, which are prior to the conception of the idea of the object before us, no presentation of the particular object can be conceived. However, in addition to the general forms and concepts that are indispensable for the presentation of any idea of an object and that constitute its essence, there are in every presentation of a particular object some incidental and particular elements, which cannot be derived from the general forms and concepts. These particular components of an idea, which are not a part of its essence, are ascribed to something existing outside and independent of our mind. Thus, not of the essential parts, but rather of the inessential and incidental parts of the idea can it be said that they are copies of an original. But then the inessential and incidental parts of the idea cannot be an adequate copy of the original. This is the import of Maimon's statement that the conception of ideas as copies of originals must be understood "figuratively."

Maimon's criticism of the doctrine of ideas as copies of originals is closely connected with his criticism of the concept of the thing-in-itself as a metaphysical entity and with his own conception of the thing-in-itself as referring to those particular parts of an object that have not been rationalized and completely mastered by the mind. Those irrational elements of our consciousness, related to an object, which constitute a problem for further investigation, are attributed to something outside the mind. The term "outside" means precisely outside intellectual comprehension. It has been conceived, however, to imply the existence of an entity outside the mind in a metaphysical sense, i.e., a thing existing in itself, independent of our mind. But the particular, irrational aspects of an object are immanent to consciousness, not outside it in the sense of transcendence. Thus the "material" components of our consciousness, namely, those particular elements of it that have not

[24] *Ibid.*, pp. 337 f.

been categorized and rationalized, are attributed to something outside us and designated as a thing-in-itself.

Similarly, it can be shown with reference to the general laws of nature established by the human mind that those particular phenomena that cannot be derived from the general law are attributed to a thing outside us. So, for instance, the essence of a certain force is determined by the law according to which this power is operative. Thus the force of attraction is determined by the Newtonian law of gravitation, that bodies attract each other by a force in direct relation to their masses and in inverse relation to the square of the distance between them. This does not mean, however, that all bodies will actually attract each other in accordance with the general law of gravitation. Owing to incidental circumstances in which certain particular bodies exist, these bodies may not harmonize with the general law of gravitation. But this does not invalidate the general law. The law in its essence remains, and the deviation from it of the particular bodies constitutes a problem that will have to be explained by some subsidiary hypothesis unless these deviations accumulate to such an extent that the general law is no longer practical and cannot be maintained. The same is true with reference to our perceptive capacity by which we produce presentations and ideas of objects. Its essence is determined by the general forms and concepts that are indispensable for the process of presentation as such. But the particular components of our ideas cannot be derived from general forms and concepts, just as the attraction of particular bodies to each other cannot always be derived from the general law of gravitation.

The process of presentation (*Vorstellung*) of objects is determined by general forms and concepts, such as causality, substance and various forms of relation, without which it would be impossible. This is the essence of presentation in general. The actual presentation of a certain object here and now is grounded in the particular object presented, which is the material of the presentation. The actual presentation of a certain object presupposes the general form, i.e., the essence, of presentation as such.

Now, when Schulze, following Hume, maintains that presentations of objects are grounded in impressions made by the objects on our mind, or that they are copies of originals, he can refer only to the actual presentations as they arise in our consciousness, that is, the material of the presentation. But the essence of presentation as such, which is determined by general forms, is logically prior to the actual presentation of a certain object. We have, therefore, to distinguish between the possible and the actual presentation. "Possible" implies the essence of the process of presentation in general; "actual" refers to a particular act of presentation, and the latter presupposes the former.[25]

The concept of "possibility" does not denote here potentiality as it is understood by Aristotle; it means rather transcendental possibility in the Kantian sense. Possibility implies here logical necessity. That is to say, those logical forms and presuppositions that are indispensable for the comprehension of a concept and make it possible are its necessary conditions. Possibility thus precedes actuality in the sense of being logically prior. While for Aristotle possibility precedes actuality in a temporal sense, every phenomenon prior to becoming actual must be in a potential state, i.e., it must be possible before it is realized in actuality, with Kant as well as with Maimon the relation between possibility and actuality is tantamount to the relation between the general transcendental forms and their realization in objects of experience. The former is not prior in time to the latter; it is only logically prior, for it is the necessary condition of the particular realization in actuality.

Now, since the possibility of presentation as such, i.e., its essence, is logically prior to, and presupposed by, the actual presentation of a particular object, "it is wrong to say that the objective truth of the presentation is grounded in the particular object; rather the reverse is true, that the particular object is determined as a real object by the general forms."[26]

Hume's position with reference to the concept of causality is that this concept cannot be derived from the impressions of objects on our mind. The idea of a necessary connection between two objects – that when A is given, B *must* follow – is entirely different from the perception of a mere sequence in time of B after A. Nor can it be maintained that necessity is involved in the perception of a sequence, that is to say that the impression of necessity is given in the perception of objects following each other. If this were so, we should have perceived the necessary nexus at the first perception of the sequence of the objects. The fact that repetitious observation is required for the conception of a necessary connection between the objects sufficiently establishes that necessity is not involved in the perception. It is rather a logical conclusion on the basis of the perception. However, the inference of logical necessity from the perception of a temporal sequence is a leap that

---

[25] *Ibid.*, p. 338.
[26] *Ibid.*

cannot be justified. Hence, Hume states that the concepts of necessity and causality are the results of a psychological illusion. Owing to a certain capacity of our imagination, the perception of an association of phenomena frequently following one upon the other is transformed into a concept of a necessary connection between them. The logical concept of necessity is grounded in the psychological effect of habit on our imagination.

Against this derivation of the concept of causality Maimon raises the following objection. As the objective reality of the concept of causality is not admitted, objective truth as such is subject to doubt. According to Hume, objective truth is nothing else but that our ideas and presentations of objects are due to the impressions made on our mind by the objects outside us. But since the reality of a causal relation is denied, we have no criterion of objective truth.[27]

The import of Maimon's criticism seems to consist in the detection of an inner contradiction in Hume's position. If causality is not real but merely a psychological illusion, then the connection between the effects of objects upon our mind in the form of impressions and the ideas we form of the objects lacks a basis in reality. Such a connection presupposes the concept of causality. In Hume's doctrine of ideas as resulting from the effect of objects, the reality of the concept of causality is implied. The supposition of a necessary connection between impressions and ideas is unthinkable without the concept of causality; and in the psychological derivation of the idea of necessity, causality is presupposed, since "habit and custom" are declared by Hume to be the root and the cause of the idea of necessity and causality.

It is of interest to recall here that Schulze tries to defend Hume against similar criticism. He refers to the general conception prevalent among Hume's critics, that his skepticism is based on the fundamental principle of empiricism, which holds that all human knowledge is derived exclusively from sensations. Consequently, the critics consider that they have refuted Hume by pointing out that "either the concept of a necessary connection implied in the concept of causality is real in some of our experience [namely, the experience of the causal relation between sensations and our ideas and between external objects and their effects on our mind], or the concepts of necessity and causality have their root in a source other than sensations..."[28] Schulze, however, regards such a conception of Hume's skepticism as based on a misunderstanding.

---

[27] *Ibid.*, 340.
[28] Schulze, *op. cit.*, p. 117, note.

If Hume's position were grounded in the empirical doctrine that all knowledge is derived directly or indirectly from impressions made on our mind by objects, Hume would have been guilty of a gross inconsistency. Such a doctrine presupposes the truth of the principle of causality as an objective law of nature or of things-in-themselves. It is inconceivable for one who is acquainted with the writings of Hume, which are distinguished by depth of thought, to ascribe to him such inconsistent thinking. Actually, the real import of Hume's skepticism is this, that by doubting the objective reality of the principle of causality, the empirical doctrine is *ipso facto* undermined. By denying the reality of causality, the principle of a real ground as such is implicitly denied. Hume directs the arrows of his criticism against causality, but they are intended also to hit the doctrine of empiricism that our ideas are grounded in sensations produced by external objects.

However, according to Schulze, the reason why Hume developed his position on the assumption of the fundamental empirical principle, that all our knowledge is derived from sensations and impressions produced by objects, is to be explained by the philosophical situation of his time. It is conditioned by historical circumstances. British philosophy was then dominated by the empiricism of Locke; nothing exists in the mind that has not been previously in the senses. All human knowledge is derived from sensuous impressions, and the reality of our cognitions is grounded in and caused by something existing outside the mind. Considering the philosophical spirit of the time, Hume could pave the way for his position only on the assumption of Locke's sensualism. He discusses the problem of objective reality *kat anthropon* and tries to show, on the basis of the philosophical doctrines prevalent among his contemporaries, that causality has no objective reality. But his arguments are implicitly, if not explicitly, directed against Locke's fundamental empirical principle. For if the truth of the causal connection has no basis in reality, but is due to a psychological illusion, human knowledge cannot be derived from impressions made by objects, and our cognitions cannot be the result of the reaction of our senses to the stimuli of external objects, as Locke maintained. But Maimon's criticism of Hume, as we understand it, is not invalidated by Schulze's defense of him. For if the idea of necessity and causal connection as such has no real basis, either in the world of external objects or as an indispensable principle of thought, we have no criterion of objective truth, and there can be no explanation of the presence of the concept of causality in our mind. The explanation of the rise of this idea as a psychological illusion presupposes the concept of causality. The very distinction between illusion and objective truth presupposes a criterion of objective truth and its reality. In other words, the import of Maimon's criticism of Hume and of Schulze's defense of Hume's skepticism can be summed up thus: The very attempt to explain the idea of causality as a psychological phenomena does not accord with a radical skepticism denying objective truth as such.

Maimon's position deviates from Hume's in that he assumes the reality of *a priori* concepts. The idea of a necessary connection is real with regard to mathematical objects, and the propositions determining mathematical objects are synthetic propositions. The idea of a causal necessity as such is *a priori* and has reality in the realm of mathematics. It is only with reference to empirical objects of experience that its reality can be doubted. An *a priori* idea, which has reality in the realm of mathematics, has been transferred to the realm of empirical objects by a psychological illusion.

Schulze tries to show that Kant has not succeeded in solving the problem raised by Hume.[29] According to Kant, scientific experience is possible only because necessary synthetic propositions are not derived from empirical objects but are grounded in forms of understanding. If these propositions were derived from empirical objects, they could not be of a necessary nature. From the fundamental principle of empiricism, that all our knowledge derives exclusively from the effect of empirical objects upon our mind, Hume's skepticism naturally follows. The *Critique* therefore proposes that synthetic propositions have their root in the necessary forms of understanding. Empirical objects given to our senses become objects of cognition owing to those constitutive forms that are indispensable for cognition. Necessary synthetic propositions are thus the necessary conditions of the cognition of empirical objects.

Now, Schulze's objection to this position consists in the following. Granted that our mind is in possession of necessary synthetic propositions and that they are grounded in the constitutive forms of the capacity of our understanding, we still have to prove their reality in the realm of objects. From the subjective existence of the forms in our mind the *Critique* draws the conclusion of the reality of synthetic propositions with reference to empirical objects. Thus the idea of a necessary causal relationship, which is a form of thought, is considered the real ground

---

[29] See the chapter in *Aenesidemus*, p. 130: "Has the Skepticism of Hume Really Been Refuted by the *Critique of Pure Reason?*"

for causation in the empirical realm of objects. The original forms of the human mind constitute the real ground, i.e., the source, of necessary synthetic propositions. And since the capacity of presentation is the ground of these propositions, it follows, according to Kant, that the mind is also the ground of the reality of these propositions. The principle of sufficient reason is thus employed to prove not only the subjective association of our ideas and presentations in our mind, but also their objective reality in the connection of things themselves. The subjective nature of our mind is considered the real ground of the objective reality of necessary synthetic propositions. The *Critique* thus tries to "refute Hume's skepticism merely by assuming the certainty of those propositions, the reliability of which is doubted by Hume."[30]

Maimon considers this criticism to be based on a misunderstanding of the whole tenor and purport of the *Critique*. The *Critique* by no means concludes from the constitutive nature of the concepts in our mind that they are necessarily real in the realm of objects. It by no means determines our mind as the cause of the necessary synthetic proposition.[31] According to Schulze, Kant tries to solve the problem of the possibility of necessary synthetic propositions by declaring the mind to be the efficient cause of these propositions. That there are such propositions we know from scientific experience, and the mind is the cause of their reality.[32]

Maimon, however, maintains that Kant does not determine the mind as the cause and is not concerned with the question of the cause and the source of synthetic propositions. His purpose is only to determine the general modes of the function of our understanding, or the laws of cognition. It is the same with natural laws established by science. Newton's law of gravitation, for instance, should not be regarded as referring to the force of attraction as something outside objects, which is supposed to be the cause of the mutual attraction between objects. It determines only the general mode of the function of attraction as manifested in things. The same is true of the Kantian doctrine that the forms of understanding are grounded in the cognitive capacity. The forms of cognition are the general modes or laws of the function of cognition; Kant does not declare the subjective mind as the cause of these forms. The question of the cause of the forms of understanding and of necessary synthetic propositions is beyond the scope and purview of Kant.[33]

[30] *Ibid.*, p. 133.
[31] *Ibid.*, p. 347.
[32] *Ibid.*, p. 137.
[33] *Logik*, p. 347.

The importance of Maimon's criticism of Schulze seems to lie in his recognition that in the conception of the mind as the cause of the forms of understanding, the mind is considered a metaphysical entity, a thing-in-itself. The mind is thus conceived of as the substance of all reality. The purpose of the *Critique*, however, is, according to Maimon, not to replace the material substance with a mental substance, but merely to establish the function of the cognitive capacity in the ordering process of the phenomena of experience.

Maimon concludes his criticism of Schulze with this remark: "We generally think of the mind as subject and cause of cognition, but we do not determine it as such."[34] This seems to imply that it is psychologically natural for us to think of the mind as the cause of its function, but the task of philosophy is confined solely to determining the function of the mind, i.e., the forms of understanding as they manifest themselves in the phenomena of experience ordered by these forms. To look for a cause of the cognitive function and to consider the mind as a metaphysical entity that is the cause of this function, is a psychological lapse, against which philosophy has to guard us.

The contemporary relevance of Maimon's understanding of the essence of the *Critique* will be fully realized when it is compared with various expositions, contemporary and otherwise, of Kant. It is true that Kant has shifted the center of the philosophical investigation from the object to the subject, provided the subject is understood, not as a substance, but as a process in which the cognitive function is grounded. To be sure, Kant declared the subject, not the object, to be the ground of our cognition. But this does not mean that the subject is to be understood as a fixed metaphysical entity, a thing-in-itself. Rather, the subject and the object are both in a process of movement; they are the end results of the cognitive act, of the function of cognition. And this is what Maimon is driving at when he points out that the subject should not be considered the cause of the forms of understanding.

The generally prevailing view, however, is that by recognizing the subject as the ground of cognition Kant has conceived of it as the fundamental reality, as the substance out of which the forms of understanding flow and manifest themselves in the determination of objects. Such a view led to the conception of the essence of the *Critique* as a kind of subjectivism. Hence the Kantian distinction between phenomenon and noumenon is understood to imply the distinction between subjective and objective knowledge. The Kantian doctrine that we can know

---

[34] *Ibid.*, p. 348.

only phenomena is tantamount to stating that all knowledge is subjective; we cannot know noumena because there can be no objective knowledge. Further, according to such an interpretation of Kant, there is no essential difference between Kantian and Berkeleyan idealism; both are subjective idealism. This is the prevailing conception of the essence of Kantianism especially among some of his Anglo-Saxon expositors. It is the contribution of Neo-Kantianism – anticipated by Maimon – that it has sought to demonstrate the untenability of such a view.

According to Schulze, Kant assumes the reality of things-in-themselves, which affects our empiric perceptions. But since the categories of thought are, according to the *Critique*, confined to the realm of experience, i.e., phenomena, it is illegitimate to assume the reality of things-in-themselves as affecting our empiric perceptions. Things-in-themselves play a positive role in our experience, since they are the cause of our perceptions. And this, maintains Schulze, contradicts the basic doctrine of the *Critique*, that the concepts of cause and effect can be applied only to objects of experience, not to things-in-themselves.[35]

In Maimon's concept of experience there is no place for things-in-themselves. Experience is not the result of the effect of the things upon our mind. Experience, i.e., organized and cognized experience, is the exclusive result of *a priori* concepts of thought. We are aware, however, in the cognition of phenomena of experience, of some components that cannot be deduced from *a priori* concepts: our imagination ascribes these irrational components to something outside the mind. Things-in-themselves are thus defined negatively, not positively, that is to say, they are not determining experience but are grounded in the consciousness of something irrational and uncategorized. Hence, to say that our mind is affected can mean no more than awareness of irrational components in our cognition of experience. In this sense does Maimon understand the concept of experience as implied in the *Critique*.

Schulze argues further against Kant that it is illegitimate to conclude from the fact that synthetic propositions are necessary conditions of cognition of experience, their reality in things as they are outside the mind.[36] This, however, is based, according to Maimon, on a misunderstanding, for the *Critique* draws from the fact of such propositions in scientific experience the conclusion as to their reality only as necessary conditions of the possibility of experience, for the necessary conditions

[35] Schulze, *op. cit.*, pp. 263 f.
[36] *Ibid.*, pp. 142 ff.

of the possibility of experience are the necessary conditions of objects of experience. It does not infer the reality of such propositions in things as they are in themselves outside their relation to our cognitive capacity. Objects of experience are objects cognized by the mind. These are the objects with which scientific experience is concerned. Objects as they are in themselves outside their relation to our cognitive capacity are not objects of experience. It is therefore incorrect to suggest with Schulze that the *Critique* tries to prove the reality of synthetic propositions in things as they exist outside their relation to our cognition.[37]

Herein lies the essential difference between critical and dogmatic philosophy: The former tries to prove the reality of synthetic propositions with reference to objects of experience, i.e., objects in relation to our cognitive capacity; the latter tries to conclude, from the mode of our thinking of the objects, their existence in themselves outside their relation to our mind. In this way dogmatic philosophy proves the existence of the soul. Since it is impossible to think of the soul otherwise than as a simple subject, it must exist as such. But this is an unwarranted conclusion. From the analysis of the idea of the soul as a simple subject its existence as such does not follow. The assumption of the existence of the soul is not impossible in itself, but it has no ground in experience, and it cannot be deduced from the mode of our thinking of it.[38] The *Critique* has shown that existence cannot be deduced analytically from the concept of thought. Hence synthetic propositions are conceived as necessary conditions only of objects of experience not of things-in-themselves. There is no basis for the assumption of the reality of these propositions with reference to things as they exist in themselves. Moreover, the assumption of the existence of these propositions in things-in-themselves is self-nullifying. For if these propositions were real in things-in-themselves, "they would be given to us by the things, and they could not then be necessary propositions," since ideas given through objects can be only factually, not necessarily true.[39]

According to Maimon, Schulze's criticism of Kant is based on an incorrect conception of the relation between critical and dogmatic philosophy. Schulze seems to assume that the relation between Kant and Hume is similar to the relation of Leibniz' method of philospohizing to that of Locke. Locke and Leibniz are both concerned with the problem of the real origin of our cognition of objects. While the former

[37] *Logik*, p. 350.
[38] *Ibid.*, pp. 349 f.
[39] *Ibid.*, p. 350.

derives all knowledge from empiric sensuous impressions, the latter deduces knowledge of objects from innate ideas inherent in our mind. Since necessary and generally valid principles cannot be derived from empiric experience, Leibniz assumes the mind to be the source and origin of the necessary concepts. But he does not explain the ground of his assumption. The doctrine of innate ideas is merely a hypothesis that is preferable to the empirical hypothesis, as it avoids the difficulties of the latter; for if all knowledge is grounded in sense data and perceptions, how can we attain certitude of cognition, i.e., knowledge grounded in necessary and generally valid principles?[40]

The Critique of Pure Reason, on the other hand, does not search for the source, nor does it determine the cause of cognition; rather it investigates merely the content of cognition. The starting point of the critical mode of philosophizing is the fact of synthetic propositions with reference to objects of experience. This fact is given through the reality of natural science; it is thus a fact of cultural consciousness. The *Critique* then seeks to show its possibility by deducing it from the concept of an object of experience in general. The reality of objects of experience, i.e., ordered and scientific experience, is not a hypothesis but a demonstrable fact. The possibility of synthetic propositions with reference to objects of experience is demonstrated by a method of deduction and not a mere hypothesis. This is the difference between the critical and the dogmatic modes of philosophizing.[41]

The implications of Maimon's understanding of the *Critique* are far-reaching and have contemporary relevance. We have already referred to the generally accepted view that the Critique of Pure Reason promulgates a kind of subjective idealism. Instead of given objects determining the cognizing subject, the subject decisively affects the objects. The subject is thus understood as the source of being, i.e., as the ground and cause of all reality.

Now, Maimon's decisive distinction between the dogmatic, rational mode of philosophy, as represented by Leibniz, and the critical mode of philosophy, emphasizes that the task of the latter consists in the search for the laws governing the process of cognition of objects, not in the establishment of the subject as the source and cause of our cognition. The subject is not a thing-in-itself, a fixed entity with ready-made forms of thought, which are imposed upon and spread over the sensuous objects of experience. The *Critique* is concerned with the

---

[40] *Ibid.,* p. 354.
[41] *Ibid.,* p. 355.

analysis of ordered objects of experience as presented by natural science in order to discover those concepts that cannot be derived from "given" objects and that are indispensable for systematic experience, i.e., experience comprehended as an organized unity. This process of analysis implies that the concept of subject is not to be understood as a metaphysical entity, as an existing thing, but as a creative agent. Concepts of thought derived by analysis of objects of experience are creative forms that arise in and through the struggle with the problems of experience.

Maimon does not fully develop this thought; he only intimates it. He thus anticipates a line of thought that is later more fully elaborated by Hermann Cohen, Paul Natorp, and others. Maimon thus constitutes the first link in a chain of thought leading to a conception of the essence of the *Critique* and of critical philosophy that has contemporary relevance and is vitally important for our own time. It is the essence of Hermann Cohen's "Logic of Origin" (*Ursprung*) and Paul Natorp's concept of *fieri* as the central idea of critical philosophy, i.e., that the subject is not to be understood as a thing-in-itself, but as a continuously creative agent. The subject, by creatively ordering objects of experience, is in constant movement, and in creating the world of objects as an organized and systematic unity, the subject recreates itself. The meaning of the concept of "origin" (*Ursprung*) is essentially different from that of "source." While source implies a sort of being, origin means creation out of nothing. The same is true of the concept of *fieri*, which implies continuous creation.

According to the *Critique*, it is impossible to attain knowledge of things-in-themselves, for the categories of thought are confined to the cognition of objects of experience. Schulze argues that since things-in-themselves are entirely unknown to us, it is impossible to know what effect they may have upon our mind. The possibility is therefore not excluded that *a priori* propositions in our cognition of objects of experience are determined by, and correspond to things as they are in themselves. "Who knows what purpose 'nature in itself' may have destined for man and his cognitive capacity?"[42]

This is a question frequently raised against Kant even in contemporary philosophy. Now, Maimon's objection to this kind of argument is that such a supposition is an empty and useless hypothesis. Suppose that the entirely unknown things have an effect upon our mind in the con-

---

[42] Schulze, *op. cit.*, p. 152.

ception of *a priori* propositions. Of what use would such a hypothesis
be to us, as long as the mode of this effect and the manner in which
things-in-themselves determine our mind is unknown to us? Since it
cannot possibly be known how the *noumena* affect our cognition of
phenomena, nothing is gained by assuming such an affect. Moreover, it
may be added (though Maimon does not explicitly state it in this connection) that nothing is gained by positing the reality of things-in-themselves. What, Maimon asks, would be the reaction to an astronomer
who suggests that, though the Newtonian system explains the world
by the general laws of attraction, there can be another system of laws
by which the phenomena of motion and the relation between the
heavenly bodies can be explained? Our objection to such a suggestion
would be: This is, in principle, not impossible, but so long as such a
system has not been evolved, the supposition of such a possibility is
of no use.[43]

Here Maimon evolves a conception of hypothesis whose validity is
dependent upon its verifiability and function. A hypothesis that cannot
be verified fulfills no function; it is therefore valueless. Hence it is useless
to posit the reality of things-in-themselves, which are beyond the scope
of the possibility of experience, and to assume an order in things-in-
themselves corresponding to the order of objects of experience as
cognized by the mind with its forms of sensibility and concepts of
thought. That which transcends the limits of experience is not subject
to any categorization, and any hypothesis about its nature is worthless,
i.e., it is of no theoretical value, for a philosophical account of the
essence of the world. Even the category of existence cannot be applied
to things-in-themselves. The supposition of a correspondence between
the order of phenomena and the order of noumena is baseless. Things-
in-themselves must therefore be completely left out of our considerations
concerning the essence of cognition and the world.

With regard to the conception of the subject, the difference between
Schulze's and Maimon's interpretation of the *Critique of Pure Reason*
consists in the following: Schulze holds that according to the *Critique*
the mind as a subject is either a thing-in-itself, or a noumenon, or a
transcendental idea.[44] In the first case, the real existence of a thing-in-
itself is the cause of the reality of necessary propositions. But such a view
does not harmonize with the main doctrine of the *Critique*, that a thing-
in-itself cannot be a cause of phenomena of experience. A thing-in-itself

[43] *Logik*, p. 353.
[44] Schulze, *op. cit.*, p. 154.

cannot be an object of knowledge. It is therefore a self-contradiction to maintain, on the one hand, that the subject is a thing-in-itself and, on the other hand, to consider it the cause of necessary propositions.

Likewise, if the subject as a *noumenon*, i.e., an intelligible object that can only be imagined but not known by our understanding, is the cause of necessary propositions, how can the function of causality be attributed to an unknown entity? Even the category of existence, as conceived by the human mind, cannot be attributed to a *noumenon*. How, then, can such an empty concept be considered the cause of the necessary propositions of our cognition? The category of causality is confined to objects of experience; it cannot be employed with reference to objects transcending experience, i.e., *noumena*.[45] Similarly, if the subject is a transcendental idea, the same question arises: How can the subject be defined as the source of certain components of our cognition, since a transcendental idea is not an object of experience? "The mind and its activity are not given in our empiric intuition."[46] Hence it is incongruous, according to the *Critique*, to attribute the origin of our cognition to the mind, which is beyond the possibility of experiential knowledge. According to Kant, the transcendental ideas, such as God as the first cause and the world as totality, are legitimately employed only for the purpose that the experiential knowledge attained by our understanding shall realize completeness. But no cognition is possible of transcendental ideas as objects existing in themselves, transcending the limits of experience.[47] Thus the conception of the mind as a subject, in which necessary propositions have their ground and source involves us, according to Schulze, in a contradiction with the main doctrine of the *Critique*.

According to Maimon, Kant in the *Critique of Pure Reason* determines the mind neither as a thing-in-itself nor as a *noumenon*. The concept of mind implies nothing other than an entirely undetermined subject of presentations (*Vorstellungen*). That is to say, the mind is posited as an undefined, uncategorized entity, to which presentations are referred as their bearer. The concept of subject as a thing-in-itself would render it an object presented by itself. The subject is therefore to be considered only as a subject of presentations, i.e., as a necessary condition of presentations. Just as an object can be thought of only in relation to a

---

[45] *Ibid.*, p. 160. As to the meaning of the term *noumena*, Schulze is inclined to understand it as a thing-in-itself, which seems to be implied in Kant. See Schulze, *op. cit.*, pp. 161 n.

[46] *Ibid.*, pp. 170 f.

[47] *Ibid.*

subject, so a subject can be thought of only in relation to the presentation of objects. Thus the mind is a logical subject that must be posited as a bearer of presentations. But the subject cannot be subsumed under the category of existence or of reality; it is therefore neither a thing existing in itself nor a *noumenon*.[48]

(c) MAIMON AND FICHTE

Fichte's arguments against the reality of a thing-in-itself show unmistakably his relation to Maimon. Fichte was acquainted with Maimon's work prior to his formulation of the *Wissenschaftslehre*. Some aspects of his reasoning are so similar to Maimon's in content as well as in formulation that a direct influence of the latter upon his thought is most likely.

Fichte evolved a system of subjective idealism by way of an analysis of the sensuous capacity of man leading to a complete elimination of the concept of a thing-in-itself. His subjective idealism is developed for the purpose of demonstrating the untenability of things in themselves. This position is, however, only a methodological device, for, in the course of his investigations, Fichte arrives at the conception of absolute idealism by way of the idea of a super-ego. His arguments against a metaphysical transcendent entity and his criticism of the supposition of such a reality are gounded in the same motives underlying Maimon's thought. "The senses grant us," writes Fichte, "merely subjective sensations. What we know about reality comes through the medium of our senses and feelings."[49] Our cognition of an object is grounded in the perception of subjective relations. "Without 'feeling' (*Gefühl*) the presentation of an object beyond us is impossible."[50]

Fichte is critical of the Kantian use of the term "impression" (*Empfindung*) to describe the relation of our sensibility to the given objects. "Impression" implies the idea of a relation between two entities, a subject and an object, assuming thus the reality of a thing-in-itself. Herein, according to Fichte, lies Kant's empirical "realism," which is to be transformed into "transcendental idealism" when thought out consistently.[51] While "impression" means being affected by something outside the subject, "feeling" is exclusively subjective. To have a sensation of sweet or red implies merely a consciousness of the state of the

[48] *Logik*, p. 355.
[49] See Johann Gottlieb Fichte's *Sämtliche Werke*, Berlin, 1845, I, 313 f.
[50] *Ibid.*, p. 314.
[51] *Ibid.*, p. 490.

subject; it does not refer to the reality of something outside the subject. As the term "feeling" foes not imply a reaction to something given from without, but is exclusively confined to the subjective sphere, it is to be preferred to the term "impression" as a designation of the root and source of cognition. "The material as such does not come into the senses; it can be projected or thought of only by the productive capacity of the imagination."[52] Also, the feeling of resistance by the object in the sense of touch is due to the sense of hindrance to our will, which is subjective. "The sense of resistance by an object is not directly felt [gefühlt] but concluded [geschlossen]."[53]

The subjective nature of our sense perceptions rules out the possibility of deducing them from something outside the subject; they are to be deduced exclusively from within human subjectivity. Sense perception is due to a spontaneous act of the soul; it is therefore to be "considered as a priori," while impressions are due to receptivity, which presupposes a thing-in-itself, as a particular receptive act produces an impression. This is the basis of the dogmatism of some Kantians, such as Beck and Reinhold.[54]

In line with his subjective idealism, Fichte says that for a complete and consistent idealism the difference between a priori and a posteriori loses its meaning and vanishes. They are not two different sources of cognition; they differ only in the method of approach, corresponding to the level of consciousness.[55] Those cognitions which are a posteriori for the lower level of consciousness, that is, the empirical, common-sense mind, are a priori for a higher level of consciousness, that is, the philosophic mind, which penetrates to the source and origin of our ideas by which the objects of cognition are generated. Since our perceptions are grounded in the productive capacity of the soul, it is absurd to try to deduce them from something else. It is the dogmatism of the Kantians to explain the original productive act of feeling and sensing by referring to something outside the mind.[56] We should not, therefore, speak of an "affection" by a thing-in-itself upon our mind. The explanation of our sensations and feelings as a direct affection by things-in-themselves is a dogmatic assumption without warrant. We are faced, according to Fichte, with the following alternative: Either the presupposition of transcendental idealism, that is, its very basis, is incorrect, or its

[52] *Ibid.*, p. 315.
[53] *Ibid.*
[54] *Ibid.*, p. 490.
[55] *Ibid.*, p. 447.
[56] *Ibid.*, p. 490.

particular presentation is faulty in that it does not give a full account of the spontaneous, creative role of the subject, the ego.[57]

Fichte's criticism of the followers and expositors of Kant for assuming the reality of a thing-in-itself is aimed at all of his contemporaries – Schulze, Beck, and Reinhold – with the exception of Maimon, of whom he writes to Reinhold: "For the abilities of Maimon I have boundless respect. I am firmly convinced, and am ready to prove, that the Kantian philosophy, as it is generally understood and interpreted by you, has been shaken by Maimon to its very foundations."[58] In another context, Fichte writes with reference to Maimon that he is "one of the greatest thinkers of our time, who, as I see it, teaches the same doctrine concerning the doctrine of reality as a thing-in-itself, that it is a consequence of a deception of our capacity of the imagination."[59]

According to Fichte, the productive capacity of the ego and the faculty of the imagination produce spontaneously and creatively, and the whole process of the faculty of sensibility and that of understanding is exclusively dependent upon the ego. To assume a reality in and by itself which affects the ego would make the latter dependent on and determined by something that is radically different and distinct from it. The spontaneous and creative ego and the thing-in-itself are so disparate that there can be no determination of the former by the latter. There can be no connection and no causal relation between heterogeneous entities. It is a rude and obtuse dogmatism to posit things in themselves as the cause of our perceptions.[60] Such an assumption is a "distortion of reason,"[61] an "irrational concept,"[62] "a complete chimera,"[63] a "nothing" (*Unding*).[64]

Fichte recognizes that Kant must bear his share of the responsibility for the causal connection that was presupposed by his followers to obtain between things-in-themselves and our subjective impressions. Kant's frequently repeated distinction between things as they appear to us and things as they are in themselves is the ground of the misunderstanding that the latter are the cause of the former. Such a conception is impossible. The distinction between appearance and thing-in-

[57] *Ibid.*, p. 447.
[58] See *Johann Gottlieb Fichtes Leben und literarischer Briefwechsel, herausgegeben von seinem Sohne Immanuel Hermann Fichte*, 1862, p. 511.
[59] Fichte, *Sämtliche Werke*, I, p. 227.
[60] *Ibid.*, pp. 482 ff.
[61] *Ibid.*, p. 472: "*Verdrehung des Verstandes.*"
[62] *Ibid.*: "*Unvernünftiger Begriff.*"
[63] *Ibid.*, p. 19: "*Unfug.*"
[64] *Ibid.*, p. 472.

itself should be understood as a logical distinction; it has a methodo-logical function. In order to make clear what appearances are, Kant introduces the distinction between things as they appear and things as they are in themselves, thus defining and delimiting the concept of appearance. Its sole purpose is to show that the source and origin of all knowledge reside in the subject; it does not mean to imply the reality of things-in-themselves as the determining cause of our impressions and cognitions.

The denial of the possibility of a causal relation between a thing-in-itself and appearances, the elimination of the reality of a thing in and by itself outside the subject, and the discovery of the exact location of the idea of a thing-in-itself in the immanent human consciousness, are ideas promulgated by Maimon in similar terms and by similar arguments.

There are logical reasons for the impossibility of such a causal relation-ship. The thing-in-itself as a *noumenon*, writes Fichte, is something that is thought by us, that is superimposed by our mind on the appearances; thus it originates in our thinking, and this *noumenon*, or thing-in-itself, is used by the interpreters for something else. The idea of the thing-in-itself is grounded in impressions, and the ground for impressions is now found in the thing-in-itself.[65] The globe of these interpreters "rests on the great elephant, and the great elephant rests on the globe. The thing-in-itself, which is a mere thought, is now declared to affect the ego. Have they forgotten the first part of the statement? The thing-in-itself, which is a mere thought, is now something other than thought. In all seriousness, how can the predicate of reality, that of affecting, be ascribed to a mere thought? What, then, were the astounding discoveries of the great genius, i.e., Kant, whose light has illumined the declining philosophical century?"[66] The rejection of the Kantian thing-in-itself is thus rooted in the recognition of the impossibility of assuming a causal relation between the thing-in-itself and our impressions, and in ascribing to the *noumena*, which are mere thoughts, the predicate of reality pos-sessing the power of affecting our ego.

Fichte opposes the realistic notion of an object that is outside the mind and is neither produced nor determined by our thought but exists independently according to its own laws, yet corresponding to our idea, our image of it. It is difficult, he writes, to find justification for such an assertion, nor can we account for it "unless we have an immediate intuition of the thing." "If we are, however, convinced of

---

[65] *Ibid.*, p. 482.
[66] *Ibid.*, p. 483. The same argument is used by Maimon. See above, p. 54, n. 2.

the need of such an immediate intuition, we must also be convinced of the thing being within us."[67] As an explanation of this argument of Fichte, it should be added that an act of intuition must be immanent to the mind. Fichte then proceeds: "The complete determination is the ground of the relation between the image and the thing."[68] That is to say, the full comprehension of a thing in its totality is the thing-in-itself, and the relation of our image to a thing is the relation of our conception of a thing to its complete determination. Or, in Maimon's terms, the relation between the mental presentation and the thing is a relation between the "partial presentation" of the thing and its "complete presentation." Fichte has thus formulated his standpoint of immanence in terms similar to those of Maimon.

In his criticism of Schulze-Aenesidemus, Fichte tries to show the impossibility of the idea of a thing existing in and by itself, independent of our modifying sensibility. A being existing in itself, independent of the modes of our thought, is naturally not cognizable. Moreover, the idea of such a thing is unthinkable. "Aenesidemus' conception of a thing possessing reality and qualities, which is independent not only of the human capacity of presentation but of all possible intelligences, has not been thought by any man... nor is such a thought possible. For the self-consciousness of the mind thinking such an object and striving for its cognition always accompanies the thought of the thing... Leibniz, therefore, endowed his thing-in-itself, i.e., the monads, with the capacity of presentation."[69] The logical argument, that we cannot think of an object without at the same time being conscious of the self-thinking of the object, has its origin in Maimon's analysis of consciousness as consisting of various components. In his criticism of Reinhold's fundamental principle of consciousness, Maimon shows that consciousness of an object is always accompanied by the self-consciousness of the thinking subject.

(d) THE CORRESPONDENCE BETWEEN FICHTE AND MAIMON

Some of the letters that Maimon and Fichte exchanged have been preserved, and they bear testimony to a relationship of friendship and mutual respect between them. The correspondence is also of relevance for an understanding of their philosophical attitudes, their agreements and dissensions. In a letter to Fichte, dated August 16, 1794,[70] Maimon

---

[67] *Ibid.*, p. 377.
[68] *Ibid.*, p. 378.
[69] *Ibid.*, pp. 19 f.
[70] See Fichte, *Leben und literarischer Briefwechsel*, II, 443 ff.

acknowledges with thanks the receipt of a copy of Fichte's work, *"Über den Begriff der Wissenschaftslehre."* He then develops the idea of a "theory of science" (*Wissenschaftslehre*), its method and goal, in the following manner.

Philosophy was for a long time considered to be an *a priori* science dealing with the capacity of cognition, but it was not clearly and sufficiently distinguished from other sciences, which are based partly on empirical principles. Kant set himself the task of demonstrating the pure character of philosophy as a science and of distinguishing it from other sciences. Some followers of Kant, however, have committed the mistake of concluding that since philosophy is a pure science, it is to be completely isolated from other branches of scientific knowledge; they have treated philosophy as a totally isolated, self-sufficient and independent science. They have failed to recognize that, while philosophy is indeed a pure science dealing with the forms of thought and not with its content, it should not be treated in complete isolation from the content of thought.

Philosophy is not merely a canon, but also an organon of scientific thought. The difference between canon and organon consists in that the former merely organizes the various branches of knowledge into a unified system, while the task of the latter is to derive the various subjects of thought from principles explaining their generation. In other words, canon has an organizing and ordering function; organon has a creative and generating function. The principles of philosophy must be formulated with reference to their application to science and with a view to their relevance to objects of scientific experience. "Instead of getting support and sustenance from other branches of human knowledge, philosophy, by its isolation, has entangled itself in its own web." "It is time to call back philosophy from heaven to earth." The desideratum of philosophy is not in a highest principle from which to deduce the relationship between subject and object, as Reinhold thought he had discovered in his principle of consciousness. Rather, philosophy requires a principle of a lower order, the subject matter of which is the limit or the border between formal and real thought, that is to say, a principle from which the transition from formal to real thought (*reales Denken*) can be explained and deduced. Maimon then refers to the investigation of this principle in a book of his, a copy of which he had sent to Fichte.[71]

It is clear that Maimon has in mind his principle of determinability,

[71] I.e., *Versuch einer neuen Logik.*

which is the criterion of synthetic judgments. Just as the law of contradiction is the criterion of analytic judgments in the realm of formal thought, so the principle of determinability is the criterion of synthetic judgments. But according to Maimon, the principle of determinability suffices only for the deduction of synthetic judgments in mathematics, not of synthetic judgments in the realm of experience. Therein, Maimon feels, is the desideratum of philosophy: to find a principle that would explain the possibility of synthetic judgments in the realm of real thought (*reales Denken*), i.e., thought in relation to objects of experience.

Maimon's letter concludes with a personal note worth mentioning. He complains of the fate of his writings and the lack of understanding for his philosophy, as shown by his critics. He expresses a hope for a fair appraisal of his work in the *Allgemeine Literaturzeitung* by the author of the *Critique of All Revelation*... [i.e., Fichte].

In another letter to Fichte[72] thanking him for an invitation to become a collaborator in the *Allgemeine Literaturzeitung*, Maimon writes: "With joy and anticipation I look forward, as you do, to the time when philosophy will become a systematic science. For my part, I shall try to contribute to the best of my ability towards the attainment of this goal. We shall meet each other on the way, as we proceed in opposite directions on the road to our common destination. Whereas your point of departure is the formulation of an abstract concept of science in general, thus descending from the highest principle to the concrete sciences, my intention is to proceed in the opposite direction, starting from the concrete objects of science and ascending to the general principle."

Elsewhere Maimon defined more fully his philosophical method as the way from below upwards, not from the top downwards. "I recognize," he writes, "the value of formal thought merely as the *sine qua non* for real thought; my chief purpose, however, is the comprehension of the latter. It is my conviction that critical philosophy has already been completed by Kant. The improvement, however, which can be undertaken consists, not in the ascent to higher principles, but rather in the descent to lower principles and in trying to connect them as much as possible with the principles of critical philosophy." The consideration of the particular methods of thought of the various sciences can here open the way for us. The various sciences must first be studied for the cognition of the truths contained therein; "then they must be investigated again

---

[72] Dated October 16, 1794. See Fichte, *Leben und literarischer Briefwechsel*, p. 444.

with a view to determining the way of the human spirit, its manifold procedures for the invention, ascertainment, and expansion of the truth, and finally, it must all be presented in the complete systematic form of a science."[73]

In a letter dated August 3, 1795, to G. Hufeland (Professor of Law in Jena), one of the editors of the *Jenasche Allgemeine Literaturzeitung*,[74] Fichte consents to write a review of Kant's *Kritik der reinen Vernunft*, third and fourth editions, but asks for more time on various grounds together with the following explanation: "... as, apart from that, I owe to the *Literaturzeitung* important reviews such as that of Maimon's Logic."[75] This letter is of great interest for the understanding of some of the problems with which Fichte was engaged – as Richter, the editor of the letter, has pointed out – and which have a relation to Maimon. It contains references to his conception of the inadequacy of the *Critique of Pure Reason* and the *Critique of Judgment* to supplement Kant's theoretical philosophy as presented in his first *Critique*. Kant was driven to the further development of his thought by his own recognition of the lack of a unifying principle in his first *Critique*. In all this, Fichte follows in the trend of thought already indicated by Maimon. According to Maimon, the dualism of sensibility and understanding cannot be dissolved except by declaring sensibility also as a function of understanding and by the introduction of the idea of an infinite mind. Maimon's idea of an infinite mind is replaced by Fichte with the idea of an absolute Ego. The role and function of both are to overcome the dualism of sensibility and understanding, to eliminate the "given," and to bring about a relativization of the distinction between the *a posteriori* and the *a priori*. In this respect, however, Maimon is not as radical as Fichte. Fichte also writes that through the study of Hume he has learned to understand the motives and intentions of Kant's first *Critique* in a better light. That is to say, through a deeper understanding of skepticism he has realized the insufficiency of the Kantian solution of the problem of knowledge because of its lack of a unifying principle. Fichte's conception of the Ego as the unifying principle is the result of his greater appreciation of skepticism. In this he was influenced by

---

[73] See Maimon, *Str.*, p. 187.

[74] This letter is not included in the collection of Fichte's letters published by hin son; it was published by Raoul Richter in the *Kantstudien*, V, 116, under the heading, "Ein ungedruckter Fichte Brief."

[75] "Weil ich ohne dem auch der Literaturzeitung so wichtige Rezensionen, als Maimons Logik, schuldig bin." It seems, however, that Fichte did not write the promised review on Maimon's *Logik*, as the editor, R. Richter, noted. See *Kantstudien*, V, 118, note 1.

Maimon and Aenesidemus-Schulze, as he himself testifies.[76]

Skepticism, however, was not the ultimate position either for Fichte or for Maimon. It was for Fichte merely a method leading to a positive metaphysical doctrine of speculative idealism as expressed in the central concept of an absolute ego, a super-reason, projecting the non-ego. For Maimon skepticism was an alternative position as well as a method leading to critical idealism with a metaphysical undertone, as is evident in his doctrine of an infinite mind.

[76] See *ibid.*, note 2.

XV CONCLUDING REMARKS

Both Maimon and Fichte undertook a transformation of Kantian idealism. This transformation concerned, first, the concept of "subject" in relation to which the world is a phenomenon. The subject cannot mean the individual subject. It is the view of both Maimon and Fichte that the individual psychic subject is in itself a phenomenon; like all phenomena of experience, it is a creation of an objectifying act of our object-forming thinking. The forms of the world, that is, the forms in which we conceive phenomena, cannot be thought of as dependent upon the subjective human mind with its casual, incidental frailties. Critical idealism is objective idealism; it is not compatible with subjectivism and psychologism. Hence the conception of the human subject as the ground of any cognition of the objects of reality is to be eliminated as incompatible with transcendental, critical idealism. Kant himself has clearly shown in his refutation of idealism that the individual subject is to be replaced with the idea of a super-individual subject as the ground of our conception of phenomena. The creative function of thought, producing objective laws governing the phenomena of experience, is to be attributed to a "general consciousness" (*Bewusstsein überhaupt*) and not to the individual subjective consciousness. The "general consciousness" is to be understood as objective, scientific thought manifesting itself in the various stages of scientific development.

For Maimon and Fichte the individual subject is not an absolute reality. The subject is a phenomenon, like all other objects. Space and time and the categories of understanding are not the product of the individual subject, nor are they to be understood as immanent in the individual psyche. The forms of intuition and cognition are the necessary forms of cognition in general; they are the product of a general consciousness. To overcome anthropologism and psychologism the fundamental principles of cognition are to be conceived of as super-individual principles, otherwise they could not have objective validity. Likewise, the transcendent thing-in-itself as the cause and source of the material of sensation is to be eliminated; if it were not, the validity of the application of the pure forms of cognition would be determined by something "given." Thus the general validity of concepts would be impaired, for cognition which is dependent on, and derived from, an experience given cannot claim universal validity.

These motives were fully developed by Maimon and Fichte. Fichte posited an absolute ego, instead of the individual empirical ego, as the creator of the world-phenomenon. The absolute ego is not dependent upon the reception of material given from without. The phenomena of the world are immanent, not in the individual, but in the super-individual ego. The singular individual ego is in itself the result of a positive act of the absolute super-ego. The Kantian concept of things-in-themselves is done away with by declaring the super-ego to be the creator of phenomena, including the empirical individual ego. The phenomena of the world bear the impress of the absolute ego. The possibility of the application of *a priori* concepts to phenomena is attributable to the participation of the individual ego in the absolute super-ego which is the projector of the phenomena. The conformity of *a priori* knowledge with the phenomena of the world is the result of the fact that both are projections of the super-ego.

We have here a metaphysic of an absolute reality. The pure and absolute ego is thought of as a reality existing in itself and as the source of all existing things. The idealistic thesis that an object has reality only for a thinking subject and that the object is constituted through the "general" subject is not valid for the absolute ego, which has existence in and by itself. The validity of the idealistic thesis of the necessary correlation between subject and object, (i.e., that there are no objects except for a subject and no subject except as a constituent principle of the forming of objects), which is the essence of the principle of immanence, is confined to the realm of experience. The absolute subject, the super-ego, is exempt from this law. The super-ego has absolute existence in itself and by itself; it is thought of as a substance. Fichte's transformation of Kantian critical idealism into speculative idealism resulted from his attempt to solve the difficulties in the Kantian formulation of critical philosophy. In the process, however, he transformed the critical position into speculative metaphysics.

Maimon's idea of an infinite mind of which our mind is a part is the basis of Fichte's doctrine that the absolute ego projects the non-ego. However, Maimon proposed this metaphysical idea in order to grant reality to our synthetic propositions. Maimon does not conceive of the infinite mind as an existing reality in itself without relation to objects of experience. Just as the human, restricted subject is a cognizing subject, so is the infinite mind. It is a mind conceiving all objects in terms of analytic propositions, It may therefore be suggested that the fundamental law governing the subject-object relation – that objects are unthinkable without a subject and subject is inconceivable without objects – applies also to the infinite mind.

Moreover, the assumption that synthetic propositions are all analytic in relation to an infinite mind implies a function for men: to strive for the resolution of synthetic propositions into analytic ones. The idea of an infinite mind that imposes a function on the human mind is no longer a transcendent thing-in-itself.

A refinement of critical idealism was undertaken by Neo-Kantianism of the Marburg School (Hermann Cohen, Paul Natrop and others). According to this school of thought, all being is constituted by cognition; a thing is what it is through cognition. There is no object without a subject of cognition. Cognition, however, is not to be understood as a psychological, temporal process performed by individual subjects, but as an objective process, such as takes place in scientific thought. The opposition of subject and object is not to be presupposed prior to cognition. If the objects and the subject were presupposed as pre-existing entities, cognition would then be contingent upon both subject and objects; and knowledge of objects would be conditioned, but not generated by the forms of cognition. The question would then arise as to the grounds of conformity between subject and object. The system of conformation is rooted in such metaphysical assumptions as the idea of a preestablished harmony, as history of philosophy amply demonstrates. In order to avoid such assumptions the opposition of subject and object is to be understood as arising in and through the process of cognition. The correlation of subject and object is fundamental for both subject and object. Both are constituted by the forms of cognition. Like any object the subject is constituted by conceptually determinating forms of thought. Prior to the process of cognition there are no determined objects. Subjective idealism and psychologism are thus precluded. It is an illusion to think of "facts" of experience and of objects given to our perception prior to the process of cognition. What is supplied to our perception are not mere sensations and impressions, for even these have already been touched by thought. Even that which Kant designates as the "manifold" of sensibility is not wholly given and passively received by the mind, for this manifold has already been fashioned and determined somew Such a manifold is regarded as wholly given only by the unreflective and uncritical mind, i.e., by the common sense attitude toward reality.

What is given is actually only an undetermined X. Cognition alone posits all being and all determinations. A critical analysis of reality as it is conceived and perceived by us will lead to the conclusion that nothing precedes thought. The "facts of perception" do not determine our thought. Rather, our thought, through its conceptual processes, produces and determines the "facts of perception."

Likewise, time and space are not fixed intuitions, as they are for Kant, but concepts set by the mind for the cognition of objects. We are not concerned here with notions of time and space as perceived by our psyche on the level of our "natural" attitude toward reality, but with time and space as conceived by mathematics and physical science. The possibility is thereby granted that a new concept of time and space (such as the theory of relativity, which conceives of time and space as a four-dimensional entity) may be posited for the ordering of phenomena of experience. The new development of the conception of time and space is a refutation of the original Kantian conception of these notions as fixed forms of intuition, but not of the neo-Kantian doctrine of time and space as pure concepts of thought. Cognition of the world is an endless process, and new forms and categories of thought may arise in the struggle with the problems of reality. Scientific cognition generates objects in the endless process of objectification. The completely determined being is not a given fact; it is rather the endless task of cognition. The fundamental principles of critical idealism as developed by this school of thought invest the "Copernican Revolution" in philosophy with a new meaning. This "Revolution" is usually regarded as consisting in the doctrine that the subject determines the object rather than that the object determines our concept of it. In a consistently critical system of thought, however, this "revolution" is to be understood as the doctrine that it is objective cognition, as evidenced in scientific thought, and not the individual subject, that generates objects. It is the objective Logos that produces and generates objects of cognition.

In this refinement of critical idealism the principle of restriction, concerning the impossibility of metaphysics as a science, is secondary to the positive doctrine which grants the function of creating objects of cognition to the exact sciences, in which the pure creative process of thought is manifest. Kant now appears, not as the "all destroyer" (*der alles-zermalmende*), but as the master builder. The core of critical idealism is not its criticism of classical metaphysics, but its account of the basic principles of reality as grounded in the creative concepts of mind. The criticism of metaphysics, which is the negative aspect of critical philosophy, is but a consequence of its positive doctrine that all being is grounded in the fundamental concepts of understanding.

The main problem that arises from the Kantian *Critique* is how to validate the pure *a priori* concepts, which are not derived from experience, for the things of experience. How can pure concepts, posited by the mind, be the real ground for phenomena of experience? Generally valid concepts must be *a priori*, for *a posteriori* cognitions derived from experience cannot claim general validity and universality. This is the basic assumption of the *Critique*. Now the crucial difficulty is that pure *a priori* concepts have validity for reality; that is to say, concepts which are not taken from experience are nevertheless valid for ordering phenomena of experience.

Fichte addressed himself to this problem by proposing a monistic-pantheistic solution. To be sure, the spatio-temporal world of our experience is a reality independent of our individual cognition, but it is in itself the immanent product of a super-individual reason, a super-ego. This cosmic ego is the intelligent and creative principle of the universe and of the empirical individual ego. The things of the world are projections of the super-ego, and our mind can apply pure concepts *a priori* to objects of experience, for by the comprehension of *a priori* concepts we become conscious of the all-pervasive cognitions of the super-ego. Universal reason is the source of *a priori* concepts and of the fundamental principles of reality; universal intelligence grants to the human individual mind its laws and cognitions. Pure *a priori* concepts can therefore be applied to objects of experience and mold them because the latter, being the product of a super-reason, have in themselves their real ground in the pure cognitions of the universal super-reason. This is the essence of Fichte's metaphysical conception of idealism. It was thus that speculative absolute idealism replaced critical idealism.

Another approach to the solution of our problem is represented by the Neo-Kantianism of the Marburg school. According to this school of thought, the ordered world of our scientific experience conforms to *a priori* concepts because the phenomena acquire objectivity only through these concepts. It is through the methodical thinking of science that the objective world is generated. The process of objectification is however never completed; it is an endless process. The human mind, through the development of scientific thought, is constantly striving for more adequate objectification. The ultimate correspondence of objects of reality with *a priori* principles of thought is an ideal goal; it is an endless task. This conception of the essence of the "Critique" aims at a formulation of critical idealism in its purity, avoiding meta-physical assumptions.

In their denial of psychologism and subjectivism Fichte and Neo-Kantianism are of one mind. They differ radically, however, in their solution of the problem of the possibility of applying pure forms of thought to objects of experience. For Fichte the application is made possible by positing an absolute mind, a super-ego, which is the ground of reality and of the human mind. This super-reason is placed at the beginning. For Neo-Kantianism, however, the ultimate realization of pure concepts, that is, the complete mastery of objects of experience in accordance with pure principles *a priori* is envisioned as being at the end of the historical process. The struggle with the problems of reality is an endless struggle. The final solution of all problems by the scientific process of objectification is a goal for the future.

Maimon's position is intermediate between the speculative meta-physics of Fichte and the rigorous critical view of Neo-Kantianism. On the one hand, Maimon conceived the idea of an infinite mind, of which the human mind is a part; on the other hand, the idea of an infinite mind is for him a goal to strive for. Synthetic propositions have reality, inasmuch as we can hope for their resolution into analytic propositions. Maimon does not place the infinite mind at the beginning of the process, but rather at the end. In the solution of the problem of antinomies, where the human mind strives to transcend the realm of experience, man manifests a metaphysical aspect; here we have to consider the human mind as a part of the infinite mind. It is at this point that Maimon comes close to the speculative metaphysics of Fichte. But in the realm of cognition of experience the infinite mind serves the function of an idea, that is, an ideal goal. Here Maimon approaches the Neo-Kantian position. Let us recall Maimon's words in a letter to Fichte: "We shall meet each other on the way, as we proceed in opposite directions on the road to our common destination. Whereas your point of departure is the formulation of an abstract concept of science in general, thus descending from the highest principle to concrete sciences, my intention is to proceed in the opposite direction, starting from the concrete objects of science and ascending to the general principle." What Maimon means is that while Fichte attempts to descend from the speculative conception of a super-ego, a universal reason, to the realm of experience, he, Maimon, is trying to ascend from objects of experience cognized in terms of synthetic propositions to the ultimate ideal of analytic knowledge.

INDEX